A Spanish
Learning
Grammar

Third Edition

A Spanish Learning Grammar

Pilar Muñoz and Mike Thacker

Routledge
Taylor & Francis Group

LONDON AND NEW YORK

First edition published 2001 by Hodder Education

Third edition published 2012 by Routledge
2 Park Square, Milton Park, Abingdon, Oxon OX14 4RN
711 Third Avenue, New York, NY, 10017, USA

Routledge is an imprint of the Taylor & Francis Group, an informa business

British Library Cataloguing-in-Publication Data
A catalogue record for this book is available from the British Library.

Library of Congress Cataloging-in-Publication Data
A catalog record for this book is available from the Library of Congress.

ISBN: 978-1-444-15733-8

Illustrations drawn by Marta Muñoz.
Cover photo: © Luis Carlos Jiménez — Fotolia.
Typeset by Integra, India

Contents

Acknowledgements

The authors would like to express their gratitude to the following readers for suggestions for improvements to the first edition, many of which have been incorporated in this new edition: Barbara Ayling, Bernard Bentley, Noelia Alcarazo and Antonia Moreira Rodríguez. A special 'thank you' must go to Linda Hartly (University of Dundee) for her generous contribution. The authors are especially grateful to Bianca Knights, of Hodder Education, for her advice and encouragement during the revising of the book, and to Marta Muñoz for drawing such beautiful illustrations.

The publishers would like to thank the following for permission to include copyright material:

Diario El País, S.A. for an extract from *La tele*, El País Semanal (1993).

Intellect Ltd for permission to reproduce an extract from Paddy Woodworth 'The war against terrorism: the Spanish experience from ETA to al-Qaeda', *International Journal of Iberian Studies*, 17.3, pp.169–182.

Mercedes Casanovas and the author for an extract from © *Corazón tan blanco*, Javier Marías (1992) and an extract from © *Todas las almas*, Javier Marías (1989).

Plaza Janés for an extract from *La casa de los espíritus*, Isabel Allende (1995).

Ray Loriga, *La pistola de mi hermano*, Plaza y Janés, 2000, p. 87.

Clío Año 5 número 50

Every effort has been made to trace copyright holders of material reproduced in this book. Any rights not acknowledged here will be acknowledged in subsequent printings if notice is given to the publisher.

Introduction

This third edition of *A Spanish Learning Grammar* has been revised, 10 years after its first publication, mainly to reflect changes in everyday Spanish since 2001, especially in the language of new technology. Our aim, when explaining grammar points and in the practice exercises, has therefore been to exemplify Spanish as it is now, and to do so in as student- and teacher-friendly a fashion as possible. We have also borne in mind, where appropriate, the Royal Spanish Academy's *Nueva Gramática de la lengua española* (2009), which establishes best usage across the Hispanic world. Further, we have brought up to date the drawings used to illustrate grammar visually and added several new ones, across both parts of the book.

A Spanish Learning Grammar was written in the belief that grammar is the key to real communication. The innovative structure of the book, which is in two parts, corresponding to 'Core knowledge' and 'More advanced knowledge', seeks to encourage a full understanding of grammatical concepts; at the same time the book acts as a traditional reference grammar.

We believe that the two-part division of the book will provide learners with a means of gaining a secure understanding of the language. They will gradually extend their possibilities of expression, whether spoken or written, through enjoyable and disciplined practice. Our method of explaining how grammar works in English and then in Spanish enables students to grasp the fact that Spanish, like all languages, has different ways of creating its grammatical rules, which derive from a distinctive cultural and linguistic tradition.

Part I establishes the *concept* and the *particular features* of each of the grammar points, providing the structures needed for *ab-initio* and intermediate courses. Part II is suitable for more advanced learners, covering more sophisticated and complex structures.

Part I follows, typically, a set sequence:
(i)   Each point is explained initially by reference to *English grammar*.
(ii) An *illustration* follows, which shows the concept in visual terms and uses authentic Spanish language.
(iii) Parallels between English and Spanish are then pointed out in a contrastive way and the key ideas relating to areas of Spanish grammar are systematically set out.
(iv) The essential *uses* of the grammar area are then explored, with examples.
(v)   Finally, a sequence of *exercises* at the end of each section gives ample *practice*. Part I exercises aim to create good habits and ensure a solid foundation rather than test the creative use of language.

Part II builds on the concepts established in Part I:
(i)   The learner is reminded of the *essential points* of the grammar areas.
(ii) The *more complex aspects*, which are met by students when they have grasped the concept properly, are explained and exemplified.
(iii) More demanding *exercises* are placed at the end of Part II chapters, many of which offer a challenge to the student to use grammar creatively. The exercises tend to be more contextualised than those in Part I.

In this edition the structure of Parts 1 and 2 has been harmonised so that readers can locate the grammar they are looking for more easily on the Contents page.

A Key to all exercises is provided at the end of each part of the book.

Two important symbols are used throughout the book:

 Key ideas (the fundamental ideas which inform each grammatical point).

 Common errors (errors which persist if not eradicated early in the learning process).

Recommended reading

The following is useful for a more advanced study of Spanish grammar: J. Butt and C. Benjamin, *A New Reference Grammar of Modern Spanish*, Fifth Edition (Hodder Education, 2011). Special reference to this text will be made in specific chapters of the book.

Glossary of Grammatical Terms

Active and passive sentences Sentences are either active or passive. In an active sentence, the subject carries out the action of the verb, e.g. **El fuego destruyó el hotel** (Fire destroyed the hotel). In the passive version of this example, what was the object (hotel) of the active sentence becomes the subject of the passive verb and the *agent* (fire) appears after **por: El hotel fue destruido por el fuego** (The hotel was destroyed by fire). Verbs which take a direct object (transitive verbs) can be used in either an active or a passive way.

Adjective Adjectives are words used to identify or describe nouns. In Spanish, adjectives agree with nouns in number and gender, e.g. **Dos caballos blancos** (Two white horses); **blancos** is a masculine plural adjective.

Adverb Adverbs give more information about a verb or an adjective. Adverbs can tell you how, when, where and to what degree something happens or is, e.g. **Trabajó bien/tarde/allí/mucho** (He worked well/late/there/a lot); **Está totalmente obsesionado** (He is totally obsessed).

Affirmative sentence An affirmative or positive sentence is one in which we assert a fact or state agreement to something, as opposed to a *negative* one in which we refuse, deny, or contradict something.

Antecedent In a relative clause the antecedent is the preceding noun to which the relative pronoun or adjective refers. In **La mujer que viste ayer es mi esposa** (The woman [whom] you saw yesterday is my wife), **La mujer** is the antecedent and **que** the relative pronoun.

Augmentative An augmentative is a suffix (e.g. **-ón/ona**), added to the end of a word to convey the meaning of greater size or vulgarity, e.g. **mujer** (woman) > **mujerona** (big woman).

Auxiliary verb An auxiliary verb is a verb which combines with a participle or an infinitive e.g. to form a compound tense using **haber** plus the past participle, as in **He traído tus discos** (I've brought your discs).

Clause A clause is the part of a sentence which contains its own verb, but which does not necessarily make complete sense. There are two types of clause, 'main' and 'subordinate'. A main clause has an independent meaning within the sentence; a subordinate clause cannot function independently without another clause. In **Me desperté antes de que sonara el despertador** (I woke up before the alarm went off), **Me desperté** can stand on its own as the main clause; **antes de que sonara el despertador**, as the subordinate clause, depends on the main clause.

Comparative Comparatives are adjectives and adverbs which emphasise a particular quality by comparing the *degree* to which two nouns possess that quality: **Londres es más grande que Madrid** (London is bigger than Madrid).

Compound tense *See* **Tense**

Conjugation A conjugation is a grouping of verbs. There are three such groupings in Spanish, which are distinguished by their infinitive endings. These are verbs ending in: **-ar**, **-er** and **-ir**, e.g. **hablar, comer, vivir.**

Conjunction Conjunctions are words like **y**, **pero** and **porque** that link words, phrases or clauses, e.g. **Ha venido porque quiere pasar la noche aquí** (He has come because he wants to stay the night here).

Continuous tense *See* **Tense**

Definite article The definite article (English 'the') is used to indicate a previously known person, animal, thing or idea, e.g. **el chico** (the boy), **los perros** (the dogs), **la manzana** (the apple), **las ideas** (the ideas).

Demonstrative The demonstratives are used when identifying something, e.g. **este** (this) and **aquel** (that). They can be either adjectives or pronouns.

Diminutive A diminutive is a suffix (e.g. **-ito/a**) added to the end of a word to convey the meaning of smallness or cuteness e.g. **casa** (house) > **casita** (little house).

Diphthong A combination of two vowels in the same syllable, e.g. **a + i** in **aire**.

Direct object *See* **Object**

Gender Words in Spanish are either masculine or feminine in gender, e.g. **el ordenador** (computer), **la calle** (street).

Gerund The Spanish gerund is a form of the verb ending in **-ando** or **-iendo**, e.g. **hablando** (speaking), **riendo** (laughing). It normally functions as part of continuous tenses in Spanish, e.g. **Están hablando** (They're speaking), or as an adverb, e.g. **Salieron riendo** (They went out laughing).

Imperative mood *See* **Mood**

Impersonal verb Impersonal verbs are verbs whose subject has no particular identity, or whose identity is not revealed, e.g. **Nieva** (It is snowing), **Se dice que Chile es muy hermoso** (It is said that Chile is very beautiful).

Indefinite article The indefinite article (English 'a/ an/some') is used to indicate a person, animal, thing or idea that has not been previously mentioned or known, e.g. **un chico** (a boy), **unos perros** (some dogs), **una manzana** (an apple), **unas ideas** (some ideas).

Indefinites Indefinite nouns and adjectives are words that do not refer to anything or anybody in particular, like **alguno** (some, any), **alguien** (somebody, anybody) and **cualquier** (any).

Indicative mood *See* **Mood**

Indirect object *See* **Object**

Infinitive The infinitive is the form of the verb which is not inflected. In English the infinitive consists of the word 'to' plus the verb, e.g. 'to eat'. The Spanish infinitive ends in either **-ar**, **-er** or **-ir**, e.g. **encontrar** (to find), **hacer** (to do/make), **salir** (to go out).

Interrogative Interrogative pronouns and adjectives are words used to introduce questions, like **¿qué?** (what?), **¿cuántos?** (how many) and **¿quiénes?** (who?).

Intransitive verb *See* **Transitive and intransitive verbs**

Irregular verb *See* **Regular and irregular verb**

Main clause *See* **Clause**

Modal verb Modal verbs are **auxiliary** verbs, like **poder** (can) and **deber** (must), *which are followed by the infinitive*. Modal verbs communicate a particular mood or intention to the verb which follows. **No puedo ayudarte** (I can't help you); **No debo ayudarte** (I mustn't help you).

Mood There are three moods of the verb, which are used to express ideas and emotions. These are:

- *Indicative*. This mood is used for statements of fact and certainty: **Come yogur cada mañana** (He eats yogurt every morning).
- *Imperative*. This mood is used for giving commands. Commands are made both in the positive: **¡Hazlo!** (Do it!) and the negative: **¡No lo hagas!** (Don't do it!)
- *Subjunctive*. This mood is for uncertainty, unreality, wishes and hopes: **Espero que ganemos el partido** (I hope we win the match).

Negative sentence A negative sentence is one in which we refuse, deny, contradict or say 'no', e.g. **No vamos nunca a la playa** (We never go to the beach).

Noun A noun is the name that we give to a person, animal, thing or idea. There are two types of noun: *common*, e.g. **mujer** (woman), **libro** (book), **cosa** (thing) and *proper*, which refer to particular persons, places, or objects, e.g. **Aurelia**, **D. Quijote**, **Microsoft**.

Number Number refers to words being singular or plural, e.g. **el árbol** (tree), **los árboles** (trees), **la fiesta** (party), **las fiestas** (parties).

Object A **direct object** is a word which receives the action of the verb directly, e.g. **la pelota** in **¡Coge la pelota!** (Catch the ball!). An **indirect object** is one which receives the action of the verb indirectly. In **Da caramelos a los niños** (She gives sweets to the children), **los niños** is the indirect object and **caramelos** the direct object.

Orthographic-changing verb These are verbs which change their spelling in order to maintain the correct sound, e.g. **buscar** (to look for) becomes **busqué** (I looked for) in the preterite.

Passive sentence *See* **Active and passive sentences**

Past participle The past participle is the form of the verb ending in **-ado** or **-ido**, e.g. **pasado** (passed), **comido** (eaten). It has two main functions: as an adjective, e.g. **la puerta cerrada** (the closed door), and as part of a verb, as in the passive and the perfect tense e.g. **Es bien sabido que** ... (It is well known that ...), **He terminado** (I have finished).

Person Verb endings are always related to a subject, which can be in the first, second or third person, singular or plural:

yo (I) first person singular

tú (you) familiar second person singular

usted (you), formal second person singular

él, ella (he, she, it) third person singular

nosotros (we) first person plural

vosotros (you) familiar second person plural

ustedes (you) formal second person plural

ellos, ellas (they) third person plural

Personal pronoun *See* **Pronoun**

Positive sentence *See* **Affirmative sentence**

Possessive Possessive adjectives and pronouns tell us who is the possessor of something or show a relationship between different people, or people and things/ideas, e.g. **mi**, **su** and **nuestras**, adjectives, in **mi bicicleta** (my bicycle), **su padre** (her father), **nuestras vacaciones** (our holidays); and **mía**, pronoun, in **es mía** (it's mine).

Preposition A preposition links a noun or noun phrase with the rest of the sentence, e.g. **cerca de** in **El museo está cerca de la catedral**. (The museum is near the cathedral). By changing the preposition we change the meaning of the sentence, e.g. by replacing **cerca de** with **lejos de** (far from), **en** (in) or **frente a** (opposite) in the example.

Pronoun Pronouns stand in the place of nouns whenever it is unnecessary to refer to the noun. Personal pronouns appear in four main places in a sentence: as the subject, **yo** (I); as the direct object, **me** (me); as the indirect object, **le** (to him/her/it); after a preposition, **para él** (for him).

Other types of pronouns are: demonstrative, e.g. **aquel** (that one); relative, e.g. **que** (what, which, who); interrogative, e.g. **¿cuál?** (which?); reflexive, e.g. **se** (himself, etc.), etc.

Radical-changing verb A feature of the Spanish verb system is that certain verbs change the spelling of the stem of the verb, e.g. **pensar** (to think) becomes **pienso** (I think) in the first person of the present indicative. In the same way, **encontrar** (to find) becomes **encuentro** (I find) and **pedir** (to ask for) becomes **pido** (I ask for).

Reflexive verb These are verbs that are accompanied by a reflexive pronoun, such as **me** (myself), **te** (yourself) and **se** (himself, themselves). The verb will only be reflexive if the subject is the same as the object. For example, **Se lavó rápidamente** (He washed himself/got washed quickly).

Regular and irregular verb Regular verbs, e.g. **hablar**, **comer**, **vivir**, conform to predictable models for the formation of the different tenses. If you know that a verb is regular you can work out from the model the form that you need. Irregular verbs do not always conform to a predictable model for their formation so it is important to learn them. Many common verbs, such as **decir**, **saber** and **ir**, are irregular. See pages 324–334 for tables of irregular verbs.

Relative clause Relative clauses are subordinate clauses introduced by relative pronouns like **que** (what, who, etc.) and **quien** (who). They refer back to a previous noun, called the antecedent, and they link two clauses together, e.g. **Mi padre, que está en Caracas, llamó ayer** (My father, who is in Caracas, phoned yesterday).

Subject The subject is the word or group of words which determines the verb ending, e.g. in **Los chicos jugaban en la calle** (The children were playing in the street), the subject (**Los chicos**) is plural so the verb is in the plural. In active sentences the subject usually carries out the action of the verb: **Juan me dio un disgusto** (Juan upset me). In passive sentences the subject receives the action of the verb: **El paquete fue traído por Pepe el cartero** (The parcel was brought by Pepe the postman).

Subjunctive mood *See* **Mood**

Subordinate clause *See* **Clause**

Superlative The superlative is an adjective or adverb used when we are referring to a quality in its greatest possible degree, e.g. **[el] más rico** in **Los Estados Unidos es el país más rico del mundo**. (The United States is the richest country in the world).

Tense Tense means the relative time the verb refers to, whether present, future or past. Tenses can be *simple*, i.e. consist of one word, or *compound*, i.e. consist of more than one word.

- In Spanish the *simple* tenses are: Present, Future, Conditional, Preterite and Imperfect. The Present and Imperfect exist in both the indicative and the subjunctive mood.

- *Compound* tenses consist of the auxiliary verb, e.g. a form of **haber** (to have) or **poder** (to be able), plus a participle or an infinitive, e.g. **Juan había llegado** (Juan had arrived), **No puedo salir esta noche** (I can't go out tonight).

- Spanish has a range of *continuous* tenses. These forms are used to emphasise what is (was, will be, etc.) happening at the moment of the action: **Está cantando en la ducha** (He's singing in the shower).

Transitive and intransitive verb A verb is called transitive when it normally requires a direct object, as in **Necesitamos** (we need). The meaning would be completed with the addition of more information, as in **Necesitamos pan y leche** (We need bread and milk). Some verbs, however, make complete sense on their own without needing an object to complete their meaning, e.g. **Juana duerme** (Juana is sleeping). Verbs of this kind are called intransitive. Certain verbs can be both transitive and intransitive, e.g. **Mira** (Look); **Mira aquel pájaro** (Look at that bird).

Glossary of Computing & Mobile Phone Technology

.com (dot.com)	.com (punto.com)
'pay as you go'	tarjeta prepago f.
anti-virus	antivirus m.
at (@)	arroba (@)
attach file (tab)	adjuntar archivo
bar	barra f.
battery	batería f.
BlackBerry	BlackBerry m.
broadband	banda ancha f.
cartridge	cartucho de tinta m.
CD	CD (ce, de) m.
charge (verb)	cargar
chat (verb)	chatear
chatroom	chat m.
click on (verb)	hacer clic
close (verb)	cerrar
computer	ordenador m. computadora (Lat.Am.) f.
contacts	contactos m.
copy (verb)	copiar
copy and paste (tab)	copiar y pegar
credit (to have/ not to have)	saldo [(no) tener...]
cursor	cursor m.
delete (verb)	borrar
download (verb)	bajar(se); descargar
draft (tab)	borrador
DVD	DVD (de, uve, de) m.
e-book	libro electrónico/e-book m.
e-mail	correo electrónico/e-mail m.
file	archivo/fichero m.
forward (tab)	reenviar
forward (verb)	reenviar
from:	de:
hacker	hacker m.f.
hard disk	disco duro m.
charger	cargador m.
headphones	auriculares m.
icon	icono m.
in/outbox	bandeja de entrada/salida f.
internet shopping	comercio electrónico m.
internet	Internet m.f.
iPad	iPad m.
iPod	iPod m.
IT	informática f.
junk mail	correo basura m.
key	tecla f.
keyboard	teclado m.
laptop	portátil m.
link	enlace, m.
memory stick	pen (drive) m.; memoria USB (u, ese, be) f.
message	mensaje, m.
missing call	llamada perdida f.
mobile	móvil m., celular (Lat. Am.) m.
modem	módem m.
mouse	ratón m.
open (verb)	abrir
password	contraseña f.
paste (verb)	pegar
pin (number)	pin m.
post (message) (verb)	postear
press a button (verb)	pulsar
print (verb)	imprimir
printer	impresora f.
recipient	destinatario m.
record (verb)	grabar
recorder	grabadora f.
remote control	mando a distancia m.
reply	respuesta f.
router	router m.
save (verb)	guardar
scan (verb)	escanear
scanner	escáner m.
screen	pantalla f.
search engine	buscador m.
sent (tab)	enviado
server	servidor m.
social network	red social f.
software	software m.

spam	correo no deseado/spam *m.*	to:	para:
speaker	altavoz *m.*	tool bar *(tab)*	barra de herramientas *f.*
spelling check	corrector ortográfico *m.*	user friendly	entorno amigable *m.*
stand by	en espera	user name *m.*	usuario *m.*
subject *(tab)*	asunto *m.*	www	www (uve doble, uve doble, uve doble)
surfer	internauta *m.f.*		
switch off *(verb)*	apagar	web page	web, sitio web *m.*
switch on *(verb)*	encender	wifi	wifi *f.*
tab	pestaña *f,*	wireless	inalámbrico/a
tablet	tableta *f.*	word processor	procesador de datos *m.*
text message	mensaje de texto, SMS (ese, eme, ese) *m.*		

Part I

Core Knowledge

1

Pronunciation, accents, spelling and punctuation

1.1 The Spanish alphabet

Symbol		Symbol		Symbol	
a	a	j	jota	r	erre
b	be	k	ka	s	ese
c	ce	l	ele	t	te
d	de	m	eme	u	u
e	e	n	ene	v	uve
f	efe	ñ	eñe	w	uve doble
g	ge	o	o	x	equis
h	hache	p	pe	y	i griega/ye
i	i	q	cu	z	zeta

Note: Letters of the alphabet (las letras del abecedario) are **feminine**.

ñ

In Spanish *ñ* is a separate letter of the alphabet. In dictionaries niñez comes after ninguno.

k and w

Very few words contain *k* and *w*. Most of them are imported from other languages, e.g. karate, whisky.

1.2 Pronunciation

Consonants

Some consonants are pronounced in a markedly different way from their equivalent in English. The most important of these differences are as follows:

1 *b* and *v* have the same sound:

bueno   barba   vino   varios

2 *c*

a Before *a*, *o* and *u*: *c* is a hard sound (as in 'come'):

campo   arranca   coste   banco   Cuba   cuando

b Before *e* and *i: c* is a soft sound

In Castilian Spanish (spoken mainly in the north and the centre of Spain) this sound is like English 'th' in 'thin'. In much of Spain and Spanish America the sound is 's':

| cena | acento | cine | incidente |

3 *g*

a Before *a, o* and *u: g* is a hard sound (as in 'go'):

| garaje | ganar | gordo | gol | gusto | gusano |

b Before *e* or *i: g* is a sound made in the throat, like *ch* in Scottish 'loch':

| gente | gerente | giro | gitano | dirige |

c *gu* followed by *a* is pronounced 'gw' (as in 'Gwen'):

| guapo | agua | guardar |

d *gu* followed by *e* or *i* is a hard sound (as in 'go'); *u* is silent:

| guerra | llegué | guitarra | Miguel |

e In the combinations *güe* and *güi* a diaeresis is placed over the *u*. This indicates that the sound is 'gw' (as in 'Gwen'):

| averigüé | vergüenza | argüir |

4 *h*

h is always silent: **hombre** is pronounced 'ombre', **hotel** 'otel', etc.:

5 *j*

j is a sound made in the throat, like *ch* in Scottish 'loch':

| hijo | jardín | Jorge | paja | Méjico |

6 *ll*

ll is pronounced like *lli* in 'pillion':

| llave | calle | llegar | hallar |

7 *r*

a A single *r* at the beginning of a word is normally 'trilled' or 'rolled', e.g. the *r* in *el río*. Otherwise it is a single trill or 'flap', as in *cara*.

b *rr*, as in *burro, sierra*, is not considered to be a separate letter. It cannot be split to form part of two different syllables. It is always a rolled sound, like a 'Scottish' *r*.

The difference between these two sounds can be heard clearly when comparing *pero* (but) and *perro* (dog).

8 *x*

x is pronounced

a between vowels: can be either 'ks' (as in 'expect') or 'gs' (as in 'example'):

| elixir | existir | éxito |

or

b before a consonant: 'ks' or, more usually, 's':

| excepto | exclamar | experiencia |

9 *z*

In Castilian Spanish (spoken mainly in the north and centre of Spain) this sound is pronounced like 'th' in 'thin'. In much of Spain and Spanish America the sound is 's':

| zona | zigzag | zozobra |

Vowels

The five vowels are **a, e, i, o** and **u**. Wherever a vowel appears in a word it has the same sound value, unlike in English, where the same vowel can be pronounced in several different ways, and may not even be pronounced at all, e.g. the three 'e's in 'vegetable'. The two 'a's in the Spanish word Sara have exactly the same sound, whereas in the English 'Sara', the two '**a**'s are different sounds.

Spanish vowel sounds are normally shorter than in English. This can be seen by comparing the way in which *sombrero* is pronounced in English and Spanish. In the English word the last two vowels, **e** and **o,** are much longer.

No Spanish vowel sound is exactly the same as the English equivalent. The exact sounds are learned best by listening to native speakers of Spanish.

1   **a**   similar to *a* in 'rather', but shorter:

cara	haba	gato	meta	parada

2   **e**   similar to the *a* sound in 'say' but without the *y* sound:

feo	pero	comer	real	beneficio

3   **i**   similar to the *ee* sound in 'bee', but shorter:

sino	así	cinco	rico	límite

4   **o**   similar to the *o* in 'lost':

oro	pero	negro	olé	corona

5   **u**   similar to *oo* in 'wood':

puro	ducha	cura	puse	saludo

1.3 Accents

Rules of stress

In both English and Spanish, when saying a word of two or more syllables, it is natural to stress one syllable more than the other(s). When saying *Barcelona*, in both languages the main stress is on the syllable **lo**. Spanish, however, stresses the first syllable in *Cádiz* and the second in *pintor*. In the equivalents of these words in English the stress lies on the second syllable in *Cadiz* and the first in *painter*.

Stress affects the sound of a word. If you try moving the stress from the first to the second syllable, e.g. by pronouncing *dis*co or *veg*etable as *disco* or *vegetable*, you will see that the word sounds wrong. The same is true of Spanish. If you do not stress words correctly, you may fail to communicate the meaning, since a Spanish speaker will have to make a special effort to understand you. It is therefore essential to know the rules of stress. In Spanish the basic rules of stress are:

1   The stress is on the **penultimate syllable:**

   a   in words ending in a vowel:

padre	fol**le**to	**chi**ca	co**ro**na	**pu**ro

   b   in words ending in **n** or **s**:

i**ma**gen	**te**men	**chi**cas	**so**los	**duer**men

A word with the stress on the penultimate syllable is known as *llana* or *grave*.

2   The stress is on the **last syllable** in words ending in a consonant *other than* **n** *or* **s**:

ca**paz**	ciu**dad**	ho**tel**

A word with the stress on the last syllable is known as *aguda*.

3   The above two rules are overridden by the presence of a **written accent** (´):

fácil	**á**guila	in**glés**	en**tré**	ha**bló**	cham**pú**

4   Words may be stressed on the **antepenultimate,** or third-from-last, syllable:

fan**tás**tico	**má**gico	ki**ló**metro	**pá**jaro

A word with the stress on this syllable is known as *esdrújula*.

Notes on the use of the written accent

1 When words form a *plural* they must keep the stress on the same syllable as the singular. In order to do this they have, in certain cases, either to lose or gain a written accent, in accordance with the rules of stress.

a Words ending in *-ión, -án, -én, -ín, -ón, -ún* and *-és* lose their accent in the plural:

singular	plural
intención	intenciones
montón	montones
francés	franceses
jardín	jardines
terraplén	terraplenes

b Words ending in *-en* place the stress on the antepenultimate syllable in the plural:

imagen	imágenes
joven	jóvenes
examen	exámenes

c Note that the following two words are exceptional in that they stress a different syllable in the plural:

carácter	caracteres
régimen	regímenes

2 Words which introduce a question, like cómo, qué, quién and dónde, bear an accent, whether the question is direct or indirect:

¿Cómo estás?	How are you?
Le pregunté quién era.	I asked him who he was.

3 Monosyllables do not normally bear an accent (but see 4 (ii) below):

fui   vio   de   ya   tan

4

a The written accent can change the meaning of a verb form:

hablo	I speak	habló	he spoke
trabajara	he worked (imperfect subjunctive form)	trabajará	he will work

b The written accent is used to distinguish the meaning of two words which are otherwise spelt the same:

el	the	él	he, him, it
mas	but	más	more
mi	my	mí	me
se	(one) self (reflexive pronoun)	sé	I know, be (imperative)
si	if	sí	yes, (one)self
te	you (object)	té	tea
tu	your	tú	you (subject)

Vowels and stress

The five vowels are divided into two types, strong and weak:

strong vowels: *a*, *e* and *o*
weak vowels: *i* and *u*

1 When *one strong and one weak vowel* or *two weak vowels* are combined they form a *diphthong*. A diphthong counts as **one syllable**:

a (strong) + *i* (weak)	e.g.	ba**i**le
a (strong) + *u* (weak)	e.g.	L**au**ra
e (strong) + *i* (weak)	e.g.	s**ei**s
e (strong) + *u* (weak)	e.g.	**eu**ropeo
i (weak) + *a* (strong)	e.g.	Bol**i**via
i (weak) + *e* (strong)	e.g.	c**ie**lo
i (weak) + *o* (strong)	e.g.	biolog**í**a
i (weak) + *u* (weak)	e.g.	v**iu**da
o (strong) + *i* (weak)	e.g.	**oi**ga
u (weak) + *a* (strong)	e.g.	g**ua**po
u (weak) + *e* (strong)	e.g.	h**ue**vo
u (weak) + *i* (weak)	e.g.	r**ui**do

2 When two strong vowels are combined, they form two separate syllables:

a + e	maestro	(compare English 'maestro')
e + a	Seat	(compare English 'seat')
e + o	peor	
o + e	roer	

3 When a weak and a strong vowel are combined, a written accent is required if the stress is on the weak vowel and the two vowels are pronounced as separate syllables:

i + a	el día
o + i	el oído
u + a	continúa

4 When two weak vowels are combined, the emphasis is on the second vowel and no accent is required:

u + i	construido
i + u	ciudad

5 *i* is replaced by *y* at the end of words:

muy   hay   soy

1.4 Changes of spelling

In certain circumstances changes of spelling in verbs take place in order to preserve the sound of consonants, e.g. buscar (to look for) becomes busqué (I looked for), in the first person of the preterite tense (see Part I, 26.2).

Double letters

1 Words in Spanish which contain a single consonant will often have a double consonant in the equivalent word in English.

Compare:

Spanish	English
(im)posible	(im)possible
necesario	necessary
inmediatamente	immediately
letra	letter
difícil	difficult
burbuja	bubble
budista	Buddhist

2 The consonants *c* and *n* may be doubled. When this happens they form part of two separate syllables and each consonant is pronounced:

a In words which contain **-cc-** the first *c* is hard, the second soft:

ac|ción   introduc|ción

b Only a handful of words contain **-nn-**. In these words both '*n*'s are sounded:

in|necesario   in|novador

c *ll* and *rr* are very frequent:

llegar   calle   barrio   carretera

Capital letters

In Spanish capital letters (mayúsculas) are used far less than in English. Note that the following have small letters (minúsculas):

1 Adjectives derived from proper nouns, e.g. adjectives of nationality and those denoting regional identity:

proper noun		**adjective**	
Inglaterra	England	inglés	English
Andalucía	Andalusia	andaluz	Andalusian
Lorca	Lorca (the playwright)	lorquiano	of Lorca

2 Nouns and adjectives denoting religious or political groups:

¿Por qué tuvo el comunismo tanta influencia en Cuba?
Why did Communism have so much influence in Cuba?

En el siglo dieciséis Inglaterra se convirtió en un país protestante.
In the sixteeenth century England became a Protestant country.

3 Days of the week and months of the year:

lunes   Monday
septiembre   September

4 Official titles:

la reina de Inglaterra   The Queen of England
el papa   The Pope
el presidente de los Estados Unidos   The President of the United States

5 Titles of books, plays and films:

La vida es sueño, de Calderón.   *Life is a Dream*, by Calderón.
Mujeres al borde de un ataque de nervios, de Pedro Almodóvar.   *Women on the Verge of a Nervous Breakdown*, by Pedro Almodóvar.

1.5 Punctuation

The main punctuation marks are:

.	el punto	full stop
,	la coma	comma
:	dos puntos	colon
;	el punto y coma	semicolon
¿?	los signos de interrogación	question marks
¡!	los signos de admiración	exclamation marks
« »	las comillas	quotation marks
( )	los paréntesis	brackets
-	el guión	hyphen
_	la raya	dash
…	los puntos suspensivos	ellipsis

a) Notes on punctuation

1 In numbers, the full stop is used like the English comma.

1.415.322 (Spanish) = 1,415,322 (English)

2 In decimals, the comma is used where English would use a decimal point.

37,3% (Spanish) = 37.3% (English)

3 A feature of Spanish is the placing of interrogation and exclamation marks at the beginning and the end of questions and exclamations. Note that the inverted question or exclamation mark can be in the middle of a sentence:

¡Qué desastre! ¡ No me han reparado el coche!　What a disaster! ¡They haven't repaired my car!

Dime, ¿qué demonios vamos a hacer ahora?　What on earth are we going to do now?

4 The *raya* (–) is used to introduce direct speech where in English there would be inverted commas:

–Si no vuelves antes de las nueve –dijo　'If you don't come back before nine,' said
Pedro –no tendremos tiempo para ir al cine.　Pedro, 'we won't have time to go to the cinema.'

5 *Comillas* (« ») are used for quotations within sentences:

El Gobierno español va a comprar　The Spanish Government is going to buy
30 películas del Hollywood clásico para　30 classic Hollywood films in order to
inculcar en los jóvenes « caballerosidad,　instil 'chivalrous behaviour, heroism and ideals
el heroismo e ideales por los que luchar ».　worth fighting for' into young people.

Note: these days English-style inverted commas are often used in journalism instead of *comillas*.

6 The *guión* is used less frequently than the English hyphen. Its main uses are:

a Word division at the end of a line. When a word is divided in this way the next line must start with a new syllable:

Aquel día, las fuerzas de la República　That day the Republican army knew
sabían que las tropas del ejército ene-　that the enemy soldiers were going to
migo iban a retirarse.　retreat.

b Compound words consisting of two nouns:

el coche-bomba　car bomb
la palabra-clave　key word

Exercises

Note: Although beginners will find some of these exercises difficult, it is important to attempt them. The first five exercises are especially useful for the sound and stress of the words.

1 Practise saying the following words out loud:

a **l** and **ll**

| calle | cal | llamar | lamer | hallé | alarma | llego | ligar | ilegal | hallar |

b **b** and **v**

| vino | bien | vaca | barca | IVA | iba | avería | haber | uva | hubo | ver |

c **j**

| jota | hija | ojo | jamón | jardín | ejercicio | bajo | ejército | brujo | jaleo |

d **r** and **rr**

pero   perro   río   real   cara   para   parra   parar   oro   barra   porro

e **x**

experto   existe   excepto   éxito   exponer   extra   sexo   asfixia   examen

2 Work with a companion who will read the first half of the following list for you to write down; change roles for the second half of the list:

aquella	corriente	esquema	inquieto	corona	inquisitivo
asqueroso	requiero	encuesta	caracol	quimera	bikini
bacalao	vaquero	etiqueta	requiebro	escueto	anticuado
trinquete	quinqué	maniqueo	acuático	frecuente	pesquisa

3 Write separate lists of the words which contain **a** a hard **c**; **b** a soft **c**; and **c** a hard and a soft **c**:

cena	calor	ciudad	campo	palacio
destrucción	caramba	cinco	policía	acceso
cerilla	ciencia	bicicleta	cicatriz	conciencia
celos	dice	circunstancia	cubo	obsceno

4 Write lists of the words which contain **a** a hard **g**; **b** a **g** which sounds like Spanish **jota**; and **c** a **g** which sounds like 'gw':

agua	girasol	gerente	gol	guapa
gordo	averiguar	elegante	gitano	Miguel
vergüenza	pegué	liga	orgullo	genial
guardián	guerra	lugar	gimnasta	halagüeño

5 Some of the following words contain a diphthong, others do not. Place each word in the appropriate group:

Diphthong	***Yes***		***No***	
Example:	*ruina*		*correo*	
feo	ruina	variable	miedo	correo
caer	pues	destruido	peatón	poner
cara	chimenea	hacia	pienso	leer
luego	Ceuta	ciudad	neurosis	jaleo

6 Of the words in the following list, 15 have a written accent, the other 15 do not. Place each word in the appropriate group:

	Accent	***No accent***
Example:	*también*	*dijo*
aguila	fue	tambien
dijo	ambicion	heroe
encantador	ambiguedad	saludable
destruido	maestra	arroz
jardin	general	autobus
comian	interes	riquisimo
capaz	sofa	visiones
imagenes	examen	bailar
telefono	ausencia	local
subterraneo	espejo	caido

7 Classify the following words in three groups according to where the stress goes: on the last syllable, on the penultimate syllable and on the antepenultimate syllable. Add a written accent where necessary:

gato	caramba	critica	renegon
rapaz	apendice	retruecano	alferez
golondrina	Sevilla	cantaro	repique
autobus	acordeon	Luis	coliflor
mantequilla	paella	pozo	antilope
dormitorio	atencion	alberca	Corcega
lucero	reposteria	datiles	altimetro

8 There are 15 accents missing from words in the following passage. Put the accents back in the correct places:

Isabel II es la numero 60 de los reyes de Inglaterra, y la sexta reina. Su tio fue Eduardo VIII, quien abdico en 1936 para casarse con una divorciada. Su padre, Jorge VI, dejo de ser duque de York para convertirse en rey despues de aquella abdicacion. Durante la dramatica segunda guerra mundial la familia real se quedo en Londres, a pesar de la posible invasion alemana de la capital. Un año antes de los Juegos Olimpicos de Londres en 1948, Isabel habia contraido matrimonio con el griego Felipe, quien renuncio a sus derechos al trono griego. Existe parentesco entre el principe Felipe y la reina Sofia de España. (written by the authors)

9 In Spanish, words frequently begin with lower-case letters where in English they do not. In the following passage pick out the 10 English words beginning with a capital letter which in Spanish begin with a lower-case one. Make a list, as in the example:

	English	*Spanish*
Example:	*Monday*	lunes

On Monday 15th March I met my French friend Marie in the Mallorca Bar. We both study Spanish-American Literature in Bogotá. We talked about one of the books we like best, García Márquez's novel *A Hundred Years of Solitude*. This is the story of the life of a Colombian family over 100 years, in which fantasy and reality are mixed. The novel is full of colourful characters and extraordinary events. After a while two of our friends came along. They persuaded us to go the Odeon to see *Requiem for a Spanish Peasant*, a film based on the novel by Ramón Sender, an Aragonese writer of the middle of the twentieth century.

10 Rewrite the following passage with the correct Spanish punctuation, accents and capital letters.

The passage begins: – ¿Dígame?
　　　　　　　　　 – Buenos días. Es ahí …

digame buenos dias es ahi la embajada americana no señor esto es el restaurante banderas esta ud seguro me han dado este numero para la embajada americana y se trata de un asunto muy urgente mire señor le digo que esto no es la embajada esto es el 91 4617901 un restaurante mejicano y si no tiene intencion de reservar una mesa lo mejor sera que cuelgue ud perdone buenas tardes buenas tardes

2 Articles

What is an article?

An article is a word used before a noun to indicate whether it is *non-specific* (i.e. it has not been mentioned before):

> Andrew has bought *a* house

or *specific* (i.e. it has been mentioned before):

> Which one?

> *The* pretty one on *the* hill

There are two types of articles in English, **indefinite**, 'a/an/some' and **definite**, 'the'.

There are significant differences between Spanish and English in the way the articles are used.

Note:- Burladero: barrier behind which the bullfighter takes refuge

2.1 The definite article

	singular	plural
masculine	el	los
feminine	la	las

Key ideas

In English there is one form of the definite article, 'the', whereas in Spanish there are four forms. The definite article agrees with the noun in number and gender:

el calor del verano — the summer heat
los jugadores del Barça — the Barça players
la mejor actriz — the best actress
las mejores ofertas — the best offers

- **a** and **de**, when followed by **el**, become a single word:

  a + el = al
  de + el = del

  –¿Has visto **al** vecino **del** quinto? Es guapísimo.
  'Have you seen the man who lives on the fifth floor? He's very good-looking.'
  –Claro, es jugador **del** Atlético y va **al** campo a entrenarse todos los días.
  'Sure, he plays for Atlético and goes to the ground to train every day.'

- The other forms of the definite article, **la**, **los** and **las**, remain unchanged after **a** and **de**:

  Hay un mensaje **de los** amigos de Tony en el contestador. Le esperan **a las** cuatro **de la** tarde en la estación.
  There's a message from Tony's friends on the answering machine. They'll be waiting for him at the station at 4 p.m.

- The definite article is used with nouns **in a general sense** or to indicate **a unique person or thing**:

  Las casas están más baratas ahora.
  Houses are cheaper nowadays.
  El vino en **las** comidas es bueno para el corazón.
  Wine at mealtimes is good for the heart.
  Me encanta **el** cine pero no me gustan **las** películas de miedo.
  I love cinema but I don't like horror films.
  En **los** países fríos todos **los** edificios **tienen** calefacción.
  In cold countries all buildings have central heating.
  La inocencia es algo precioso.
  Innocence is a precious thing.
  Los medios de comunicación tienen mucho poder.
  The media have a lot of power.
  Las biografías de celebridades se venden muy bien.
  Celebrities' biographies sell very well.

The definite article is used in the following circumstances:

1 When referring to a person or thing whose identity is known to the speaker:

Vamos a ver **la** película de la que hablamos ayer.
Let's go and see **the** film we talked about yesterday.

2 With the **names of languages**, except when they follow *hablar*, *saber* and *aprender* directly:

Carlos sabe francés, alemán y ruso. **El** inglés y **el** italiano los está aprendiendo ahora. Tiene mucha facilidad para **las** lenguas.
but
Juana ha aprendido muy bien **el** chino.

Carlos knows French, German and Russian. He's learning English and Italian now. He has a gift languages.

Juana has learned Chinese very well.

3 Before **titles**, except when you are addressing the person directly:

–Que pase **la** *Señora Galindo*; **el** Doctor Ruiz la espera.

'Mrs Galindo is next; Dr Ruiz is waiting for her.'

–Buenas tardes **Señora Galindo**. *¿Cómo* se encuentra hoy?

'Good afternoon, Mrs Galindo. How are you today?'

–Mejor, **Doctor Ruiz**, mucho mejor, muchas gracias.

'Better, Dr Ruiz, much better, thank you.'

4 With **days of the week**, translating 'on' in English:

El Museo de Arte Contemporáneo abre **los** lunes y **los** martes por la mañana; **los** miércoles y **los** jueves por la tarde; **los** viernes y **los** sábados por la mañana y por la tarde. Todos **los** domingos está cerrado.

The Museum of Contemporary Art opens on Mondays and Tuesdays in the morning; on Wednesdays and Thursdays in the afternoon; on Fridays and Saturdays in the morning and afternoon. It is closed on Sundays.

5 With a number of common expressions:

a/en la cárcel	to/in prison
a/en la escuela	to/at school
en el espacio	in space
en el hospital	in hospital
en la televisión	on television

The definite article is not used in the following circumstances:

1 With roman numbers after the names of monarchs and popes:

Felipe II (segundo) de España y la reina Isabel I (primera) de Inglaterra reinaron en el mismo siglo.

Philip II (the Second) of Spain and Elizabeth I (the First) of England reigned in the same century.

2 With **countries,** as in English:

Me gusta pasar las vacaciones en **Europa**.
En invierno voy a esquiar a **Suiza** o a **Francia** y en verano voy al sur, a **Grecia** o a **España.**

I like spending my holidays in Europe.
In winter I go skiing in Switzerland or France and in the summer I go to the south, to Greece or Spain.

But note that there are some exceptions, e.g. la India, el Salvador, el Japón, la China, el Perú, el Reino Unido, los Estados Unidos. However, more often than not, Spanish newspapers now drop the definite article, except for la India and el Salvador.

The definite article is used if the country is qualified by a phrase or an adjective:

La España de la democracia
La Inglaterra victoriana

Democratic Spain
Victorian England

3 When **in apposition**:

A phrase which is in *apposition* gives more information about the preceding noun:

Juan, hijo único de María y Carlos, ...
López, nuevo portero del Barcelona, ...

Juan, the only son of María and Carlos, ...
López, the new Barcelona goalkeeper, ...

2.2 The indefinite article

The **indefinite** article refers to a noun that has not been specified (and so is considered 'indefinite').

	singular	plural
	(a/an)	(some)
masculine	un	unos
feminine	una	unas

Key ideas

In Spanish there are four forms of the indefinite article. The definite article agrees with the noun in number and gender:

un coche rápido	a fast car
una chica colombiana	a Colombian girl
unos niños traviesos	some naughty children
unas mujeres del campo	some country women

The indefinite article is used in the following circumstances:

1   **un/una** are used when the identity of the person or thing you are referring to is not already known:

Un hombre y **una** mujer entraron en el hotel y pidieron **una** habitación con baño.	A man and a woman went into the hotel and asked for a room with a bath.

2   The plural form **unos/unas** is often either not translated at all, or translated more satisfactorily by 'a few', or 'approximately':

Han ido a tomar **unas** cervezas al bar de la esquina.	They've gone to have a few beers in the local bar.

3   **unos/unas** mean 'approximately', 'about', **with numbers**:

Nos quedan **unos** mil euros.	We have about a thousand euros left.

The indefinite article is not used in the following circumstances:

1   With **professions** or **occupations** after **ser**, unless the noun is qualified in some way:

Picasso fue pintor. Fue **un** pintor muy importante porque inició el Cubismo.	Picasso was a painter. He was a very important painter because he started the Cubist movement.
Es médico pero no **un** médico cualquiera; es el premio Nobel de Medicina de este año.	He's a doctor, but not any old doctor; he's this year's Nobel Prize winner in Medicine.

2   When the noun is **in apposition**:

Mandó un correo a su amigo Sánchez del Portal, tenista de mucha fama.	He sent an email to his friend Sánchez del Portal, a tennis player of great renown.

3   With **otro**, **tal**, **medio**, **qué**, **cien** and **mil**:

Dame otro ejemplo.	Give me another example.
Nunca pensé que dijera tal cosa.	I never thought he would say such a thing.
Tráiganos media botellita de vino.	Bring us half a bottle of wine.
¡Qué historia tan rara!	What a strange story!
Hace cien años.	A hundred years ago.
Préstame mil euros.	Lend me a thousand euros.

4 Omission of 'some':

Póngame azúcar y leche en el café.   Add some sugar and milk to my coffee.

Note that in French the 'partitive' article (***du*** *sucre, du lait*) would be used here.

Exercises

1 Place the correct definite article before the following words:

caballo	turistas	diccionario
nariz	deportes	detectives
flor	canciones	belleza
patata	montañas	igualdad
taxi	bolso	semáforos
profesiones	dedos	solución
anuncios	DVDs	luna

2 Choose from the following list of words your favourite 10 topics, giving the correct definite article:

artes   lectura   senderismo   música   baile   traducción   televisión   teatro
natación   ordenadores   tenis   política   fotografía   gastronomía   gramática
rock and roll   jazz   moda   compras   artes marciales   decoración   electrónica
economía   fútbol   coleccionismo   medio ambiente   idiomas   viajes   deportes

3 Make three columns, saying which characteristics are required for the three professions indicated, placing the appropriate definite article with each word:

deportista   *ejecutiva*   *político*

honestidad	control	energía	ambición	constancia
diplomacia	belleza	inteligencia	contactos	experiencia
buen corazón	elegancia	formación	rapidez	reflejos
modales	salud	resistencia	competitividad	creatividad

4 Decide whether the nouns in the following sentences need an article or not. Fill the gaps with the correct article where necessary:

a Si eres _____ estudiante o jubilado, tienes descuento en _____ peluquería.

b Ha ido a la tienda a comprar _____ pan y _____ leche.

c Ha contraído _____ enfermedad incurable.

d Este fin de semana voy a un cursillo para aprender _____ nuevo programa de Windows.

e Esta tarde voy a comprar _____ portátil nuevo porque _____ viejo no funciona bien.

f Siempre hay _____ ruido en _____ clase 23.

g ¿Has oído _____ últimas noticias?

h España ha cambiado mucho en _____ últimos tiempos.

i En Murcia se cultivan _____ melocotones riquísimos. Hay quien dice que son _____ mejores de España.

j El profesor Gómez, _____ físico famoso, murió en diciembre.

3
Nouns

What are nouns?

A noun is the name that we give to a person, animal, thing or idea. We usually distinguish between two types of nouns: **common** nouns like *car, island, writer* and *country* and **proper** nouns, which refer to particular persons, places, or objects, like *Porsche, Menorca, Cervantes, Spain*.

Key ideas

In Spanish, there are two main considerations when dealing with nouns:

- *gender*: all nouns are either **masculine** or **feminine**
- *number*: all nouns are **singular**, i.e. they refer to a single thing, or **plural**, i.e. they refer to more than one thing.
- Plurals are normally formed in Spanish by adding *-s or -es* to the singular.

Un Cuadro

" Las Meninas "

3.1 Gender

1 There are no exceptions to the rule that nouns in Spanish are either masculine or feminine in gender. Nouns are preceded by the definite or indefinite article: **el/un** for masculine singular nouns and **la/una** for feminine singular nouns. It is sometimes possible to determine the gender of a noun according to biological gender.

masculine nouns		**feminine nouns**	
el/un hombre	man	la/una mujer	woman/wife
el/un tío	uncle	la/una tía	aunt
el/un caballo	horse	la/una yegua	mare
el/un camarero	waiter	la/una camarera	waitress
el/un león	lion	la/una leona	lioness

2 In most cases there is no obvious reason for a noun being masculine or feminine, and so the gender has to be learned:

el piso	flat	la casa	house
el maquillaje	make-up	la rata	rat
el brazo	arm	la cabeza	head

3 In general, nouns ending in **-o** are masculine and nouns ending in **-a** are feminine, but there are too many exceptions to rely absolutely on this rule, as these examples show:

el día	day	una radio	radio
un mapa	map	la mano	hand
la moto	motorbike	el planeta	planet
una modelo	(fashion) model		

4 Nouns with the following endings are normally masculine: **-aje**, **-or**, as are those with a **stressed vowel**:

el garaje	garage	el ordenador	computer
el equipaje	luggage	el jabalí	wild boar
el calor	heat	el plató	(cinema) set

5 Nouns with the following endings are normally feminine: **-ión, -dad, -tad, -triz, -tud, -umbre, -nza, -cia, -ie**:

la solución	solution	la virtud	virtue
la población	population	la incertidumbre	uncertainty
la universidad	university	la esperanza	hope
la libertad	freedom	la experiencia	experience
la cicatriz	scar	la serie	series

Note: the following two exceptions to the above: **el avión** (aeroplane), and **el camión** (lorry).

6 Certain categories of noun are normally masculine, as follows:

a Rivers **(los ríos)**, seas **(los mares)**, lakes **(los lagos)**, mountains **(los montes, los picos)** and mountain ranges:

el Tajo	the Tagus
el Támesis	the Thames
el Mediterráneo	the Mediterranean
el lago Titicaca	Lake Titicaca
el Aconcagua	Mt Aconcagua
los Pirineos	the Pyrenees

Note that **montaña** (mountain) and **cordillera** (mountain range) are feminine.

b Fruit trees **(los árboles frutales)**:

el almendro	almond tree
el manzano	apple tree

Note that the fruits derived from these trees are normally feminine: **la almendra** (almond), **la manzana** (apple).

c   Cars **(los coches)**:

un viejo Seat	an old Seat
el Peugeot de mi vecino	my neighbour's Peugeot

d   Days of the week **(los días de la semana)**:

Llegó un sábado.	He arrived on a Saturday.
Solían salir los lunes.	They used to go out on Mondays.

e   Colours **(los colores)**:

El azul es mi color preferido.   Blue is my favourite colour.

f   Points of the compass **(los puntos cardinales)**:

el norte	the north	el este	the east	el noreste	the north-east
el sur	the south	el oeste	the west	el suroeste	the south-west

g   Infinitives **(los infinitivos)**:

The infinitive is always masculine when it has the function of a noun (see Part I, 32.1).

El ir y venir de la gente.   The coming and going of people.

7   Certain categories of noun are normally feminine:

a   Letters of the alphabet **(las letras del abecedario)**:

En castellano la ce se pronuncia como la zeta. In Spanish the letter **c** is pronounced the same as **z.**

b   Islands, roads **(las islas, las carreteras)**:

Las Islas Canarias	The Canary Islands
La M30 The M30	

8   The gender of currencies varies:

el dólar   la libra esterlina   el yen   el euro

3.2 Number

Nouns in Spanish form their plurals as follows:

1   Nouns ending in a vowel add **-s**:

la hamburguesa	las hamburguesas	hamburger/s
la impresora	las impresoras	printer/s
el pescado	los pescados	fish (on a plate)
el pie	los pies	foot/feet

2   Nouns ending in a consonant add **-es**:

el árbol	los árboles	tree/s
la ciudad	las ciudades	town/s
el color	los colores	colour/s
el móvil	los móviles	mobile/s
la ley	las leyes	law/s
el país	los países	country/-ies

Note that:

a   Nouns ending in **z** change the ending to **-ces** in the plural:

la voz	las voces	voice/s
el pez	los peces	fish (live)

b   Nouns which have an accent on the last syllable lose the accent in the plural:

un inglés	unos ingleses	English person/s
el pantalón	los pantalones	trousers
la razón	las razones	reason/s
una región	unas regiones	region/s

c Nouns ending in **-en** which are stressed on the penultimate syllable add an accent in order to keep the stress on the same syllable:

el examen	los exámenes	examination/s
la imagen	las imágenes	image/s
el origen	los orígenes	origin/s

d The following two words alter their stress in the plural:

| el carácter | los caracteres | character/s |
| el régimen | los regímenes | regime/s |

3 In both English and Spanish, nouns can be classified according to whether they can be counted or not. A *count* noun, for example 'apple', is different from a *mass* noun, such as 'salt' or 'vengeance'. We can say 'two apples' but we would not normally say 'two salts' or 'five vengeances'.

Spanish makes plurals of mass nouns more readily than English:

singular		*plural*	
la noticia	a piece of news	**las noticias**	news
el pan	bread	**los panes**	loaves of bread

Exercises

1 Place each noun in its group, as in the example:

| | **masculine** | **feminine** |
| Example: | color | maldad |

coraje	mano	gripe	tren
maldad	moda	cerveza	corbata
salud	sensibilidad	foto	biblioteca
color	discusión	estrés	policía
costumbre	mapa	ojo	mercado
tendencia	dolor	televisión	cena

2 Write the masculine or feminine form of the following nouns, as appropriate:

el profesor	....
la amiga	....
el jefe	....
el escocés	....
la perra	....
el socio	....
un nadador	....
la andaluza	....
una cubana	....
un programador	....

3 Give the plural of the following nouns, as in the example:

el francés	los franceses	la verdad	....
un tsunami	....	la piel	....
la madre	....	la posibilidad	....
el atleta	....	el revés	....
un lápiz	....	una vez	....
el rey	....	el violín	....
la situación	....	la nación	....

4 Make two lists of the nouns in this passage, one of the common nouns, the other of the proper nouns:

> Angel tuvo buena suerte. Era el pequeño de siete hermanos y su madre tenía que trabajar y estaba poco en casa. La gente pensaba que acabaría con problemas pero se equivocaron. Le gustaba ir a la escuela y su maestro, Don Ricardo, le buscó una beca para ir al Instituto Antonio Machado. Allí resultó que le gustaban mucho el inglés y las matemáticas y por fin fue a la Universidad de Zaragoza para estudiar informática. Ahora tiene un trabajo muy bueno y la esperanza de conseguir un cargo de director en una gran compañía como Microsoft.
> (written by the authors)

5 Fill the gaps using the words in the box with either the definite or indefinite article in the correct gender:

mano	día	patente	cliente
traje	tapices	televisión	mapa

a Mi cumpleaños es _____ 8 de marzo.

b La empresa tiene _____, así que puede comercializar el producto.

c Cogió la pelota con _____ derecha.

d Si quiere saber el tiempo vea _____ a las 10.

e Si no sabes donde está Uruguay búscalo en _____.

f Los toreros siempre llevan _____ de luces cuando lidian.

g Antiguamente la gente rica solía colgar _____ en la pared para mostrar su riqueza.

h ¿Qué hacemos cuando _____ se niega a pagar la factura?

4
Adjectives

What are adjectives?

Adjectives are words used to identify or describe nouns. When we say: 'Simon lives in a house', we communicate no information about his house or his living conditions. One way to give this information is by using adjectives.

If we place an adjective before the noun 'house' – 'Simon lives in a *small* house' – we learn something more about what the house is like.

Each of the adjectives describes or defines the house further, and can even tell us what Simon is like.

In English, adjectives can be placed: **before the noun** (as in the above examples) or **after the verb,** as in 'That house looks *pretty*', etc.

Mis Hermanos

Iñaki es el mayor, altísimo, estudioso y casi calvo.
Imanol tiene el pelo largo, es corto de vista y le gusta la ropa moderna.
Amaia tiene el pelo rizado, es gordita y muy aficionada a la música
Garbiñe es la más pequeña, delgadísima, alegre y deportista.

Key ideas

In Spanish, adjectives are generally used in the same way as in English, i.e. next to the nouns they describe and as the complement of the verb, but there are several significant differences:

- Adjectives agree with the noun in *gender*:

  La cena resultó **desastrosa** ... la sopa estaba **fría**, el pan **duro**, el vino era **barato** y los comensales **aburridos**.

  Dinner was disastrous ... the soup was cold, the bread stale, the wine cheap and the guests boring.

- Adjectives agree with the noun in *number*:

  En España los meses **fríos** suelen ser enero y febrero. En marzo, generalmente hace un tiempo **fresco** pero **soleado**. En verano las temperaturas son muy **altas** y el sol **ardiente**.

  In Spain the cold months are usually January and February. In March it is generally cool but sunny. In summer the temperatures are very high and the sun is hot.

- Adjectives are normally placed *after* the noun:

  La mitología **griega** contiene personajes **imaginarios** e historias **increíbles**.

  Greek mythology contains imaginary characters and incredible stories.

4.1 Formation

1 Many adjectives in Spanish end in **-o** (masculine) or **-a** (feminine); the plural forms are **-os /-as**. Thus:

masc. sing.	fem. sing.	masc. plural	fem. plural
electrónico	electrónica	electrónicos	electrónicas

2 Adjectives which do not end in **-o/-a** usually have the same form for masculine and feminine in the singular:

Lleva un pantalón gris.	He is wearing grey trousers.
Lleva una falda gris.	She is wearing a grey skirt.

In the plural, adjectives which end in **-e** add **-s** and most of those which end in a consonant add **-es**.

masc. sing	fem. sing.	masc. plural	fem. plural	
dulce	dulce	dulces	dulces	sweet
gris	gris	grises	grises	grey
azul	azul	azules	azules	blue

Me gustan el café y el vino dulces.   I like sweet coffee and sweet wine.

3 Adjectives ending in **-z** change the **z** to **c** in the plural:

masc. sing	fem. sing.	masc. plural	fem. plural	
feliz	feliz	felices	felices	happy
capaz	capaz	capaces	capaces	capable

4 Adjectives ending in **-án, -ón, -ín** and **-or** (except comparatives) add **-a/-as** to make the feminine:

masc. sing	fem. sing.	masc. plural	fem. plural	
holgazán	holgazana	holgazanes	holgazanas	lazy
mandón	mandona	mandones	mandonas	bossy
encantador	encantadora	encantadores	encantadoras	charming

–Sr Antúnez, la Srta. López es una empleada difícil; es un poco holgazana y prefiere dejar el trabajo a las otras empleadas. No le digo más que todas la llaman 'la mandona'.
–Sí, pero es encantadora con los clientes.

'Mr Antúnez, Mrs Lopez is a difficult employee; she's rather lazy and prefers to let others do the work. Everybody calls her "the boss"; I'll say no more.'
'Yes, but she's charming with the clients.'

5 Adjectives which denote the region or country that a person comes from add **-a** in the feminine:

masc. sing	fem. sing.	masc. plural	fem. plural	
español	española	españoles	españolas	Spanish
inglés	inglesa	ingleses	inglesas	English
castellano	castellana	castellanos	castellanas	Castilian
andaluz	andaluza	andaluces	andaluzas	Andalusian
vasco	vasca	vascos	vascas	Basque

Su padre es alemán y su madre francesa pero sus abuelos, por parte del padre, eran daneses y su otra abuela sueca; es lo que se dice una verdadera europea.

Her father is German and her mother French, but her other grandparents, on her father's side, were Danish and her other grandmother Swedish; she's what you'd call a true European.

6 Comparative adjectives do not have a separate feminine form. (See Part I, 5.1):

masc. and fem. sing.	masc. and fem. plural	
mejor	mejores	better
peor	peores	worse
superior	superiores	superior

4.2 Position of adjectives

Adjectives are normally placed after nouns in Spanish, with the following key exceptions:

1 A number of common adjectives:

bueno	good
malo	bad
pequeño	small
gran(de)	big, great

–Buenos días, Don Julián.
–Buenos no, Don Ricardo, malos días.
–¿Qué le pasa, hombre?
–Que tengo un virus en el ordenador y eso me está dando un gran dolor de cabeza.

'Good day, Don Julian.'
'It's not a good day, Don Ricardo, it's a bad one.'
'What's the matter with you?'
'I've a virus in my computer which is giving me a big headache.'

2 Cardinal and ordinal numbers, and **último**:

El primer cuento de las 'Mil y una noches' habla de Scheherezade, una princesa árabe que se libró de ser ejecutada en el último minuto, gracias a su habilidad para contar cuentos interesantísimos.

The first tale in *A Thousand and One Nights* is about Scheherezade, an Arabian princess who escaped execution at the last moment thanks to her ability to tell fascinating stories.

4.3 Shortening (or 'apocopation') of adjectives

1 Certain common adjectives lose the final **-o** when they come before a masculine singular noun. This is called 'apocopation'. These adjectives are:

alguno	>	algún	any	primero	> primer	first
bueno	>	buen	good	tercero	> tercer	third
malo	>	mal	bad	uno	> un	one, a
ninguno	>	ningún	no			

–¿Han dejado **algún** paquete para mí? 'Has someone left a parcel for me?'
–No, aquí no hay **ningún** paquete. 'No there's no parcel here.'
–Qué raro, el **primer** paquete llegó 'How strange, the first parcel arrived safely and then
muy bien y después nada. Las compras nothing more. Internet shopping is a good idea but
en Internet son una buena idea pero as the postal service is so bad it can get very
como hay tan **mal** servicio de correos annoying.'
pueden resultar muy enojosas.

2 **Grande** shortens to **gran** before masculine and feminine singular nouns:

El gran futbolista, Messi. The great footballer, Messi.
Acudan a la gran rebaja en los grandes Come to the big sale at the department
almacenes 'El Corte Inglés'. store 'El Corte Inglés'.

Exercises

1 Fill the gaps with a suitable adjective from the box:

rayadas	difíciles	fácil	electrónico	moreno
dulce	abierta	rápido	sanos	idénticos

a el pelo _____
b unos programas _____
c un coche _____
d dos móviles _____
e una música _____
f el juego _____
g las camisas _____
h la puerta _____
i unos hombres _____
j una tarea _____

2 Change the following phrases into the plural:

Example: un chico inglés chicos ingleses

a un ratón electrónico _____
b una ciudad española _____
c una tarea difícil _____
d un tren francés _____
e un pinchadiscos bueno _____
f un museo encantador _____
g una mañana gris _____
h un gobierno corrupto _____
i una mañana primaveral _____
j un gran artista _____

3 Turn the following phrases and sentences into the masculine:

Example: Mi madre es generosa. Mi padre es generoso.

a Mi perrita es muy simpática. _____
b Su madre era feliz. _____

c La chica es trabajadora. _____

d Tu amiga es carpintera. _____

e La gata no estaba enferma. _____

f Una mujer extraordinaria. _____

g La niña bilingüe. _____

h Una señora gallega. _____

4 Write the correct adjective of nationality:

a La Reina Isabel es (de Inglaterra) _____

b Han venido mis amigos (de Alemania) _____

c Igor es (de Rusia) _____

d Barcelona es una ciudad (de Cataluña) _____

e Me encanta la cocina (de Portugal) _____

f Mariluz es (de España) _____

g Umbria es una región (de Italia) _____

h Gérard es (de Francia) _____

5 Answer the following questions, using one or more adjectives:

a ¿De qué color son tus zapatos? _____

b ¿Cómo es tu habitación? _____

c ¿Cómo es tu casa? _____

d ¿Cómo son tus mejores amigos? _____

e ¿Cómo es tu pueblo/ciudad? _____

f ¿De qué color tienes el pelo? _____

6 Pau and Xavier's story is rather sad; on the other hand, Gerardo's and Leo's, although very similar, is much happier. Construct Gerardo's and Leo's story by filling the gaps with the adjectives in the box:

> Pau y Xavier son *jóvenes e inteligentes*. Sus padres fueron *inflexibles* con ellos porque sacaban *malas* notas. La verdad es que eran muy *perezosos*. Después de llevar una vida *horrible* en casa decidieron independizarse. Ahora tienen un trabajo *temporal* y viven en una casa *abandonada*. Sus amigos son *pobres* como ellos. *Algunas* veces organizan fiestas *simpáticas* aunque por lo general están bastante *deprimidos*. Es *triste* que hayan tenido tan *mala* suerte.

generosos	ocupados	muchas	fantástico	carísima
guapos y felices	muy protegida	excelentes	muy bien pagado	
buena	importantes	elegantes	aplicados	

Gerardo y Leo son _____. Sus padres fueron _____ con ellos porque sacaban _____ notas. La verdad es que eran _____. Después de llevar una vida _____ en casa decidieron independizarse. Ahora tienen un trabajo _____ y viven en una casa _____. Sus amigos son _____ como ellos. _____ veces organizan fiestas _____ aunque por lo general están bastante _____. Es _____ que hayan tenido tan _____ suerte.

5

Comparison

What is comparison?

There are two important terms used for comparison, *comparative* and *superlative*.

Comparative

When we looked at adjectives we said that they were words used to identify or describe nouns, in order to express particular qualities.

> *Fresh* fruit is *good* for you.

Sometimes we want to emphasise a particular quality by comparing the **degree** to which two nouns possess that quality:

> Fresh fruit is *better* for you than chocolate.

A comparison takes place when we say that somebody or something possesses a quality to a *greater* degree:

> Tony is more creative *than* Adam.

Or to a *lesser* degree:

> Tony is *less* clever *than* Adam.

Or to the *same* degree:

> Adam is *as* reliable *as* Tony.

A teacher speaking about these two students might say:

> Tony is more creative than Adam but Adam is cleverer; the one is as reliable as the other.

In the above example we are using the adjectives *creative* and *clever* in their **comparative** forms.

We frequently link two people, things or ideas in this way to compare them for their size, shape, importance, character, etc. When we do this in English we use *more/less … (than),* or we add *-er* to the word if it is short, e.g. 'smaller', 'quicker'.

Superlative

The superlative is used when we are referring to a quality **in its greatest possible degree**.

We use *most/least* (the most/least intelligent, stupid, beautiful, etc.), or we add *-est* to the word if it is short ('the busiest', 'the greatest' etc.):

> English is the most popular language.

> Albania is one of the poorest countries in Europe.

The second part of the comparison is either understood (first example) or the group to which the noun belongs is mentioned, e.g. countries in Europe (second example).

In the above examples we are using 'popular' and 'poor' in their **superlative** forms.

Key ideas

In Spanish comparisons follow the same principles as in English. There are three kinds:

- Comparison of superiority
- Comparison of inferiority
- Comparison of equality

5.1 Comparative

Comparison of superiority

When we want to say that one thing, person or animal possesses a particular quality to a higher degree than another we use:

más ... que

Inglaterra es **más** verde **que** España.   England is greener than Spain.

Comparison of inferiority

When we want to say that one thing, person or animal possesses a particular quality to a lesser degree than another we use:

menos ... que

En Inglaterra hace **menos** sol **que** en España.   It's less sunny in England than in Spain.

Comparison of equality

When the qualities compared are of the same or similar value we use:

tan ... como

El tráfico es **tan** malo en España **como** en   The traffic is as bad in Spain as in
Inglaterra.   England.

When the comparison refers to quantity, the adjectival form *tanto/a/os/as* is used, agreeing with the noun to which it refers:

En Barcelona hay **tantos** coches **como** en   There are as many cars in Barcelona as in London.
Londres.
En España se leen **tantas** revistas **como** en   As many magazines are read in Spain as in
Inglaterra.   England.

los españoles se acuestan más tarde que....

..... Los Ingleses.

Special comparative forms

1 Adjectives of comparison

The most common adjectives we use for comparison have special comparative forms:

adjective	comparative
bueno	mejor
malo	peor
mucho	más
poco	menos
grande	mayor
pequeño	menor

Note: mayor and **menor** normally refer to the age rather than the size of a person (for the use of **más grande/más pequeño** instead of **mayor/menor** (see Part II, 5.2):

Carlos está mejorando: su último examen es **mejor** que el anterior; seguramente ha estudiado con **más** interés que antes.	Carlos is improving: his latest examination is better than the previous one; he's certainly studied with greater interest than before.
Sin embargo su hermana **menor** ha sacado **peores** notas.	However, his younger sister has had worse marks.
Desde que juega al baloncesto trabaja con **menos** frecuencia.	Since she's been playing basketball she's been working less.

2 Adverbs of comparison

a The most common adverbs we use for comparison have special comparative forms:

adverb	comparative
bien	mejor
mal	peor
más	más
poco	menos

These forms are **invariable**:

Guisas la paella mejor que cualquier restaurante.	You cook paella better than any restaurant.
La compañía va de mal en peor.	The company is going from bad to worse.
No puedo decirte más; es un secreto.	I can't say any more; it's a secret.
Cada día gasto menos.	Every day I spend less.

b For comparisons of equality **tanto como** (as much as), is used:

Él no hace deporte **tanto como** ella.	He doesn't play sports as much as her.
No ve la tele **tanto como** piensas.	She doesn't watch TV as much as you think.

5.2 Superlative

Key ideas

- In Spanish the superlative expresses a quality in its greatest possible degree, as in English.
- There are *two* ways of expressing the superlative: **el/la más** (**grande**, etc.), and by the addition of **-ísimo/a**.

Formation

The superlative is formed:

1 *Either* by placing the definite article before the noun whose quality we are describing, and adding the comparative adjective after the noun:

Inmaculada es la persona **más simpática** de su familia.	Inmaculada is the nicest person in her family.

or by placing the definite article before the comparative adjective:

Inmaculada es **la más simpática** de la familia.	The nicest person in the family is Inmaculada.

2 *Or* by adding the suffix **-ísimo/-ísima** to the adjective to intensify its meaning.

When **-ísimo** is added, the final vowel is normally removed:

grande	big	grandísimo	enormous
claro	clear	clarísimo	extremely clear
feo	ugly	feísimo	very ugly

Andalucía es una región **hermosísima.**	Andalusia is an extremely beautiful region.
¡Estoy **cansadísimo**!	I'm exhausted.
Es cierto que aquella chica es **guapísima**.	It's true that that girl is very pretty.

Notes

a Spelling changes occur with certain endings:

adjectives ending in **-co/-ca** and **-go/-ga** become **-quísimo/a** and **-guísimo/a** respectively, in order to preserve the sound:

rico	rich, tasty	riquísimo	very rich, tasty
largo	long	larguísimo	very long

Inmaculada es **simpatiquísima**.	Inmaculada is really nice.

b Adjectives ending in **-z** change the **z** to **c**:

feliz	happy	felicísimo	very happy

c

When the superlative follows the noun, *you do not repeat the definite article before the adjective,* as you do in French:

Dicen que Andalucía es la región más hermosa de España.

They say that Andalusia is the most beautiful region of Spain.

d

The English 'in' after a superlative is expressed by **de** in Spanish:

el edificio más alto **del** mundo

the tallest building *in* the world

Exercises

1 Make sentences comparing the following:

Example: Inglaterra   España

En Inglaterra hace menos sol que en España.

a un elefante	un ratón
b Estados Unidos	Mónaco
c el azúcar	la sal
d los ingleses	los españoles
e un lobo	una oveja
f un coche	una bicicleta
g el sol	la luna
h una naranja	un plátano
i las montañas	las colinas
j un policía	un criminal

2 Carlos and Charo are two quite different young people. Can you compare them?

Example: Carlos es mayor que Charo.

Carlos	**Charo**
Tengo 17 años.	Tengo 15 años.
Tengo tres hermanos.	Tengo cinco hermanos.
Vivo en un piso pequeño.	Vivo en un chalet en el campo.
Me gusta mucho mi trabajo.	No me gusta mucho mi trabajo.
Soy un poco perezoso.	Soy muy trabajadora.
Soy aficionado al cine.	Me gusta ver la tele.
No le tengo miedo a nada.	Me gusta la aventura.
Salgo mucho por la noche.	Siempre me acuesto a las once.
Sólo tengo un amigo británico.	Escribo muchas cartas a mis amigos británicos.

3 Fill the gaps using **tan** … **como** or **tanto/a/os/as** … **como**:

a Hoy en día no hay _____ bibliotecas _____ antes.

b Marisol es _____ alta _____ su hermana.

c San Francisco no tiene _____ habitantes _____ Nueva York.

d El río Manzanares no es _____ ancho _____ el Tajo.

e Tu tío bebe _____ cerveza _____ tú.

f Paco es _____ rico _____ su padre.

g Estos zapatos no son _____ elegantes _____ aquellos.

h El pescado es un alimento _____ natural _____ la carne.

i Yo tengo _____ experiencia laboral _____ tu hermano.

4 Correct the following sentences using the comparative or the superlative form:

Example: Bilbao es más grande que Madrid.

No, Madrid es más grande que Bilbao.

a América del Sur es más rica que Europa.

b Estados Unidos es el país más pobre del mundo.

c Holanda es tan montañosa como España.

d Finlandia es un país tan antiguo como Grecia.

e La monarquía española tiene más poder que la británica.

f Alemania es el país más pequeño de Europa.

g Una copa de vino cuesta menos que un coñac.

h La moda italiana es tan elegante como la sueca.

i Los coches franceses son más potentes que los alemanes.

j Bilbao es la ciudad menos contaminada de España.

5 The following words and phrases are answers to questions. Make up a question for each answer, using a superlative:

Example: El Amazonas   ¿Cuál es el río más largo del mundo?

a El monte Everest

b William Shakespeare

c España

d China

e El móvil

f El sol

g El invierno

h El verano

i Los Beatles

j El continente africano

6 Clara and Elena have been interviewed for the job of air hostess. Which of the two should get the job? Write 10 sentences comparing their CVs. Use various ways of comparing them:

Example: Clara es más joven que Elena.

Clara	**Elena**
19 años	27 años
habla inglés y español	habla español, francés y alemán
mide 1,60 metros	1,78 metros
diploma de la escuela de azafatas	experiencia de cinco años con IBERIA
soltera	madre de un niño de cinco años
tímida pero sonriente	dio las respuestas correctas

6
Numerals

We use numbers for counting, doing sums and ordering things. Numbers can be expressed in the international language of figures (2 + 2 = 4), in a written form (two plus two equals four) or in a spoken form.

There are three types of numbers:

● those we use for *counting* (1, 2, 25, 101, 1000, etc.), called **cardinal** numbers
● those we use for ordering things in a sequence (1st, 2nd, 3rd, 4th, etc.), called **ordinal** numbers
● those we use for collections of things, e.g. 'dozen', 'a pair', called **collective** numbers.

Numbers in English and Spanish come as individual words (e.g. 'seven') and in combination (e.g. 'seventy-seven'). In English the first 12 numbers have one component, the next seven are combinations of a number plus 10 (thirteen, fourteen, etc.). Comparison with English numbers is useful up to point, but there are many differences between the languages in both the way numbers are formed and in the way they are perceived.

Key ideas

- Spanish, like English, has cardinal, ordinal and collective numbers.
- In Spanish numbers are adjectives (except for **un millón** and collective numbers): many of them have masculine and feminine forms, e.g. **uno/a** (one).
- All Spanish numbers except **uno/a** are plural so are used with the plural form of the verb:

¿Cuánto *es*?	How much is it?
Son sesenta y cinco euros.	**It's** sixty-five euros. (cardinal)
el primer día de Carnaval	the first day of Carnival (ordinal)
media docena de huevos	half a dozen eggs (collective)

6.1 Cardinal numbers

1–15 these numbers have to be learned by heart:

1	uno/una	6	seis	11	once
2	dos	7	siete	12	doce
3	tres	8	ocho	13	trece
4	cuatro	9	nueve	14	catorce
5	cinco	10	diez	15	quince

16–19 are a combination of 10 and another number. Note that the **z** of **diez** changes to **c** and that the two words are linked by **i**:

16	dieciséis	18	dieciocho
17	diecisiete	19	diecinueve

20–29 are formed by a special combination of **veinte** and the other number, linked by **i**:

20	veinte	24	veinticuatro	27	veintisiete
21	veintiuno/una	25	veinticinco	28	veintiocho
22	veintidós	26	veintiséis	29	veintinueve
23	veintitrés				

30–99 the tens have to be learned, but other numbers are formed by a combination of the tens and units:

30	treinta	50	cincuenta	70	**setenta***
31	treinta y uno	55	cincuenta y cinco	78	setenta y ocho
32	treinta y dos	56	cincuenta y seis	80	ochenta
40	cuarenta	60	**sesenta***	89	ochenta y nueve
43	cuarenta y tres	67	sesenta y siete	90	**noventa***
44	cuarenta y cuatro				

* **Note** the unpredictable nature of the spelling of these three numbers: **seis** (6) > sesenta; **siete** (7) > setenta; **nueve** (9) > noventa.

100–1.000.000

The numbers 100, 1000 and 1,000,000 should be learned by heart; other numbers are combinations of previous numbers:

100	cien(to)	900	novecientos/as
101	ciento uno/una	1000	mil
102	ciento dos	1001	mil uno/una
155	ciento cincuenta y cinco	1347	mil trescientos cuarenta y siete
200	doscientos/as	1999	mil novecientos noventa y nueve
300	trescientos/as	2007	dos mil siete
400	cuatrocientos/as	44.510	cuarenta y cuatro mil quinientos diez
500	quinientos/as	100.000	cien mil
600	seiscientos/as	723.000	setecientos veintitrés mil
700	setecientos/as	1.000.000	un millón
800	ochocientos/as	5.000.000	cinco millones

Notes:

- Numbers up to 30 are written as one word:

dieciséis	16
veintinueve	29
But treinta y cinco	35

- There are some peculiarities in the spelling of words containing the number 5:

5 cinco	15 quince	50 cincuenta	500 quinientos

- Long numbers are formed as follows:

  125.673:

ciento	veinticinco	mil	seiscientos	setenta	y tres
1(00)	25		6(00)	7(0)	3
a hundred	and twenty-five	thousand	six hundred	and seventy	-three

Uno/una

Uno becomes **un** before a masculine singular noun. This is true of all numbers which end in **uno**. **Una** remains the same before a feminine singular noun:

un chico	one boy (or **a** boy)
una chica	one girl (or **a** girl)
cincuenta y un años	fifty-one years
Hay veintiuna alumnas en la clase.	There are twenty-one girls in the class.

Note: **uno** keeps the final **o** when it stands on its own:

¿Cuántos billetes te quedan?	How many tickets have you got left?
Sólo uno.	Only one.

Masculine and feminine forms

Cardinal numbers containing **un(o)** and multiples of **ciento** have a masculine and a feminine form; other numbers do not:

¿Cuántas personas había? Había cuatro: **un** hombre, **una** chica y **dos** mujeres.	How many people were there? There were four: one man, one girl and two women.
En España se estrenan **trescientas cincuenta** películas nuevas cada año.	Three hundred and fifty new films are screened in Spain each year.
–¿Cuánto cuesta tu abono?	How much is your season ticket?
–**Mil quinientos** euros.	One thousand five hundred euros.
Ha heredado quinientas mil libras, **que son** casi quinientos mil euros.	He has inherited five hundred thousand pounds, which is nearly five hundred thousand euros.

The position of y

Spanish places **y** between **tens and units** (unlike English, which places 'and' between thousands/hundreds and tens). Note that **y** is never placed after *hundreds* or *thousands* when a zero follows:

doscientos treinta **y** ocho	238	two hundred ***and*** thirty-eight
quinientos noventa **y** uno	591	five hundred ***and*** ninety-one
doscientos ocho	208	two hundred ***and*** eight
mil tres	1,003	one thousand ***and*** three

Ciento, mil and un millón

1 **Ciento** is shortened to **cien** before a noun or an adjective but not before another number, except **mil**:

cien metros	a hundred metres
las cien mejores películas	the hundred best films
ciento treinta kilómetros para Santillana	a hundred and thirty kilometres to Santillana
ciento cincuenta mil hombres	a hundred and fifty thousand men
cien mil soldados	a hundred thousand soldiers

2 **Cien** and **mil** are not preceded by the indefinite article, unlike in English:

cien aviones	a hundred aeroplanes
mil litros	a thousand litres

3 Multiples of a hundred (spelt as one word) agree in gender and number:

quinient**as** personas	five hundred people

4 **un millón** (a million) is preceded by the indefinite article as in English, but must be followed by **de**:

un millón de habitantes	a million inhabitants

6.2 Ordinal numbers

1st	1º/1ª	primero/a	10th	10º/10ª	décimo/a
2nd	2º/2ª	segundo/a	11th	11º/11ª	undécimo/a
3rd	3º/3ª	tercero/a	12th	12º/12ª	duodécimo/a
4th	4º/4ª	cuarto/a	13th	13º/13ª	decimotercero/a
5th	5º/5ª	quinto/a	20th	20º/20ª	vigésimo/a
6th	6º/6ª	sexto/a	30th	30º/30ª	trigésimo/a
7th	7º/7ª	séptimo/a	100th	100º/100ª	centésimo/a
8th	8º/8ª	octavo/a	1000th	1000º/1000ª	milésimo/a
9th	9º/9ª	noveno/a			

Form

1 Ordinal numbers, like cardinal ones, are adjectives so they agree with the noun in number and gender:

los primeros días de la primavera	the first days of spring
la tercera edad	the third age
el sexto piso	the sixth floor
las tres primeras horas	the first three hours (note the word order here)

2 **Primero** and **tercero** drop the final **o** before a *masculine* singular noun (see Part I, 4.3.1):

el primer paso	the first step
el tercer día	the third day

But

la primera/tercera vez	the first/third time

3 Ordinal numbers are normally used up to ten; subsequently cardinal numbers are used:

Isabel Segunda	Elizabeth II (the second)
el siglo quinto	the fifth century

But

Alfonso trece	Alfonso XIII (the thirteenth)
el siglo veintiuno	the twenty-first century

6.3 Collective numbers

The following nouns are frequently used to express a collective idea:

un centenar/una centena (de)	a hundred
cientos (de)	hundreds of
una decena (de)	ten
una docena (de)	a dozen
un millar (de)	a thousand
miles de	thousands of
un millón (de)	a million
un par de	a couple of
una veintena (de)	a score of

Most of these collective numbers usually have the meaning of 'approximately':

una docena de personas	about a dozen people
miles de problemas	thousands of problems
un par de amigos	a couple of friends

6.4 Expressing the time, dates, years and telephone numbers

The time

When telling the time cardinal numbers are used. The singular of **ser** is used to tell the time with **la una**, the plural with all other times:

¿Qué hora **es**?	What time is it?
Es la una.	It's one o'clock.
Son las seis y media.	It's half-past six.

Note: the 24-hour clock is used for timetables:

El avión despegó a las 21.30.	The aeroplane took off at 21.30/9.30 p.m.

Alternatively 'de la mañana' (a.m.) and 'de la tarde/noche' (p.m.) are placed after the number:

las cinco de la mañana	5 a.m.	las diezde la noche	10 p.m.

Dates

Cardinal numbers are used except for the first of the month, where the ordinal number is used sometimes:

el siete de mayo	7th May
el primero de enero	1st January

(It is also possible to say **el uno de enero**.)

Note that when writing the date it is usual to insert **de** before the month and year:

el 25 de febrero de 1940	25th February 1940

Years

In Spanish, years are expressed by listing thousands, hundreds, tens and units. In English, on the other hand, years are expressed as two 'blocks': 19|50 = nineteen|fifty:

mil ochocientos ocho	eighteen (hundred and) eight
mil novecientos, noventa y nueve	nineteen (hundred and) ninety-nine
dos mil dos	two thousand and two

Telephone numbers

In Spain telephone numbers are expressed in blocks of two:

Example   Alicante 25 87 59

Alicante	25	87	59
	veinticinco	ochenta y siete	cincuenta y nueve

Exercises

1   Write the number which corresponds to the word:

veinticuatro	ciento nueve	dieciséis
cincuenta y cuatro	mil novecientos nueve	catorce
setecientos setenta y cinco	treinta y ocho	veintitrés
un millón mil ciento seis	cuarenta y nueve	quinientos siete

2   Write the following numbers as words, then say them out loud and check your pronunciation with your teacher:

7 15 21 29 37 53 69 79 103 286 1039

85 48 332 14 8 99 113 500 906 100 1.000.000

3   Write the following numbers as words, read them out loud and check your pronunciation with your teacher:

1°   3°   10°   4°   2°   7°

4   Write out the following in words:

16 libros	100 cigarrillos	500 dólares	31 botellas
250 litros	75 niños	1.000.000 de años	900 pesetas

5   Say in Spanish the departure and arrival times of each train and write the answers to the following questions in words. Give the times in two forms, using the 24-hour clock and a.m./p.m.:

	Salida	Llegada
Madrid–Toledo	10.05	11.10
Córdoba–Sevilla	11.15	12.00
Madrid–Bilbao	15.54	19.40
Barcelona–Gerona	20.00	20.35
Alicante–Valencia	22.07	00.15

Example: At what time does the train arrive at Bilbao?

        A las diecinueve cuarenta.   A las siete y cuarenta de la tarde.

a   At what time does the train leave Alicante?

b   At what time does the train arrive at Seville?

c   At what time does the train arrive at Valencia?

d   At what time does the train leave Córdoba?

e   At what time does the train arrive at Gerona?

6 Complete the sentences, writing the numbers in words:

**LIGA
ESPAÑOLA**

	Partidos	Ganados	Perdidos	Empatados	Goles+	Goles–	Puntos
Barcelona	38	25	5	8	87	34	58
R. Madrid	38	24	5	9	75	28	57
Deportivo	38	22	6	10	67	33	54
Valencia	38	19	9	10	60	33	48
Tenerife	38	15	9	14	59	47	44
Atlético	38	16	11	11	52	42	43
Sevilla	38	17	12	9	46	44	43

a El Barcelona terminó en .... lugar con .... puntos.

b El Valencia ganó .... partidos y marcó .... goles.

c El Deportivo terminó en .... lugar y perdió .... partidos.

d El Tenerife perdió .... partidos y terminó con .... puntos.

e El Real Madrid empató .... partidos y marcó .... goles.

f El Sevilla terminó en .... lugar y terminó con .... puntos.

7 Write the information requested in Spanish, in figures and in words:

a your age

b the year of your birth

c the number of people in your family

d the number of questions in this exercise

e your telephone number

f the number of your house

g yesterday's date

h the number of days in a year

i the number of students in your class

j a baker's dozen

7
Personal pronouns

What are personal pronouns?

Pronouns **stand in the place of nouns** whenever it is unnecessary to mention the noun again. For example, when you are talking about a friend, you might give her name at first:

'Laura came round last night'

in order to identify her, and then use 'she' or 'her' subsequently:

'*She* brought Sophie with *her*'.

We all use pronouns as a kind of shorthand to avoid clumsy or needless repetition. A pronoun does not tell you anything more about the noun it is replacing; it simply acts as a neat and shorter substitute.

Pronouns may appear in four main places in a sentence:

- as the **subject** (English 'I', 'he')
- as the **direct object** (English 'me', 'them')
- as the **indirect object** (English 'you', 'us'), preceded by a preposition such as 'to'
- **after a preposition** (English 'after you', 'above it')

The form taken by a pronoun depends on what function it has in the sentence (subject 'we', direct object 'us', etc.).

Key ideas

- Spanish personal pronouns agree in gender and number with the nouns that they replace
- They are either subject, direct object, indirect object or they follow prepositions, as in English
- Pronouns can also be 'reflexive', i.e. they are object pronouns **which refer back to the subject of the sentence**. In English the reflexive pronouns are 'myself', 'yourself', etc.

Note the difference between:

María me compra un audiobook todas las semanas.
Maria buys me an audiobook every week. (not reflexive)
and
María se compra un audiobook todas las semanas.
Maria buys herself an audiobook every week. (reflexive)

Forms of the personal pronoun

	subject	direct object	indirect object	after prepositions
1st person sing.	**yo**	**me**	**me**	**mí**
	I	me	to me	me
2nd person sing. **familiar**	**tú**	**te**	**te**	**ti**
	you	you	(to) you	you
2nd person sing. **formal**	**usted**	**le/lo** (masc) **la** (fem)	**le**	**usted**
	you	you	(to) you	you
3rd person sing.	**él**	**le/lo**	**le**	**él**
	he/it	him/it	(to) him/it	him/it
	ella	**la**	**le**	**ella**
	she/it	her/it	(to) her/it	her/it
1st person plural	**nosotros/as**	**nos**	**nos**	**nosotros/as**
	we	us	(to) us	us
2nd person plural **familiar**	**vosotros/as**	**os**	**os**	**vosotros/as**
	you	you	(to) you	you
2nd person plural **formal**	**ustedes**	**les/los** (masc) las (fem)	**les**	**ustedes**
	you	you	(to) you	you
3rd person plural	**ellos**	**les/los**	**les**	**ellos**
	ellas	**las**	**les**	**ellas**
	they	them	(to) them	them

Important note: The **vosotros** form for the 2nd person plural is used **in Spain only**. In parts of Latin America the formal plural form, **ustedes**, is also used for the informal second person plural. Thus the sentence 'And are you coming to the beach then?' will be, in Spain, Pues vosotros, ¿venís o no a la playa?, but in Latin America, Pues ustedes, ¿vienen o no a la playa?

7.1 Subject pronouns

Key ideas

- Subject pronouns stand for the person, thing or idea which is the subject of the verb.
- The subject pronoun is normally **implicit in the form of the verb**: thus voy means 'I am going/coming'; comieron means 'they ate'.
- The major difference between English and Spanish lies in the frequency with which subject pronouns are used: in English they are used automatically, in Spanish **they are used in only a limited number of situations**: for *emphasis, contrast, avoidance of ambiguity* and *when they stand on their own*:

–¿Juegas al tenis conmigo?
–No, yo no juego contigo; yo juego con Andrés. Tú juegas con Candela.
–Pero yo prefiero jugar contigo porque juegas mejor.
–Bueno, primero juegas con ella y luego conmigo.

'Will *you* play tennis with me?'
'No, *I'm* not playing with you; *I'm* playing with Andrés. *You* are playing with Candela.'
'But *I* prefer to play with you because *you* play better.'
'OK, **you** play with her first and then with me.'

The familiar and the formal subject pronoun

1. Note that there is a familiar and a formal second person, in the singular and plural:
   - **tú** and **vosotros** are the familiar forms
   - **usted** and **ustedes** the formal (polite) forms.

   Usted and **ustedes** are **always followed by the third person form of the verb**.

2. People use the familiar and the formal forms according to status and seniority, as in the following examples, where the person in a subordinate position uses **usted** to address a person in a senior position to them and a person uses **tú** to address a friend or relative:

   Pase Vd., Sr director. Estamos encantados de verle. Come in, sir. We are delighted to see you.
   Pasa, Gloria. ¡Qué contentos estamos de verte! Come in, Gloria. We are so pleased to see you!

   It should be noted that in recent years the use of the familiar form has become more and more prevalent and is now the norm in many situations previously regarded as formal.

Use of the subject pronoun

The subject pronoun is used:

1. When the person referred to needs to be emphasised:

   Que **yo** sepa … As far as *I* know ….
   Y ¿qué crees **tú**? And what do *you* think?

2. For contrast:

   Cuando salimos a cenar **yo** como pescado siempre y **ella** nunca. When we go out to eat I always eat fish and she never does.

3. To avoid ambiguity:

   Usted conducía a demasiada velocidad. You were speeding.
   Me temo que tengo que ponerle una multa. I am afraid I have to give you a fine.

   Here the inclusion of **usted** is justified in order to make it absolutely clear who is being addressed. The third-person form of the verb can mean 'he/she/it' or 'you'. It is unnecessary to repeat **usted** in the second sentence, since there is no further likelihood of ambiguity.

(4) As a 'free-standing' pronoun:

–Has ganado la lotería.	You've won the lottery.
–¿**Yo**? Me tomas el pelo.	Me? You're pulling my leg.

7.2 Direct object pronouns

Key ideas

- Direct object pronouns stand for a person, thing or idea which is the object of the verb
- Unlike the subject pronouns, the object pronouns in Spanish are used as frequently as in English. The difference is that in Spanish object pronouns **are usually placed before the verb**, whereas in English they come after the verb:

  Lo bajé todo de Internet.   I downloaded it all from the Internet.

Position

(1) Direct object pronouns are usually placed before the verb in Spanish:

Te vi en la calle.	I saw you in the street.
No la conozco.	I don't know her/ I haven't met her.

(2) Despite the above rule, the direct object pronoun may be added to the end of an **infinitive** or **gerund**. Alternatively, it may be placed before the auxiliary verb that the infinitive or the gerund accompanies:

Vamos a contratar**los** mañana.	We are going give them the contract tomorrow.
or **Los** vamos a contratar mañana.	
Estaba observándo**la** con atención.	He was watching her attentively.
or **La** estaba observando con atención.	

Note that an accent has to be added in the second example, in order to preserve the stress (see Part I, 1.3).

(3) The direct object pronoun must be added to the end of the positive imperative (see Part I, 25.5). It is, however, always placed before a negative imperative:

Conécta**lo**.	Connect it	BUT	No **lo** conectes.	Don't connect it.
Déja**la** venir.	Let her come.	BUT	No **la** dejes venir.	Don't let her come.
Vámo**nos**.	Let's go.	BUT	No **nos** vayamos.	Let's stay.

Lo/la/le and los/las/les

(1) The singular pronouns **lo**, **la** and **le** and the plural ones **los**, **las** and **les**, have two meanings: they can act as both third person **and** second person formal pronouns:

lo and **le** can mean either 'him' or 'you' (masculine singular)
la can mean either 'her' or 'you' (feminine singular)
los and **les** can mean either 'them' or 'you' (masculine plural)
las can mean either 'them' or 'you' (feminine plural)

(2) Note that **lo/los** and **le/les** are **interchangeable** in either meaning:

Lo/Le llamaré a las ocho.	I'll call **him/you** (masculine, singular, formal) at eight o'clock.
La veré mañana.	I'll see **her/you** (feminine, singular, formal) tomorrow.
Los/Les voy a enseñar a bailar.	I'm going to teach **them/you** (masculine, plural, formal) to dance.
Las vi ayer.	I saw them/you (feminine, plural, formal) yesterday.

Where it is not clear whether the pronoun refers to 'him/them' or 'you', Spanish inserts a personal pronoun preceded by **a**:

Le/lo veré **a él** mañana.	I'll see him tomorrow.
Le/lo veré **a usted** mañana.	I'll see you tomorrow.

Important note: There is a great deal of variation in the use of **le** and **lo** for the direct object in different parts of the Spanish-speaking world. (For a discussion of this point see Butt and Benjamin, 5th edition, 2011, 154)

'Redundant' direct object pronoun before the verb

When the direct object comes **before** the verb, it is often 'repeated' as a pronoun:

Esa ópera **la** cantó Maria Callas mejor que nadie.	Maria Callas sang that opera better than anybody.
Mi número pin no **lo** sabe nadie.	Nobody knows my pin number.
Esos programas **los** actualicé ayer.	I updated those programs yesterday.

Note: This does not happen when the direct object comes after the verb.

7.3 Indirect object pronouns

Key ideas

Indirect object pronouns in Spanish correspond to the English pronoun preceded by 'to' in sentences like 'I gave it *to him*'. In this sentence 'it' is the *direct object* (because it receives the action of the verb 'gave' directly) and 'him' is the *indirect object* (because it receives the action of the verb 'gave' indirectly).

Position

The rules for the position of indirect object pronouns are identical to those for direct object pronouns: usually they are placed before the verb but they may be added to the end of the infinitive or the gerund. They **must** be added to the end of positive imperatives:

Le mandé un mensaje.	I sent him (i.e. 'to him') a text.
Estaba escribiéndole *or* Le estaba escribiendo un mail cuando se apagó la pantalla.	I was writing an email to him when the screen went blank.
Van a venderle el piso *or* Le van a vender el piso el año que viene.	They're going to sell (to) him the flat next year.
Dame tu dirección de correo electrónico.	Give me (i.e. to me) your email address.

Order of object pronouns

Where a sentence contains both a direct and an indirect object pronoun, **the indirect one always comes first in sequence**, whether the two pronouns precede the verb or are added on to the end of it:

Me lo dio ayer.	She gave it to me yesterday.
Mándamelo mañana.	Send it to me tomorrow.

In each of the above sentences **me** is the indirect object pronoun and **lo** the direct object pronoun.

Indirect object pronoun replaced by se

In sentences where there is both a direct and indirect object in the third person, the indirect object pronoun becomes **se**, so as to avoid two initial **l-** sounds coming together (**le/lo, les/lo**, etc.). This happens in both the singular and the plural:

No se lo preguntes.	Don't ask him (it).
¿Se lo mandaste ayer?	Did you send it to them yesterday?
Díselo en seguida.	Tell them (it) at once.

'Redundant' indirect object pronoun before the verb

Spanish often places an indirect object pronoun before the verb even though there is an indirect object noun after it:

Les dije a tus amigos que estabas ocupado.	I told your friends that you were busy.
¿No **le** importa a tu novio que salgas con tus amigas?	Doesn't your boyfriend mind that you go out with your friends?

7.4 Pronouns after prepositions

Key ideas

Pronouns are commonly used after prepositions, as in English. These pronouns are called 'disjunctive' since, unlike the other pronouns, they are not closely connected to the verb.

1 The forms of the prepositional pronouns are the same as the subject pronouns, except for **mí** and **ti**.

2 Prepositional pronouns are used after any preposition:

¿Por qué no vas al cine con ellos?	Why don't you go to the cinema with them?
Sin él vamos a perder el partido.	Without him we'll lose the match.
Para mí no hay otra posibilidad.	For me there's no other possibility.

3 **Con** combines with **mí, ti** and **sí** to make the special forms **conmigo** (with me), **contigo** (with you) and **consigo** (with himself, etc.):

¿Por qué no vienes **conmigo** a Barcelona?	Why don't you come to Barcelona with me?
Porque **contigo** nunca lo paso bien.	Because I never have a good time with you.

4 The neuter pronoun, **ello**, is frequently used after prepositions to refer to an idea and not to a specific noun:

No estoy de acuerdo con ello.	I don't agree with that.
¿Qué esperas conseguir con ello?	What do you hope to achieve by that?
No voy a contar con ello.	I am not going to count on that.

7.5 Reflexive pronouns

Key ideas

Reflexive pronouns are object pronouns which refer back or 'reflect' the action of the verb onto the subject of the sentence. In the sentence 'He cut himself' in English the reflexive pronoun 'himself' reflects back to 'He', the subject. Spanish reflexive pronouns also reflect back to the subject but the construction used is different (see Part I, 31.1).

Forms of the reflexive pronoun

1st person singular	me	myself
2nd person singular **familiar**	te	yourself
2nd person singular **formal**	se	yourself

3rd person	se	himself, herself, itself
1st person plural	nos	ourselves
2nd person plural **familiar**	os	yourselves
2nd person plural **formal**	se	yourselves
3rd person plural	se	themselves

1 The reflexive pronouns are the same as the direct object pronouns **except** in the third person and the formal second person, for which **se** is used.

Creo que Federico se ha alegrado de vernos.   I think that Federico was pleased to see us.

2 The reflexive pronoun normally precedes the verb:

Se vio en el espejo.   She saw herself in the mirror.
Me pregunté lo que debía hacer.   I asked myself what I should do.

3 After prepositions the third person and second person formal pronoun is **sí**. **Sí** combines with **con** to make **consigo**, meaning 'with (for, to, etc.) him/her/it/yourself' (singular) and 'with (for, to, etc.) themselves/yourselves' (plural):

No lo quieren para sí (mismos).   They don't want it for themselves.
Está hablando consigo (mismo).   He's talking to himself.

Exercises

1 Rewrite the sentences, changing the words in brackets into direct object pronouns:

Example: Subieron (la montaña). *La subieron.*

a Echamos (el correo) en el buzón.

b ¿Has plantado (las flores)?

c Compramos (los zapatos).

d Borramos (el texto).

e Ha traído (los discos).

f Metí (la llave) en la cerradura.

g Ha buscado (la información) en la red.

h No conozco (a la presidenta).

i No he leído (el folleto).

j Han sacado (el dinero) del cajero automático.

k ¿Has visto (películas) en 3D?

2 Rewrite the sentences, changing the words in brackets into indirect object pronouns:

Example: Conté la historia a mi padre. *Le conté la historia.*

a Devolveré el libro (a tu profesor).

b Saludaremos (a Juana y Carmen).

c ¿Instalamos los televisores a los clientes nuevos?

d Pagué el alquiler (al dueño).

e Elisa va a hacer un pastel de fresas y chocolate (a su nieto).

3 Rewrite the sentences, changing the words in brackets into direct and indirect object pronouns:

Example: Dieron (el dinero a Sara) *Se lo dieron*.

a Dio (las medicinas a los enfermos).

b Carlos devolvió (la llave a María).

c Daré (a mis colegas la enhorabuena).

d Entregaremos (las entradas a tu padre).

e He comprado (unos pendientes a mi hija).

4 Turn the words in brackets into pronouns:

Example: Compré un regalo para (tu hermano). *Compré un regalo para él.*

a Paseamos delante de (la playa).

b Según (el parte meteorológico) el tiempo va a empeorar.

c Mi casa nueva está aún sin (cortinas).

d Cecilia compró un regalo para (mí y para mi amigo).

e Detrás de (las casas) había un huerto.

5 Answer the question as in the example using an object pronoun:

Example: ¿Conoces a María? *Sí, la conozco.*

a ¿Tienes el coche?

b ¿Has cambiado tu número de móvil?

c ¿Le has dado el CD a Conchi?

d ¿Les ha contado el cuento a tus hermanos?

e ¿Vas a decirle a Alberto lo que tiene que hacer?

6 Answer the questions, using the imperative with object pronouns as in the example, (a) in the positive imperative and (b) in the negative imperative:

Example: ¿Te traigo la revista? (a) *Sí, tráemela* (b) *No, no me la traigas.*

a ¿Te doy el dinero?

b ¿Te pongo una cerveza?

c ¿Le doy un mapa?

d ¿Les devuelvo la invitación?

e ¿Te llevo el desayuno a la cama?

8

Demonstrative adjectives and pronouns

What are demonstratives?

'I don't like *this* red car. I prefer *that* blue one over there.'

'Do you remember *that* meal we had in Paris? *This one* is even better.'

We use the demonstratives *this/that* and *these/those* when we want to identify something. In English we use *this* for objects that are near to us and *that* for objects that are further away from us, in both *space* and *time*.

Demonstratives can be either:

> **adjectives** ('this/these' and 'that/those'), which qualify a noun: 'this car', 'in those days'
>
> or
>
> **pronouns** ('this [one]/those [ones]', 'that [one]/those [ones]'), which refer back to a noun.

8.1 Demonstrative adjectives

Key ideas

- In Spanish demonstrative adjectives agree in gender and number with the noun they qualify:

  este reloj   this watch
  esa falda   that skirt
  aquellas manzanas   those apples

- There are **two** ways of saying 'that/those' in Spanish. You use either **ese**, etc., or **aquel**, etc., depending on the meaning.

masc. sing	fem. sing.		masc. pl.	fem.pl.	
este	esta	this	estos	estas	these
ese	esa	that	esos	esas	those
aquel	aquella	that	aquellos	aquellas	those

Este, esta, estos/as

Este/esta is the equivalent of 'this' in English, referring to something close to the speaker, either in space or time. **Estos /estas** is the equivalent of 'these' in English:

Este señor quiere comprar un nuevo televisor.	This gentleman wants to buy a new television.
Esta mañana tendremos que limpiar la casa.	We'll have to clean the house this morning.
Me gustan mucho estos pasteles.	I really like these cakes.
Estas calles necesitan más luz por la noche.	These streets need more light at night.

Ese, esa, esos/as and aquel/aquella, aquellos/as

To express the English idea of 'that'/'those', one of two words is used, depending on the meaning:

ese, etc., meaning 'that (thing)' which is *near to the listener*

aquel, etc., meaning 'that (thing)' which is *distant from both the speaker and the listener*

–¿Te gusta esta falda?	'Do you like this skirt?'
–Sí, pero esos pantalones te sientan mejor.	'Yes, but those trousers suit you better.'

Esos, not **aquellos**, is used here because 'those trousers' are nearer to the listener (who asked the question):

Aquel día en la Feria lo pasamos de maravilla.	We had a wonderful time at the Fair that day.

Aquel, not **ese** (*día*) is used because the day is distant (in time) from the people involved.

Mira, **aquella** montaña todavía tiene nieve en la cumbre.	Look, that mountain still has snow on the top.

Aquella, not **esa** (**montaña**) is used because the mountain is distant (in space) from the people involved.

Note: in written language it is not always possible to determine whether **ese** or **aquel** has to be used, so in many cases either may be valid.

8.2 Demonstrative pronouns

Key ideas

- Spanish, demonstrative pronouns agree in gender and number with the noun they refer to.
- There are two ways of saying 'that one'/'those ones' in Spanish: **ese**, etc. and **aquel**, etc.
- The demonstrative pronoun has the same form as the demonstrative adjective, but students should note that they will often see a written accent on the first **e** of the demonstrative pronouns, i.e., **éste, ése, aquél** etc. (See also Butt and Benjamin, 5th edition, 2011, 82-3).

masc. sing.	fem. sing.		masc. pl.	fem. pl.	
éste	esta	this (one)	estos	estas	these (ones)
ése	esa	that (one)	esos	esas	those (ones)
aquél	aquella	that (one)	aquellos	aquellas	those (ones)

Note In English, demonstrative pronouns are often conveyed by the addition of the word 'one(s)', e.g., 'that one', 'these ones'.

Este/a, estos/as

This pronoun is used like the English 'this one':

–¿Cuál de las dos películas prefieres? 'Which of the two films do you prefer?'
–Pues, me gustaría más ver esta que esa. 'Well, I'd rather watch this one than that one.'

Ese/a, esos/as *and* aquel/aquella, aquellos/as

The difference between meanings of 'that'/'those' in demonstrative adjectives is also true for demonstrative pronouns. Either of two words may express the idea of *that one/those ones*:

ese, meaning 'that one', near to the listener
aquel, meaning 'that one', distant from both the speaker and the listener:

A Pásame ese libro.   A Pass me that book.
B ¿Cuál, **este**?   B Which, this one?
A Sí, **ese**.   A Yes, that one.
B Y pásame **aquel** en la estantería, el azul. B And pass me that blue one in the bookcase.

A is speaking about a book which is close to B so **ese** is used for the demonstrative adjective 'that' (book). B refers to the book as 'this one', **este**, since it is nearer to him. A confirms that it is 'that one', **ese** (nearer B) and then she asks for a blue book that is not close to either speaker, **aquel**, 'that one'.

Neuter form

A neuter form of the demonstrative pronoun exists:

esto (this)   **eso** (that)   **aquello** (that)

1 The neuter form refers not to a specific object but to an *indeterminate idea*; it is therefore neither masculine nor feminine.

2 Since these pronouns do not refer to a specific noun they are translated by 'this/that (business/ affair/ thing/matter)':

No me gusta eso.   I don't like that. (The thing that is disliked is not specified by the speaker.)
¿Cómo hiciste esto?   How did you do this? (The thing that has been done is not specified.)

Accentuation

 The incorrect inclusion or omission of an accent often changes the meaning or function of a word. Do not confuse: **esta** 'this', demonstrative adjective, feminine singular with **está** '(s)he/it is', third person singular of **estar**, present tense.

Exercises

1 Complete with all the correct demonstrative forms: (a) **este, esta, estos, estas;** (b) **ese, esa, esos, esas;** and (c) **aquel, aquella, aquellos, aquellas:**

____ botellas	____ tema	____ artista
____ cuello	____ manos	____ día
____ pulmones	____ hotel	____ niñas
____ moto	____ peces	____ cárcel
____ té	____ foto	____ rincón

2 Fill the gaps using the correct demonstrative:

a Dame ____ mapa que está en la estantería.

b ¿Qué pastel prefieres, ____ o aquel?

c ¿Qué modelo te gusta más? Pues, ____, el que está a tu lado.

d ¿Prefieres este coche o ____?

e ¿Dónde pongo ____ CDs?

f En ____ época vivimos mejor.

9
Possessive adjectives and pronouns

What are possessives?

When we make a statement like 'Sorry, that's *my* pen' or 'This one's *yours*' we are using the possessive adjective ('my') or the possessive pronoun ('yours'). The adjective tells us who is the 'possessor' of the noun which follows; the pronoun takes the place of the noun as well as indicating who 'the possessor' is .

We use possessives in two ways:

- to show **possession or property**
- to show **a relationship between people and (a) things (b) ideas or (c) other people,** as in 'That's *my* favourite record', 'It's *his* responsibility', or 'She's *their* boss' (*my, his* and *their* are possessive adjectives)

In both Spanish and English there are separate forms for possessive adjectives and pronouns.

Forms of the possessive adjective and pronoun

personal pronouns	possessive adjectives		possessive pronouns	
	singular	**plural**	**singular**	**plural**
yo I	**mi** my	**mis** my	**mío/a** mine	**míos/as** mine
tú you *singular familiar*	**tu** your	**tus** your	**tuyo/a** yours	**tuyos/as** yours
él he	**su** his	**sus** his	**suyo/a** his	**suyos/as** his
ella she	**su** her	**sus** her	**suyo/a** hers	**suyos/as** hers
usted you *singular formal*	**su** your	**sus** your	**suyo/a** yours	**suyos/as** yours
nosotros we	**nuestro/a** our	**nuestros/as** our	**nuestro/a** ours	**nuestros/as** ours
vosotros you *plural familiar*	**vuestro/a** your	**vuestros/as** your	**vuestro/a** yours	**vuestros/as** yours
ellos they	**su** their	**sus** their	**suyo/a** theirs	**suyos/as** theirs
ellas they	**su** their	**sus** their	**suyo/a** theirs	**suyos/as** theirs
ustedes you *plural formal*	**su** your	**sus** your	**suyo/a** yours	**suyos/as** yours

9.1 Possessive adjectives

 ## Key ideas

Spanish possessive adjectives work like English ones:

Me encanta mi perro.   I love *my* dog.

but there are **important differences** relating to the agreement of the possessive adjective and noun.

In English the adjective refers to and agrees with **the possessor**:
Jane always collects **her** children from school.

In Spanish the adjective, while referring to the possessor, agrees in number and gender with **the thing possessed**:

Jane siempre recoge a **sus** niños del colegio.

mi casa	my house (singular possessive adjective/singular noun)
mis documentos	my documents (plural possessive adjective/plural noun)
vuestras amigas	your (female) friends (feminine possessive adjective + plural noun)

Nuestro(s) and vuestro(s)

Note that the equivalents of 'our' and 'your' (familiar plural) have four forms, depending on whether the following noun is masculine, feminine, singular or plural:

vuestro turno	your turn	**nuestra lengua**	our language
vuestros libros	your books	**nuestras preocupaciones**	our worries

The translation of 'your'

The table on p. 52 shows that the possessive adjective 'your' can be either **tu(s), vuestro/a/os/as** or **su(s)** depending on whether you are referring to the other person(s) using the formal or familiar mode of address (see Part I, 7.1.1). for an explanation of this distinction). Thus, depending on who you are talking to, the question 'Have you got your passport(s)?' could be any of the following:

¿Tienes tu pasaporte? (addressing one friend)
¿Tenéis vuestros pasaportes? (addressing more than one friend)

or

¿Tiene su pasaporte, señor? (addressing a relative stranger)
¿Tienen sus pasaportes, señores? (addressing a group of relative strangers)

The possessive replaced by the definite article

In Spanish the definite article is used with parts of the body, clothing or possessions where in English there would be a possessive adjective:

Le robaron el reloj.	They stole his watch.
¡Nunca te lavas la cara!	You never wash your face!
Me duele la cabeza.	My head aches.

This kind of construction is frequently used with reflexive and impersonal verbs, as in the last two examples.

9.2 Possessive pronouns

We use a possessive pronoun to replace a noun, in order to avoid repetition of that noun.

In the sentence 'That car is Juan's', **Aquel coche es de Juan**, the idea of possession is rendered in Spanish by **de** with the noun.

In 'That car is *his*', the possessive pronoun 'his' is used to replace 'Juan's' in English: **Aquel coche es suyo**. We know that the word 'his' is the possessive pronoun (and not the adjective) because it is not followed by a noun.

 ## Key ideas

- As with the possessive adjective, the possessive pronoun agrees in number and gender with the object possessed:

  Sus padres viven en Badajoz; los míos viven en Madrid.
  His/her/their parents live in Badajoz; mine live in Madrid.

  A Laura le gusta más el piso de Juan, porque el suyo es muy pequeño.
  Laura prefers Juan's flat because hers is very small.
  (In this example, **el suyo** is masculine because it refers to **el piso**, the thing possessed. The fact that the possessor (Laura) is feminine is not relevant.)

- When the pronoun is preceded by the verb 'to be', the definite article is omitted:

  Este coche es nuestro.   This car is ours.
  Un día esta casa será tuya, hijo.   One day this house will be yours, son.

- **el suyo**, etc., can mean 'his', 'hers', 'yours' or 'theirs'. Where a possible ambiguity arises with the third person, Spanish often substitutes **de él/ella/usted**, etc., or the name of the person, for greater clarity:

  ¿Esta bicicleta es suya/de usted?   Is this bicycle yours?
  Aquel piso es suyo/de ella/de Ana.   That flat is hers/Ana's.

Exercises

1 Fill the gaps with the correct possessive adjective:
Example: (Yo) ...... lápiz: *Mi lápiz*

a (ella) _____ gafas

b (Vd.) _____ hijo

c (nosotros) _____ casa

d (vosotros) _____ amigo

e (ellas) _____ coche

f (tú) _____ vecino

g (él) _____ revista

h (nosotros) _____ compañeros

i (Vds.) _____ libros

j (Vd.) _____ documentos

2 Fill the gaps with the correct possessive adjective:

a Juan no sabía dónde vivía _____ nueva amiga (*his*).

b Les dijo a _____ hijos (*her*) que la cena estaba lista.

c Decidimos no volver a _____ hotel (*our*).

d Van a visitar a _____ abuela (*their*).

e La mujer había perdido _____ bolsa (*her*).

f Muchachos, ¿dónde está _____ casa (*your*)?

g Clara, ¿qué piensa _____ mamá (*your*) del novio?

h ¿Sabes que _____ pasaportes (*our*) están caducados?

i Mañana vamos a reunirnos en la oficina de _____ jefe (*her*).

j No pude encontrar _____ datos personales (*their*).

3 Complete the sentences with the correct possessive pronoun:

a Estas revistas son _____ (de Juan)

b El futuro es _____ (de nosotros)

c El sombrero era _____ (de usted)

d La idea era _____ (de mí)

e Los vídeos son _____ (de vosotros)

f Las manzanas son _____ (de ti)

g Aquella granja es _____ (de ustedes)

h Este coche es _____ (de ella)

i El balón es _____ (de él)

j El ordenador es _____ (de mis hermanos)

10
Relative clauses

What are relative clauses?

Each of these sentences contains a relative clause:

The person *who answered the phone* was very polite.
The film *(that) we watched last night* was extremely violent.
The Picasso painting, *which we saw at the MOMA last month*, has been stolen in New York.

Relative clauses are clauses introduced by words like 'who', 'that' and 'which'. These words are **relative pronouns**. They have two important functions:

- As pronouns, they refer back to a previous noun. In the above sentences the noun that is referred to ('person', 'film', 'painting') stands immediately before the relative pronoun, and is called the **antecedent.**

- They link two clauses together. The clause which is introduced by the relative pronoun is called a **subordinate clause.**

The most frequently used Spanish relative pronouns are:

que	who, (whom), (which), (that)
el que, la que, los que, las que	(whom), (which), (that)
quien(es)	who, whom
lo que, lo cual	what, which

Note: The English relative pronouns 'whom', 'which' and 'that' are often 'hidden': the sentence 'The novel I gave you is a masterpiece' could equally well be 'The novel *which/that* I gave you is a masterpiece'. Similarly, 'The girl I saw ...' may be 'The girl *whom/that* I saw ...'.

Key ideas

There are several important differences between the meaning and the use of relatives in English and Spanish:

- In Spanish the relative pronoun is **never omitted**:

La novela **que** te di es una obra maestra.	The novel (that/which) I gave you is a masterpiece.
Todo **lo que** come le engorda.	Everything (that) he eats makes him fat.

- The relative pronoun is always placed a close as possible after its antecedent.
- **Quien** is used only for people
- When a preposition is used with a relative pronoun, it **always precedes** it:

El piso en **el que** vivíamos tenía tres dormitorios.	The flat (which) we lived in/in which we lived had three bedrooms.

10.1 Que: who, whom, which, that

Que is by far the most frequently used of the relative pronouns. It is invariable in its form. **Que** is used in the following circumstances:

1 As a ***subject pronoun*** for human and non-human antecedents:

Esa chica **que** acaba de llegar ha traído las pizzas.	That girl who has just come has brought the pizzas.
Mira aquel perro **que** está debajo de la mesa.	Look at that dog that is under the table.
El castillo del Duque, **que** era uno de los más antiguos de España, fue destruido por el fuego.	The Duke's castle, which was one of the oldest in Spain, was destroyed by fire.

2 As an ***object pronoun,*** **que** is used for non-human antecedents:

El coche **que** compré ayer no tiene aire acondicionado.	The car (that/which) I bought yesterday hasn't got air conditioning.
Los libros **que** has sacado de la biblioteca no me sirven.	The books (that/which) you took out of the library are no use to me.
No corras. El tren **que** tenías que coger ha salido ya.	Don't run. The train (that) you had to catch has already left.
El abuelo ya ha tomado el café **que** le hiciste.	Grandpa has already drunk the coffee you made him.

10.2 El que, la que, los que, las que: whom, which, that

This form of the relative is used most frequently **after prepositions**:

La ciudad, de **la que** había estado ausente diez años, parecía una maravilla.	The town, which he'd been away from for 10 years, seemed wonderful.
El coche en **el que** iba el general se paró de súbito.	The car (that) the general was travelling in stopped suddenly.
Una chica, a **la que** no conocía, vino a saludarle.	A girl, whom he did not know, came to greet him.
Estas son las razones por **las que** está enfadada.	These are the reasons why (for which) she's upset.

10.3 Quien(es): who, whom

Quien has a plural form: **quienes**. It is used **for human antecedents only**, in the following circumstances:

1 As a **subject pronoun**:

Pablo, **quien** diseña nuestras páginas en la red, se ha casado con Puri.	Pablo, who designs our web-pages, has married Puri.
Alfredo y Ramón, quienes dicen ser expertos en informática, acaban de encontrar trabajo en Madrid.	Alfredo and Ramon, who claim to be IT experts, have recently found work in Madrid.

In both of these sentences **que** may be used instead of **quien(es).**

2 As an **object pronoun**:

Voy a mandar una carta a mis amigos franceses, a **quienes** conozco desde hace mucho tiempo.	I'm going to send a letter to my French friends, whom I have known for a long time.

Note: **que** can also translate the object pronoun for human antecedents 'that' or 'whom', if personal **a** is omitted (see Part I 37.3):

La dependienta **que** conocías se ha marchado.	The shop assistant (whom) you knew has left.

(In this sentence you could also put 'La dependienta a la que *or* a quien conocías ...'.)

3 **After prepositions:**

Clara, para **quien** todos los hombres son unos machistas, acaba de discutir con su jefe.	Clara, for whom all men are chauvinists, has just had an argument with her boss.
El hombre con **quien** trabajo es ingeniero electrónico.	The man (whom) I work with (i.e., 'with whom I work') is an electronic engineer.
La chica a **quien** vimos ayer es sueca.	The girl (whom) we saw yesterday is Swedish.
A **quien** corresponda	To whom it may concern

10.4 Lo que, lo cual: what, which

Lo que and **lo cual** mean 'what' or 'which', referring back to a **whole idea**:

¡No hagas caso de **lo que** ha dicho!	Don't take any notice of what he said!
Lleva una capa, **lo cual** es raro de ver en Madrid estos días.	He wears a cloak, which is unusual to see in Madrid these days.
¿Has entendido **lo que** te he dicho?	Did you understand what I said to you ?

Exercises

1 Match the phrases in List A with those in List B to make full sentences:

List A		List B	
A	Ayer vimos al profesor Morales,	1	que habla cinco idiomas.
B	Estoy buscando el paraguas	2	que le invitó a tomar una copa.
C	Ayer Nacho se encontró con un colega	3	en el que hemos puesto muchas flores.
D	Conozco a una estudiante de traducción	4	quien salía del colegio.
E	La casa tiene un balcón	5	que dejé en la tienda.

2 Fill the gaps with **el que**, **la que**, **los que** or **las que**:

a La casa en _____ vivíamos antes se ha vendido.

b El colegio en _____ estudiaba Manolo lo han cerrado.

c Las chicas a _____ conociste en Málaga han salido para Granada.

d La mujer con _____ se casó es hija de una amiga de mi juventud.

e Todos los países en _____ las empresas invierten muchas de sus ganancias son más ricos.

3 Fill the gaps with the correct relative pronoun:

a Alfredo buscaba algo _____ había dejado en el coche.

b No conozco a la mujer _____ te llamó anoche.

c Las verdaderas amistades son _____ uno escoge.

d Mi abuelo, _____ tiene en su memoria toda la historia de la familia, vuelve a su ciudad natal.

e El día en _____ va a tener lugar la huelga de los pilotos teníamos intención de volver a Inglaterra en avión.

f No le digas a Mario _____ vamos a hacer mañana.

g La dependienta a _____ viste en el Corte Inglés es vecina nuestra.

h Fui a ver a Mariana, _____ estaba en la cocina preparando la cena.

i Vino a nuestra casa un chico _____ era amigo de mi hermano.

j _____ tienes que hacer es comprarte un nuevo ordenador.

4 Combine each of the following pairs of sentences with a relative clause to make one sentence:

Example: Juan volvió a la una. Juan había cenado en el restaurante Rialto.

Juan, quien había cenado en el Restaurante Rialto, volvió a la una.

a Vimos llegar al cartero. El cartero nos traía muchas cartas.

b He visto un nuevo software. El software te ayuda a bajar material de Internet.

c Hemos alquilado un piso antiguo. El piso nos encanta.

d La puerta fue forzada. La puerta no tenía buena cerradura.

e Carmen es una chica simpática. Carmen canta flamenco los jueves por la noche.

f Nacho acaba de llamar. Nacho no sabía quién había ganado la copa.

11

Interrogatives and exclamations

What are interrogatives?

Interrogatives are words used to introduce questions. In English these are 'what?', 'where?', 'who?', etc. Interrogatives can be pronouns, adverbs and adjectives.

The interrogatives in Spanish are:

¿qué?	what?
¿cuál? ¿cuáles?	which? what?
¿(de/a) quién/quiénes?	(of)who(m)/whose?
¿cómo?	how? what?
¿(a)dónde?	where?
¿por qué?	why?
¿cuándo?	when?
¿cuánto(a/os/as)? (adverb and adjective)	how much/many?

Key ideas

- Interrogative words **always** bear an accent
- In direct questions interrogatives are preceded by an inverted question mark, as well as being followed by a normal one

11.1 Interrogatives

¿Qué?

¿Qué? acts as both pronoun and adjective. **¿Qué?** means 'what?'

(1) **¿Qué?** as a pronoun:

¿Qué te parece?	What do you think?
¿Qué es el cricket? Es un deporte inglés.	What is cricket? It's an English sport.
Y ¿qué?	So what?

(2) **¿Qué?** as an adjective:

¿Qué hora es?	What is the time?
¿De qué color son tus zapatos nuevos?	What colour are your new shoes?
¿Qué tipo de película es? Si es de miedo, no me interesa.	What kind of film is it? If it's a horror film I'm not interested.

¿Cuál? ¿cuáles?

¿Cuál? can mean both 'which?' and 'what?'

(1) **¿Cuál?** meaning 'which?' implies a choice between two or more possibilities:

¿Cuál de los dos prefieres, el té or el café?	Which of the two do you prefer, tea or coffee?
–¿Cuál has elegido? –El de Monet.	'Which have you chosen?' 'The one by Monet.'
–He traído los periódicos.	'I've brought the newspapers.'
–¿Cuáles?	'Which ones?'
–El País y La Vanguardia.	'El País and La Vanguardia.'

(2) 'What?' can be translated by both **¿cuál?** and **¿qué?** In general, **¿cuál?** translates 'what?' with the verb 'to be' when asking for opinions.

¿Cuál es tu opinión sobre este tema?	What do you think about this topic?

¿Quién(es)? and ¿de quién(es)?

(1) **¿Quién(es)?** means 'who?' or 'whom?':

–¿Quién es?	'Who is it?'
–Es Chimo.	'It's Chimo.'
¿Con quién hablaba tu primo?	To whom was your cousin talking? (Who was your cousin talking to?)

When **quién** is the direct object it must be preceded by personal **a** (Part 1, 37.3):

¿A quién te refieres?	Who are you referring to?

(2) **¿De quién(es)?** means 'whose?', of possession and 'of/for/about whom?':

¿De quién es esta cartera?	Whose is this wallet?
¿De parte de quién?	Who's calling? (lit. 'on behalf of whom?')

¿Cómo?

¿Cómo? usually means 'how?' but may also be translated by 'what?':

¿Cómo conociste a tu mujer?	How did you meet your wife?
¿Cómo es tu amiga, Marisa?	What is your friend like, Marisa?

¿Dónde? and ¿adónde?

¿Dónde? means 'where?' and **¿adónde?** 'where to?':

¿Dónde está mi camiseta nueva?	Where is my new t-shirt?
¿Adónde vamos mañana?	Where are we going (to) tomorrow?

¿Por qué?

¿Por qué? means 'why?':

¿Por qué duermen los españoles la siesta?	Why do Spaniards have a siesta?
¿Por qué me miras así?	Why are you looking at me like that?

Note: **porque** ('because') is one word; **¿por qué?** ('why?') is two words.

¿Cuándo?

¿Cuándo? means 'when?':

¿Cuándo vamos a recibir los resultados de los exámenes?	When will we get our exam results?
Pablo, ¿cuándo tuvo lugar la guerra civil española?	Pablo, when was the Spanish Civil War?

¿Cuánto?

1 As a pronoun **¿cuánto?** means 'how much?':

¿Cuánto cuestan las naranjas?	How much are the oranges?
¿Cuánto vas a tardar?	How long are you going to be?

2 As an adjective **¿cuánto/a/os/as?** means 'how much?' or 'how many?':

¿Cuántas mujeres hay en el Gobierno español?	How many women are there in the Spanish Government?
¿Cuántos habitantes tiene Jaca?	How many inhabitants are there in Jaca?

11.2 Exclamations

What are exclamations?

Exclamations are emphatic statements of surprise, anger, delight, pain, etc., introduced by an exclamation word such as 'what!' 'how!' In Spanish the following words are used to introduce exclamations:

¡cuánto(a/os/as)! 'how much/many!', used both as an adverb and an adjective
¡qué! 'what a … !' 'how!', is used as an adjective only.
¡cómo! 'how!' 'what!', used as an adverb.

Key ideas

- Exclamation words **always** bear an accent
- Exclamations are preceded by an inverted exclamation mark, as well as being followed by a normal one

¡Cuánto!

1 as an **adverb**:

¡Cuánto me duele el pie!	How my foot hurts!
¡Cuánto me alegro!	I'm really delighted! (lit. how pleased I am!)
¡Cuánto tiempo sin verte!	It's such a long time since I saw you last!

2 as an **adjective**:

¡Cuántas veces te he dicho que no puedes salir!	How many times have I told you you can't go out!
Mario, ¡cuántos papeles tienes en el suelo!	What a lot of papers you have on the floor, Mario!
¡Cuánta alegría me ha dado tu visita!	I was really happy that you came! (lit. how much pleasure your visit has given me!)
¡Cuánto calor hemos pasado en Córdoba!	What hot weather we've had in Cordoba!

¡Qué!

¡Qué lata!	What a nuisance!
¡Qué me dices!	You don't say!
¡Qué bonita es esa sortija!	How beautiful that ring is!
¡Qué disparates dices!	What nonsense you are talking!

¡Cómo!

¡Cómo habla aquel tío!	How that fellow talks!
¡Cómo me gusta esa música!	How I love that music!

Exercises

1 Match the following questions with a suitable answer:

A	¿Dónde está el restaurante japonés?	1	Soy Jorge.
B	¿Cuándo ocurrió la Reforma protestante?	2	Desde el año pasado.
C	¿Quién eres?	3	De la vida de los gitanos andaluces.
D	¿Qué significa 'carrera'?	4	Está en la calle Fuencarral.
E	¿De qué trata el *Romancero gitano* de Lorca?	5	Los años universitarios y la trayectoria profesional.
F	¿Por qué no me llamaste?	6	60 euros el kilo.
G	¿Cuánto valen los pimientos?	7	En el siglo XVI.
H	¿Desde cuándo tienes el SEAT?	8	Porque estaba en Roma.

2 Fill the gaps in the following sentences with a suitable interrogative or exclamatory pronoun.

a ¿ _____ dices? No te oigo.

b ¿ _____ de los dos suéters te gusta más?

c –¿ _____ es Casilda? –Es mi prima.

d ¿ _____ quiere decir la palabra 'castizo'?

e ¿ _____ de los argumentos te ha impresionado más?

f ¡ _____ piso tan pequeño!

g ¿ _____ es su plato preferido?

h ¿De _____ parte de España es usted?

i ¡_____ veces he intentado convencerle!

j ¿Viste a Pura? ¿_____ estaba?

k ¿_____ vas esta noche, al cine o a la discoteca?

l ¿_____ me preguntas eso? Yo no sé nada.

m ¿_____ cuesta el alquiler del coche por día?

n ¿Con _____ sales ahora, con Nuria o con Conchi?

o ¿En _____ siglo vivió Shakespeare?

3 Invent questions for the answers below, as in the example:

Example: Estaban en el parque. *¿Dónde estaban tus padres?*

a 30 euros el kilo.

b Estaban hablando con el director.

c La una y cuarto.

d Vivimos en el Barrio Santa Cruz.

e Muy bien, gracias.

f Porque estuve allí el año pasado.

g Soy María.

h Digo que si no comemos pronto me voy a morir de hambre.

i Vamos a la piscina.

j 17 años.

12 Indefinites

What are indefinites?

In the sentence 'I can't find anybody to lend me some money', 'anybody' is an indefinite pronoun and 'some' is an indefinite adjective. By definition, 'anybody' is no one in particular, and the adjective 'some' does not indicate a *precise* amount of money. Adjectives, pronouns and adverbs of this kind, which do not refer to a particular person or thing, are called **indefinites**. They usually refer to a vague or imprecise quantity of something. Words like 'some', 'any', 'someone', 'whatever', 'few' and 'enough' are indefinites.

Key ideas

- In Spanish, indefinites refer to people, places or things that are not specific
- Indefinites can be either pronouns, adjectives or, in some cases, adverbs:

¿Hay **alguien** en casa?	Is there *anyone* at home?
Algún día iré a Cuba.	*Some* day I'll go to Cuba.
Habla **demasiado**.	She/He talks *too much*.

- Negative words are indefinites in Spanish (see Part I, 35). If the verb is negative in Spanish the indefinite will also be negative:

No puedo ver **nada**.	I can't see *anything*.
No hay **nadie** en casa.	There isn't *anybody* at home.

The following words in Spanish are usually considered to be indefinites:

uno/una/unos/unas	a/some
alguno/a/os/as	some, any
alguien	someone, anyone
algo	something, anything
cada	each, every
cualquiera/cualesquiera	any (adj.); anyone (noun)
demás	other(s)
otro/a/os/as	other
varios/as	several
mucho/a/os/as	much, many
poco/a/os/as	small, few, little
bastante/s	enough
demasiado/a/os/as	too much, too many
todo/a/os/as	all, any, every

12.1 Uno/una/unos/unas

1   For the use of **uno/a** as an indefinite article see Part I, 2.2.

2   **Unos/as** means 'some' or 'a few'. **Unos pocos** or **unos cuantos** is frequently used as a variant:

Unos críos estaban jugando al fútbol.	Some/A few kids were playing football.
–¿Cuántas entradas tienes?	'How many tickets have you got?'
No sé. Sólo me quedan unas pocas.	'I don't know. I've only a few left.'

12.2 Alguno/a/os/as

1   In the masculine singular **alguno** shortens to **algún**, as in **algún día**, 'some day'.

2   In the singular, **alguno** usually means 'some':

¿Has visto alguna mejora en los nuevos ordenadores?	Have you seen some/any improvement in the new computers?
Sí, tienen más memoria.	Yes, they have more memory.

3   The English 'some' or 'any' before 'mass' nouns (see Part I, 3.2) is **not** translated by **alguno**:

Tráigame pan.	Bring me some bread.
¿Quieres café?	Do you want some/any coffee?

4   In the plural **algunos/as** means the same as **unos/as**:

Te he traído algunas/unas manzanas del huerto de mi vecino	I've brought you some/a few apples from my neighbour's orchard.

5   Alguno/a/os/as can also act as a pronoun:

Algunos de mis amigos van a correr el maratón.	Some/A few of my friends are going to run the marathon.
¿Conoces a alguna de las chicas que viven en el piso de enfrente?	Do you know any of the girls who live in the flat opposite?

12.3 Alguien

Alguien, meaning 'somebody' or 'anybody' (in questions), is **invariable**:

Busco a alguien que me pueda ayudar.	I'm looking for someone to help me.
¿Ha contestado alguien al anuncio?	Has anyone answered the advertisement?

12.4 Algo

Algo, meaning 'something' or 'anything' (in questions) is **invariable**:

¿Tiene algo que declarar?	Have you anything to declare?
Algo bueno va a pasar, te lo prometo.	Something good is going to happen, I promise you.

12.5 Cada

1   **Cada** is an invariable adjective meaning 'each', 'every':

Cada miembro del grupo contribuyó a la tarea.	Each member of the group contributed to the task.
Nos reunimos cada tres semanas.	We meet every three weeks.

2   **Cada uno/a** is a pronoun and means 'each one', 'every one':

Cada uno de los estudiantes aprobó el examen.   Each/every one of the students passed the examination.

3   The phrase **cada vez más/menos** is used to indicate an increasing or decreasing degree ('more and more'/ 'less and less'):

Hay cada vez más coches en las carreteras.   There are more and more cars on the roads.

4   'Every' emphasising the meaning of 'all' (together), as opposed to 'each' (individually), is normally rendered by using **todo/a/os/as** (see Part 1, 12.13):

Aquel invierno, todos los días eran iguales.   That winter, every day was (i.e., all the days were) the same.

12.6 Cualquiera/cualesquiera

1   When the adjective **cualquiera** precedes a noun it normally loses the final **a**:

Hoy día cualquier persona puede aspirar a ser Presidente, sin tener en cuenta su origen social.   Nowadays anyone can aspire to be President, regardless of their social origin.

2   As an adjective **cualquiera** means 'any' in the sense of 'whatever', whoever':

En cualquier momento Juan puede estar aquí.   Juan may arrive at any moment.
Cualquier vuelo me conviene. ¡Escógelo tú!   Any flight suits me. You choose!

3   When it acts as a pronoun **cualquiera** does not drop the final **a**:

Cualquiera puede aprender a usar Internet.   Anyone can learn to use the internet.
Puede elegir cualquiera de los hoteles sin pagar nada por adelantado.   You may choose any of the hotels without paying anything in advance.

4   The plural **cualesquiera** is little used in speech:

Cualesquiera que fueran sus acciones ...   Whatever his actions were ...

12.7 Demás

Demás acts as both an adjective and a pronoun. It means the same as **otro/a/os/as** and is **invariable**:

Dejemos las demás cosas aquí y volvamos a buscarlas mañana.   Let's leave the other things here and come back for them tomorrow.
Vinieron sus amigos y demás gente.   Her friends came and some other people, too.
Los demás se han negado a firmar el contrato.   The others have refused to sign the contract.

12.8 Otro/a/os/as

Otro, meaning 'other', 'another', varies in gender and number. Note that **otro** is *never* preceded by the indefinite article:

Me serviré otra copa, con tu permiso.   I'll have another drink, if you don't mind.
A unos les gusta la gramática, a otros no.   Some people like grammar, others do not.
Volveremos otro día.   We'll come back another day.

12.9 Varios/as

Varios, meaning 'several', can act both as adjective and pronoun:

He intentado ponerme en contacto contigo varias veces, pero sin éxito.	I've tried to contact you several times, but without success.
Vino mucha gente a la fiesta. Varios llegaron antes del comienzo.	Lots of people came to the party. Several arrived before it was due to start.

12.10 Mucho/a/os/as and poco/a/os/as

Mucho/a/os/as ('much', 'many', 'great') and **poco/a/os/as** ('small', 'few', 'little') may act as adjective or pronoun. They vary in gender and number. **Mucho** and **poco** may also act as adverbs, in which case they are **invariable**.

1 As an adjective:

Tu mucha experiencia te ayudará a conseguir un empleo.	Your great experience will help you to get a job.
Con la poca suerte que tengo, me van a suspender otra vez.	With the bad (i.e. little) luck I have, I'll fail my exams again.
Tiene pocos amigos.	He has few friends.

2 As a pronoun:

Muchos se han atrevido a circunnavegar el mundo; pocos han tenido éxito.	Many have dared to sail round the world; few have succeeded.
Muchas mujeres reciben todavía un sueldo inferior al de los hombres por el mismo trabajo.	Many women still receive a lower salary than men for the same work.

3 As an adverb:

Me importa poco que tu socio no se ponga de acuerdo conmigo.	It matters little to me that your partner does not agree with me.
Andalucía me impresionó mucho.	Andalusia impressed me a lot.

12.11 Bastante/s

Bastante meaning 'enough', may act as an adjective or a pronoun. It has a plural form but is **invariable** in gender. **Bastante** may also act as an adverb, in which case it is **invariable**.

1 As an adjective:

Si no tenemos bastante cerveza, iré a buscar más.	If we haven't enough beer, I'll go and get some more.
No hay bastantes sillas para todos.	There aren't enough chairs for everybody.

2 As a pronoun:

–¿Te hacen falta más libros?	'Do you need any more books?'
–No, hay bastantes.	'No, there are enough.'

3 As an adverb:

Se ha portado bastante bien.	He's behaved quite well.

12.12 Demasiado/a/os/as

Demasiado meaning 'too much', 'too many', may act as an adjective or pronoun. It varies in gender and number. **Demasiado** may also act as an adverb, in which case it is **invariable**.

1   As an adjective:

Hay demasiada gente aquí. Tengo que salir fuera.

There are too many people here. I must get outside.

En aquella empresa hay demasiados jefes.

There are too many bosses in that company.

2   As a pronoun:

Alfredo tiene muchos enemigos. En verdad, tiene demasiados.

Alfredo has a lot of enemies. In truth, he has too many.

3   As an adverb:

Bebes demasiado, Lola.

You drink too much, Lola.

12.13 Todo/a/os/as

Todo, meaning 'all', 'any', 'every', may act as an adjective or a pronoun. It varies in number and gender.

1   As an adjective:

Todo sevillano conoce el refrán 'El que se va a Sevilla, pierde su silla'.
De todos modos …

Every citizen of Seville knows the saying: *'El que se va a Sevilla, pierde su silla'*.
In any case …

Note: When **todo(s)** means 'the whole (of)', 'all', 'every', a following noun is usually preceded by the definite article:

Todos los chicos estaban jugando con el Wii.
Pasamos todo el día hablando.
Iba a París todas las semanas.

Every boy was/All the boys were playing with Wii.
We spent the whole day talking.
He used to visit Paris every week.

2   As a pronoun:

todo = everything ; **todos** = everyone:
Me gusta todo lo que veo en Barcelona.
Todos llegaron al mismo tiempo.

I like everything I see in Barcelona.
Everyone arrived at the same time.

Exercises

1   Fill the gaps using **algo, alguien, alguno/a/os/as** or **algún**:

a ¿Llamó _____ anoche?

b Tiene habitaciones? Sí, me quedan _____.

c ¿Tiene _____ que declarar?

d Has visto _____ vez un eclipse del sol?

e Pasa _____ raro aquí que no entiendo bien.

f Estuve con él _____ tiempo antes de marcharme.

g Conozco a _____ que puede reparar el coche.

h _____ historias personales son muy tristes.

i ¿Hay _____ noticia nueva?

j Los jóvenes en paro estaban buscando _____ diputado que les escuchara.

2 Fill the gaps using either **bastante/s, demasiado/a/os/as** or **todo/a/os/as**:

a Estamos cansadísimos. Hemos trabajado _____.

b No es necesario traer más papel para la impresora. Ya tenemos _____.

c _____ lo que ha dicho es un disparate total.

d En el tercer mundo hay _____ gente pobre.

e Sabemos _____ que comer fruta nos sienta bien.

f Trabajó mucho para los exámenes y le salieron _____ bien.

g Puede que no sea bueno pensar _____.

h _____ las niñas estaban jugando en la calle.

i Los aviones volaron por encima de la ciudad _____ la noche.

j Sabe lo _____ sobre Internet como para buscar información, pero nada más.

3 Fill the gaps using **otro/a/os/as, mucho/a/os/as** or **poco/a/os/as**:

a Por favor, ¡no me lo digas _____ vez!

b Trabajábamos _____ para poder terminar temprano.

c En el verano quedaba _____ agua en los ríos.

d Es _____ probable que el tren se retrase.

e _____ gente cree en Dios.

f Vamos _____ veces al cine porque nos gusta.

g Adiós. Hasta _____ día.

h Mis amigos creen que hablo bien el francés, pero de verdad sólo conozco unas _____ palabras.

i Faltan sólo dos días. Es _____ tiempo.

j Ya éramos cinco personas, y entonces vino _____.

Verbs

What are verbs?

The verb is the central part of a sentence: it usually carries several different messages within it.

In the sentence 'She drinks coffee every morning' the verb 'drinks' tells you, first and foremost, the action that takes place. The sentence also carries several pieces of information concerning who is carrying out the action and when it takes place. It tells you four things in particular:

WHAT: the action that takes place, *drinking*.

WHEN: the drinking is in *present time* (if it were in past time we would say 'she drank')

WHO: the subject of the verb 'she' is in the *third person* (if it had been in another person the verb would not have an 's' on the end, e.g. 'I drink', 'you drink')

HOW MANY: the verb is in the *singular* (if it had been in the plural it would not have had an 's' on the end, e.g. we drink, they drink)

In Spanish the verb carries even more messages within it. For instance:

The time of the action is specified in more detail, by using different *tenses* of the verb. For example, the English sentence *Celia drank coffee* is in past time. It could be translated into Spanish using either the preterite tense, Celia **bebió** café, if we know when in the past she drank it, or the imperfect tense, Celia **bebía** café, if she did so regularly in the past.

In Spanish you don't always need to include the subject pronoun with the verb. The endings of the verb are different depending on whether the subject is 'I', 'You', 'we', etc. In Bebo café, the ending indicates that *I*, the speaker (1st person singular), drink coffee; beb**emos** café tells us that *we* (1st person plural) drink coffee; beb**es** café informs us that *you* (2nd person singular, informal) drink coffee. In English the same word, 'drink', is used every time, with the exception of the 3rd person singular ('drink**s**'), so it is necessary to specify the subject.

Verbs also very according to their *mood*. In Spanish it is possible to be direct and to the point when stating a fact, by using the **Indicative** mood: Quiero un café (I want a coffee). But it is also possible to express nuanced language relating to, for example, wishes, future ideas or possibility, by using the **Subjunctive** mood: Quiero que tomes un café conmigo (I want you to have a coffee with me). For orders and requests, the **Imperative** mood is used: Por favor, bebe tu café porque tenemos prisa (Please drink up your coffee, because we're in a hurry).

The combination of all different tenses and moods forms a conjugation. In Spanish there are three conjugations:

- *First conjugation:* verbs whose infinitive ends in AR.
- *Second conjugation:* verbs whose infinitive ends in ER
- *Third conjugation:* verbs whose infinitive ends in IR

Finally, verbs are also divided into *regular*, when they follow a predictable pattern, and *irregular*, when they deviate from it.

14

Present tense

What is the present tense?

The present tense refers to actions that take place in the present time. There are two forms: 'He speaks' and 'He is speaking'.

The first of these forms is used to talk about actions **which are habits** or **which happen all the time**:

'He goes out every Friday.'

'They both speak French.'

The second form is usually for actions **which are happening at the time of speaking**:

'He is swimming like a champion.'

'You are not speaking clearly enough.'

Spanish, like English, has two basic forms: the simple present: **habla** (he speaks), and the present continuous: **está hablando** (he is speaking) (see Part I, 23.1).

¿Ves lo solo que está siempre? Pues en Facebook tiene 1500 amigos.

Key ideas

The simple present tense is used:

- to describe a state of affairs which exists at the time of speaking
- to describe a habit
- for statements generally held to be true
- for future intention

14.1 Formation of the present tense

Regular verbs

-ar verbs: the stem + *-o, -as, -a, -amos, -áis, -an*
-er verbs: the stem + *-o, -es, -e, -emos, -éis, -en*
-ir verbs: the stem + *-o, -es, -e, -imos, -ís, -en*

	hablar to speak	**comer** to eat	**vivir** to live
yo	habl**o**	com**o**	viv**o**
tú	habl**as**	com**es**	viv**es**
él, ella, Vd.	habl**a**	com**e**	viv**e**
nosotros/as	habl**amos**	com**emos**	viv**imos**
vosotros/as	habl**áis**	com**éis**	viv**ís**
ellos, ellas, Vds.	habl**an**	com**en**	viv**en**

Irregular verbs

Irregular verbs typically have a special form in the **first person singular:**

estar (to be): estoy, estás, está, estamos, estáis, están
hacer (to do/make): hago, haces, hace, hacemos, hacéis, hacen
poner (to put): pongo, pones, pone, ponemos, ponéis, ponen
salir (to go out): salgo, sales, sale, salimos, salís, salen

For the present tense of irregular verbs see the Verb tables on pages 323–334.

Radical-changing verbs

Many verbs change the spelling of the last syllable of the stem of the verb in the first three persons of the singular and the third person plural.

cerrar (to shut): cierro, cierras, cierra, cerramos, cerráis, cierran
volver (to return): vuelvo, vuelves, vuelve, volvemos, volvéis, vuelven
pedir (to ask for): pido, pides, pide, pedimos, pedís, piden
seguir (to follow): sigo, sigues, sigue, seguimos, seguís, siguen

For a full account of radical-changing verbs see Part I, 26.1.

Orthographic-changing verbs

Some verbs contain other spelling changes in the present tense:

vencer (to conquer): venzo, vences, vence, vencemos, vencéis, vencen
coger (to catch): cojo, coges, coge, cogemos, cogéis, cogen

conocer (to know): conozco, conoces, conoce, conocemos, conocéis, conocen
construir (to build): construyo, construyes, construye, construimos, construís, construyen
continuar (to continue): continúo, continúas, continúa, continuamos, continuáis, continúan

For a full account of orthographic-changing verbs see Part I, 26.2.

14.2 Use of present tense

The present tense is used in the following contexts:

1 To state **what is happening or what is true now**:

Hace sol.	The sun is shining.
Viene en coche.	He's coming by car.
Estoy en forma.	I'm fit and well.

2 To describe something that **happens habitually**:

Voy al cine todos los sábados.	I go to the cinema every Saturday.
Llueve mucho en Galicia.	It rains a lot in Galicia.
Me levanto a las siete todos los diás menos los domingos.	I get up at 7 o'clock every day except on Sundays.

3 To refer to **features which are inherent** to a person or thing:

Guillermo es serio y tiene muy buen corazón.	Guillermo is serious and very good-hearted.
Ramón habla por los codos.	Ramón talks nineteen to the dozen.

4 To make statements that are **generally considered to be true**:

El tiempo pasa.	Time passes.
El caviar es carísimo.	Caviar is very expensive.
Todos los gobiernos son corruptos.	All governments are corrupt.

5 To refer to an **immediate future action** or a **future intention** (see Part I, 15.1). Note that in this sense English frequently prefers to use the present continuous form:

Salimos a las ocho.	We're going out at eight.
El avión llega a las 21 horas.	The plane gets in/is getting in at 9 p.m.
Me marcho mañana.	I'm leaving tomorrow.
–¿Qué haces este verano?	'What are you going to do/doing this summer?'
–No estoy segura pero espero pasar tres semanas en Barcelona.	'I'm not sure but I hope/I'm hoping to spend three weeks in Barcelona.'

Exercises

1 Create sentences using the words given:

Example: Mis vecinos   español   hablar

        Mis vecinos hablan español.

a	Los niños	mucho	dormir
b	(Tú)	novelas	escribir
c	(Vosotros)	a las seis	terminar
d	D. Ramón	en pipa	fumar
e	(Yo)	en Iberia	trabajar
f	La plaza	en el centro	estar
g	(Ellos)	a las ocho	desayunar

h	(Nosotros)	mucho	correr
i	Maruja	la televisión	ver
j	Jaime y yo	a la piscina	ir

2 Fill the gaps with the correct form of the verb in the present tense:

Me _____ (llamar) Esperanza. _____ (ser) extremeña. _____ (Vivir) con mi familia en un piso grande cerca del centro de Cáceres. _____ (Tener) tres hermanas, que se _____ (llamar) Amelia, Adela y Milagros. Cada domingo _____ (nosotros ir) a hacer una visita a nuestra abuela, que _____ (vivir) en un pueblecito cercano. Para ir allí _____ (coger) el tren de cercanías o un taxi. A veces mi madre nos _____ (llevar) en el coche. La abuela nos _____ (preparar) una comida muy rica, que _____ (comer) a las tres de la tarde. Nos _____ (quedar) con la abuela hasta las seis de la tarde, cuando _____ (volver) a casa.

3 Match the two halves to make a full sentence:

A	Los martes	1	del nuevo tren de alta velocidad?
B	En el invierno	2	porque el profesor es malo.
C	¿Qué piensas	3	siempre pido calamares.
D	No aprendemos mucho	4	vamos al cine porque venden las entradas con descuento.
E	Cuando comemos en el restaurante Torres	5	nos divertimos mucho.
F	¿Quién sabe	6	historias divertidas.
G	Los fines de semana	7	nieva mucho en los Pirineos.
H	Enrique me cuenta siempre	8	cómo resolver el problema?

4 Fill the gaps with the correct form of the present tense:

a _____ (ser) de Manchester.

b _____ (tener) 19 años.

c Mis amigos y yo _____ (vivir) en un piso grande que _____ (tener) ocho habitaciones.

d _____ (nosotros ir) a una universidad que _____ (estar) cerca de nuestra casa.

e Todos los viernes por la noche Juan y yo _____ (salir) para ir al cine. Siempre _____ (volver) tarde a casa.

f Cada verano mi familia _____ (ir) de vacaciones a Santander, en el norte de España.

g Cuando _____ (yo estar) en España _____ (yo nadar) en el mar todos los días.

h _____ (hablar) castellano con un amigo español.

5 All the verbs which appear in the box are radical-changing (see Part I, 26.1. Make a list of the infinitives of these verbs, then complete the sentences below using the verbs in the box:

pensamos	cierran	piensas	empieza	se calienta
cuestan	vuelvo	prefieres	suelen	me acuesto
se encuentran	tienen	jugamos	tenéis	calienta

a El sol no _____ mucho en invierno

b Roberto y yo _____ al tenis todos los días.

c Los últimos modelos de teléfonos móviles _____ mucho más que los antiguos.

d La catedral y el castillo _____ en el casco antiguo de la ciudad.

e _____ temprano cuando tengo que trabajar por la mañana.

f La presentación _____ tarde, así que tenemos tiempo para cenar antes.

g ¿ _____ el vestido azul o el rojo? ¿Cuál te gusta más?

h Estás muy callada. ¿En qué _____?

i Los bancos _____ a la una de la tarde.

j El mundo _____ poco a poco debido a los gases invernaderos.

k Voy a la Universidad a las nueve de la mañana y _____ a las cinco de la tarde.

l Los perros pequeños _____ ser muy nerviosos.

m Vamos a marcharnos pronto. ¿ _____ todos vuestros pasaportes?

n Solo algunas zonas _____ cobertura para wifi.

o Eva y yo _____ viajar a la India el año que viene.

6 A Spanish TV presenter, Marta Sánchez, filled in the following questionnaire. On the basis of the answers, write a few simple sentences about her habits using the first person (**yo**). Then rewrite the sentences using the third person (**ella**):

Example: Leo muchos libros pero no escucho música pop.

Marta lee muchos libros pero no escucha música pop.

leer libros	sí
montar a caballo	no
cocinar	no
ir al campo	no
acostarse temprano los días laborables	sí
escuchar música pop	no
jugar al tenis	sí
nadar	sí
divertirse los fines de semana	sí
comer en restaurantes	no

15
Future tense

What is the future tense?

We use the future when **we are predicting or giving information about what is going to happen**, as in 'It will be cold today' and 'We will (or We'll) arrive at 7 p.m.'. In English we place the auxiliary verb 'will' or 'shall' before the verb to form the future. Another way of referring to the future is by using the present continuous of 'to go' plus the infinitive of the verb, as in 'It is going to be cold today' and 'We are going to arrive at 7 p.m.'.

15.1 Formation of the future tense

A major difference between English and Spanish is that in English the future is made up of two words (an auxiliary and a verb) whereas in Spanish it is one word, formed by adding the following endings to the infinitive: **-é, -ás, -á, -emos, -éis, -án**. Thus 'I will speak' is **hablar + é = hablaré**; 'you will eat' is **comer + ás = comerás**, etc.

	hablar	**comer**	**vivir**
yo	hablar**é**	comer**é**	vivir**é**
tú	hablar**ás**	comer**ás**	vivir**ás**
él, ella, Vd.	hablar**á**	comer**á**	vivir**á**
nosotros/as	hablar**emos**	comer**emos**	vivir**emos**
vosotros/as	hablar**éis**	comer**éis**	vivir**éis**
ellos, ellas, Vds.	hablar**án**	comer**án**	vivir**án**

Key ideas

In Spanish there are three principal ways of expressing the future, using:

- The future tense, **to state or predict that something definitely will (or will not) happen**:

  El Manchester United **jugará** | Manchester United will play
  mañana en Barcelona. | in Barcelona tomorrow.
  En junio me **examinaré** de gramática. | I'll take my grammar exam in June.
  Mañana **hará sol** en la costa. | It will be sunny on the coast tomorrow.

- **ir + a** followed by the infinitive, especially to indicate **future intention**. This construction is often interchangeable with the future tense, especially in colloquial language:

  El Manchester United **va a jugar** manaña | Manchester United will play in
  en Barcelona. | Barcelona tomorrow.
  En junio me **voy a examinar** de gramática. | I'll take my grammar exam in June.
  Mañana **va a hacer** sol en la costa. | It will be sunny on the coast tomorrow.

- The present tense (see Part I, 14.2(5)):

  Vamos a Méjico este verano. | We're going to Mexico this summer.
  ¡Ya **voy**! | I'll be right there!
  Nos **vemos** a las dos. | We'll meet at 2 o'clock.

Note: for a detailed discussion of the future tense see Butt and Benjamin (fifth edition, 2011), 216-19.

15.2 Irregular forms of the future

Twelve verbs have an irregular future *stem*. All these verbs have the same endings as the regular verbs.

caber	cabré, etc.	**poder**	podré	**salir**	saldré
to fit, to be contained		to be able		to go out	
decir	diré	**poner**	pondré	**tener**	tendré
to say		to put		to have	
haber	habré	**querer**	querré	**valer**	valdré
to have (*auxiliary*)		to want		to be worth	
hacer	haré	**saber**	sabré	**venir**	vendré
to do, to make		to know		to come	

Verbs that derive from these verbs also have an irregular stem (see the Verb tables on pages 323–334):

deshacer (to undo): desharé etc.   **suponer** (to suppose): supondré etc.

detener (to stop): detendré etc.

Exercises

1 Complete the table with the correct form of the verb in the future:

infinitive	yo	tú	él/ella/Vd.	nosotros/as	vosotros/as	ellos/ellas/Vds.
mirar						
escribir						
perder						
tener						
salir						
querer						
hacer						

2 Fill the gaps using the future tense of the verbs in the infinitive:

a ¿Cuándo _____ (tú ir) al médico?

b _____ (yo escribir) la carta esta noche.

c En el restaurante Mariquilla _____ (nosotros comer) bien, te lo prometo.

d ¿ _____ (volver vosotros) la semana que viene?

e No _____ (yo hacer) nada hasta que llegues.

f A las tres de la tarde _____ (haber) manifestación en la plaza San Antonio.

g Mario no _____ (levantarse) antes de las once.

h El fin de semana _____ (hacer) frío en Asturias.

i Si me escuchas bien te _____ (yo dar) la solución a tu problema.

j Mariluz, ¿ _____ (poder) acompañarme a la agencia de viajes mañana?

3 Fill in the gaps with the verb in the future, as in the example:

Example: ¿Te has limpiado los zapatos?   No, los limpiaré mañana.

a ¿Has hablado con tu padre?

No, _____ con él a las ocho de la tarde.

b ¿Han venido tus colegas de Buenos Aires?

No, _____ esta noche.

c ¿Has ido a Menorca?

No, _____ este verano.

d ¿Os habéis examinado ya?

No, nos _____ la semana que viene.

e ¿Ha echado las cartas?

No, pero las _____ enseguida.

f ¿Le has dicho a Carlos que vuelva?

No, se lo _____ pronto.

g ¿Ha llamado a María?

No, le _____ mañana por la mañana.

16 Conditional tense

What is the conditional tense?

In the sentence 'If she worked harder she would be the best in her class', the verb 'would be' is *conditional*. The conditional tense, as its name suggests, is mainly used to describe events which would only take place if specific conditions were met. In this case the girl's success as a student depends on how hard she works. The conditional is also used when expressing oneself politely, as in: 'Would you like a Coca-Cola?'; and for expressing the future as seen from the past, as in 'He said he would leave'.

In English we place the auxiliary verb 'would' or 'should' before the infinitive to form the conditional.

16.1 Formation of the conditional tense

The major difference between English and Spanish is as follows: in English an auxiliary verb is used **before** the verb, whereas in Spanish the conditional is formed by adding an ending to the infinitive.

The verb endings are as follows: **-ía, -ías, -ía, -íamos, -íais, -ían**. Thus, 'I would speak' is **hablar + ía = hablaría**; 'you would write' is **escribir + ías = escribirías**, etc.:

	hablar	comer	vivir
yo	hablaría	comería	viviría
tú	hablarías	comerías	vivirías
él, ella, Vd.	hablaría	comería	viviría
nosotros/as	hablaríamos	comeríamos	viviríamos
vosotros/as	hablaríais	comeríais	viviríais
ellos, ellas, Vds.	hablarían	comerían	vivirían

Key ideas

The conditional tense is used:

- to express oneself politely:

¿**Podría** decirme la hora, por favor?	Could you tell me the time, please?
¿Te **molestaría** que llegara el jueves?	Would it be all right if I arrived on Thursday?
¿Qué **preferirías hacer,** ir al cine o al teatro?	Which would you rather do, go to the cinema or the theatre?

- after 'if-clauses' (see Part I, 24.2), to describe **events which could happen**:

Si ganara la lotería **abandonaría** mi empleo.	If I won the lottery I would give up my job.
Si fuera menos presumida **sería** más agradable.	She would be nicer if she were not so conceited.

- to report past events which were originally expressed in the future tense:

Villa dijo que **participaría** en la Copa Mundial.	Villa said that he would take part in the World Cup.

(In direct speech this would have been: Villa dijo: 'Participaré en la Copa Mundial'.)

16.2 Irregular forms of the conditional

As with the future, 12 verbs have an irregular *stem:*

caber	cabría, etc.	**poder**	podría	**salir**	saldría
to fit, to be contained		to be able		to go out	
decir	diría	**poner**	pondría	**tener**	tendría
to say		to put		to have	
haber	habría	**querer**	querría	**valer**	valdría
to have (auxiliary)		to want		to be worth	
hacer	haría	**saber**	sabría	**venir**	vendría
to do, to make		to know		to come	

Verbs that derive from these verbs have the same stem:

deshacer (to undo): desharía etc.   **suponer** (to suppose): supondría etc.
sostener (to support): sostendría etc.

Note: The translation of 'would' by the imperfect.

The auxiliary verb 'would' in English can be used to recount an event that took place habitually in the past (in the sense of 'used to'). In this case the correct equivalent tense in Spanish is the imperfect, not the conditional.

Cuando vivíamos en Madrid paseábamos por el Retiro cada domingo.	When we lived in Madrid we would go for a walk in the Retiro Park every Sunday.

Exercises

1 Complete the table with the correct verb form of the conditional:

infinitive	yo	tú	él/ella/ Vd.	nosotros/as	vosotros/as	ellos/ellas/ Vds.
cerrar						
pedir						
volver						
tener						
poder						
hacer						
sabe						

2 Fill the gaps with the correct form of the conditional:

a Le preguntó si _____ (tomar) té o café.

b Nos _____ (encantar) ir a Canarias.

c No me _____ (molestar) que Mónica nos acompañara al cine.

d Pedro y Carmen _____ (dar) cualquier cosa por hacerse modelos.

e Si yo fuera tú, no les _____ (contestar).

f No sé si _____ (vosotros poder) llegar a tiempo.

g Les _____ (nosotros aconsejar) que firmaran el contrato cuanto antes.

h Si tuviera tiempo, _____ (yo hacer) más deporte.

i Si Jorge me lo pidiera le _____ (yo decir) cómo preparar la paella.

j Si fuera rica _____ (ella viajar) por todo el mundo.

3 Give advice in response to the following statements, using the conditional, as in the example:

Example: No sé si ir de vacaciones a Italia o Francia
            Yo, en tu lugar, iría a Francia.

a No sé si ponerme el vestido rojo o el azul. ¿Qué piensas?

b No sé si cambiar de empleo o quedarme en Apple.

c No sé qué comprarle a Lucía para su cumpleaños.

d No sé qué universidad escoger, la Autónoma o la Complutense.

e No sé si decirle a Elena que la quiero.

4 Fill the gaps using the conditional:

¿Qué _____ (yo hacer) si ganara la lotería? Primero, mis amigos y yo _____ (tener) una gran fiesta. Luego _____ (vender) mi piso y _____ (comprar) otro en el barrio Salamanca. Después _____ (ir) con mis padres a Grecia. Ellos _____ (no poder) rechazar mi invitación si yo lo pagara todo. Finalmente _____ (yo buscar) otro empleo más interesante. ¿ _____ (yo estar) más contenta? No sé, pero si el tener tanta riqueza me cambiara demasiado, creo que _____ (acabar) regalando todo el dinero a las sociedades benéficas.

5 Rodrigo is a very confident boy. He was making plans as if nothing could possibly change them. Unfortunately he became ill and he could not carry them out. Change the story that follows, adding at the beginning 'Si no estuviera enfermo, este año terminaría …':

Este año terminaré el curso y obtendré unas notas magníficas. Luego iré a las islas Galápagos y veré todos los animales interesantes que hay allí. Nadaré con los delfines y contemplaré el perfecto cielo azul desde las rocas. De las islas me trasladaré a Costa Rica y pasearé por el parque natural más hermoso de Centro América. A mi vuelta a Tarragona tendré tiempo de disfrutar de mis amigos y también me prepararé para el próximo curso. El año que viene será el último de mi carrera y entonces seré biólogo.

17

Perfect tense

What is the perfect tense?

In the sentence 'He has broken the window' the verb used is in the perfect tense. This tense combines the *auxiliary verb* ('has') and the *past participle* of the verb ('broken'). The perfect tense is used to describe **actions that have begun in the past and carry through to the present.** What we are interested in is that the window is broken *now*.

Key ideas

- In Spanish the perfect tense is used in the same way as in English, to describe past actions that are still 'alive' in the present. If the past action has finished, the perfect cannot be used. Compare:

En el siglo XX hubo dos guerras mundiales pero en el siglo XXI no ha habido ninguna. | In the twentieth century **there were** two world wars but in the twenty-first century there **haven't been** any.

The first verb (**hubo**), which is in the preterite, describes a completely finished past situation; the second, in the perfect tense ([**no**] **ha habido**), refers to an absence of action i.e, world wars, which is still relevant at the time of speaking.

- Typically, the perfect tense is used with adverbs related to the present, such as **ahora, esta mañana, todavía no** and **hoy**.

Todavía no ha traído los libros. | She hasn't brought the books yet.
Hoy le ha tocado el gordo a don Manuel. | Today Don Manuel has won the jackpot (in the lottery).

Esta mañana hemos llegado al final de nuestra investigación. | We have got to the end of our research this morning.

- The Spanish perfect may also be used for events that took place in the very recent past (usually that day). As long as the time in the sentence includes the present moment, the perfect can be used. In this context Spanish use differs from English, which may use a past simple rather than a perfect tense:

Hoy ha trabajado bien. | He has worked well today.
¿Has visto el Palacio Real? | Have you seen/Did you see the Royal Palace?

Esta mañana no he desayunado. | I didn't have breakfast this morning.
Yo no he dicho eso. | I didn't say that/I haven't (ever) said that.

- The auxiliary verb (**haber**) and the past participle may not be split as in English:
  Nunca ha estado en Valladolid.   She has never been to Valladolid.
- The past participle, when part of the perfect tense, is **invariable** in number and gender.

17.1 Formation of the perfect tense

The perfect tense is formed from:

The auxiliary verb **haber** *plus* the past participle of the verb, either ending in **-ado** (**-ar** verbs) or **-ido** (**-er** and **-ir** verbs): **he hablado, he comido, he vivido**.

	hablar	comer	vivir
yo	he hablado	he comido	he vivido
tú	has hablado	has comido	has vivido
él, ella, Vd.	ha hablado	ha comido	ha vivido
nosotros/as	hemos hablado	hemos comido	hemos vivido
vosotros/as	habéis hablado	habéis comido	habéis vivido
ellos, ellas, Vds.	han hablado	han comido	han vivido

17.2 Irregular past participles

The following verbs have irregular past participles:

abrir	to open	**abierto**	opened
cubrir	to cover	**cubierto**	covered

decir	to say	**dicho**	said
escribir	to write	**escrito**	written
freír	to fry	**frito**	fried
hacer	to do/make	**hecho**	done/made
imprimir	to print	**impreso**	printed
morir	to die	**muerto**	dead
poner	to put	**puesto**	put
prender	to catch	**preso**	caught
resolver	to resolve	**resuelto**	resolved
romper	to break	**roto**	broken
satisfacer	to satisfy	**satisfecho**	satisfied
ver	to see	**visto**	seen
volver	to return	**vuelto**	returned

Verbs derived from the above verbs are also irregular:

descubrir (to discover)	**descubierto**	**devolver** (to give back)	**devuelto**
deshacer (to undo)	**deshecho**	**disolver** (to dissolve)	**disuelto**
prever (to foresee)	**previsto**	**suponer** (to suppose)	**supuesto**

¿Todavía no has hecho los deberes?   Haven't you done your homework yet?
El Rey ha muerto.   The King has died.
Todavía no han vuelto de sus vacaciones. They haven't come back from their holidays yet.

Exercises

1 Give the correct form of the perfect tense of the following verbs, as in the example:

Example: mirar (tú) *has mirado*

a encontrar (yo) ....

b querer (tú) ....

c limpiar (vosotros) ....

d ir (ellos) ....

e poner (él) ....

f romper (nosotros) ....

g abrir (tú) ....

h volver (ella) ....

i absolver (yo) ....

j decir (nosotros) ....

k traer (él) ....

l levantarse (ellas) ....

2 Make sentences from the following words, using the perfect tense:

Example: Conchi ya *resolver* el problema. *Conchi ya ha resuelto el problema.*

a todavía no *empezar* las clases

b todavía no *despertarse* Aitana

c Javier *preparar* hoy la cena

d ya *comenzar* el partido de baloncesto

e hoy Charo *acostarse* temprano

f Rodrigo *ganar* una medalla en las Olimpiadas

g (yo) no *ver* las llaves

h Paco y José no *tener* vacaciones este año

i Mila y yo *escribir* la carta

j Julián *investigar* un caso muy serio de corrupción

3 Ask questions using the perfect tense, as in the example:

Example: ver (tú) la foto de Carlos *¿Has visto la foto de Carlos?*

a comenzar (tú) las clases de yoga

b volver (ellos) de París

c poner (él) la mesa

d cenar (vosotros)

e hacer (usted) el viaje a Marruecos.

f hablar (tú) con el encargado

g ver (vosotros) el accidente

h oír (ellos) la noticia

i recibir (Vd.) un mail

j resolver (Vds.) el caso

4 Change the infinitives into the perfect tense:

En años recientes los españoles _____ (construir) unas obras de ingeniería y unos edificios magníficos. El Museo Guggenheim de Bilbao ya _____ (atraer) a millones de personas y _____(llegar) a ser la atracción turística más visitada del mundo. También _____ (terminarse) la autopista de Madrid a Valencia, vínculo simbólico y real entre dos grandes ciudades. _____ (comenzar) finalmente la línea de trenes de alta velocidad entre Barcelona y Madrid. Todos estos proyectos _____ (ser) muy costosos.

18

Preterite tense

What is the preterite tense?

In the sentence 'We flew to Barcelona yesterday' the action of the verb is in the past, and we use a single word 'flew' to describe this action. In English this form is known as the 'simple past'.

Key ideas

In Spanish the **preterite** tense, as with the simple past in English, consists of a single word indicating a past action which happened at a clearly defined time and which is now over. The preterite tense has to be distinguished from the imperfect tense, which also indicates a past action.

The preterite is used in the following circumstances:

- to recount a completed action in the past. The important thing to remember is that the time period is regarded as over and done with:

    La semana pasada **escribí** a   Last week I wrote to
    mis amigos españoles.   my Spanish friends.

- to narrate a sequence of single events which took place at a well-defined time in the past: this happened, then that, then that, etc.:

    Ayer **vino** mi amiga Juana y **fuimos**   Yesterday my friend Juana came and
    a la piscina. Después **tomamos** un café   we went to the swimming pool. Afterwards
    en el bar Zurich y   we had coffee in the Zurich Bar and
    luego **volvimos** a casa.   then we went back home.

- for actions which took place over a long period in the past, when the beginning and end of that period are clearly defined:

    El rey Felipe II **reinó** de 1556 a 1598.   King Philip II reigned from 1556 to 1598.

18.1 Formation of the preterite tense

Regular verbs

-ar verbs: add **-é, -aste, -ó, -amos, -asteis, -aron** to the stem of the verb
-er and **-ir** verbs: add **-í, -iste, -ió, -imos, -isteis, -ieron** to the stem of the verb

	hablar	comer	vivir
yo	habl**é**	com**í**	viv**í**
tú	habl**aste**	com**iste**	viv**iste**
él, ella, Vd.	habl**ó**	com**ió**	viv**ió**
nosotros/as	habl**amos**	com**imos**	viv**imos**
vosotros/as	habl**asteis**	com**isteis**	viv**isteis**
ellos, ellas, Vds.	habl**aron**	com**ieron**	viv**ieron**

Note: In **-ar** verbs the first person plural (**hablamos**) has the same form in the preterite as in the present tense:

Hablé con ella ayer pero no encontramos una solución.

I spoke to her yesterday but we did not find a solution.

Elisa volvió sola de Granada.

Elisa came back alone from Granada.

¿Cuánto tiempo viviste en Sevilla?

How long did you live in Seville?

Irregular preterites

Many of the most commonly used verbs in Spanish have irregular preterite forms, involving a change in the spelling of the stem of the verb. Once the first person of the verb is learnt there should be little difficulty in learning the remaining persons, since they normally follow a predictable pattern, as for regular **-er** and **-ir** verbs above. For example, the preterite of **dar** is: **di, diste, dio, dimos, disteis, dieron**.

The most common irregular preterites are listed below (for a full list of verb forms, see Verb tables on pages 323–334. As an aid to learning the irregular preterite tenses those with similar forms have been grouped as follows:

	infinitive	first person singular	third person singular	third person plural	
1	dar	di	dio	dieron	to give
	ir	fui	fue	fueron	to go
	oír	oí	oyó	oyeron	to hear
	ser	fui	fue	fueron	to be
	ver	vi	vio	vieron	to see
2	andar	anduve	anduvo	anduvieron	to walk
	estar	estuve	estuvo	estuvieron	to be
3	caber	cupe	cupo	cupieron	to fit, be contained
	haber	hube	hubo	hubieron	to have (auxiliary)
	saber	supe	supo	supieron	to know
	poder	pude	pudo	pudieron	to be able
	poner	puse	puso	pusieron	to put
	tener	tuve	tuvo	tuvieron	to have
4	decir	dije	dijo	dijeron	to say
	hacer	hice	hizo	hicieron	to do/make
	querer	quise	quiso	quisieron	to want, wish
	traer	traje	trajo	trajeron	to bring
	venir	vine	vino	vinieron	to come

5	Another common group, ending in **-ucir** has **-j-** as the final consonant:				
	conducir	conduje	condujo	condujeron	to drive
	Other verbs which follow this pattern are:				
	introducir	to introduce	**producir**	to produce	
	reducir	to reduce	**traducir**	to translate	

Notes

(1) The verbs **ir** and **ser** have exactly the same form in the preterite.

(2) The third person singular of **hacer** is **hizo**.

(3) The first and third person singular of **dar, ir, ser** and **ver** are single syllables. No accent is needed.

(4) Any verb with a preterite stem ending in **-j**, as in **decir > dije, traer > traje**, 'loses' the following **i** in the third person plural: **dijeron, trajeron**.

(5) Verbs derived from the above verbs have the same irregularities in the stem, e.g. **proponer** (to propose): **propuse/propuso/propusieron; detener** (to stop): **detuve, detuvo, detuvieron** (for a full list of these verbs see Verb tables on pages 323–334):

Fue a Lima para comprar objetos de plata.	He went to Lima buy silver objects.
Me fue imposible viajar a Madrid.	It was impossible for me to travel to Madrid.
Ayer fuimos a Barcelona en avión.	We flew to Barcelona yesterday.
(Yo) no lo hice.	I didn't do it.
¿Qué les dijiste?	What did you say to them?.
Miguel estuvo en Tarragona durante las fiestas.	Miguel was in Tarragona for the festivities.
Vieron a Tomás en febrero.	They saw Tomás in February.
Estudié toda la noche y aproveché mucho el tiempo.	I studied all night and I made good use of the time.

18.2 The preterite and time references

The preterite is used when a specific time in the past is clearly defined, i.e. the beginning and the end of the period are known. It is therefore used with words which indicate a definite time period, such as **durante**, **ayer, el año pasado, hace dos días,** etc. More often than not, however, the time reference is understood, not stated:

Durante más de veinte años fui periodista. | I was a journalist for more than 20 years.
Aquella noche, después de cenar en el | That night, after dining in the restaurant, I
restaurante, de repente me sentí enferma. | suddenly felt ill.
Cuando salí de casa, vi a un tipo sospechoso. | When I went out of the house, I saw a
Pasé de largo y me metí por la primera calle | suspicious-looking person. I went straight
a la izquierda. | past him and turned down the first road
on the left.

(In the last example it is understood that the actions took place in the past, but the writer does not state when.)

18.3 The use of the Spanish preterite and the French perfect tense

It is important for students of both Spanish and French to distinguish between the uses of the perfect tense in these two languages. Students who take up Spanish after they have learned French frequently use the Spanish perfect where they should use the preterite. In general the French perfect tense has a similar use to the preterite in Spanish. Thus 'I said' would normally be **dije** (and not **he dicho**) in Spanish but *j'ai dit* in French. Similarly, 'They spoke to me' would be **me hablaron** (and not **han hablado**) but *Ils m'ont parlé* in French.

Exercises

1   Fill the gaps in the table with the correct forms:

Example: Subieron (la montaña). *La subieron.*

Infinitive	yo	tú	él/ella/ Vd.	nosotros/ as	vosotros/ as	ellos/ellas/ Vds.
llevar	llevé			llevamos		
volver		volviste			volvisteis	
ocurrir			ocurrió			ocurrieron
mirar		miraste				miraron
coger	cogí			cogimos		
hacer			hizo		hicisteis	
salir	salí		salió			
querer		quisiste				quisieron
poner			puso	pusimos		
venir	vine				vinisteis	vinieron
ver		viste				
ir	fui			fuimos		
ser			fue		fuisteis	
saber			supo			supieron
comprar		compraste	compró			
llamar	llamé				llamasteis	
traer	traje		trajo			
tener				tuvimos		tuvieron
romper	rompí				rompisteis	
irse		te fuiste				se fueron

2   Give the preterite form of the following:

a compro ....   f obtenéis ....

b va ....   g pasas ....

c llamamos ....   h escondemos ....

d corre ....   i deshago ....

e hacen ....   j parece ....

3   Fill the gaps with the correct form of the preterite:

a Ayer _____ (nosotros chatear) en Internet con Marta.

b El mes pasado _____ (yo conseguir) un empleo en el Bar Roque.

c Anoche _____ (ellos beber) demasiado.

d _____ (nosotros hablar) castellano durante dos horas.

e El sábado _____ (yo salir) a ver una película.

f ¿_____ (tú trabajar) con la agencia el verano pasado?

g ¿_____ (vosotros recibir) el paquete?

h No te _____ (ellos contactar) porque no sabían tu número de teléfono.

i No _____ (haber) ganancias este año.

j Cristina _____ (decir) que no iba a venir en coche.

4   Fill the gaps using one of the verbs in the box in the correct form of the preterite:

reconocer	traer	poner	contestar	dar
empezar	aburrir	aprobar	perder	estar

a La Segunda Guerra Mundial _____ en 1939.

b Fuimos al cine para disfrutar, pero la película nos _____.

c Los terroristas _____ una bomba en la estación.

d Llamé dos veces pero nadie me _____.

e Cuando Juan _____ los exámenes sus padres le _____ una bicicleta nueva.

f En 2009 Mercedes y yo _____ mucho dinero en la Bolsa.

g Emilio, ¿_____ en París con María la semana pasada?

h Los amigos de Pablo _____ que no tenían razón.

i Pilar _____ dos botellas de vino a la fiesta.

5   Armando tells a story to his little sister to send her to sleep. Fill the gaps with the correct form of the preterite of the verbs in brackets:

Cuando la hormiga _____ (descubrir) aquel grano de trigo tan enorme, _____ (ir) a llamar a sus compañeras. Entre todas _____ (conseguir) transportarlo a su hormiguero pero aquel grano gigante no _____ (poder) pasar por la entrada. La hormiga jefe _____ (tomar) el mando de la operación y _____ (llamar) a una hormiga forzuda con patas muy fuertes y la _____ (ordenar) cavar con una pala una entrada más grande. Después de trabajar toda la noche el grano _____ (entrar) en el hormiguero y las hormigas _____ (celebrar) con una gran fiesta el hecho de que ya no pasarían hambre en todo el invierno.

19

Imperfect tense

What is the imperfect tense?

When we talk about the past in English we choose between several different forms of the verb. For example, if we want to stress the *continuous* nature of past action like 'playing tennis' we might say 'We *were playing* tennis in the park'. If we want to convey the idea that the same action was being *repeated* or was *habitual* we use the auxiliary verb 'used to': 'We *used to play* tennis in the park'. Both forms can have a different meaning from the simple past 'we played tennis'.

Key ideas

In Spanish the imperfect tense is used for continuous or habitual actions in the past. This is a different tense from the preterite (see Part I, 18.2).

The imperfect tense is used:

- when the speaker has **no particular interest in when the action started or when it was going to finish**, i.e. the beginning and the end of the action are not clearly defined:

Juan **jugaba** al tenis.	Juan was playing tennis. (We are not told when he started or when he finished.)
No **sabíamos** qué hacer.	We did not know what to do.

- to indicate **habits or repeated events in the past**:

Todos los días **íbamos** a la biblioteca, y **volvíamos** a casa con un montón de libros.	We used to go to the library every day and we would come back home with a big pile of books.

- for **descriptions rather than events in the past**:

Era alto y **llevaba** una chaqueta azul.	He was tall and was wearing a blue jacket.

- to say **what was happening when a particular event in the preterite occurred**:

Estábamos todos en la cocina cuando oímos la explosión.	We were all in the kitchen when we heard the explosion.

19.1 Formation of the imperfect tense

Regular verbs

-ar verbs: add **-aba, -abas, -aba, -ábamos, -abais, -aban** to the stem of the verb.
-er and **-ir** verbs: add **-ía, -ías, -ía, -íamos, -íais, -ían** to the stem of the verb.

	hablar	comer	vivir
yo	habl**aba**	com**ía**	viv**ía**
tú	habl**abas**	com**ías**	viv**ías**
él, ella, Vd.	habl**aba**	com**ía**	viv**ía**
nosotros/as	habl**ábamos**	com**íamos**	viv**íamos**
vosotros/as	habl**abais**	com**íais**	viv**íais**
ellos, ellas, Vds.	habl**aban**	com**ían**	viv**ían**

Irregular imperfects

Only three verbs have irregular forms: **ir** (to go), **ser** (to be), **ver** (to see), and their compounds, as follows:

ir	ser	ver
iba	era	veía
ibas	eras	veías
iba	era	veía
íbamos	éramos	veíamos
ibais	erais	veíais
iban	eran	veían

No sabía que hablabas francés.	I didn't know you spoke French.
Desde la ventana se veía la Sierra Morena.	The Sierra Morena could be seen from the window.
Escuchábamos la radio mientras desayunábamos.	We listened to the radio while we ate breakfast.
Siempre llevaba puestos los auriculares de su iPod.	She always had her iPod earphones on.
Éramos tres: Juan, Carlos y yo.	There were three of us: Juan, Carlos and me.

Exercises

1 Fill the gaps in the following table with the correct form of the imperfect tense:

infinitive	yo	tú	él/ella/ Vd.	nosotros/ as	vosotros/ as	ellos/ellas/ Vds.
encontrar	encontraba	encontraba				
saber		sabías		sabíamos		
escribir			escribía		escribíais	
decir			decía			decían
ver	veía			veíamos		
ser		eras			erais	
pasar			pasaba			pasaban
querer	quería			queríamos		
dar		dabas				daban
salir			salía		salíais	

2 Fill the gaps with the correct form of the imperfect tense, as in the example:

Example: Hoy mis padres viven en Cádiz pero antes *vivían* en Córdoba.

a Ahora vivimos en Zamora pero antes _____ (vivir) en Valencia.

b Hoy hay muchos partidos políticos en España pero antes no _____ (haber) ninguno.

c Antes de tener acceso a los procesadores de texto, el trabajo para el instituto _____ (ser) mucho más lento.

d Mientras _____ (nosotros pasear) por la Calle Alcalá hubo un accidente cerca del semáforo.

e Cuando _____ (yo ser) niño, mis padres se _____ (mudar) de casa cada tres años.

f Desde la ventana de la habitación donde _____ (nosotros alojarse), _____ (verse) las montañas.

g Cuando _____ (él viajar) en avión (siempre) _____ (leer) el periódico o _____ (dormirse).

3 Fill the gaps using the verbs in the box in the imperfect tense:

salir	ser	estudiar	charlar	visitar	estar
tener	llevar	ganar	trabajar	acercarse	permanecer

a Los dos hombres _____ abrigos idénticos de color negro.

b Mi anterior jefe _____ un hombre con grandes dotes de mando.

c Cuando _____ 15 años fui a Francia.

d Mientras mis amigos y yo _____ a la fiesta, Ana _____ en la cama con gripe.

e Siempre que Carmen _____ a Laura, _____ con la abuela.

f No fui al colegio ayer porque _____ enfermo.

g Cuando Juan _____ en Alemania _____ muchísimo dinero.

h Cuando _____ los exámenes, los estudiantes _____ mucho por la noche.

4 Complete the sentences placing the verbs in brackets in the correct form of the imperfect:

Example: Ahora me gustan mucho los toros pero antes no me gustaban nada.

a Desde que me compré el coche nuevo salgo de excursión todos los fines de semana; antes no _____ (poder) porque el coche _____ (estropearse) cada dos por tres.

b Hoy en día hay que tener cuidado y poner alarmas antirrobo; antiguamente no _____ (haber) tanta delincuencia.

c Actualmente las comunicaciones son excelentes; en el pasado, con sólo el correo no _____ (ser) fácil estar en contacto.

d Antes no _____ (nosotros tener) mucha elección con las tarifas de los móviles.

e Ahora es riquísimo pero su familia _____ (trabajar) en el campo y no _____ (tener) casa propia.

f En la universidad me cuesta entender a los profesores pero cuando _____ (estar) en el colegio les _____ (entender) a todos perfectamente.

g Hace tiempo que no veo a Carmina. Cuando _____ (nosotros vivir) cerca _____ (ir) a merendar juntas todas las tardes.

h Hay que ver lo contenta que está Montse estos días. Antes de romper con Josep no _____ (reírse) nunca y _____ (tener) mala cara.

i Hoy los días son muy cortos. Cuando era pequeña cada día _____ (parecer) una eternidad.

j En invierno _____ (navegar) por Internet todos los días pero en verano _____ (coger) la bicicleta y se _____ (ir) a dar paseos largos por el campo.

20

The preterite and imperfect tenses contrasted

How do we know when to use the preterite and the imperfect tenses?

The imperfect and the preterite are frequently contrasted in the same context, to indicate the difference between something *that was going on* (imperfect) and *something specific that happened* (preterite). In these cases, the preterite often expresses a completed action, whereas the imperfect is a 'background' descriptive tense (for the basic uses of these two tenses see Part I, 18 and 19. In written and spoken Spanish you often have to choose which of these two tenses to use when referring to the past. The contrast can be seen clearly in storytelling, where very often a story starts with a general description (imperfect) followed by an action that occurred (preterite).

imperfect	preterite
Cuando tenía 14 años,	heredé una fortuna de mi tío de Argentina.
When I was 14,	I inherited a fortune from my uncle in Argentina.
Mientras trabajaba en McDonald's	Carlos conoció a su primera novia.
While he was working in McDonald's	Carlos met his first girlfriend.
Cuando vivía en Sevilla	me saqué el carnet de conducir.
When I lived/was living in Seville	I got my driving licence.

Exercises

1 Read the following passage and identify the past tenses used. In each instance decide why the writer has used the preterite or the imperfect tense:

Cuando salí de la peluquería, sabía que no tenía ganas de volver a casa. Hacía un tiempo precioso y las terrazas de los cafés estaban llenas de gente. Caminaba despacio porque quería disfrutar el ambiente. El calorcito del sol en la cara me hacía sentirme bien. Decidí sentarme y tomar un helado. Llamé al camarero que vino enseguida. Cuando volvió con el helado, tropezó con una silla y me lo tiró sobre mi camiseta nueva. Se disculpó muchísimo y al final me trajo un helado más grande y no me dejó pagar.

2 Underline the correct verb in the following sentences. In some sentences there is more than one right answer:

a La moto *se acercó/acercaba* y los policías la *esperaron/esperaban* en su coche.

b *Hubo/Había* un ruido enorme muy cerca, al que *siguió/seguía* un silencio profundo.

c *Se bebió/bebía* el vaso de un trago y *se marchó/marchaba*.

d Todos los días *me levanté/levantaba* a las ocho y *me marché/me marchaba* a las nueve.

e Cuando *vimos/veíamos* la noticia en Internet, *estuvimos/estábamos* todos sentados mirando el ordenador.

f *Me puse/ponía* de pie enseguida; ya no *aguantó/aguantaba* más.

g El viernes *salimos/salíamos* de compras, pero las tiendas *fueron/estaban* cerradas.

h *Conocí/Conocía* a Sara en Londres, cuando los dos *asistimos/asistíamos* a un cursillo de programadores.

i La semana pasada *llamó/llamaba* a la puerta de Conchi pero no *estuvo/estaba*.

j El chico *se cayó/caía* del muro y *se rompió/rompía* el brazo.

3 Fill the gaps using either the preterite or the imperfect tense:

a Cuando _____ (ellos viajar) por Méjico _____ (descubrir) unos restos aztecas.

b Mientras Manolo _____ (dormir), los ladrones le _____ (robar) el coche del garaje.

c En el año 2000 se _____ (construir) una nueva torre de telecomunicaciones en Valencia.

d ¿Qué _____ (hacer) cuando el jefe te _____ (decir) que _____ (ir) a despedirte?

e El lunes pasado Javier _____ (comerse) todo el chocolate que _____ (haber) en la cocina.

f De pronto _____ (sentirse) cansadísima y _____ (tener) que descansar.

g _____ (Hacer) mucho tiempo que le _____ (nosotros esperar) en el aeropuerto.

h Cuando Carmela _____ (venir) a casa, siempre _____ (yo jugar) al ajedrez con ella.

i Los domingos siempre le _____ (yo invitar) a Pablo a tomar una copa.

j En 2011 _____ (nosotros estar) dos veces en Santiago de Chile.

4 The following story is written in the preterite. Place sentences **a** to **g** in the correct place in the story so as to give background information:

> El ladrón entró por la puerta, subió al piso de arriba y cogió todas las joyas. El ladrón lo dejó todo en orden y salió. Los dueños tardaron mucho tiempo en darse cuenta del robo.

a ya que se trataba de un ladrón muy considerado

b porque a Doña Luisa no le gustaba ponerse joyas

c que estaba abierta

d y que tenían un valor sentimental incalculable

e mientras D. Benito y Doña Luisa charlaban tranquilamente en el salón

f que había en una caja en el armario

21 Compound tenses

What are compound tenses?

If we compare the sentences 'She *went* to the party' with 'She *has gone* to the party' we see that in the first sentence the verb consists of one word, whereas in the second the verb consists of two words. The second type is known as a **compound verb,** so called because it consists of two or more parts. In the example, 'has' is the *auxiliary verb*, and 'gone' the *past participle*. This section deals with compound perfect tenses of this kind.

Key ideas

- In Spanish, as in English, perfect compound tenses are made up of two or more parts, e.g. the auxiliary verb **haber** and the past participle, e.g. **hablado, venido, sabido, roto** etc. (See Part I, 33.1).

- In a compound perfect tense the past participle is **invariable**, that is, it does not change in gender or number.

- In a compound tense **haber** should *never* be split from the past participle, as can happen in English: 'I had always believed that' is **Siempre había creído esto.**
- There are five compound tenses using **haber** in Spanish, as follows:

  perfect
  pluperfect
  future perfect
  conditional perfect
  past anterior
- The perfect and pluperfect forms exist in both the indicative and the subjunctive; the other three tenses have only an indicative form

 Whereas the past participle with **haber** is invariable, a past participle with the auxiliary verbs **ser** and **estar** *always agrees in number and gender with the subject*, e.g. **Estamos casados** (We are married); **La casa fue destruida** (The house was destroyed).

21.1 Perfect tense

This tense and its formation are explained in Part I, 17 (general use) and in Part I, 22.2 (subjunctive use). It is formed from the *present tense* of **haber** and the past participle:

he
has
ha   hablado/comido/vivido
hemos
habéis
han

Dile que no **han llegado** todavía.   Tell him they have not arrived yet.
¿Has terminado el trabajo?   Have you finished the job?

21.2 Pluperfect tense

This tense is used to indicate an action which occurred *before another action in the past*. The English equivalent is 'I *had* (spoken, etc.)'.

The pluperfect is formed from the *imperfect tense* of **haber** and the past participle of the verb:

había
habías
había .   hablado/comido/vivido
habíamos
habíais
habían

Cuando volvimos al garaje el mecánico   When we got back to the garage the
ya **había terminado** la reparación.   mechanic had already carried out the repair.
Las encuestas no confirmaron lo que los   The polls didn't confirm what the politicians
políticos **habían dicho.**   had said.

21.3 Future perfect tense

This tense indicates a future action which will have happened.

The future perfect is formed from the *future tense* of **haber** and the past participle of the verb :

habré
habrás
habrá
habremos   hablado/comido/vivido
habréis
habrán

Tus amigos **se habrán marchado** antes de que llegues.	Your friends will have gone before you arrive.
Cuando organices tu nuevo contrato de móvil, las tarifas ya **habrán bajado.**	When you get your new mobile contract prices will have come down.

21.4 Conditional perfect tense

This tense indicates a past action which would have happened.

The conditional perfect is formed from the *conditional tense* of **haber** and the past participle of the verb:

habría
habrías
habría
habríamos   hablado/comido/vivido
habríais
habrían

Habría sido preferible que lo hubieras entregado a tiempo.	It would have been better if you'd handed it on time.
El jardín **habría estado** más bonito si hubiera llovido un poco más.	The garden would have been more beautiful if it had rained a little more.

Exercises

1   Supply the missing parts of the following verbs:

infinitive	yo	tú	él/ella/Vd.	nosotros/ as	vosotros/ as	ellos/ellas/ Vds.
hablar	he hablado			hemos hablado		
conocer		has conocido			habéis conocido	
ir			ha ido			han ido
poner	he puesto			hemos puesto		
vivir		has vivido			habéis vivido	

2 Supply the missing parts of the following verbs:

infinitive	yo	tú	él/ella/Vd.	nosotros/as	vosotros/as	ellos/ellas/Vds.
mirar		habías mirado			habíais mirado	
poder	había podido			habíamos podido		
volver			había vuelto			habían vuelto
escribir	había escrito				habíais escrito	
romper		habías roto		habíamos roto		

3 Supply the missing parts of the following verbs:

infinitive	yo	tú	él/ella/Vd.	nosotros/as	vosotros/as	ellos/ellas/Vds.
cerrar	habré cerrado					habrán cerrado
venir		habrás venido			habréis venido	
beber			habrá bebido	habremos bebido		
abrir	habré abierto				habréis abierto	
decir		habrás dicho		habremos dicho		

4 Supply the missing parts of the following verbs:

infinitive	yo	tú	él/ella/Vd.	nosotros/as	vosotros/as	ellos/ellas/Vds.
comer	habría comido			habríamos comido		
sacar		habrías sacado			habríais sacado	
hacer			habría hecho			habrían hecho
ver	habría visto			habríamos visto		
cubrir		habrías cubierto			habríais cubierto	

5 Underline the correct tense:

a Mi padre se enojó conmigo porque no *he hecho/había hecho* los deberes.

b Hoy me *he despertado/había despertado* a las seis.

c Cuando llegamos al aeropuerto el avión *ha aterrizado/había aterrizado* hacía cinco minutos.

d *Había/ Habría esperado* una mejor película de ese director.

e El jefe tuvo que cambiar la decisión que *ha hecho/había tomado* media hora antes.

f Cuando llegué al aparcamiento no pude encontrar el coche que *he dejado/había dejado* allí por la mañana.

g Para cuando termine el verano ya te *has puesto/habrás puesto* bastante morena.

6 Fill the gaps with the correct form of the pluperfect:

Ayer Consuelo me contó lo de su viaje a Italia. Parece que su novio y ella _____ (ir) al aeropuerto en un coche alquilado. Luego ella descubrió que _____ (perder) su pasaporte. Lo _____ (poner) sobre la mesa del vestíbulo antes de marcharse y se le _____ (olvidar). La pareja _____ (tener) que volver a casa para buscarlo. Cuando llegaron a casa el coche se _____ (averiar). Finalmente, _____ (volver) al aeropuerto en tren y _____ (coger) el avión cinco minutos antes de la salida.

7 Complete with the correct form of the future perfect as in the example.

Example: Carmen come siempre a las dos. Ya son las tres, entonces *habrá terminado* de comer.

a Mercedes suele ir a la oficina a las nueve. Son las nueve y diez, así que _____ (llegar) ya.

b Vas a ver la película a las diez de la noche, así que a la una, ya _____ (salir) del cine.

c Como en febrero van a despedir a 200 empleados, para marzo _____ (crearse) más paro en la ciudad.

d En abril pagamos los impuestos. En mayo ya los _____ (pagar).

e Están avanzando mucho con la nueva carretera. Dentro de tres meses _____ (abrir) otro tramo.

22
The subjunctive

What is the subjunctive mood?

In English when we say 'If I *were* you', 'I wish it *were* possible' we are using the verb 'to be' in the English subjunctive. The subjunctive is one of the three *moods* of the verb, the other two being the indicative and the imperative. The moods are differentiated by their use: broadly speaking, the imperative is used for *commands*, the indicative for statements of *fact* or *certainty* and the subjunctive for *unreality* or *uncertainty*.

Of the three moods of the verb the subjunctive is without doubt the one which poses the greatest challenge for the student of Spanish, since its uses are often subtle and do not have recognisable equivalents in English. The subjunctive is a robust form in Spanish, unlike in French, where its use is limited, or in English, where it is barely alive.

 ## Key ideas

In Spanish the subjunctive is used to communicate meanings which are often subjective or less 'secure' than those communicated by the indicative mood. The meaning can vary according to whether the speaker chooses the indicative or the subjunctive. For example, after **aunque** ('although', 'even if') either the indicative or the subjunctive may be used, depending on the degree of uncertainty. Compare:

Aunque llueve a cántaros, me voy.	Although it's raining cats and dogs, I'm going.
Aunque llueva a cántaros, me iré.	Even if it's raining cats and dogs, I'll go.

In the first case, *it is a fact* that it is raining therefore we use the indicative. In the second case *it is uncertain* whether it is going to rain or not, so (although the person will go in any case) the subjunctive is used.

For a more detailed account of the meaning of the subjunctive see Butt and Benjamin (fifth edition, 2011), 242–245.

22.1 Characteristics of the subjunctive

1 The subjunctive is in principle used in **subordinate** clauses. It is occasionally also found in main clauses (see Part II, 22.3)

2 If the subject of the subordinate clause is not the same as the subject of the main verb, **que +** subjunctive is used.

Quiero que me vea.	I want him to see me. (Different subjects, therefore subjunctive construction.)

3 While the indicative is used for actions that are *real, factual, and that actually take place,* the subjunctive is associated with, for example:

a possibility and impossibility

Es (im)posible que nos veamos mañana en el concierto.	It's (im)possible for us to meet tomorrow at the concert.

b hopes and desires

Espero que Emilio vuelva pronto. Me apetece que nos veamos mañana en el concierto.	I hope Emilio will come back soon I'd like us to meet at the concert tomorrow.

c necessity

Es importante que nos veamos mañana antes del mediodía.	It's important for us to meet tomorrow before midday.

4 The subjunctive is also used after conjunctions like **cuando** ('when'), indicating future actions:

Ya hablaremos mañana cuando nos veamos.	We'll speak when we meet tomorrow.

The subjunctive is obligatory after some conjunctions, such **como si** ('as if') and **para que** ('in order that'):

Se comportaba como si fuera el jefe. Voy a darme prisa en terminar para que no lleguemos tarde.	He was behaving as if he was the boss. I'll finish quickly so that we won't be late.

22.2 Formation of the subjunctive

There are four subjunctive tenses, the **present**, the **perfect**, the **imperfect** and the **pluperfect**. They are formed as follows:

Present subjunctive

a   Regular verbs

Add the following endings to the stem of the infinitive:

-ar verbs: **-e, -es, -e, -emos, -éis, -en**
-er and **-ir** verbs: **-a, -as, -a, -amos, -áis, -an**

Thus the **endings** of **-ar** verbs look like the present indicative endings of **-er** verbs, and those of **-er** and **-ir** verbs look like the present indicative endings of **-ar** verbs.

hablar	comer	vivir
hable	coma	viva
hables	comas	vivas
hable	coma	viva
hablemos	comamos	vivamos
habléis	comáis	viváis
hablen	coman	vivan

b   Radical-changing and irregular verbs

The present subjunctive of radical-changing and irregular verbs is formed by removing **o** from the end of the stem of the first person singular of the present indicative and adding the endings listed above. Irregular verbs keep the final consonant of the first person singular stem for all persons. Radical-changing verbs follow the pattern of the present indicative. Thus the present subjunctive of:

* the irregular verb **tener** is **tenga, tengas, tenga,** etc.
* the **-ar** verb **cerrar** is **cierre, cierres, cierre,** etc.
* the **-er** verb **volver** is **vuelva, vuelvas, vuelva** etc.
* the **-ir** verb **repetir** is **repita, repitas, repita,** etc.

There are some important exceptions to this rule, as follows:

dar (to give)	**estar** (to be)	**haber** (to have)	**ir** (to go)	**saber** (to know)	**ser** (to be)
dé	esté	haya	vaya	sepa	sea
des	estés	hayas	vayas	sepas	seas
dé	esté	haya	vaya	sepa	sea
demos	estemos	hayamos	vayamos	sepamos	seamos
deis	estéis	hayáis	vayáis	sepáis	seáis
den	estén	hayan	vayan	sepan	sean

For a more complete list of forms see Verb tables (see pages 323–334).

Perfect subjunctive

The perfect subjunctive is formed from the present subjunctive of **haber** plus the past participle.

hablar	comer	vivir
haya hablado	haya comido	haya vivido
hayas hablado	hayas comido	hayas vivido
haya hablado	haya comido	haya vivido
hayamos hablado	hayamos comido	hayamos vivido
hayáis hablado	hayáis comido	hayáis vivido
hayan hablado	hayan comido	hayan vivido

Imperfect subjunctive

The imperfect subjunctive is formed for all verbs, regular and irregular, by taking the stem of the third person plural of the preterite tense and adding one of the following two endings:

-ar verbs:	either	**-ara, -aras, -ara, áramos, -arais, -aran**
	or	**-ase, -ases, -ase, -ásemos, -aseis, -asen**
-er and **-ir** verbs:	either	**-iera, -ieras, -iera, -iéramos, -ierais, -ieran**
	or	**-iese, -ieses, -iese, -iésemos, -iesies, -iesen**

The **-ara/-ase** and **-iera/-iese** endings are **interchangeable.**

hablar	comer	vivir
hablara/ase	comiera/iese	viviera/iese
hablaras/ases	comieras/ieses	vivieras/ieses
hablara/ase	comiera/iese	viviera/iese
habláramos/ásemos	comiéramos/iésemos	viviéramos/iésemos
hablarais/aseis	comierais/ieseis	vivierais/ieseis
hablaran/asen	comieran/iesen	vivieran/iesen

Note that irregular verbs conform to the same rule.:

infinitive	third person plural of preterite	imperfect subjunctive
hacer (to do/ make)	**hicieron**	**hiciera/iese, hicieras, etc.**
estar (to be)	**estuvieron**	**estuviera/iese, estuvieras**, etc.
decir (to say)	**dijeron**	**dijera/ese, dijeras**, etc.

Pluperfect subjunctive

The pluperfect subjunctive is formed from the imperfect subjunctive of haber plus the past participle:

hablar	comer	vivir
hubiera/iese hablado	hubiera/iese comido	hubiera/iese vivido
hubieras/ieses hablado	hubieras/ieses comido	hubieras/ieses vivido
hubiera/iese hablado	hubiera/iese comido	hubiera/iese vivido
hubiéramos/iésemos hablado	hubiéramos/iésemos comido	hubiéramos/iésemos vivido
hubierais/ieseis hablado	hubierais/ieseis comido	hubierais/ieseis vivido
hubieran/iesen hablado	hubieran/iesen comido	hubieran/iesen vivido

22.3 Four uses of the subjunctive

The subjunctive is used in four main ways:

To form the negative imperative and the formal positive imperative

The subjunctive is used to form all persons of the negative imperative, and the formal second person (singular and plural) of the positive imperative as in, **¡No mires!** (Don't look!); **¡No lo haga!** (Don't do it!); **¡Que vuelvan mañana!** (Come back tomorrow!) (See Part I, 25.2, 25.4.)

In subordinate clauses introduced by *que*

This section explains the most common and straightforward uses of the subjunctive in **que** clauses.

Subordinate **que** clauses frequently contain the subjunctive, for example:

main clause	subordinate clause
No me gusta	que siempre hablen francés.
I don't like	them speaking French all the time.
Quiero	que comas conmigo.
I want	you to have lunch with me.
No creo	que lo encuentren en la red.
I don't believe	that they will find it on the web.

The subjunctive is used:

a   After impersonal expressions of **possibility** and **probability**, such as **es posible que** and **es probable que**:

No es posible que te acompañemos.   It's not possible for us to go with you.
Es probable que le den un trabajo   He will probably be offered a job
en Vodaphone.   at Vodaphone.

b   After verbs and expressions indicating an **emotion** such as **querer** (to want), **desear** (to want/wish), **esperar** (to hope), **temer** (to fear), **alegrarse de** (to be pleased), **es una pena** (it's a pity).

Note that the subjunctive construction is not used when the subject of the main verb is the same as the subject of the subordinate clauses:

Quiero que leas esta carta.   I want you to read this letter.
                                        but
Quiero leer esa carta.   I want to read that letter.
Esperamos que Pedro consiga un   We hope Pedro will get a
buen resultado en la carrera.   good result in the race.
Me alegro que hayas venido.   I'm pleased you have come.
Es una pena que hayan perdido   It's a pity they have missed such a good opportunity.
una oportunidad tan buena.

c   After verbs and expressions of **influence, requests** and **necessity**, such as **es importante que** (it is important that), **será mejor que** (it will be better that), **hacer** (to make), **pedir** (to ask), **es necesario que** (it is necessary that), **decir** (to tell):

Es muy importante que cumplas tu promesa.   It's very important that you keep your promise.
Los diplomáticos se ocuparon de que todo   The diplomats got everything ready for the
estuviera preparado para la boda de la princesa. wedding of the princess.
Será mejor que salgas inmediatamente.   It will be better for you to leave at once.
Le pedí que me diera su dirección.   I asked him to give me his address.
No es necesario que Carmelo traiga los CDs It's not necessary for Carmelo to bring the CDs.

d   Verbs of **permitting** and **prohibiting** such as **dejar** (to let/allow), **permitir** (to permit), **prohibir** (to forbid):

Deja que te acompañe a parada del autobús.	Let me go with you to the bus-stop.
El juez permitió que el padre visitara a sus hijas los fines de semana.	The judge permitted the father to visit his daughters at weekends.
El médico le ha prohibido que fume.	The doctor has forbidden him to smoke.

e   With verbs of **saying** and **thinking, used in the negative**, such as **no decir** (not to say), **no creer** (not to think), **no parecer** (not to appear):

No digo que ella no sea simpática.	I'm not saying that she's not nice.
El director del banco no cree que tenga yo suficiente dinero como para comprar un piso.	The bank manager does not believe that I have sufficient money to buy a flat.
No me parece que haga mucho ejercicio.	I don't think that he does much exercise.

After conjunctions

The most common conjunctions which are used with the subjunctive are those indicating time, like **cuando**, and purpose, like **para que** (in order that).

a   Conjunctions of time

The subjunctive is used in clauses introduced by a 'time' conjunction, such as **cuando, hasta que** (until), **en cuanto** (as soon as), **mientras** (while), provided these conjunctions communicate **a future meaning**:

Cuando vengas mañana iremos al parque con los niños.	When you come tomorrow we'll go to the park with the children.
Estaré contenta mientras sigas siendo tan considerado.	I'll be happy as long as you keep taking me into account.
Llámame en cuanto sepas el resultado de tu examen.	Ring me as soon as you know your exam result.

Notes:

1   If the meaning after the time conjunction is not the future, the indicative is used:

Cuando va al cine siempre compra palomitas.	When (i.e. every time that) she goes to the cinema she always buys popcorn.

2   The indicative is always used when **cuando** introduces a question:

¿Cuándo nos vas a sacar una foto?	When are you going to take our photo?
¿Cuándo va a llegar esa maldita pizza?	When is that wretched pizza going to arrive?

b   Conjunctions of purpose

Para que, meaning 'so that', 'in order to' or simply 'to', is the most frequently used conjunction of purpose:

Te doy la llave para que me cuides el piso mientras esté fuera.	I'm giving you the key so you can look after my flat whilst I'm away,
Dale de comer al perro para que acabe de ladrar.	Feed the dog so that he stops barking.
Échale una mano al jardinero para que plante todas las rosas.	Give the gardener a hand so he can plant all the roses.
He traído fresas para que nos las comamos de postre.	I've brought some strawberries so that we can have them for pudding.

In main clauses

The subjunctive is used principally after words meaning 'perhaps':

Quizás las baterias duren hasta mañana.	Perhaps the batteries will last until tomorrow.

Exercises

1 Supply the missing parts of the following verbs in the present subjunctive:

infinitive	yo	tú	él/ella/Vd.	nosotros/as	vosotros/as	ellos/ellas/Vds.
mirar	mire			miremos		
creer		creas			creáis	
escribir			escriba			escriban
saber		sepas		sepamos		
ir	vaya					vayan
poner			ponga		pongáis	
querer		quieras		queramos		
encontrar			encuentre		encontréis	
pedir	pida			pidamos		
ser		seas			seáis	
poder	pueda			podamos		
abrir		abras			abráis	
dar			dé			den
preferir		prefieras			prefiráis	
venir	venga			vengamos		

2 Supply the missing parts of the following verbs in the imperfect subjunctive:

infinitive	yo	tú	él/ella/Vd.	nosotros/as	vosotros/as	ellos/ellas/Vds.
dar		dieras		diéramos		
desear	deseara				desearais	
tener			tuviera	tuviéramos		
necesitar		necesitaras				necesitaran
decir	dijera				dijerais	
beber			bebiera			bebieran
poner		pusieras		pusiéramos		
poder	pudiera				pudierais	
haber			hubiera			hubieran
estar		estuvieras				estuvieran
hacer	hiciera			hiciéramos		
llamar		llamaras			llamarais	
conocer			conociera			conocieran
traer		trajeras		trajéramos		
parecer	pareciera					parecieran

3 Fill the gaps in the following sentences using the present subjunctive of the verb in brackets:

a Quieren que _____ (tú cantar) ahora.

b No creemos que nos _____ (ellos decir) que no.

c Me alegro de que _____ (tú estar) contenta con el nuevo piso.

d ¡Deja que Pedro y yo _____ (ir) contigo al baile!

e Cuando _____ (venir) Raquel dile que estamos en el bar.

f Abre la ventana para que _____ (entrar) un poco de aire.

g Juana, espero que mañana te _____ (ir) bien en el examen.

h Es necesario que _____ (los niños dejar) de jugar con los videojuegos despues de una hora.

i ¡Qué pena que Alberto no _____ (saber) nadar!

j Es importante que _____ (nosotros comer) mucha fruta.

4 Match the phrases in List A with the most suitable ones from List B:

List A	List B
a Quiero que me	**g** Paco tenga facilidad para las lenguas.
b Ana no cree que	**h** gastemos los recursos de la tierra.
c Cuando llegue el verano	**i** ocurra si los gobiernos no hacen nada.
d Es muy importante que no	**j** sea de Córdoba.
e Temo que un desastre ecológico	**k** iremos de vacaciones a Santander.
f Es probable que Juan	**l** traigas las gafas.

5 Fill the gaps in the following sentences using the imperfect subjunctive:

a Quería que mis hermanos _____ (ir) a la fiesta conmigo.

b Estaba en la calle, esperando que alguien _____ (abrir) la puerta.

c Cuando el padre fue despedido fue necesario que toda la familia _____ (hacer) sacrificios.

d Era necesario que Laura _____ (trabajar) cuando _____ (terminar) la universidad para poder pagar el préstamo.

e Le enseñó el ordenador para que _____ (poder) ver cómo funcionaba

6 Complete the sentences using a present subjunctive:

a Es importante que …

b Queremos que …

c Es probable que …

d No es necesario que …

e No me gusta que …

f Mis padres no creen que …

g Me alegro de que …

h Le he dado la llave para que …

i Deseo que …

j Deja que …

Continous forms of the verb

What are continuous forms of the verb?

Compare the two sentences 'She's eating an apple' and 'She eats an apple every day.' Each sentence describes the same action, but the two sentences look at present time in a different way. The first one stresses that the eating is happening **now**; the second that the action is **a habit**, which is not necessarily happening now.

The first sentence is an example of the *continuous* (or *progressive*) form. We choose this form of the verb when we are interested in the fact that that action is continuing.

Key ideas

In Spanish the continuous forms are used:
- only for actions which are/were/will be, etc., *actually in progress*
- mainly with the present and the imperfect

23.1 Formation of continuous tenses

Continuous tenses are formed from the verb **estar** followed by the gerund (see Part I, 29):

Está trabajando.	She is working.
Los chicos estaban comiendo.	The children were eating.

¿Policía?
Mire, estoy temblando...
Están robando en el
piso de enfrente y
se lo están
llevando todo.

¿Bromeando?
No, no estoy
bromeando.

23.2 Uses of the continuous tenses

1 To convey the idea of an action that is/was/will be, etc., in progress:

En este momento están hablando con el jefe.	At this moment they're talking to the boss.
Estamos esperando que abran la puerta.	We're waiting for them to open the door.
Lo estoy pensando.	I'm thinking about it.
Ya se estaba haciendo tarde.	It was already getting late.
Aquel día estaban pasando cosas sorprendentes.	Surprising things were happening that day.

2 To denote an action that is being repeated over a period of time:

¿Está escribiendo una novela?	Is he writing a novel?
Yo estaba esperando que llegara de un momento a otro ...	I was hoping that she would arrive from one moment to the next ...

3 The verbs **estar, ir, ser, tener, venir, volver** are **not** normally used in the continuous form:

Ahora viene.	He's coming now.
¿Adónde vamos?	Where are we going?
Volvían del aeropuerto cuando se encontraron con sus amigos.	They were returning from the airport when they met their friends.

4 The continuous form is **not** used to indicate a future tense, as in English:

¿Qué haces la semana que viene?	What are you doing next week?
Vamos a Francia en octubre.	We are going to France in October.
Llegan a las ocho.	They're arriving at eight.
¡Ya voy!	I'm coming.

Exercises

1 Put the following verbs into the continuous form of the present tense:

Example: hablamos > *estamos hablando*

anda	comen	escribes ....
hago	bebemos	lees ....
se levanta	miráis	hablaba ....
estudiábamos	cae	jugabas ....
pide	destruyen	abrimos ....

2 Underline which is the more suitable of the two verbs:

a Actualmente Jorge *pinta/está pintando* un retrato de su novia.

b El niño *duerme/está durmiendo* todos los días hasta las seis de la mañana.

c Te *hablo/estoy hablando* de lo que pasó hace ocho días.

d *Trabaja/está trabajando* en Nueva York desde junio.

e ¿Qué *hacéis/estáis haciendo* en agosto?

f Cuando entramos en el teatro vimos que una cámara *grababa/estaba grabando* la función.

g Montse llegó cuando me *duchaba/estaba duchando*.

h El cartero *viene/está viniendo* a las ocho de la mañana.

i *Desayunábamos/Estábamos desayunando* en la cocina cuando dieron la noticia del atentado terrorista.

j Continuamente me *llaman/están llamando* por teléfono para venderme cosas.

3 The following narrative describes what happens every day before a concert. Rewrite the description as if it is happening now. Start like this: **Los músicos se están preparando ...:**

(En este momento) los músicos se preparan para el concierto. El pianista practica unas escalas y los miembros de la orquesta le escuchan. Como siempre, todos esperan la llegada del director, un señor muy distraído. Mientras tanto este busca en vano dónde aparcar el coche. Los espectadores entran poco a poco a la sala. Todos visten sus mejores ropas y piensan que el concierto será excelente. Todos charlan animadamente y encargan bebidas para el intermedio. Los acomodadores llevan a los espectadores a sus respectivos asientos. Todos, músicos y público, desean que empiece el concierto.

24

If-Clauses

What are 'if-clauses'?

In the sentence 'If the company wins the contract we'll all keep our jobs' there are two parts, or clauses. The first part, beginning with 'if', expresses a condition for the second sentence to happen.

There are three kinds of condition:

- **Open**, i.e. it might or might not happen but, if it does, the result is certain:

  If Matty comes, we'll have a party.

- **Unlikely or impossible**:

  If I won the lottery I'd buy a fantastic villa in Spain.

  This condition expresses a wish rather than a real possibility.

- **'Missed opportunity' in the past**:

  If I'd known how efficient she was, I'd have given her the job.

  This condition expresses a wish that has not been fulfilled and so is contrary to fact.

Key idea

In Spanish the degree of possibility is important when choosing the verb for a conditional sentence. There are predictable rules for the use of verbs with the three types of if-clause listed above:

24.1 Open conditions

An open condition is one which might or might not be fulfilled. The action in the main clause will take place in the future.

Si + present indicative

The most common type of open condition points forward to the future, but the tense we use in the if-clause is the **present indicative.** In the main clause is used either the **present** or **future indicative** or the **imperative.**

NEVER use the present subjunctive after *si*.

SI + PRESENT INDICATIVE	PRESENT INDICATIVE
Si hace demasiado calor.	podemos dormir la siesta.
If it's too hot.	we can have a siesta.
SI + PRESENT INDICATIVE	FUTURE INDICATIVE
Si Juan necesita los documentos.	tendrás que sacarle una copia.
If Juan needs the documents.	you'll have to make him a copy.
SI + PRESENT INDICATIVE	IMPERATIVE
Si no te gusta la comida.	déjala.
If you don't like the food.	leave it.

Si with a past tense in the indicative

We use **si** with a past tense in the indicative, followed by a present or future tense in the main clause, in order to indicate doubt.

SI + PERFECT	FUTURE INDICATIVE
Si han llegado ya	empezaremos la reunión
If they've arrived	we'll begin the meeting
SI + PRETERITE	PRESENT INDICATIVE
Si el presidente firmó el acuerdo ayer	podemos cerrar el contrato.
If the president signed the agreement yesterday	we can finalise the contract.

24.2 Unlikely or impossible conditions

Spanish uses the same structure for: (a) conditions which are unlikely to be fulfilled and (b) conditions which may be impossible. For this type of sentence the **imperfect subjunctive** is used in the if-clause and the **conditional** in the main clause.

SI + IMPERFECT SUBJUNCTIVE	CONDITIONAL
Si tuviera mucho dinero	te compraría un coche.
If I had a lot of money	I'd buy you a car.
Si fueras mayor	me casaría contigo.
If you were older	I'd marry you.

There is some possibility that the first condition may be fulfilled, but it seems unlikely to the speaker. In the second example, the condition cannot be fulfilled since the person cannot be any older than he or she is.

Note: the **-ra** and **-se** endings of the imperfect subjunctive are interchangeable (see Part I, 22.2).

24.3 Missed opportunity

These are conditions which have not been fulfilled. For this type of sentence the **pluperfect subjunctive** is used in the if-clause and the **conditional perfect** in the main clause.

SI + PLUPERFECT SUBJUNCTIVE	CONDITIONAL PERFECT
Si me hubieran dado el empleo	habría organizado una fiesta.
If I'd got the job	I'd have thrown a party.
Si hubieras escrito un e-mail en lugar de una carta,	el mensaje les habría llegado enseguida.
If you'd written an e-mail instead of a letter,	the message would have reached them instantly.

Exercises

1 Fill the gap with the correct form of the present tense of the verb in brackets:

Example: Si te _____ (molestar) la tele, apágala.

Si te molesta la tele, apágala.

a Si te _____ (escribir) desde Granada, contéstame.

b Si no te _____ (gustar) la carne, hazte vegetariano.

c Si (ellos) os _____ (invitar) a cenar, aceptad.

d Si (el) _____ (ser) impertinente, no le hagas caso.

e Si (vosotras) _____ (pasar) mucho tiempo en el ordenador, salid a dar paseos con frecuencia.

f Si te _____ (gustar) esos zapatos, cómpratelos.

g Si (yo) no _____ (llegar) a las ocho, no me esperéis.

h Si _____ (hacer) mucho sol, ponle un sombrero.

i Si _____ (estar) enfermo, cuídale.

j Si ya _____ (ser) las once, no subas el volumen.

2 Give the correct form of the verb in brackets:

Example: Si Carmen ha terminado los exámenes, pasaremos unos días con ella.

a Si aún no han dado las noticias, no _____ (ser) aún las nueve y media.

b Si el PSOE ha ganado las elecciones, tu padre _____ (estar) de buen humor.

c Si ha salido con esta lluvia, _____ (mojarse) de arriba abajo.

d Si te has gastado todo el dinero que te di, _____ (tener) que esperar hasta la próxima semana.

e Si te has entrenado lo suficiente, _____ (correr) el maratón sin problemas.

f Si has estado en los Picos de Europa, _____ (saber) que es uno de los paisajes más bellos de España.

g Si has hablado con Carmina, te _____ (haber) contado lo de Puri.

h Si ya ha salido el tren, _____ (nosotros coger) el próximo.

i Si te han instalado banda ancha, _____ (poder) conectarte a Internet en cualquier momento.

j Si no has visto la película en el cine, la _____ (poder) ver más tarde en DVD.

3 Change the tenses of the verbs in Exercise 2, as in the example:

Example: Si Carmen hubiera terminado los exámenes, habríamos pasado unos días con ella.

4 Fill the gaps with the correct form of the verb in brackets:

a Si _____ (nosotros tener) más tiempo, podríamos terminar el juego de ajedrez.

b Si pudiera, ¡ _____ (dar) mi vida por la suya!

c ¿Qué harías tú, si alguien te _____ (regalar) flores por la calle?

d Si yo fuera tú, _____ (cambiar) de coche cuanto antes.

e Si estuvieras en Madrid, esta noche _____ (tú venir) a cenar con nosotros en el restaurante peruano.

f Si ustedes no _____ (vivir) en la ciudad, se sentirían menos estresados.

g Si tuviera trabajo, no _____ (estar) siempre tan preocupado.

h ¿Qué contestaría usted si le _____ (ellos pedir) su opinión sobre la eutanasia?

i Si supieras que el precio de los pisos iba a subir, ¿qué _____ (hacer)?

j No habría tanto crimen en las costas si _____ (haber) más vigilancia policial.

25
The imperative

What is the imperative?

'Look at that!' and 'Don't move!' are examples of imperatives or commands.

The first example is a *positive* command, the second a *negative* one. The mood that is used for commands is called *imperative*. In English we recognise the written imperative in two ways: there is not normally a subject pronoun and there is often an exclamation mark at the end of the sentence. The spoken imperative is recognised by the tone of the voice.

First person plural commands are less direct and seem more like an attempt to persuade than to give an order. 'Let's go out tonight', 'Let's not argue!' are imperatives of this type.

 ## Key ideas

Spanish speakers use the imperative more than English speakers, who tend to use less direct language.

- In order to choose the correct form for the person(s) being addressed we have to differentiate between
  - *familiar* and *formal* modes of address (**tú/vosotros** and **usted/ustedes**)
  - *positive* and *negative* forms
- all imperatives, except the positive forms for **tú** and **vosotros**, are taken from the relevant person of the *present subjunctive*:

  Pase, pase, don Ramón.   Come in now, Don Ramon.

- the positive imperatives of **tú** and **vosotros** have their own independent forms:

  Tú también Ramoncín, pasa, pasa.   And you, come in too, young Ramon.

The forms of the imperative are as follows:

	positive	negative
tú	imperative	no + present subjunctive
vosotros	imperative	no + present subjunctive
usted	present subjunctive	no + present subjunctive
ustedes	present subjunctive	no + present subjunctive

25.1 Tú and vosotros: positive commands

Tú

This form is used to address a person with whom you are on familiar terms (see Part I, 71), e.g. a friend, a close relative, someone younger than yourself:

¡Pepe! ¡Coge el paraguas, que va a llover!   Pepe! Get the umbrella; it's going to rain.

To form the **tú** positive command, remove the last letter from the **second person singular of the present indicative**:

present indicative	imperative
(second person singular)	
hablas	habla
comes	come
vives	vive
cierras	cierra
mientes	miente

Nine verbs have irregular forms, as follows:

irregular verb		**imperative**
decir	to say	di
hacer	to do, make	haz
ir	to go	ve
oír	to hear	oye
poner	to put	pon
salir	to go out	sal
ser	to be	sé
tener	to have	ten
venir	to come	ven

Note: verbs derived from the above verbs are also irregular in their form, e.g. **deshacer** (to undo) > *deshaz*; **disponer** (to dispose) > *dispón*; **detener** (to stop) > *detén* (for a list of these compound verbs see Verb tables on pages 323–334).

Vosotros

This form is used to address more than one person with whom you are on familiar terms, e.g. your family as a group, your friends, your fellow-students.

¡Brindad por los novios!	(Drink) to the bride and groom!

To form the **vosotros** positive command, replace the final **-r** of the infinitive with **-d**. Note that the final **-d** is omitted from reflexive forms:

infinitive	**imperative**
hablar	hablad
comer	comed
escribir	escribid
cerrar	cerrad
mentir	mentid
hacer	haced
acordarse	acordaos
ponerse	poneos

Note: the only exception to the rule for reflexive verbs is **irse**, which becomes **idos** in the imperative.

In the singular:

Habla conmigo.	Speak to me.
Come rápido porque tenemos prisa.	Eat quickly because we are in a hurry.
¡Levántate!	Get up!
Hazme el favor de poner la mesa.	Lay the table, please
¡Dímelo ahora mismo!	Tell me right now!

In the plural:

Hablad en voz baja.	Speak quietly.
¡Escribid enseguida!	Write straight away!
¡Acostaos!	Go to bed!

25.2 Tú and vosotros: negative commands

Tú

The formation of the familiar negative imperative is very different from that of the positive imperative. Singular form: *no* + **the second person singular of the present subjunctive** (see Part I, 22.3):

¡No hables tan alto!	Don't speak so loudly!
¡No comas tan deprisa!	Don't eat so quickly!
No lo borres.	Don't delete it.
No salgas con ella.	Don't go out with her.
¡No me digas!	You don't say!

Vosotros

Plural form: *no* + **the second person plural of the present subjunctive:**

¡No habléis todos a la vez!	Don't all speak at once!
¡No comáis con los dedos!	Don't eat with your fingers!
No os acostéis tarde.	Don't go to bed late.
No crucéis la calle.	Don't cross the road.

25.3 Usted and ustedes: positive commands

This form is used to address people with whom you are on formal terms, e.g. a person in authority, such as a policeman, a judge, somebody older than yourself, people you don't know.

The singular and plural are formed from **the third person (*usted/ustedes*) of the present subjunctive** (see Part I, 22.3).

In the singular:

¡Mire!	Look!
Por favor, firme aquí.	Sign here please.
Por favor, espere un momento.	Wait a moment please.
Dígame su nombre por favor.	Tell me your name please.

In the plural:

¡Miren!	Look!
Por favor, firmen aquí.	Sign here, please.
Por favor, esperen un momento	Wait a moment, please.
Díganme sus nombres, por favor.	Tell me your names, please.

It is advisable to use polite expressions as a sign of respect, like **por favor**, **si es Vd. tan amable** with the formal imperatives, both positive and negative.

Disculpe, señor/caballero	Excuse me, sir.
¡Tenga cuidado!	Be careful!
Reciban un atento saludo	Yours sincerely
Por favor, dejen los abrigos en el guardarropa.	Please leave your coats in the cloakroom.

25.4 Usted and ustedes: negative commands

The singular and plural are formed from *no* + **the third person singular or plural of the present subjunctive.**

In the singular:

No me haga esperar mucho.	Don't make me wait too long.
¡No se fatigue, D. Federico!!	Don't exhaust yourself, Don Federico!
¡No corra tanto!	Don't run so fast!
No se preocupe, Sr Director.	Don't worry, sir.

No se moleste, por favor.	Please don't worry.
¡No lo ponga allí!	Don't put it there!

In the plural:

¡No miren!	Don't look!
¡No beban!	Don't drink!
¡No se muevan! ¡Esto es un atraco!	Don't move! This is a hold-up!
¡No pisen el césped!	Don't walk on the grass.
¡No se rían!	Don't laugh!

25.5 The position of object pronouns (see Part I, 7.2.3)

Positive commands: Pronouns are added to the imperative:

¡Vete!	Go away! (tú)
¡Váyase!	Go away! (usted)
Háblame en voz baja.	Talk to me quietly.
¡Diviértete!	Enjoy yourself!
Acuérdate de mí.	Remember me.
¡Dénmelos!	Give me them!

Negative commands: Pronouns precede the verb:

¡No te vayas!	Don't go away! (tú)
¡No se vaya!	Don't go away! (usted)
¡No me hables así!	Don't talk to me like that!
No te levantes.	Don't get up.
No se olvide de mí.	Don't forget me.
No me los den.	Don't give me them.

Exercises

1 Turn the following verbs into the positive form of **a** the familiar imperative singular (**tú**); and **b** the formal imperative singular (**usted**):

	tú	usted
a mirar el avión		
b hablar castellano		
c subir la escalera		
d poner el vino en la mesa		
e beber la Coca-Cola		
f acostarse temprano		
g dormir		
h salir		
i levantarse		
j callarse		
k poner la tele		
l vestirse rápidamente		
m venir acá		

2 Turn the following verbs into the positive form of (a) the familiar imperative plural (**vosotros**); and (b) the formal imperative plural (**ustedes**):

		vosotros	ustedes
a	Llamar a la puerta		
b	Mandar un SMS		
c	Ingresar dinero		
d	Pagar aquí		
e	Poner fertilizante		
f	Cerrar la puerta		
g	Comprar en las rebajas		
h	Cambiarse de ropa		
i	Venir cuanto antes		
j	Divertirse		

3 Put the following positive familiar commands into the negative, as in the examples:

Example: Corre > *No corras*   Hablad en voz baja > *No habléis en voz baja*

a Mira la pintura ....

b Escribe la tarjeta ....

c Lee el periódico ....

d Decid lo que pensáis ....

e Escuchad música ....

f Conéctate a Internet ....

g Sal a la calle ....

h Cierra la ventana ....

i Coge la pelota ....

j Saca la foto ....

k Id al colegio ....

l Pon la tele ....

m Elige un contrato de prepago ....

n Cuéntame cómo pasó ....

o Haz la cama ....

p Huye ....

q Echa la piedra ....

r Recarga el móvil ....

s Buscad la llave ....

t Limpia el suelo ....

4 Put the following commands into the negative, as in the example:

Example: Dame el libro > *No me des el libro*

a Dime tu número ....

b Coje el teléfono ....

c Págalo en metálico ....

d Levantaos ....

e Despídete ....

f Démelo mañana ....

g Acomódese ....

h Olvídate del pasado ....

i Divertíos ....

j Vete ya ....

5 You meet a tourist in a street in Granada, who is looking for the Alhambra Hotel. In order to get there, she will have to follow your directions. Translate what you say to her. Remember to use the 'usted' form.

Continue (**seguir**) walking along the street she is in, take (**tomar**) the second on the right, turn (**torcer**) left at the petrol station, go down (**bajar**) a hill, go up (**subir**) a flight of steps, then turn right. You will see the hotel in front of you.

Write down what you told her in Spanish, remembering to use the **usted** form.

26
Spelling changes in verbs

This section describes where and how particular spelling changes occur in Spanish verbs. There are two principal types of spelling changes: **radical** and **orthographic**. Most of the verbs listed in this chapter are in other respects regular. Irregular verbs are listed in Verb tables on pages 323–334.

26.1 Radical-changing verbs

'Radical'-changing verbs are verbs in which the spelling of the *stem* (i.e. the verb minus the **-ar**, **-er** or **-ir** ending) varies in certain circumstances. The last vowel in the stem is always the part affected: thus in **cerrar** the **e** in **cerr-** 'splits' into **ie**: **cierr-**, but only in certain persons of the verb.

Radical changes affect **-ar**, **-er** and **-ir** verbs. It is not easy to predict whether a given verb undergoes a radical change or not.

-ar and -er verbs

a   In the **present indicative tense** of these verbs, the single vowel of the stem splits into two. The change from **e > ie** and **o > ue** takes place in the first, second and third persons singular and the third person plural:

cerrar	encontrar	perder	volver
to close	to find	to lose	to return
cierro	encuentro	pierdo	vuelvo
cierras	encuentras	pierdes	vuelves
cierra	encuentra	pierde	vuelve
cerramos	encontramos	perdemos	volvemos
cerráis	encontráis	perdéis	volvéis
cierran	encuentran	pierden	vuelven

b   In the **present subjunctive** of these verbs changes take place in the same persons of the verb:

cierre	encuentre	pierda	vuelva
cierres	encuentres	pierdas	vuelvas
cierre	encuentre	pierda	vuelva
cerremos	encontremos	perdamos	volvamos
cerréis	encontréis	perdáis	volváis
cierren	encuentren	pierdan	vuelvan

c   The stem also changes in the **tú** (familiar) form of the **imperative**:

cierra	encuentra	pierde	vuelve

d Other common **-ar** and **-er** verbs which follow the same pattern are:

e > ie

-ar verbs		*-er* verbs	
atravesar	to cross	atender	to attend to, see to
calentar	to heat	defender	to defend
comenzar	to begin	encender	to switch on, light
despertar	to wake	entender	to understand
empezar	to begin	querer	to wish, want
gobernar	to govern	verter	to pour
*helar	to freeze		
manifestar	to demonstrate		
negar	to deny		
*nevar	to snow		
pensar	to think		
quebrar	to break		
recomendar	to recommend		
sentar	to sit down		
temblar	to tremble		

*these verbs are used only in the third person singular

o > ue

-ar verbs		*-er* verbs	
acordarse de	to remember	cocer	to cook, to boil
acostarse	to go to bed	disolver	to dissolve
avergonzar	to put to shame	doler	to hurt
colgar	to hang	*llover	to rain
contar	to count, tell	morder	to bite
costar	to cost	mover	to move
forzar	to force	oler	to smell
mostrar	to show	poder	to be able
probar	to prove, taste	resolver	to resolve
recordar	to remember	soler	to do habitually
renovar	to renew	torcer	to twist
rogar	to ask		
soltar	to release		
sonar	to sound		
soñar	to dream		
volar	to fly		

*llover is used only in the third person singular

e Exceptionally, **jugar** (to play), with a stem vowel **u,** follows the same pattern as verbs with a stem vowel **o:**

j**ue**go, j**ue**gas, j**ue**ga, jugamos, jugáis, j**ue**gan.

-ir verbs

There are three types of radical-changing **-ir** verbs. Each has a distinctive pattern in the present tense, but in other tenses they sometimes follow the same pattern:

- verbs which change the stem vowel in the present tense from **e** to **i**, such as **pedir** (to ask for)
- verbs which change the stem vowel in the present tense from **e** to **ie**, such as **sentir** (to regret)
- verbs which change the stem vowel in the present tense from **o** to **ue,** such as **dormir** (to sleep)

a In the **present indicative** the changes take place in the first, second and third persons singular and the third person plural, when the stress falls on the stem:

e > i	*e > ie*	*o > ue*
pedir	sentir	dormir
to ask for	to regret	to sleep
pido	siento	duermo
pides	sientes	duermes
pide	siente	duerme
pedimos	sentimos	dormimos
pedís	sentís	dormís
piden	sienten	duermen

b In the **present subjunctive** of these verbs the change of spelling in the stem takes place in *all* persons of the verb. Note especially the change in the **nosotros** and the **vosotros** forms: verbs that change from *e > ie* and *e > i* in the present indicative change from *e > i* in these two persons, and verbs that change from *o* to *ue* change from *o > u* in these two persons:

pida	sienta	duerma
pidas	sientas	duermas
pida	sienta	duerma
pidamos	sintamos	durmamos
pidáis	sintáis	durmáis
pidan	sientan	duerman

c In the stem of the **preterite** in the third persons singular and plural, *e* changes to *i; o* changes to *e* in the same places:

pedí	sentí	dormí
pediste	sentiste	dormiste
pidió	sintió	durmió
pedimos	sentimos	dormimos
pedisteis	sentisteis	dormisteis
pidieron	sintieron	durmieron

d Since the **imperfect subjunctive** is formed from the third-person plural of the preterite, the *i* and *u* of the stem is present in every person of the verb: **pidiera** (or **pidiese), pidieras, pidiera, pidiéramos, pidierais, pidieran; sintiera** (or **sintiese), sintieras**, etc.; **durmiera** (or **durmiese), durmieras**, etc.

e The stem also changes in the **tú** (familiar) form of the **imperative**, following the pattern of the present indicative:

pide	siente	duerme

f The gerund makes the spelling change from *e > i* and *o > u*:

pidiendo	sintiendo	durmiendo

g Other common verbs which follow the *e > i* pattern are:

medir	to measure	corregir	to correct	reñir	to quarrel
repetir	to repeat	elegir	to choose	seguir	to follow
vestir	to dress				

h Compounds of these verbs (i.e. with a prefix) follow the same rule:

conseguir	to succeed	despedir	to dismiss	desvestir	to undress

i Other common verbs which follow the *e > ie* pattern are:

advertir	to warn	invertir	to invest
concernir	to concern	mentir	to lie
convertir	to convert	preferir	to prefer
divertir	to entertain	requerir	to require
herir	to wound	referir	to refer
hervir	to boil	sugerir	to suggest

j   The only verbs to follow the **o > ue** pattern are:

dormir   to sleep
morir   to die

-eír verbs

Note the spelling of verbs ending in **-eír**:

present indicative: río, ríes,ríe, reímos, reís, ríen
present subjunctive: ría, rías, ría, riamos, riáis, rían
preterite: reí, reíste, rió, reímos, reísteis, rieron
imperative: ríe, reíd
gerund: riendo

Two other common verbs follow this pattern:

sonreír (to smile)   freír (to fry)

26.2 Orthographic changes in verbs

Two types of spelling change affect:

● the consonant before the verb ending, in order to maintain the correct sound
● the use of the accent, in order to maintain the required stress on a vowel

-ar verbs:

These changes occur before the vowel **e**, in the present subjunctive and the first person singular of the preterite:

a   *c > qu*

buscar: present subjunctive: busque, busques, busque, etc.
to look for   preterite: busqué, buscaste, etc.

b   *g > gu*

llegar: present subjunctive: llegue, llegues, llegue, etc.
to arrive   preterite: llegué, llegaste, etc.

c   *z > c*

empezar   present subjunctive: empiece, empieces, empiece, etc.
to begin   preterite: empecé, empezaste, etc.

d   *gu > gü*

averiguar   present subjunctive: averigüe, averigües, averigüe, etc.
to verify   preterite: averigüé, averiguaste, etc.

-er and -ir verbs

These changes occur before the vowel **o**, in the first person singular of the present indicative and before **a** in the present subjunctive:

a   *c > z*

vencer   present indicative: venzo, vences, etc.
to conquer   present subjunctive: venza, venzas, venza, etc.

b   *g > j*

coger   present indicative: cojo, coges, etc.
to take   present subjunctive: coja, cojas, etc.

c *gu > g*

| seguir | present indicative: | sigo, sigues, etc. |
| to follow | present subjunctive: | siga, sigas, siga, etc. |

d *qu > c*

| delinquir | present indicative: | delinco, delinques, etc. |
| to break the law | present subjunctive: | delinca, delincas, delinca, etc. |

e -**er** and -**ir** verbs where a vowel precedes the ending of the infinitive

Examples of these verbs are **leer** (to read) and **caer** (to fall). These verbs insert **y** rather than **i** in the third persons of the preterite, the imperfect subjunctive and the gerund:

preterite   **imperfect subjunctive**

leí	caí	leyera/se	cayera/ese
leíste	caíste	leyeras	cayeras
leyó	cayó	leyera	cayera
leímos	caímos	leyéramos	cayéramos
leísteis	caísteis	leyerais	cayerais
leyeron:	cayeron	leyeran	cayeran

gerund

| leyendo | cayendo |

Verbs ending in -uir

Insert **y** in the following circumstances: in the first, second and third person singular and in the third person plural of the present indicative and throughout the present subjunctive. For example:

huir   **present indicative**   **present subjunctive**
to flee

	huyo	huya
	huyes	huyas
	huye	huya
	huimos	huyamos
	huís	huyáis
	huyen	huyan

In the third persons singular and plural of the preterite and throughout the imperfect subjunctive:

	preterite	**present subjunctive**
	huí	huyera/huyese
	huiste	huyeras
	huyó	huyera
	huimos	huyéramos
	huisteis	huyerais
	huyeron	huyeran

In the **tú** form of the imperative and the gerund:

| **imperative** | huye |
| **gerund** | huyendo |

Other common -**uir** verbs are: **destruir** (to destroy) and **construir** (to build).

Verbs ending in -cer and -*cir*

This large group of common verbs has an irregular first person singular of the present indicative. It follows that the present subjunctive, since it takes its form from the first person singular of the indicative, has the same irregularity.

parecer:	present indicative: **parezco, pareces, parece**, etc.
(to appear)	present subjunctive: **parezca, parezcas, parezca**, etc.
conocer	present indicative: **conozco, conoces, conoce**, etc.
(to know)	present subjunctive: **conozca, conozcas, conozca**, etc.
conducir	present indicative: **conduzco, conduces, conduce**, etc.
(to drive)	present subjunctive: **conduzca, conduzcas, conduzca**, etc.

Other common verbs which follow this pattern are:

agradecer	(to thank)	ofrecer	(to offer)
aparecer	(to appear)	nacer	(to be born)
apetecer	(to crave)	padecer	(to suffer)
compadecer	(to pity)	permanecer	(to stay)
desaparecer	(to disappear)	pertenecer	(to belong)
enriquecer	(to enrich)	producir	(to produce)
establecer	(to establish)	reconocer	(to recognise)
favorecer	(to favour)	reducir	(to reduce)
merecer	(to deserve)	traducir	(to translate)
obedecer	(to obey)		

Verbs ending in -ñer, -ñir and -llir

These verbs drop the **i** in the gerund, the third persons singular and plural of the preterite and the imperfect subjunctive, e.g. **reñir** (to quarrel), **zambullirse** (to dive), **tañer** (to strum).

gerund:	riñendo
preterite:	riñó, riñeron
imperfect subjunctive:	riñera/iese, riñeras, riñera, etc.

Addition of an accent in order to maintain the correct stress

a Verbs ending in **-uar** and **-iar**

These verbs do not have an accent in their infinitive form but they add an accent in the first, second and third persons singular and in the third person plural of the present indicative, the subjunctive and in the **tú** form of the imperative:

continuar **enviar**
(to continue) (to send)

present indicative

continúo	envío
continúas	envías
continúa	envía
continuamos	enviamos
continuáis	enviáis
continúan	envían

present subjunctive

continúe	envíe
continúes	envíes
continúe	envíe
continuemos	enviemos
continuéis	enviéis
continúen	envíen

imperative (second person singular)

| continúa | envía |

Other verbs that add an accent in this way are:

| actuar | (to act) | habituar | (to accustom) |
| efectuar | (to carry out) | situar | (to situate) |

evaluar	(to evaluate)		
confiar	(to entrust)	fiar	(to trust)
criar	(to bring up)	guiar	(to guide)
desafiar	(to challenge)	vaciar	(to empty)
desviar	(to divert)	variar	(to vary)

Note: The following common **-iar** verbs do not add an accent to keep the stress: **cambiar** (to change), **limpiar** (to clean).

b **reunir** (to meet) adds an accent in the same circumstances as **-uar** and **-iar** verbs.

present indicative:	reúno, reúnes, reúne, reunimos, reunís, reúnen
present subjunctive:	reúna, reúnas, reúna, reunamos, reunáis, reúnan
imperative:	reúne

Exercises

1 Give the first-person singular, first-person plural and third-person plural of the present indicative of the following verbs:

infinitive	first-person singular	first-person plural	third-person plural
a empezar			
b poder			
c despertar			
d soñar			

infinitive	first-person singular	first-person plural	third-person plural
e querer			
f dormir			
g verter			
h torcer			
i sentir			
j conseguir			
k reír			
l conocer			
m coger			
n leer			
o satisfacer			
p destruir			
q poner			
r caer			
s conducir			
t actuar			

2 Give the first-person singular, first-person plural and third-person plural of the preterite of the following verbs:

infinitive	first-person singular	first-person plural	third-person plural
a sentir			
b caer			

c reír

d seguir

e buscar

f pagar

g comenzar

h preferir

i traducir

j reñir

k hacer

l decir

m ver

n saber

o poner

3 Put the verbs in brackets in the correct form of the present indicative:

a Pablo no _____ (tener) prisa.

b Si no _____ (tú cerrar) la puerta va a hacer mucho frío.

c Enrique _____ (perder) siempre el tren de las 7.30.

d Siempre _____ (ella acordarse) de mi cumpleaños.

e Mi abuelo siempre _____ (dormirse) viendo la tele.

f Mis amigos _____ (venir) a verme mañana.

g No _____ (encontrar) mis gafas.

h ¿Por qué no _____ (tú volver) a casa?

i _____ (yo sentir), que he metido la pata.

j Dani _____ (jugar) con su Nintendo todas las tardes.

4 Put the verbs in brackets into the correct form of the preterite:

a Les _____ (yo pedir) a los Reyes Magos que me trajeran una bicicleta.

b El dólar _____ (caer) bruscamente en la Bolsa.

c Anoche no _____ (ella dormir) en toda la noche.

d _____ (ellos divertirse) mucho durante el carnaval.

e Ayer _____ (ella medir) las ventanas para comprar cortinas nuevas.

f La semana pasada _____ (él corregir) todos los exámenes.

g Hace dos días que _____ (yo llegar) al pueblo.

h Le _____ (yo buscar) por todas partes.

i Cervantes _____ (nacer) en 1547.

j Hace un rato _____ (ellos traer) lo que compraste en eBay.

27
Modal verbs

What are modal verbs?

In the sentence 'I can play tennis' there are two verbs: 'can' and 'play'. 'Can' is known as a 'modal verb'. As an auxiliary, a modal verb is always followed by a main verb and communicates attitude and intention, affecting the meaning of the verb which follows it. In this case 'can' has two possible meanings, either 'I am able to play tennis' or 'I have permission to play tennis'.

Key ideas

- Modal verbs are auxiliary verbs followed by an infinitive
- Modal verbs colour the relationship between the subject of the sentence and the infinitive
- The main modal verbs in Spanish are as follows:

verb	meaning	translation
deber (de)	obligation, supposition	must, have to
tener que	obligation	
haber de	obligation	
haber que	obligation	
poder	ability, permission, possibility	can, could, may be able to, might

For the conjugations of these verbs see Verb tables on pages 323–334.

The four verbs which are used for obligation overlap considerably in their meaning and so are, to a certain extent, interchangeable.

27.1 Deber

Deber is used for:

a obligation, whether we like it or not (especially in a legal or moral sense):

Debemos obedecer la ley.	We must/have to obey the law.
¿Crees que deberías decírselo?	Do you think you should tell him?
Debí haber invitado a Ana también.	I should have invited Ana too.

b supposition (**deber de**):

Debe de volver mañana porque
quiere asistir a la boda de su mejor amigo.

He must be coming back tomorrow because
he wants to attend his best friend's wedding.
(i.e. this is my supposition).

Con todas las joyas que lleva
debe de ser muy rica.

With all those jewels she is wearing
she must be pretty rich.

Note: the distinction between **deber** and **deber de** is not always adhered to by native speakers in modern Spanish. **Deber** on its own is also used in the sense of supposition:

Ese hombre debe ser el padre de la novia.

That man must be the bride's father.

27.2 Tener que

Tener que often overlaps in meaning with **deber**, but the obligation felt has more of a sense of necessity imposed on the person or group.

Tenemos que ponernos al día con todos
los avances tecnológicos.
El año pasado tuve que ir a Rusia
por un asunto de negocios

We have to get up to date with all the
new technological developments.
Last year I had to travel to Russia
on business.

27.3 Haber de, haber que

a **Haber de** has the same meaning as **tener que** but is less strong.

He de limpiar los cristales.
Los estudiantes de tercero han de hacer un
esfuerzo para sacar mejores notas.
Hemos de salir pronto.

I have to clean the windows.
The third-year students must make an effort to
improve their marks.
We must leave soon.

b **Haber que** is used in the third person singular of simple tenses in the indicative and the subjunctive to indicate general, impersonal obligations: **hay que, había que, hubo que, haya que, hubiera** or **hubiese que**.

Esta vida hay que tomársela en serio.
En la España de Franco había que ir a otro país
para ver películas interesantes.
No han dicho que haya que traer el pasaporte.
Aquel año hubo que apretarse el cinturón.

One has to take life seriously.
In Franco's Spain people had to go abroad to
see interesting films.
Nobody has said we have to bring our passports.
That year we had to tighten our belts.

27.4 Poder

Poder is used for:

a ability

No puedo entender este software.	I cannot understand this software. (I am mentally unable to understand it.)
No pudo hacerlo.	He couldn't do it. (He wasn't able to do it.)

b permission

¿Puedo ir a la fiesta?	Can/May I go to the party? (Will you give me permission?)
¿Podría utilizar tu portátil?	Could I use your laptop?
¿Se puede entrar?	May I come in?

c possibility

Eso no puede ser verdad.	That cannot be true. (That cannot possibly be so.)
Podrías perder un poco de peso.	You could lose a little weight. (It would be possible for you to do it.)

Exercises

1 Write the correct form of the present tense of **tener que** in the gaps.

a No (tu) _____ ir al colegio mañana.

b ¿Por qué (nosotros) _____ llevar uniforme?

c Mi novia _____ trabajar durante todo el verano.

d No (yo) _____ volver a la oficina hasta el martes.

e ¿(vosotros) _____ ir al dentista?

f Sara acaba de recibir un SMS y _____ contestarlo.

2 Write the correct form of either **deber** or **poder** in the following sentences.

a No se _____ visitar el museo porque está cerrado.

b Juan, está lloviendo. No _____ salir a la calle porque tienes un fuerte catarro.

c No se _____ fumar en los aviones.

d Por favor, ¿_____ ir a tu fiesta?

e Mamá, ¿_____ dejar de meterte en mis cosas?

f Este ordenador es muy barato. _____ tener muy poca memoria.

g ¡Estoy cansadísimo! No _____ subir la escalera.

h Los padres _____ vigilar cuando los niños navegan por Internet.

i No (yo) _____ comer cacahuetes porque soy alérgico.

j Este coche _____ ir a 160 kilómetros por hora.

3 Write five sentences using **deber** or **tener** or **haber que** indicating things that you or your friends must or must not do:

Example: El año pasado teníamos que pagar mucho para estudiar en la universidad pero este año hay que pagar más.

4 Write five sentences using **poder** stating things that you or your friends can do or are not allowed to do.

Example: No puedo decírtelo porque es un secreto.

28

Gustar-type and impersonal verbs

Now we describe two groups of verbs that behave in a special way: **gustar**-type and impersonal verbs.

28.1 What are gustar-type verbs?

Gustar-type verbs have the same structure as the English 'It hurts me', 'That surprises me'. In this type of sentence the person who is having the experience ('me' in this case) is the direct object. Although these verbs sometimes appear to be used 'impersonally', the subject of the verb is usually identifiable.

Key ideas

- Gustar-type verbs usually involve the *reversal* of the English subject and object:

  Me gusta viajar. I like travelling (lit. 'travelling pleases me').

  The construction used with verbs like **gustar** often gives rise to difficulty. The reason for this difficulty is that learners do not 'turn the sentence round'. It is important to (a) identify the subject; (b) make the verb agree; and (c) use the correct personal pronoun.

1 The Spanish construction in the sentence **Me gusta tu reloj** (I like your watch) is the reverse of the English. This construction can be broken down as follows:

indirect object pronoun	verb	subject
Me	gusta	tu reloj
To me	is pleasing	your watch

Remember that if the subject is plural *the verb must also be plural*, as in the translation of 'I like fast cars':

Me	gustan	los coches rápidos
To me	are pleasing	fast cars

If the person is someone other than 'me', *the indirect object pronoun changes*, as in the translation of 'He likes your house' (your house is pleasing to him):

Le	gusta	tu casa
To him	is pleasing	your house

2 In this construction Spanish frequently emphasises the person by placing **a mí, a ti,** etc. before the indirect object pronoun:

A mí me gusta tu reloj.	I like your watch.
A ellos les encanta el cine.	They love going to the cinema.
A Lucía le gustan mucho las cerezas.	Lucía likes cherries very much.

Note: As in the last example, if the person has not been identified before, it is necessary to use the person's name (Lucía), in order to clarify who we are referring to. The personal pronoun can be used thereafter.

3 The infinitive is frequently the subject used in this construction:

¿A ti te gusta nadar?	Do you like swimming?
No le gusta mucho ir a clase.	He doesn't like going to lectures very much.
Les encanta ver películas de Disney.	They love seeing Disney films.

4 Other common verbs of the **gustar** type are:

alegrar	to please	**fastidiar**	to annoy
apetecer	to appeal to, to feel like	**hacer falta**	to be necessary
bastar	to be enough	**importar**	to matter to
convenir	to be fitting, desirable	**interesar**	to interest
costar	to be an effort	**molestar**	to bother
cumplir	to behove, to be one's place to	**parecer**	to seem, appear
doler	to ache, hurt	**sentar**	to suit
encantar	to be delighted	**sobrar**	to be superfluous
extrañar	to surprise	**tocar**	to concern
faltar	to be lacking, missing		

Me encantan las catedrales góticas.	I love Gothic cathedrals.
A mis vecinos les sobra dinero.	My neighbours have more than enough money.
Faltan dos cosas.	Two things are missing.
A Pedro le basta con una cerveza.	One beer is enough for Pedro.
A mí me duele la cabeza.	I've got a headache.
Les conviene quedarse en Barcelona	It suits them to stay in Barcelona.
A Lorena no le importa nada que España gane la Copa Mundial otra vez.	It doesn't matter at all to Lorena whether or not Spain wins the World Cup again.
¿Te gustaría saber lo que pasó?	Would you like to know what happened?
No me apetece nada ir a Benidorm.	I don't like the idea of going to Benidorm at all.
Te toca a ti.	It's your turn.

28.2 Impersonal verbs

What are impersonal verbs?

In the sentences 'It is snowing', 'It's your turn', the word 'it', which is the subject, has no identity. Therefore the verb that follows is called 'impersonal'. In another type of sentence, such as 'one never knows' and 'it is said that ...' the subject is not revealed or cannot be given a specific identity. This type of sentence is also commonly called impersonal.

Key ideas

In Spanish the use of impersonal constructions is widespread. They occur:

- in 'true' impersonal sentences, where the verb is normally in the third person (translated into English by 'it'):

Llueve.	It's raining.
Es posible que vuelva.	It is possible that she'll return.

- with **hay**, expressing 'there is' and 'there are' (see also 27.3):

¿Hay pan?	Is there any bread?

- where the reflexive pronoun **se** is used, which is translated as 'one, 'you' or 'they' in English:

Se puede entender esto.	One/You can understand that.
Siempre se debe empezar por el principio.	One/You should always begin at the beginning.

a Verbs indicating the weather

Many of the verbs which are truly impersonal are associated with the weather. They are used only in the third person singular. The most common ones are:

llover	to rain
nevar	to snow
hacer buen/mal tiempo	to be good/bad weather
hacer sol	to be sunny
hacer calor/frío	to be hot/cold

Estaba lloviendo a cántaros.	It was raining cats and dogs.
En Málaga hace buen tiempo todo el año.	In Malaga the weather is good all year round.
Nevó toda la noche.	It snowed all night.

b Hay, the third person singular of **haber**, is used impersonally, in the meaning of 'there is', 'there are'. **Hay** may be followed by the singular or the plural. This impersonal expression is available in all tenses: **ha habido** (perfect), 'there has/have been; **habrá** (future), 'there will be'; **habría** (conditional), 'there would be'; **había** (imperfect) and **hubo** (preterite), 'there was/were', **había**

habido (pluperfect), 'there had been'. The subjunctive forms are: **haya** (present); **haya habido** (perfect); **hubiera** (imperfect) and **hubiera habido** (pluperfect).

Cuando hay conflictos, es mejor intentar resolverlos.	When there are conflicts it's best to try to resolve them.
¿Hay algo para beber? Sí, algo habrá.	Is there anything to drink? Yes, there'll be something.
No había nadie en la parada de autobús.	There was nobody at the bus-stop.
En julio hubo fiestas en mi pueblo.	There were fiestas in my town in July.
No creo que haya gente en la calle.	I don't think there are any people in the street.
Si hubiera vuelos baratos a Argentina no dudaría en ir a Buenos Aires.	If there were cheap flights to Argentina I wouldn't hesitate to go to Buenos Aires.

Note: in Latin-American Spanish the plural form of the verb is normally used when the object is plural.

No habían demasiados problemas.	There weren't too many problems.

c   Other types of impersonal verbs

In Spanish expressions of the type **(no) es necesario (que),** etc., are considered to be impersonal. They are often followed by the infinitive or the subjunctive (see Part I, 22.3):

The most common of these expressions are:

es fácil/difícil (que)	it's easy/difficult (to)
es importante (que)	it's important (that)
es (im)posible (que)	it's (im)possible (that)
es (im)probable (que)	it's improbable (that)
es necesario/preciso (que)	it's necessary (that)

No es necesario que nos acompañes si no quieres.	It's not necessary for you to come with us if you don't want to.
Es imposible nadar y guardar la ropa.	You can't have your cake and eat it.

d   The use of *se* in 'impersonal' constructions (see Part II, 30.1)

Exercises

1   Fill the gaps with the correct form of the present tense of the verb in brackets:

a A Pedro no le _____ (gustar) bailar salsa.

b A mí me _____ (encantar) las pinturas negras de Goya.

c Le _____ (doler) la pierna.

d _____ (faltar) una mesa.

e Nos _____ (hacer) falta dos platos.

f ¿Te _____ (molestar) que fume?

g No me _____ (interesar) ese chico aunque tenga un Mercedes.

h Les _____ (gustar) cenar en un restaurante los sábados.

i ¿Por qué te _____ (costar) tanto entender a los jóvenes?

j ¿Te _____ (doler) las muelas?

2   Fill the gap with the correct pronoun.

a A _____ les gustan los viejos automóviles.

b A _____ me encanta el paisaje de Castilla.

c A _____ te interesa saber lo que pasa en el mundo?

d A Jesús, ¿ _____ importa lo que diga la gente?

e A los jugadores del Valencia no _____ conviene viajar mañana.

f A vosotros, ¿ _____ gusta el chocolate?

g A _____ nos faltan tres jugadores.

h A Juana, _____ duele la espalda.

i A _____ no me molesta que me llames de tú.

j A mi novio no _____ gusta que trabaje tanto.

3 Answer the questions using the **gustar** construction, as in the example:

Example: ¿A ti te gustan las patatas fritas? *Sí, me gustan or No, no me gustan.*

a ¿A tu profesor le gusta la música? ....

b ¿A ti te gusta el fútbol? ....

c ¿A tus padres, les molesta que salgas mucho? ....

d ¿A vosotros, os interesa el deporte? ....

e ¿A ti te gusta el vino? ....

f ¿A Bart le gusta el español? ....

29

Ser and *estar*

What is the difference between ser and estar?

 ## Key ideas

The idea of 'being' is viewed in two different ways by Spaniards, according to the context. In the sentence 'I am English', 'I am' refers to my national identity, as an intrinsic part of my nature. The verb **ser** must be used here.

In the sentence 'I am drunk', 'I am' refers to **my temporary state**, which will change when I return to sobriety. The verb **estar** must be used here.

The contrasting ideas – 'identity/nature' and 'temporary state' – help to define the different ways of looking at 'being', but no description of how these two verbs are used is entirely satisfactory. Some 'rules of thumb', however, can be given which should help the learner to understand the differences between them. (For a more detailed discussion of this difference see Butt and Benjamin, 5th edition, 2011, 408.)

29.1 Forms: present tense

ser	estar	
soy	estoy	I am
eres	estás	you are
es	está	he/she/it is, you are (formal)
somos	estamos	we are
sois	estáis	you are
son	están	they are, you are (formal)

29.2 Ser

Ser is used:

1 With a **noun, pronoun** or **infinitive**:

El gallego no es un dialecto, es una lengua.   Galician is not a dialect, it is a language.
–¿Quién estaba al teléfono? –Era un número   'Who was on the phone?' 'It was the
equivocado.   wrong number'.
Lo importante es firmar el contrato.   The important thing is to sign the contract.

2   To **identify or define** a person or thing, in order to say:

what something/somebody is, or is not: 'She's a woman.'
what something/somebody is like, or not like: 'She's intelligent.'

Ser acts as a kind of 'equals sign':

Laura es española; no es inglesa.	Laura is Spanish; she's not English.

(Laura = chica española; no = inglesa.)

(By contrast, Laura **está** relajada; **no está** nerviosa [Laura is relaxed; she is not feeling nervous] describes the state Laura is in/is not in.)

Ser must be used when referring to:

> identity (**mujer**)
> intrinsic qualities and physical characteristics (**rubia/inteligente**)
> profession/occupation (**estudiante**)
> nationality (**española**)

3   To indicate **the ownership and origin of someone or something, and the material something is made of.** In all these cases the intrinsic nature of the person or object is stressed:

Este coche es mío.	This car is mine.
¿De dónde eres? Soy de Granada.	Where do you come from? I'm from Granada.
La puerta es de madera.	The door is made of wood.

4   When speaking of *time:*

Mañana es jueves.	Tomorrow is Thursday.
Son las siete y cuarto.	It's a quarter past seven.
Ya es tarde.	It's already late.

es
Mujer
Joven
rubia
estudiosa
española.

está
en el suelo
escribiendo
relajada
sola
Contenta.

29.3 Estar

Estar is used mainly in the following contexts:

1   To indicate **where** somebody or something is, that is, for location or position. The location can be permanent or temporary:

Vigo está en Galicia.	Vigo is (situated) in Galicia.
¿Dónde estamos?	Where are we? (temporarily)
Mis gafas están en el coche.	My glasses are in the car (a temporary location).

(By contrast, Vigo **es** una ciudad gallega. **Somos** italianos. Mis gafas **son** muy caras. Vigo is a city in Galicia. We are Italian. My glasses are very expensive.)

2   To indicate a **temporary state of affairs**, such as an illness, state of mind or mood:

Estoy muy sana.	I'm very healthy (but I could become ill).
Marta estaba encantada con su marido.	Marta was very happy with her husband (temporarily).
Juan está cansado.	Juan is tired (a temporary state).
La botella no está llena.	The bottle is not full (but it can be filled up again).
¿Estás contenta?	Are you happy? (*not* Are you a happy sort of person?, *but* Are you feeling happy?)
¿Por qué estás callado?	Why are you so quiet? (the person is not normally quiet)

3 To convey *the idea of an action that is/was in progress* you use **estar** with the gerund, forming the continuous tense (see Part I, 23.1). **Estar** is used in this way with all tenses of the verb:

Está lloviendo.	It's raining.
Estaba escribiendo una carta.	She was writing a letter.

29.4 Test

Check your understanding of **ser** and **estar** by filling in the gaps using the correct form:

Los elefantes _____ enormes.	Elephants are big (they cannot be small).
Juan _____ un buen chico.	Juan is a good fellow (it is his nature).
Nosotros _____ estudiantes.	We're students (this is our occupation even if it is only for a limited time).
Mi amigo y yo _____ aburridos.	My friend and I are bored (it's our present state).
Su piso _____ a la venta.	His flat is for sale (this will change when the flat is sold).
Mi novio y yo _____ muy enamorados.	My boyfriend and I are very much in love (but this could change).

29.5 Ser and estar with adjectives

1 Some adjectives are invariably used with **ser**, others with **estar**, as listed below:

ser	estar
(in)justo	bien/mal/fatal
(in)necesario	casado
(in)conveniente	de buen/mal humor
importante	enamorado
increíble	enfadado
inocente	enfermo
inteligente	harto
lógico	lleno
trabajador	(pre)ocupado
	prohibido
	roto
	vacío

Es importante saber la respuesta.	It's important to know the answer.
¡Qué inocente eres!	How innocent you are!
Están casados desde hace tres años.	They've been married for three years.
Siempre está de mal humor los lunes.	He's always ill-tempered on Mondays.
Eso está muy bien.	That's very good.

2 Certain adjectives can be used with either **ser** or **estar**, but with different meanings. The **ser** meanings always reflect *permanent* characteristics; the **estar** meanings refer to *temporary* states. The most common of these adjectives are:

	ser meaning:	*estar* meaning:
aburrido	boring	bored
bueno	good (character)	delicious (food)
cansado	tiring	tired
listo	clever	ready
maduro	mature	ripe

	ser meaning:	*estar* meaning:
malo	bad, evil	ill
nervioso	nervous (disposition)	nervous (temporarily)
tranquilo	calm (disposition)	calm (temporarily)

Ahora ya está tranquilo.	He's calm now.
Es muy tranquilo.	He's a very calm person.
¿Estás lista, cariño?	Are you ready, darling?
Ese chico cree que el fútbol es muy aburrido.	That boy thinks football is very boring.
¿Por qué estáis tan aburridos hoy?	Why are you so bored today?

Exercises

1   Fill the gaps using either **ser** or **estar**:

a Santiago de Compostela _____ en el noroeste de España.

b Rosa, ¿por qué _____ tan contenta hoy?

c Mi mujer y yo _____ profesores.

d ¿Por qué _____ tan cansado, Pedro?

e El catalán _____ una lengua romance.

f Tu idea _____ buena, pero va a costar demasiado dinero.

g Los pisos nuevos _____ lejos, fuera de la ciudad.

h Dicen que _____ argentinos pero no me lo creo.

i Créeme, Jorge; yo no _____ así.

j Javier y Rosa viven juntos, pero no _____ casados.

k Mi reloj _____ muy caro pero _____ roto.

l _____ prohibido fijar carteles.

m Sara _____ harta de estudiar.

n ¿ _____ ustedes franceses o alemanes?

o Pero chicos, ¿no _____ listos todavía?

p _____ cierto que Juan no viene hoy.

q Montse _____ la chica más lista del grupo.

r Las chicas _____ celebrando el final del examen.

s Mi jefa _____ tan contenta conmigo que me ha subido el sueldo.

t Las puertas _____ de hierro.

2   Make sentences with **ser** or **estar**, linking the words in column A with those in column B. There are several possible combinations:

A	B
los perros	de familia muy antigua
caminar	atrasado
las películas	malísimo
el Rey	feroces
nosotros	aburridas
la silla	optimistas
este tren	hambrientos

Clara	felices
los jóvenes	cansadísima
el tiempo	de mal humor
tú	de madera
su hija	a la venta
las noticias	soltera
el País	agradable

3 Make up sentences using **ser** or **estar** with the following adjectives:

a ocupada   f enamorados

b italiano   g roto

c malo   h guapa

d abiertos   i mejor

e importante   j goloso

4 Here are two lists of adjectives describing two famous people. Complete each sentence with the correct form of **ser** or **estar**, and try to guess who the people are:

A	B
_____ español	_____ inglés
_____ soltero	_____ divorciado
_____ mallorquín	_____ tímido
_____ moreno	_____ moreno
_____ en forma	_____ tradicional
_____ tenista	_____ a veces pintando
_____ simpático	_____ reservado
_____ millonario	_____ heredero de un trono
_____ muy atractivo	_____ interesado en el medio ambiente

5 Do the crossword, using forms of **ser** or **estar**:

Horizontales

(2) Antes _____ más estudioso

(4) Mi pueblo _____ de fiesta

(5) Sí, yo _____ de Málaga

Verticales

(1) Me han dicho que _____ el hermano de Ángel.

(2) (a) Lo siento no me acordaba que _____ tu cumpleaños.

     (b) ¡Dios mío, ya _____ las doce!

(4) Llaman al teléfono, espero que _____ mi madre.

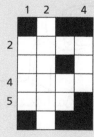

(Solution on p. 350.)

30 Active and passive

What are active and passive sentences?

The following sentence is an *active* one:

> Luisa took my bike.

The subject ('Luisa'), who carried out the action, is placed first; the verb ('took') is *active*. The object of the action ('the bike') comes after the verb.

The following sentence has the same meaning but is a *passive* one:

> My bike was taken by Luisa.

In this sentence the structure is reversed: the object of the action (the bike) becomes the subject of the verb, which changes to a *passive* one (was taken). The doer of the action 'Luisa', is known as the *agent*, the one who carries out the action. The agent comes after the verb, preceded by the preposition *by*.

Verbs which take a direct object (transitive verbs) can be used in either the active or the passive *voice* (i.e. used in either an active or a passive way).

Key ideas

- Spanish, like English, makes use of active and passive sentences, although Spanish has more varied ways of expressing a 'passive' idea and uses the construction described above less than English
- **ser**, followed by the past participle of the verb, is used to form passive sentences
- In the passive voice, the past participle after **ser** agrees in number and gender with the subject of the sentence
- The agent of the action which has been carried out is normally preceded by the preposition **por**.

Este periódico es publicado por el grupo Prisa.	This newspaper is published by the Prisa group.
Los políticos fueron criticados por el pueblo.	The politicians were criticised by the people.
La guerra ha sido declarada por el Presidente.	War has been declared by the President.

30.1 Uses of the active and passive

1 All passive sentences have an agent, normally preceded by **por**. If the agent is an unknown or a general one it can be omitted from the sentence:

La casa fue destruida (por el fuego).	The house was destroyed (by fire).
Los niños habían sido abandonados.	The children had been abandoned.

In the second example we do not know what or who were the agent(s) of the abandonment, but it is known that an agent existed. We might have chosen to express the same ideas in the active voice:

El fuego destruyó la casa.	Fire destroyed the house.
Habían abandonado a los niños.	(They (i.e. someone) had abandoned the children.

2 The passive with **ser** is usually known as the *true* passive. **Estar** is also used with the past participle, but not strictly in a passive sense, to describe the state which results from an action (see Part II, 29.2).

Compare:

Los exámenes estaban ya corregidos.	The examinations were marked already.
Los exámenes fueron corregidos por D. Alberto.	The examinations were marked by Don Alberto.

In the first example we are interested in *the state that resulted from the marking of the examinations;* in the second example we are interested in *the action which had been carried out by Don Alberto*.

Similarly:

El trabajo está terminado, así que podemos marcharnos.	The job is finished, so we can go.
El trabajo había sido abandonado sin terminar por los constructores.	The job had been left unfinished by the builders.

In the first case the result of the work is what matters and the agent is irrelevant, whereas in the second case the focus is on the action that had been carried out by the agents, the workmen. Note that **estar** + past participle is hardly ever accompanied by an explicit agent.

Exercises

1 Put the verb in the infinitive into the passive:

a La ciudad fue _____ (destruir) por las tropas del enemigo.

b El embajador ha sido _____ (trasladar) a Inglaterra.

c El edificio fue _____ (construir) por una compañía japonesa.

d El agua mineral fue _____ (derramar) por el camarero.

e El ordenador ha sido _____ (arreglar) rápidamente.

f Las llaves habían sido _____ (dejar) en la mesa.

g El pastel ha sido _____ (devorar) por el chico con gafas.

h El dinero ha sido ya _____ (devolver).

i Este libro fue _____ (imprimir) en Argentina.

2 Change the sentences from passive to active, as in the example:

Example: El terreno fue excavado en los años 90. *Excavaron el terreno en los años 90.*

a Las imágenes fueron captadas por la cámara.

b El embajador ha sido secuestrado por los terroristas.

c Las casas fueron construidas con ladrillos fabricados cerca de Madrid.

d Los restos de una iglesia visigótica fueron hallados por un grupo de arqueólogos.

e La colecta será destinada a las víctimas del terremoto.

f El autobús fue revisado por el mecánico.

g Un millón de euros será pagado para liberar al embajador.

h Ayer la crisis fue resuelta por los diplomáticos.

i Las armas fueron destruidas por una empresa británica.

j Los residuos son almacenados en depósitos de seguridad.

3 Change the sentences from active to passive, as in the example:

Example: Javier Marías publicó una nueva novela el año pasado.
El año pasado una nueva novela fue publicada por Javier Marías.

a La policía detuvo al delincuente.

b Han nombrado al señor Ramos presidente del club.

c La cena la pagó la compañía.

d El gobierno ha multado a la compañía de gas.

e El jefe cerró la oficina a las seis.

f Vendieron los pisos en febrero.

g El perro mordió al chico.

h La tecnología ha cambiado el mundo.

i Construyeron el puente en 1995.

j Todos esperaban la llegada del Rey.

k El lobo devoró a la abuela.

4 Translate into English:

Romero era un detective privado que había sido expulsado de la policía. Sus ex-compañeros sentían respeto por él ya que su mujer había sido asesinada por un psicópata y como consecuencia él se había prometido a sí mismo el dedicarse a defender a la gente inocente que era amenazada por desaprensivos. Aquella mañana, mientras se dejaba llevar por sus pensamientos, llamó a la puerta un cliente. Al decir 'adelante' entró una mujer alta, de pelo rubio largo y sedoso, exquisitamente vestida, que preguntó: ¿Es Vd. el detective Romero? Romero sintió que su vida iba a ser transformada desde ese momento.

31
Pronominal verbs

What are pronominal verbs?

Pronominal verbs are verbs that are accompanied by a reflexive pronoun. These verbs frequently communicate a 'reflexive' meaning. In the sentences 'I wash myself' and 'They love themselves', the subject and the object of the verb are the same person (I/myself; they/themselves) so the meaning is reflexive. The action is turned back on to the subject of the sentence, i.e. it is 'reflected' in it, as in a mirror. In English the reflexive pronouns are *myself, yourself, himself,* etc.

Key ideas

- In Spanish, pronominal verbs are always accompanied by a reflexive pronoun. Verbs can be made pronominal by the addition of the reflexive pronoun (see Part I, 7.5).

arreglar to get (something) ready **arreglarse** to get oneself ready
divertir to amuse (someone) **divertirse** to be amused, to amuse one another

Note that the reflexive pronoun can also have a reciprocal meaning ('each other', 'one another'). See Part II, 31.2 for this use.

- The reflexive pronoun changes according to the subject of the verb, as in the present tense of **levantarse** (to get up):

me levanto	I get up	**nos levantamos**	we get up
te levantas	you get up	**os levantáis**	you get up
se levanta	(s)he/it/you get(s) up	**se levantan**	they/you get up

¡Quiero bañarme solo!

Bien, pero yo me quedaré aquí por si no te lavas bien.

31.1 Uses of pronominal verbs

1   The pronominal verb in Spanish translates the English reflexive idea of 'self':

¡Lávate en seguida!	Wash yourself/Get washed at once!
Se cortó.	He cut himself.

2   The pronominal forms of verbs in Spanish frequently have the meaning of the English 'get', 'become', 'grow', as in the following examples:

poner	to put	**ponerse**	to put on (clothes)
alegrar	to cheer	**alegrarse**	to become cheerful
enriquecer	to enrich	**enriquecerse**	to become rich
sobreponer	to overcome	**sobreponerse**	to get over (something)
aburrir	to bore	**aburrirse**	to get bored
asustar	to frighten	**asustarse**	to become frightened
molestar	to upset	**molestarse**	to get cross, trouble oneself, bother

¡No te asustes!	Don't be frightened!
Ángela, ponte el vestido de seda.	Angela, put on the silk dress.
¡Arréglate que salimos a cenar!	Get ready. We're going out for dinner!
Si no vienes mañana, me enfadaré.	If you don't come tomorrow, I'll get upset.
No me molestes que estoy muy ocupado.	Don't disturb me. I'm very busy.

Exercises

1   Fill the gaps in the table with the correct forms of the present tense:

infinitive	yo	tú	él/ella/ Vd.	nosotros/ as	vosotros/ as	ellos/ellas/ Vds.
levantarse	me levanto			nos levantamos		
acostarse		te acuestas			os acostáis	
entenderse			se entiende			se entienden
vestirse		te vistes				se visten
hacerse	me hago			nos hacemos		
ponerse			se pone		os ponéis	
encontrarse	me encuentra		se encuentra			
sentirse		te sientes				se sienten
sentarse			se sienta	nos sentamos		
divertirse	me divierto				os divertís	

2 Fill the gaps with the correct form of the present tense of the verb in brackets:

a Siempre _____ (yo acostarse) a medianoche.

b ¿Por qué no _____ (tú bañarse) en el mar?

c _____ (nosotros verse) a las diez en el Corte Inglés.

d ¿ _____ (vosotros levantarse) o no?

e Pedro _____ (sentirse) mal porque riñó con su hermano.

f Mi madre siempre _____ (despertarse) temprano.

g Mis colegas _____ (reunirse) en el bar a la misma hora.

h _____ (yo ruborizarse) cuando recuerdo el bochorno de ayer.

i ¿No _____ (tú acordarse) de lo que pasó cuando despidieron al jefe?

j Mi novia nunca _____ (enfadarse) conmigo.

3 Write five sentences describing your typical routine in the morning up to the time you leave home. Use at least five of the following pronominal verbs: **despertarse, levantarse, lavarse, ducharse, afeitarse, vestirse, sentarse**. When you have done this, write five more sentences using pronominal verbs to describe the morning routine of a friend or a member of your family.

The infinitive

What is the infinitive?

The infinitive is the form of the verb which is not inflected. In English the infinitive consists of two words, the first of which is always 'to' and the second of which is the verb, e.g. 'to catch', 'to laugh'.

Key ideas

In Spanish the infinitive:

- consists of one word: **cantar** (to sing), **coger** (to take), **reír** (to laugh)
- ends in either **-ar, -er** or **-ir: hablar, comer, vivir**:

  No sabe leer ni escribir.   He does not know how to read or write.

- is invariable in form
- can also function as a noun:

  Vivir en Málaga es un encanto.   Living in Malaga is wonderful.

- is frequently found after prepositions:

  Después de **volver** a casa, se duchó.   After returning home he had a shower.

The perfect infinitive is formed from the infinitive of **haber** and the past participle:

  Recuerdo haberlo visto.   I remember having seen him.

32.1 Uses of the infinitive

1 **As a noun** the infinitive is always masculine and is sometimes preceded by the definite article. It can be either the subject or object of a verb:

El tomar drogas puede destruir tu vida.	Taking drugs can destroy your life.
Odio trabajar por la noche.	I hate working at night.
Me gusta viajar por Méjico.	I like travelling in Mexico.

Note that the infinitive is often translated by the English *-ing* form (see Part I, 34).

Some verbs are nouns in their own right, retaining their infinitive form, e.g. **el deber** (homework or duty), **el parecer** (opinion), **el pesar** (grief), **el anochecer** (nightfall).

2 The infinitive acts as the first component of the perfect infinitive and the passive infinitive:

Lamento haberle ofendido.	I am sorry to have offended you.
Quería ser conducido al centro de la ciudad.	He wanted to be driven to the town centre.

3 **After prepositions.**

a Prepositions, e.g. **a, de, sin, para** and **por**, are often followed by the infinitive:

Vamos a jugar al póquer.	We're going to play poker.
El modo de vivir de los españoles.	The Spanish way of life.
Se marchó sin decir nada.	He left without saying anything.
Está en París para buscar trabajo.	She is in Paris to look for work.
Por ser mi amigo, me ayudó.	He helped me because he was my friend.
Le pasó por ser tan despistada.	It happened to her because she is so forgetful.

b The construction **al** plus the infinitive is frequently used to convey the meaning 'when ...'. It refers to an action which is (almost) simultaneous with that of the main verb:

Al llegar a la estación vio que había perdido el tren.	When he arrived at the station he saw that he had missed the train.
Al levantarse Alicia no se dio cuenta de la hora.	Alicia did not realise what time it was when she got up.
Se alegró al ver que le habían preparado una sorpresa.	She was happy when she saw that they had prepared a surprise for her.

c After verbs of motion: **bajar, ir, salir, subir, venir, volver,** etc., the preposition **a** plus the infinitive is used:

Fui a Córdoba a ver la corrida.	He went to Cordoba to see the bullfight.
Vinieron a hablar con nosotros sobre el futuro.	They came to speak to us about the future.

4 The infinitive often follows an active verb:

a Directly, without the intervention of a preposition. This happens when the subject of the main verb is also the subject of the infinitive.

Tengo que limpiarme los zapatos.	I've got to clean my shoes.
Pensaba hacerlo mañana.	I intended to do it tomorrow.

b With certain verbs the infinitive can be used even if the subjects of the main verb and the infinitive are not the same (see Part II, 22.4.3):

Le mandó volver a casa.	He ordered him to go back home.
No me deja salir.	She will not let me go out.

c Preceded by a preposition, especially **a, de** and **en**:

(i) Verb + **a** (+ infinitive), e.g. **empezar a** (to begin to), **atreverse a** (to dare):

Pueden empezar a escribir el examen.	You can begin (to do) the examination.
No me atrevía a cruzar la calle por el tráfico.	I didn't dare cross the street because of the traffic.

(ii) Verb + **de** (+ infinitive), e.g. **parar de, dejar de** (to stop [doing]); **acordarse de** (to remember):

Por favor, deja de gritar.	Please stop shouting.
No paro de pensar en España.	I never stop thinking about Spain.

(iii) Verb + **en** (+ infinitive), e.g. **tardar en** (to delay, be late); **pensar en** (to think about):

La pobre tardó mucho en darse cuenta ...	The poor thing took a long time to realise ...
Sólo piensa en jugar al fútbol.	All he thinks about is playing football.

Note: A more extensive list of these verb constructions is given in Part II, 32.5).

5 The following constructions with the infinitive are very frequent:

a **tener que** (to have to) (see Part I, 27.2):

No tiene que saberlo.	He does not have to know it.
Tenéis que ordenar la casa.	You have to tidy up the house.

b **hay que** (it is necessary to, we/one must/have to) (see Part I, 27.3):

Hay que reírse un poco todos los días.	You have to laugh a little every day.

c **acabar de** + infinitive (to have just + past participle):

Acaba de escribir un libro.	She has just written a book.
Acababan de terminar la cena cuando se escapó el perro.	They had just finished the meal when the dog got out.

d **volver a** (to do something again):

No han vuelto a verla.	They haven't seen her again.
Tenemos que volver a empezar.	We have to start again.

6 Object pronouns are normally added to the infinitive:

Quisiera verle enseguida.	I'd like to see him straight away.
Esperamos reunirnos mañana.	We are hoping to meet tomorrow.

Note: Alternatively, the pronoun may be placed before the main verb in these sentences:

Le quisiera ver enseguida.	I would like to see him at once.
Nos esperamos reunir mañana.	We hope to meet tomorrow.

Exercises

1 Fill the gaps in the sentences with an infinitive from the box:

resolver	llegar	divertirse	amanecer	poner
volver	leer	ir	ver	comprar

a Después de _____ las revistas en la mesa del vestíbulo, entró en la cocina.

b No vimos toda la isla, así que tenemos que _____ a visitarla el año que viene.

c No pensamos _____ a Grecia este año.

d Al _____ al estadio nos encontramos con Paco.

e Fuimos a Bilbao a _____ el famoso Museo Guggenheim.

f Queremos _____ el problema pronto.

g Antes de _____ un nuevo ordenador, nos informamos sobre precios y calidades.

h No deja de pensar en _____.

i Acabó de _____ y todos los pájaros empezaron a cantar.

j No tengo tiempo de _____ este libro.

2 Complete the following sentences using a suitable infinitive:

a A mí me gusta..........................

b Mañana a las dos de la tarde vamos a......................

c El tren tardó una hora en.....................

d Iremos a la piscina después de.......................

e Beber demasiado puede....................

f Espero......................

g Aunque no quieras tienes que......................

h Cuando le vimos, acababa de.......................

3 Write a description of what you intend to do this weekend using the following verbs/verb constructions with the infinitive: **ir a, querer, gustar**. You could begin like this: *Esta noche vamos a ir al polideportivo porque nos gusta . . .*

4 Fill the gaps below with the infinitives in the box:

recuperar	invertir	equipar	interesar	financiar	convencer
estudiar	llegar	visitar	ser	llegar	
pedir	ser	aumentar	vender	traer	

Después de _____ todas las teorías de su tiempo, Cristóbal Colón dedujo que al _____ la tierra redonda, sería posible _____ a las Indias por el Océano Atlántico. En aquel momento lo que necesitaba era que alguien quisiera _____ su aventura. Colón se dedicó a _____ todas las Cortes europeas para _____ ayuda económica y tras _____ rechazado por los italianos y los portugueses, llegó a Castilla. Los Reyes Católicos estaban en plena política de expansión. Intentaban _____ el reino de Granada de manos de los musulmanes y esperaban _____ sus territorios en el Norte de Africa. Colón no pudo _____ al rey Fernando, pero Isabel se llegó a _____ por la propuesta del marino genovés. Como las arcas del reino estaban vacías Isabel decidió _____ sus joyas e _____ el dinero en una aventura que podría _____ grandes beneficios a Castilla. Cristóbal Colón utilizó el dinero para _____ tres carabelas que, después de muchas peripecias, consiguieron _____ a las costas americanas el 12 de octubre de 1492.

The past participle

What is the past participle?

The past participle is a special form of the verb which can act as an adjective, a part of a compound verb and a noun. The past participle in English is usually formed by adding -(e)d to the verb: *start* > *started*, *like* > *liked*, etc. There are many irregular past participles in English: *find* > *found*, *go* > *gone*, *make* > *made*, etc.

The past participle is an *adjective*, as in the phrase 'the broken window', where 'broken' is the past participle, describing the noun.

The same word acts as a *verb* in the sentence 'Dawn has broken'. Here the auxiliary verb 'has' combines with 'broken' to form the perfect tense.

A few *nouns*, such as 'a drunk' and 'the dead' are derived from past participles.

Key ideas

In Spanish the past participle, **hablado**, **comido**, etc.:

- is an essential part of compound tenses, such as the perfect (**haber** + past participle), and the passive voice (**ser** + past participle)
- can act as an adjective, describing and defining a noun
- can sometimes become a noun.

Formation of the past participle

The past participle is formed by replacing:

the **-r** of **-ar** infinitives by **-do**:	**hablar** (to speak) > **hablado** (spoken)
the **-er** of **-er** infinitives by **-ido**:	**comer** (to eat) > **comido** (eaten)
the **-r** of **-ir** infinitives by **-do**:	**vivir** (to live) > **vivido** (lived)

Irregular forms

A full list of irregular past participles, e.g. **decir** (to say) > **dicho** (said), **hacer** (to do/make) > **hecho** (done/made) etc. is given in Part I, 17.2).

33.1 Uses of the past participle

1 **As an adjective** the past participle modifies the noun and agrees in number and gender with it.

la semana pasada	last week
un árbol caído	a fallen tree
unos clientes satisfechos	satisfied customers

2 **As part of a verb** the past participle is used for:

a Compound perfect tenses consisting of **haber** + the past participle: the perfect, the pluperfect, etc. (Part I, 21.1):

¿Has visto la exposición?	Have you seen the exhibition?
Ya lo has hecho.	You have done it now.

b **Ser** + the past participle forms the passive voice (Part I, 30).

La ciudad fue destruida.	The town was destroyed.
Los cambios han sido autorizados por el gobierno.	The changes have been authorised by the government.

Note: the past participle remains **invariable** when it is part of a compound tense, whereas in the passive voice the past participle **agrees in gender and number** with the subject of the sentence.

c **Estar** is frequently used with the past participle to express the state resulting from an action (see Part II, 29.2.2).

Los bancos estaban abiertos.	The banks were open.
La entrada está prohibida.	Entry is forbidden.
La película no está autorizada para menores.	The film is not recommended for children.

Exercises

1 Give the past participles of the following verbs:

a	parar	**k**	caer
b	querer	**l**	decir
c	conseguir	**m**	permitir
d	ir	**n**	descubrir
e	escribir	**o**	ver
f	romper	**p**	hacer
g	abrir	**q**	detener
h	construir	**r**	llamar
i	oír	**s**	componer
j	leer	**t**	resolver

2 Fill the gaps in the following sentences with a past participle from the box.

roto	encontrado	cerradas	interpretada	divorciado
hecha	hablado	apagadas	traído	casada

a La puerta está _____ de madera.

b Hay muchas tiendas _____ debido a la crisis.

c Ninguna de mis amigas está _____ todavía.

d Las luces del salón estaban _____.

e Nos habíamos _____ en el bar por casualidad.

f ¿Has _____ francés con Eulalie?

g El padre _____ se quejó ante el tribunal.

h El ascensor estaba _____.

i La música fue _____ por la orquesta de RTVE.

j ¿No me has _____ ningún regalo?

34
The gerund

What is the gerund?

The term 'gerund' comes from Latin, and in English its rough equivalent is the *-ing* form (*speaking, eating*, etc.). This form is called the *present participle* in English. It is frequently used and very versatile: it can act as part of a verb, 'we were *dreaming*'; as an adjective, 'a *parking* meter'; or as a noun, '*jogging* is good for you'. In Spanish the term 'gerund' is used by Spanish grammars to describe a special form ending in **-ando** or **-iendo**.

Key ideas

The term gerund will be used to describe the Spanish verb form ending in **-ando** or **-iendo** (**hablando, comiendo**). There are similarities between the use of the *-ing* form in English and the gerund in Spanish but major differences also exist.

The Spanish gerund:

● is normally the equivalent of an **adverb,** giving more information about the action of the verb:

Salimos corriendo de la discoteca. We ran out of the disco. (lit.'We went out running …')

The gerund **corriendo** tells you about the **way** we went out.

● describes an action that is taking place *simultaneously* (or almost) with the action of the main verb:

Se pasa todo el día hablando por teléfono.   She spends the whole day talking on the phone.

● emphasises the **duration** of a verbal action:

Estaba cantando en la ducha.   She was singing in the shower.

34.1 Formation of the gerund

1 In regular verbs the gerund is formed by adding **-ando** to the stem of **-ar** verbs and **-iendo** to the stem of **-er** and **-ir** verbs. The gerund is **invariable** in form:

hablar > hablando   comer > comiendo   vivir > viviendo

2 Most irregular verbs conform to the rule for regular verbs:

poner > poniendo   saber > sabiendo   salir > saliendo

There are three exceptions:

decir > diciendo   poder > pudiendo   venir > viniendo

3 The ending of **-er** and **-ir** verbs changes to **y** when the stem of the verb ends in a vowel:

construir > construyendo   ir > yendo   caer > cayendo

4 The spelling of the stem of the gerund changes for those **-ir** verbs which change the spelling of the stem in the third persons of the preterite (see Part I, 26.1):

dormir > durmieron > durmiendo   morir > murieron> muriendo
pedir > pidieron > pidiendo   sentir > sintieron > sintiendo

5 There is a past form of the gerund, which is composed of the gerund of **haber** and the past participle (having spoken, etc.):

habiendo hablado   habiendo comido   habiendo vivido
No sé por qué te quejas, habiendo buscado   I don't know why you're complaining, having looked
las vacaciones más baratas.   for the cheapest holiday.

6 Pronouns are frequently added to the gerund (see Part I, 7.2 and 7.3). When this happens it is necessary to place an accent on the penultimate syllable of the gerund:

Estaba mirándoles.   He was looking at them.
Entró en el cuarto de estar quitándose   Taking off his jacket, he went into
la chaqueta.   the sitting room.

34.2 Uses of the gerund

1 To form **the continuous tense: estar** plus the gerund (see Part I, 23.1):

Estuvieron bailando toda la noche.	They were dancing all night.
En este momento estamos trabajando en el jardín.	At the moment we are working in the garden.

2 To indicate **how an action is being carried out**:

Fuimos andando al cine.	We walked to the cinema (lit. 'We went walking').
Siempre entraba sonriendo a la oficina.	He always went into the office smiling.
Ganó un dinerillo tocando la guitarra por los bares.	He earned some pin money playing the guitar in bars.

3 To translate the idea of *by + -ing*:

Se ganaba la vida vendiendo objetos de cuero en la calle.	He earned a living by selling leather articles in the street.
Nos entretuvimos jugando al fútbol con la pandilla.	We amused ourselves by playing football with the gang.
Se libró de la multa hablando con el policía.	By talking to the policeman he got off without paying a fine.

4 After **seguir** and **continuar** meaning 'to continue doing/to do', the gerund *must* be used:

Continuó leyendo.	He continued reading/to read.
¿Por qué sigues discutiendo?	Why do you keep on arguing?

5 **Some differences between the gerund in Spanish and the *-ing* form** (present participle) **in English**:

a When the *-ing* form acts as a verbal noun it is normally translated by the Spanish infinitive:

Ver es creer.	Seeing is believing.
No le gusta ni bailar ni pasear; sólo le gusta leer y escuchar música.	He doesn't like dancing or going for walks; he only likes reading and listening to music.

b After prepositions the *-ing* form is also translated by the infinitive in Spanish:

Después de escribir la carta, salió para echarla al correo.	After writing the letter she went out to post it.
Antes de sentarte, ¿podrías sacar la basura?	Could you take out the rubbish before sitting down?

c Strictly speaking, the Spanish gerund cannot be an adjective (see Part II, 34.2), whereas in English the *-ing* form can:

el policía sonriente/que sonríe	the smiling policeman
un traje de novia	a wedding dress
la sartén	frying pan
agua potable	drinking water
A Natacha le espera un futuro prometedor.	Natacha has a promising future.

34.3 The gerund and adjectives ending in -nte

1 It is important not to confuse the Spanish adjective which ends in **-ante**, **-ente** or **-iente** with the Spanish gerund. This form, which is derived from the verb, is often called the present participle in Spanish. Unlike the English present participle ending in *-ing*, it does *not* function as part of a verb.

2 This type of adjective is formed by replacing the final syllable of the infinitive of **-ar** verbs by **-ante** and the final syllable of the infinitive of **-er** and **-ir** verbs by either **-iente** or **-ente**. There is no reliable way of knowing which of the latter two endings applies. It is therefore necessary to learn the forms:

hablar (to speak*)* > hablante (speaking)
crecer (to grow) > creciente (growing)
sorprender (to surprise) > sorprendente (surprising)
dormir (to sleep) > durmiente (sleeping)

3 The **-nte** form corresponds to English **-ing** (e.g. burning, changing), in its function as an adjective:

agua corriente	running water
una necesidad creciente	a growing need
un crimen escalofriante	a horrifying crime
una estudiante sobresaliente	an outstanding student

Note: 'running', 'growing', etc., in the examples are English present participles which function as adjectives and are *not to be translated by the gerunds* **corriendo, creciendo**, etc., in Spanish.

4 There is a large group of nouns ending in **-nte** with, in some cases, a feminine form **-nta**:

un amante	a lover
un hispanohablante	a Spanish speaker
un/una presidente/a	a president
un/una dependiente/a	a shop assistant
un/una sirviente/sirvienta	a servant

Exercises

1 Give the gerund of the following verbs:

a esperar .... **f** poner .... **k** pedir ....

b conocer .... **g** poder .... **l** correr ....

c cumplir .... **h** creer .... **m** ir ....

d venir .... **i** elegir .... **n** destruir ....

e amanecer .... **j** herir .... **o** vestir ....

2 Fill the gaps using the gerund of the verbs in the box:

hundir	trabajar	bajar		
leer	mejorar	hacer	divulgar	avanzar

a Estaba _____ el periódico cuando su amigo entró en el bar.

b Algunas emisoras continúan _____ noticias falsas.

c Los soldados iban _____ por la selva.

d Manuel lleva mucho tiempo _____ en la fábrica de zapatos.

e Tu salud va _____ cada día más.

f En las bolsas mundiales el dólar sigue _____.

g El barco se estaba _____ sin que nadie pudiera hacer nada.

h Se está _____ de noche y se nos viene la tormenta encima.

3 Translate into English:

a La saludamos al llegar.

b Tuvo un accidente cuando cruzaba la calle.

c Este es el mejor centro comercial de la zona.

d Estaba leyendo tranquilamente cuando llegó Ana llorando.

e Suspendió el examen porque le vieron copiando.

f ¿Qué dices?

g Fumar, beber y comer demasiado es malo.

h A Carol le gusta cantar por la mañana.

i ¡Que suena el teléfono!

35
Negation

What are negative sentences?

The statements 'I want to go out tonight' and 'I don't want to go out tonight' exemplify two basic types of sentences: those in which we say 'yes', called affirmative, and those in which we say 'no', called **negative.**

There is a wide range of words which express a negative meaning. In English these are words like *not, nothing, never, nobody.* Negative words are used when, for example, we wish to refuse, deny, contradict, or say the opposite, as in 'I'm *not* going', '*Nothing* will change my mind', '*Nobody* knows the answer'.

35.1 Negative words

The most common negative words in Spanish are:

no	no, not	**ni ... ni...**	neither ... nor ...
nunca	never	**nada**	nothing, not anything
jamás	never (emphatic)	**nadie**	nobody, not anybody
tampoco	neither, nor, not either	**ninguno**	no, not any, none
ni	nor, not even	**ni siquiera**	not even

Key ideas

In Spanish, negation is grammatically more varied than in English:

- To express a simple negative statement, one negative word is placed before the verb:

No viene.	He is not coming.
Nadie sabe la respuesta.	Nobody knows the answer.
Nunca volveremos a ese restaurante.	We shall never return to that restaurant.

- With the exception of **no**, meaning 'not', negative meaning can be expressed by either *one word* or *two words*. Thus 'nobody' can be expressed as either **nadie** or **no … nadie**. Where the negative consists of two words, **no** goes before the verb and the other word after it:

Nunca voy a la playa OR **No** voy **nunca** a la playa.	I never go to the beach.
Nadie podía creerlo. OR **No** podía creerlo **nadie.**	Nobody could believe it.

- When the verb is preceded by an object pronoun, the latter must be placed between the negative word and the verb:

Nunca les manda nada.	He never sends them anything.
No me digas.	You don't say.

- In Spanish the use of **no** as the answer to a direct question is usual, whereas in English the response is often more elaborate because of the need for politeness. Thus a Spaniard might answer the question: **¿Quieres cenar conmigo esta noche?** with a simple **No.** The same question in English, 'Would you like to have dinner with me tonight?', might elicit 'No, thank you' or No, I'm doing something else'. Similarly:

–¿Ha venido el cartero?	Has the postman come?
–No.	No, he hasn't.

'Double negatives'

A 'double negative' is formed where there are two or more negative words in a sentence, one of which comes before the verb. Although in English the use of double negatives is not correct, in Spanish they are very correct. The following examples show some possible combinations of negative words:

Nunca hace **nada.**	He *never* does *anything*.
Carmen **no** sale **jamás** con **nadie.**	Carmen doesn*'t ever* go out with *anyone*/Carmen *never* goes out with *anyone*.
No había nada en las tiendas.	None of the shops had anything I liked.

No

1. **No** can be used on its own, to avoid repetition of the verb:

Pedro habla inglés muy bien, pero Juana no.	Pedro speaks English very well, but Juana doesn't.
¡Racismo no!	Down with racism!

2. **No** is used as a 'question tag', when the speaker is expecting confirmation of a statement he believes to be true. **¿no?** corresponds to a multiplicity of question tags in English, such as 'isn't he?', 'didn't you?', 'doesn't it?, etc.:

Vais a ir a Cuba este verano, ¿no?	You're going to Cuba this summer, aren't you?
El tren sale a las cinco, ¿no?	The train leaves at five, doesn't it?
Tienes los billetes, ¿no?	You've got the tickets, haven't you?

Ni ... (ni ...)

1   **Ni** followed by a second **ni** means 'neither ... nor':

No estaba ni en casa ni en el trabajo; estaba en la playa.	She was neither at home nor at work; she was on the beach.
No me gusta ni la tele ni el cine; me gusta el fútbol.	I like neither television nor cinema; I like football.

2   By itself **ni** can also mean 'not even'; alternatively, **ni siquiera** (see Part II, 38.1) may be used:

No voy a quedarme aquí ni un día más.	I'm not going to stay here even one more day.
Ni (siquiera) su mejor amigo sabía sus planes.	Not even his best friend knew about his plans.

Ninguno

Ninguno/a/os/as means 'no one', 'none', 'not ... any', 'no', and may be used both as an adjective and a pronoun.

1   As an adjective:

a   It agrees in number and gender with the noun:

Era domingo y no había ninguna tienda abierta.	It was Sunday and there were no shops open.

b   **Ninguno** shortens to **ningún** before a masculine singular noun (see Part I, 4.33):

Nunca ha tenido ningún problema.	He's never had any problem.
No había ninguna chica en la fiesta.	There were no girls at the party.

c   Note that the plural **ningunos/as** is rarely used as an adjective.

2   As a pronoun:

Ninguno is often followed by **de** with a personal pronoun: **ninguno de ellos** = 'none of them':

Ninguno de los chicos respondió.	None of the boys answered.
–¿Cuál de estos vestidos me sienta mejor ?	'Which of these dresses suits me best?'
–Ninguno de ellos.	'None of them.'

Nunca and jamás

These two words both mean 'never', 'not ... ever'. When there is another negative word in the sentence the translation is usually 'ever':

Nunca va al partido los sábados.	He doesn't ever/He never goes to the match on Saturdays.
Aquí nunca ocurre nada.	Nothing ever happens here.
Nunca lavas los platos.	You never wash the dishes.

Jamás is a stronger form of negation than **nunca**:

No quiero volver a verte jamás.	I don't *ever* want to see you again.

Note: Jamás is not used in comparisons:

Más vale tarde que nunca.	Better late than never.
Trabaja más que nunca.	He is working harder than ever.

Tampoco

Tampoco means 'neither', 'nor' and 'not ... either' and it replaces **también** (also) when the sentence is negative:

No me digas que tampoco vas a venir a cenar esta noche.	Don't tell me that you are not coming for dinner tonight either.
A mis amigos no les gusta emborracharse y a mí tampoco.	My friends don't like getting drunk and I don't either.

Exercises

1   The following sentences use a one-word negative. Rewrite each sentence using a double negative:
Example: Nadie le acompañó al cine. *No le acompañó nadie al cine.*
a   Nunca nos llama o nos manda mensajes.
b   Nada saben de la cultura del sur de España.
c   Nadie ha querido ir al festival de Benicassim conmigo.
d   Tampoco creo que vamos a ganar la copa este año.
e   Ni Fernando ni Sofía van al mercado hoy.

2   The following sentences use a double negative. Rewrite each sentence using a one-word negative:
Example: No viajo nunca en tren. *Nunca viajo en tren.*
a   Eso no lo sabe nadie.
b   No me molesta nunca que fumes.
c   Yo no lo creo tampoco.
d   No le conocemos apenas.
e   No tiene valor nada de lo que han comprado.

3   Make the following sentences negative by using an appropriate negative expression:
Example: Siempre vamos a la discoteca los viernes. *Nunca vamos a la discoteca los viernes.*
a   Federico habla siempre del pasado.
b   Los domingos siempre los paso trabajando en el ordenador..
c   Algunos de mis amigos van a Segovia conmigo mañana.
d   En la esquina hay alguien sospechoso.
e   Yo también me marcho.

4   Translate into English:
a   Nunca digo nada.
b   No habrá nada que hacer cuando volvamos a casa.
c   Nunca le había dado nadie un regalo tan bonito.
d   Vi la película anoche y no me gustó tampoco.
e   No creo en ningún político.

36
Adverbs

What are adverbs?

Adverbs give more information about the action of a verb. In the sentence 'Peter moved out' we have very limited information about the move. In 'Peter moved out *yesterday*', we find out *when* the move took place. If still more information is given, as in 'Peter moved out *unexpectedly yesterday evening*', we learn more about the *manner* and *time* of the move. The additional words are all adverbs, giving us more information about the verb.

There are four main ways in which an adverb gives extra meaning to a verb, by saying:

- **how** something is done or happens:

  She acts *beautifully*. The train stopped *suddenly*.

- **when** something is done or happens:

  They are coming *tomorrow*. See you *soon*.

- **where** something is done or happens:

  Don't eat *here*. Please step *outside*.

- **how much** something is done or happens:

  You should go out *more*. We don't earn *enough*.

In the above examples the adverb is a single word. Adverbs can also consist of groups of words, usually with a preposition followed by a noun or noun phrase. These are called 'prepositional phrases':

  They acted *in a discourteous manner.*
  They are coming *at one o'clock.*
  We saw her *in the distance.*

Key ideas

In Spanish, adverbs usually have the same function as in English. They affect the verb in four particular ways: *manner, time, place* and *degree*:

- ***manner*** **¿cómo?** (how?):

¿Cómo habla?	Habla **rápidamente.** He speaks quickly.
How does he speak?	Habla **sin pensar.** He speaks without thinking

- ***time*** **¿cuándo?** (when?):

¿Cuándo llega?	Llega **mañana.** She's arriving tomorrow.
When is she arriving?	Llega **a las dos de la mañana.** She's arriving at 2 a.m.

36.1 Adverbs ending in -mente

These adverbs consist of the feminine singular form of the adjective plus the suffix **-mente**. This form
corresponds to the English adverbial ending -*ly*:

Adjective		Adverb	
Masculine singular	**Feminine singular**		
claro	clara	claramente	clearly
estupendo	estupenda	estupendamente	wonderfully
fácil	fácil	fácilmente	easily
feliz	feliz	felizmente	happily
simultáneo	simultánea	simultáneamente	simultaneously
triste	triste	tristemente	sadly

Note: if there is a stress accent on the adjective, this must be maintained in the adverb:

El inglés es una lengua fácil.	English is an easy language.
Lo vamos a aprender fácilmente.	We'll learn it easily.
Fue una cena muy rica.	It was a splendid meal.
Hemos cenado muy ricamente.	We've dined splendidly.
En ese hotel la atención al cliente es fantástica.	In this hotel customer service is fantastic.
Nos atendieron fantásticamente.	They looked after us really well.
Es un señor muy elegante.	He's a very elegant gentleman.
Siempre viste elegantemente.	He always dresses elegantly.

36.2 Common adverbs and adverbial phrases

The most common adverbs and adverbial phrases are listed below. Note that there is an overlap of meaning occasionally between adverbs of manner and those of degree.

Manner

así	in this way, thus	**de memoria**	by heart
bien	well	**de repente**	suddenly
de costumbre	usually	**despacio**	slowly
de la misma manera	in the same way	**mal**	badly

Habla bien el inglés, pero lo escribe mal.	She speaks English well, but writes it badly.
¡Hay que aprendérselo de memoria!	You have to learn it by heart!
La puerta se abrió de repente.	The door opened suddenly.
Por favor habla más despacio, que no te entiendo nada.	Please speak more slowly because I can't understand you at all

Time

ahora	now	**luego**	then, later
a menudo	frequently	**mañana**	tomorrow
antes	before	**nunca**	never
a veces	sometimes	**pronto**	soon
ayer	yesterday	**siempre**	always
después	later, afterwards	**tarde**	late
enseguida	immediately	**temprano**	early
entonces	at that time, then	**todavía**	still
hoy	today	**ya**	already, now

A veces nada en el río.	She sometimes swims in the river.
Tráigame una cerveza … ¡Enseguida!	Bring me a beer … Immediately!
Tarde o temprano, da igual.	Early or late, it makes no difference.
Mañana por la mañana sin falta iré a reparar su lavadora.	Tomorrow morning without fail I'll be there to repair your washing machine.
Dice Andrés que pasará luego.	Andrés says he'll call by soon.
Luisa, cada día estás más guapa.	Luisa, you look more beautiful every day.

Place

abajo	down, below	**cerca**	near(by)
adelante	forward(s)	**debajo**	underneath
adentro	inside (with motion)	**delante**	in front
afuera	outside (with motion)	**dentro**	inside
allí	there	**detrás**	behind
a lo lejos/en la lejanía	in the distance	**encima**	above, on top

aquí	here	en todas partes	everywhere
arriba	above	fuera	outside
atrás	back(wards)	lejos	far

¿Vamos afuera a pasear por el parque?	Shall we go out for a walk in the park?
Subieron hasta lo alto de la colina y cuando llegaron allí, miraron atrás y vieron un paisaje precioso en la lejanía.	They walked up to the top of the hill, and when they got there, they looked back and saw a beautiful landscape in the distance.
–¿Puedo pasar?	'Can I come in?'
–Adelante, adelante.	'Come in, come in.'

Degree

bastante	enough	mucho	(very) much
demasiado	too much	muy	very
más	more	(un) poco	(a) little
menos	less	tanto	as much

–¿Hablas portugués?	'Do you speak Portuguese?'
–No mucho; sólo un poco.	'Not much; just a little.'
–Yo lo hablo bastante bien, pero mi socio casi nada.	'I speak fairly well, but my partner hardly speaks a word.'
El vino es mucho más barato en España.	Wine is a lot cheaper in Spain.
Creo que no comen bastante. Están demasiado delgadas.	I don't think they eat enough. They are too thin.

36.3 Adverbial phrases with con or de (una) manera/de (un) modo

In preference to using the adjective with the suffix -**mente** Spanish often uses a prepositional phrase with **con** or **de (una) manera/de (un) modo**:

Carlos vino a nuestra casa con frecuencia en verano.	Carlos frequently came to our house in the summer.
En caso de peligro se debe actuar con calma.	In a dangerous situation you must always act calmly.
Se comportaba de modo muy dramático.	He behaved in a very dramatic way.
Tiene un gran sentido práctico pero también puede actuar de una manera apasionada, aunque raramente lo hace.	She has a great practical sense but she can also act emotionally, although she rarely does so.
Tenemos que terminar el edificio con la mayor rapidez posible.	We have to finish the building as quickly as possible.

Exercises

1 Make adverbs ending in -**mente** from the following adjectives:

a evidente _____

b regular _____

c seco _____

d rico _____

e dulce _____

f difícil   _____

g abierto   _____

h leal   _____

i electrónico   _____

j último   _____

2   Fill the gaps with an appropriate adverb of time from those in the box—sometimes more than one adverb can be used.

> frecuentemente   hoy   después   enseguida   nunca   tarde   ayer a veces   pronto   antes   siempre

a Son muy simpáticos pero _____ están de mal humor.

b Amelia va _____ al gimnasio.

c Trajo la cena _____ .

d _____ me quito el maquillaje _____ de ir a la cama.

e Vuelve _____ que necesito el aceite.

f _____ te vi charlando con Loles.

g José María ha llevado a Rocío a la ópera porque ella no había ido _____ .

h Nos encanta tomar un café _____ de comer.

i El tren de Galicia siempre llega _____ .

j _____ hay un recital de guitarra en el casino.

3   Fill the gaps with adverbs of place from the list given in this chapter. Sometimes more than one adverb can be used:

Example: El gato está _____ _El gato está dentro/fuera/aquí/arriba._

a Ve siempre _____ y no mires _____ .

b Las zapatillas están _____ .

c Me gusta la casa porque se ve el mar _____ .

d Poneos un poco más _____ para que os saque una foto.

e Sube _____ , Toni. Alejandro está escuchando música en su habitación.

f ¡Ven _____ , Leal!

g En Benidorm había turistas _____ .

h Deja el periódico _____ .

i El Sr y la Sra Gorostiza han venido a pasar las vacaciones _____ .

37
Prepositions

What are prepositions?

Prepositions are words used to link a noun, noun phrase or pronoun with the rest of the sentence. In the sentence 'We went with Kevin', the preposition 'with' provides the link between the verb 'went' and the noun 'Kevin'. We could change the preposition to 'without' and the meaning would change: 'We went *without* Kevin'. Substitute other prepositions and the meaning changes again: 'We went *after* Kevin', 'We went *before* Kevin', etc.

Key ideas

In Spanish prepositions function in a similar way to English. The following aspects should be noted:

- When a verb follows a preposition, it must be in the *infinitive* and *not* the gerund form (the *-ing* form in English; see Part I, 34.2):

Después de **llegar** a Lima, buscaron un hotel.	After *arriving* in Lima, they looked for a hotel.
Llegaron sin **conocer** a nadie.	They arrived without *knowing* anyone.
Tras **saltar** la valla descubrieron un magnífico campo de naranjos.	After *jumping* over the fence they discovered a splendid orange grove.

- The prepositions **a** and **de** combine with the masculine singular definite article to form **al** and **del** (see Part I, 2.1):

La catedral está cerca **del** río. (**de** + **el**)	The cathedral is near the river.
Sin querer he molestado **al** profesor. (**a** + **el**)	I've annoyed the teacher unintentionally.

- the preposition **con** combines with **mí, ti** and **sí** to make **conmigo, contigo** and **consigo** (see Part I, 7.4.3):

¿Por qué no vienes **conmigo** al concierto?	Why don't you come with me to the concert?
Bueno, la verdad es que **contigo** no lo paso muy bien.	Well, the fact is that I don't enjoy myself very much when I'm with you.

- Some verbs are always followed by prepositions (see Part II, 32.5). Some of the verbs change their meaning according to the preposition which follows:

acabar con	to end with
acabar de	to have just
dar a	to give on to
dar con	to bump into, to discover
empezar a	to begin to
empezar por	to begin by

Después de este examen he acabado con las matemáticas.	After this exam I've finished with maths.
Acaban de descubrir en Holanda una nueva medicina contra el cáncer.	In Holland they have just discovered a new drug to fight cancer.
El balcón daba a la playa.	The balcony looked on to the beach.
Di con Pedro en el Rastro y tomamos una copa.	I ran into Pedro in the Rastro and we had a drink.
No pases, que han empezado a lavar el suelo.	Don't go in, they've begun to clean the floor.
Empecemos por analizar los resultados de la encuesta.	Let's begin by analysing the results of the survey.

37.1 Single-word prepositions

The single-word prepositions are as follows:

a	to, at	**hacia**	towards
ante	before	**hasta**	until, as far as
bajo	under, beneath	**mediante**	by means of
con	with	**para**	for
contra	against	**por**	by, through, for
de	of, from	**según**	according to
desde	since, from	**sin**	without
durante	during, for	**sobre**	on, about, concerning
en	in, at	**tras**	behind, after
entre	between, among		

37.2 Compound prepositions

Spanish prepositions often consist of two or more words, the last of which is **de** or, less frequently, **a**. The most common of these prepositions are:

Prepositional phrases with de

a diferencia de	unlike	**delante de**	in front of
a pesar de	despite	**dentro de**	within
a raíz de	as a result of	**después de**	after
a través de	across	**detrás de**	behind
acerca de	about	**encima de**	on top of, over
además de	as well as	**enfrente de**	opposite
al final de	at the end of	**en lugar de**	instead of
al lado de	next to	**en medio de**	in the middle of
a lo largo de	along	**en vez de**	instead of
alrededor de	around	**fuera de**	outside
antes de	before	**lejos de**	far from

| cerca de | near | más allá de | beyond |
| debajo de | under, beneath | por medio de | by means of |

Prepositional phrases with a

con relación a	in relation to	en torno a	around
con respecto a	with reference to	frente a	opposite, faced with
debido a	owing to	gracias a	thanks to
en cuanto a	concerning	junto a	next to

37.3 Uses of specific prepositions

Personal a

The direct object of the verb is preceded by the preposition **a** in the following circumstances:

a When the direct object is an actual person:

Vi **a** María ayer.	I saw Maria yesterday.
¿Conoce usted **al** director?	Do you know the manager?
Estoy esperando a Elena.	I am waiting for Elena.

Note: the direct object does not become an indirect object when this occurs.

Personal **a** is less likely to be used if the direct object has less 'individuality':

Buscamos camareros.	We are looking for waiters.
Quiero alguien que pueda ayudarme.	I want someone to help me.
Un ascensor que puede llevar 11 personas.	A lift which takes 11 people.

b When referring affectionately to an animal:

| Tengo que sacar al perro. | I have to walk the dog. |
| Lo siento, no puedo ir porque no tengo con quien dejar al gato. | I'm sorry, I can't go because I haven't got anyone to leave the cat with. |

c When referring to a noun which indicates a group of people, large or small:

| Voy a ver a la pandilla esta noche. | I'm going to see the gang tonight. |

Other uses of a

1 **A** is used to introduce the indirect object:

¡Dale el libro a tu hermano enseguida!	Give the book to your brother at once!
A mí no me gusta viajar en avión.	I don't like flying.
Pregúntale a Adela lo que quiere.	Ask Adela what she wants.

2 **A** expresses motion towards, normally translated by 'to':

Vamos a la playa a tomar el sol.	We're going to the beach to sunbathe.
Viajamos a Venezuela cada verano.	We travel to Venezuela every summer.
Van de compras al mercado.	They are going to market to shop.
Salimos a la terraza a tomar el aire fresco.	We went on to the balcony to get some fresh air.
¡Corre a la tienda que van a cerrar!	Run to the shop before it closes!

3 Translating English 'at'

'At' indicating location is usually translated by **en** in Spanish:

| Están esperando en la estación. | They are waiting at the station. |
| En este momento mis hermanos están en casa. | My brothers are at home at the moment. |

Note however, that in order to express time and rate, **a** is used for 'at' and 'per':

a *Time*

a las dos y media	at half-past two
a(l) mediodía	at midday
a los diecisiete años	at seventeen years of age

b *Rate*

El tren viajó a 300 kilómetros por hora.	The train travelled at 300 km an hour.
El alquiler son 600 euros al mes	The rent is 600 euros per month.
Los tomates se venden a tres euros el kilo.	Tomatoes are selling at three euros a kilo.
¿Cuántos mensajes mandas al día?	How many messages do you send per day?

(4) Verb constructions with **a: empezar a** (to begin to), **ayudar a** (to help); see Part II, 32.5.

(5) Expressions with **a:**

a caballo	on horseback	**a mi juicio**	in my opinion
a ciegas	blindly	**a oscuras**	in the dark
a fines de	at the end of	**a pie**	on foot
a lo lejos	in the distance	**a principios de**	at the beginning of
al fin y al cabo	after all	**al día siguiente**	on the next day
a mediados de	in the middle of	**volver a casa**	to return home

Ante, antes de and antes que

Ante means 'before', 'in the presence of', 'faced with' (e.g. a problem). It is often interchangeable with **delante de.**

(1) **Ante**

El muchacho apareció ante el director de la escuela.	The boy appeared before the head teacher.
Ante esta dificultad, ¿qué podemos hacer?	Faced with this difficulty, what can we do?
Ante todo no te pierdas.	Above all, don't get lost.

(2) **Antes de**

Antes de, which means before *in time*, must not be confused with **ante**:

Puso música antes de arrancar.	She put on some music before starting the car.
Voy a cerrar la puerta con llave	I am going to lock the door
antes de irme a la cama.	before I go to bed.

(3) **Antes que**

Antes que is normally used with the names of people or personal pronouns when a following verb is understood:

Mónica llegó antes que Paco y decidió	Monica arrived before Paco (arrived) and
comprar las entradas	decided to buy the tickets.

Bajo and debajo de

Of the two words for 'under' and 'beneath', **debajo de** and **bajo, debajo de** is used more literally. **Bajo** is more figurative and is used in set phrases:

El perro estaba escondido debajo de la mesa.	The dog was hiding under the table.
Las joyas están bajo llave.	The jewels are under lock and key.
Bajo cero.	Below zero.
Bajo los Reyes Católicos.	Under the Catholic Monarchs.

Con

Con means 'with':

Habla español con acento inglés.	She speaks Spanish with an English accent.
Siempre me he llevado fatal con mis padres.	I have always got on badly with my parents.
Las paredes estaban decoradas con fotos toreros.	The walls were decorated with photos of de bullfighters.

Contra and en contra de

1 **Contra** means 'against' in both a literal and a figurative sense:

No tengo nada contra él.   I have nothing against him.
No pongas las sillas contra la pared.   Don't place the chairs against the wall.

2 **En contra de,** for views and feelings:

Mucha gente está en contra   Many people are against the
de la despenalización de la droga.   legalisation of drugs.

De

De is the equivalent of the English 'of', indicating possession. Additionally, **de** has a wide variety of possible translations, including 'from' and 'by'.

1 **Possession**

De is normally used for **possession**, replacing the English apostrophe 's'. **De** indicates a relationship between two nouns. This relationship is sometimes expressed in English by a compound noun:

el hijo de mi amiga	my friend's son
el palacio del Rey	the King's palace
una barra de pan	a loaf of bread
un diccionario de uso del español actual	a dictionary of current Spanish usage
un hombre de 88 años	an 88-year-old man
el camino de Santiago	the road to Santiago
un hotel de la Habana	a hotel in Havana
un libro de cocina	a cookery book
un hombre de negocios	a businessman

2 **Origin**

De is also used when saying:

a Where someone/something comes from:

Hemos recibido una postal de Marisa.	We have received a postcard from Marisa.
Es de una familia monoparental.	She's from a one-parent family.
Soy de Alicante.	I'm from Alicante (i.e. it is my native town).
Vengo de Alicante.	I've come from Alicante (i.e. 'just arrived from').
Don Quijote de la Mancha.	Don Quixote of La Mancha.

b What things are made of:

una puerta de madera	a wooden door
dos tigres de bronce	two bronze tigers
una camisa de hilo	a linen shirt
un edificio de ladrillo	a brick building

3 **De** = 'about'

Estaban hablando del tiempo.	They were speaking about the weather.
No saben nada de eso.	They know nothing about that.
–¿De qué se trata?	What's it about?
–Se trata del origen del hombre.	It's about the origin of mankind.

4 **De** in comparisons. For the use of **más de** and **menos de** see Part II, 5.1.

5 **Dates**

Note the use of **de** in writing dates:

21 de enero de 2013   21 January 2013

6 With time expressions followed by parts of the day (**mañana, tarde**, etc.) **de** translates 'in':

a las cinco de la tarde	At five o'clock in the afternoon
la una y cuarto de la madrugada	1.15 a.m.

7 Expressions with **de:**

de buena/mala gana	willingly/unwillingly	**de repente**	suddenly
de día	by day	**de todas formas**	in any case
de golpe	suddenly	**de una vez**	all at once
de nada	don't mention it	**de un trago**	in one gulp
de noche	by night	**de vacaciones**	on holiday
de nuevo	again	**de vez en cuando**	from time to time
de paso	in passing		

Delante de

Delante de means 'in front of', 'before':

Todo pasó delante de mis ojos.	Everything happened before my eyes.

Dentro (de)

Dentro de has two meanings: 'inside' a space, physically, and 'within' a time limit:

1 *Inside*

Vamos dentro que va a llover.	Let's go inside because it looks like rain.

2 *Within*

Dentro de unos días salimos para Bilbao.	We will leave for Bilbao in a few days.

Desde

Desde means 'from' and 'since'. There is some overlap with **de**, but **desde** tends to be used to insist on the starting point or origin in time or space.

1 *From*

Han venido desde Buenos Aires solo para verte.	They've come from Buenos Aires only to see you.
Desde mi ventana veo los árboles del parque.	I can see the trees in the park from my window.
Aprendí desde edad muy temprana a cantar y a bailar bien.	I learned to sing and dance well from a very early age.

2 *Since*

Me rompí la pierna el año pasado y desde entonces ando cojeando.	I broke my leg last year and since then I've walked with a limp.
Vivía en Zaragoza desde el 2001.	He had lived in Zaragoza since 2001.
Desde que tuve un accidente en la piscina no hay quien me meta en el agua.	Since my accident in the swimming pool no one can persuade me to go in the water.

Note that in the first and second examples above there is a change of tense in the translation. In the first example the Spanish present tense becomes the English perfect tense; in the second example the Spanish imperfect tense becomes the English pluperfect tense.

Detrás de

Detrás de means 'behind' and 'after':

El niño se escondió detrás de la silla.	The child hid behind the chair.
Detrás del primer plato viene el postre.	After the first course comes the dessert.

Durante

Durante, meaning 'during', 'for', refers to the period of time for which an action went on.

① *During*

Durante el siglo diecinueve España perdió todas sus colonias.

During the nineteenth century Spain lost all her colonies.

② *For*

Estuve en Colombia durante tres años.
Estuvo buscándolo en la red durante mucho tiempo.

I was in Colombia for three years.
He was looking for it on the web for a long time.

En

① **en = sobre, encima de,** meaning 'on'

Ponlo en el suelo.
Puedes comprar los billetes en Internet.
En la acera de enfrente

Put it on the floor.
You can buy your tickets on the Internet.
On the opposite pavement

② **En** for location, literally and figuratively, meaning 'in' and 'at':

Estamos en el museo Picasso.
En este colegio un 25 por ciento de estudiantes son internos.
Déjame en paz.
En el Parlamento Europeo …
Después del accidente se quedaron en el hospital unos días.
Por la noche se puede viajar en coche cama.
Terminó su carrera en la Universidad de Salamanca.
En la cumbre de la montaña …

We are in the Picasso Museum.
In this school at least 25 per cent of the students are boarders.
Leave me alone/in peace.
In the European Parliament …
After the accident they stayed in hospital for a few days.
During the night it is possible to travel in a sleeping car.
He finished his degree at the University of Salamanca.
On the mountain top …

③ **Entrar en**

The verb **entrar** (to enter/go into) is followed by **en:**

Según la policía los ladrones entraron en la casa por la ventana.

According to the police the robbers got into the house through the window.

Note: in Latin-American Spanish, **entrar a** is used.

④ Expressions with **en:**

en absoluto	not at all	**en mi opinión**	in my opinion
en aquel momento	at that moment	**en ninguna parte**	nowhere
en avión	by air/aeroplane	**en resumen**	in short
en bicicleta	by bicycle	**en seguida/enseguida**	at once
en broma	jokingly	**en todo caso**	in any case
en cambio	on the other hand	**en tren**	by train
en casa	at home	**en voz alta/baja**	in a loud/low voice
en cierto modo	in a way	**estar en huelga**	to be on strike
en coche	by car	**tomar en serio**	to take seriously
en la actualidad	at the present time		

Encima de

Encima de means 'on top of', 'above', ' on'. There is some overlap between **encima de, sobre** and **en:**

Encima del edificio había dos grúas enormes.

There were two enormous cranes above the building.

Puse el libro en la mesa, encima de otro.

I put the book on the table, on top of another one.

Encima is also used figuratively:

Encima de ser millonaria,
es simpatiquísima.

As well as being a millionairess,
she is really nice.

Enfrente de and frente a

1 *Opposite*

both prepositions mean 'opposite'

Volvió a sentarse en frente de mí.
Vivimos frente a Correos.

He sat down again opposite me.
We live opposite the Post Office.

2 *In opposition to, facing*

Frente a is also used more figuratively, in the sense of 'in opposition to', 'facing':

Frente a la opinión pública, estoy de acuerdo con
la legalización del cannabis.
Frente al peligro hay que lanzarse a la acción.

Contrary to public opinion, I agree with the
legalising of cannabis.
In the face of danger we must throw
ourselves into action.

Entre

Entre means 'between' and 'among(st)'

1 *Between*

Estaba dudando entre llamar por teléfono o
presentarme sin más.
Entre tú y yo siempre habrá una buena amistad.

I was hesitating between telephoning or just
turning up.
You and I will always be friends (lit.
Between you and me there will always be a
good friendship).

2 *Among(st)*

El español se cuenta entre las lenguas mundiales
más importantes.
Me encanta pasear entre los árboles.

Spanish is among the most important world
languages.
I love walking amongst the trees.

3 *An expression*

entre semana

on weekdays

Hacia

Hacia means 'towards' and 'around'.

1 *Towards*

Hacia el año 2010.
Miró hacia arriba.
Andrés tiene una actitud muy rara hacia
los extranjeros.

Towards the year 2010.
She looked upwards.
Andrés has a very strange attitude to
foreigners.

2 *Around* in time expressions:

Van a llegar hacia las siete de la tarde.

They will arrive around 7 p.m.

Hasta

Hasta means 'until', 'as far as', 'up to':

La calle se extendía hasta el río.
Podéis jugar fuera hasta las siete.

The street stretched as far as the river.
You can play outside until seven.

Note: **hasta**, as an *adverb*, means 'even', and should not be confused with the prepositional use:

Toda mi familia, hasta el abuelo,
se interesa por la informática.

All my family, even my grandfather, is
interested in IT.

Expressions with **hasta**

hasta luego	see you later	**hasta la vista**	so long
hasta mañana	see you/till tomorrow	**hasta entonces**	until then

37.4 Para

Para, meaning 'for', 'in order to', has an underlying sense of *destination, purpose,* of *movement* towards a goal. It must not be confused with **por**, which can also be mean 'for' in English.

1 'For' of destination, purpose

When followed by an infinitive **para** means '(in order) to', '(so as) to':

Juan compró la bicicleta para dársela a su hijo.	Juan bought the bicycle for his son (i.e. to give it to him)
No sirve para nada.	It is not useful for anything.
Quiero saber para quién es este jersey.	I want to know who(m) this sweater is for.
El regalo es para darte las gracias.	The present is to say thank you.
Estudiamos la grámatica para entender la estructura de la lengua.	We study grammar in order to understand the structure of the language.
Emigró a Francia para huir de la dictadura.	He emigrated to France to get away from the dictatorship.
Vengo para preguntar la hora del concierto.	I've come to ask the time of the concert.

2 Destination in the sense of 'in the direction of a specific place':

Vamos enseguida para casa.	Let's go home at once.
Mañana salimos para Córdoba, en el tren de alta velocidad.	Tomorrow we are going to Cordoba, on the high-speed train.

3 'By' or 'for' in time expressions

a **Para** meaning 'by' in the sense of 'in time for':

Termino el trabajo para las siete.	I'll finish the work by 7 o'clock.
¿Puedes devolverme el DVD para cuando llegue mi hermana?	Can you give me back the DVD by the time my sister arrives?

b 'For' in relation to time:

Déjalo para mañana.	Leave it for tomorrow.
Queremos una habitación doble para una noche.	We want a double room for one night.

37.5 Por

Por is used when the *cause* of something is to be communicated or to show its origin in time or space. **Por** can be translated by a variety of words and expressions such as 'by', 'through', 'by means of', 'on behalf of', 'because of'.

Por must not be confused with **para**, which also means 'for' in English. The following newspaper headline illustrates the basic meanings of these two prepositions:

CUATRO AÑOS DE CÁRCEL PARA UN MÉDICO POR LA MUERTE DE UN PACIENTE

Four years' imprisonment for a doctor on account of the death of a patient

The prison sentence was for (**para**) the doctor (the recipient), because of (**por**) the death of a patient he was responsible for.

1 *Because of:*

Lo hizo por orgullo.	He did it out of pride.
Me gustas por simpático no por guapo.	I like you because you are nice, not because you are good-looking.

Me enfadé por algo que dijo ayer.	She annoyed me on account of something she said yesterday.
Se disculpó por no tener bebida en casa.	She apologised for not having any drink in the house.
Le estaban sacando fotos por haber ganado en Wimbledon.	They were taking his picture because he won at Wimbledon.
Hacía esfuerzos por hablar normalmente.	I made an effort to speak normally.
Por amor a los animales es vegetariana.	She's a vegetarian because she loves animals.
Te felicito por la promoción.	I congratulate you on your promotion.

2 'On behalf of', 'in favour of':

Estoy por la despenalización de la droga.	I am in favour of the legalisation of drugs.
Espero una llamada importante y tú no puedes contestarla por mí.	I am waiting for an important call and you can't answer on my behalf.
¡Vota por los Verdes!	Vote for the Greens!
Réquiem por un campesino español	*Requiem for a Spanish Peasant* (title of a novel)

3 'By (means of)':

Mandamos el documento por correo electrónico.	We sent the document by electronic mail.
Prefiero ponerme en contacto con mis colegas por fax que llamarles por teléfono.	I prefer to get in touch with my colleagues by fax than by phone.
Estamos muy lejos pero nos mantenemos en contacto por Skype.	We are a long way apart but we keep in touch by Skype.

4 'Via':

Salimos por la puerta principal.	We went out via/by the main door.
Fueron a Sevilla por Córdoba.	They went to Sevilla via Cordoba.
Gesticulaba por la ventanilla del coche.	He gesticulated through the car window.
Tuvieron que meter el piano por la cocina.	They had to bring the piano in via the kitchen.

5 'Times':

| dos por tres son seis | two times three equals six |

6 Time phrases:

En el sur hace muchísimo calor por la tarde, pero por la noche hace más fresco.	In the south it is very hot in the afternoon but at night it is cooler.
Voy a salir por un momento.	I am going out for a moment.
Por ahora ha hecho un tiempo estupendo.	Up to now the weather has been wonderful.

7 **Por** as agent in passive sentences:

Por is the usual equivalent of 'by' in passive sentences (see account of the passive, Part I, 30).

| Los informes fueron escritos por un catedrático de Economía. | The reports were written by a professor of economics |
| Aquella novela fue escrita por Juan Marsé. | That novel was written by Juan Marsé. |

8 Expressions with **por**:

por aquí	this way	**por (lo) tanto**	therefore
por casualidad	by chance	**por lo visto**	apparently
por ciento	per cent	**por (or para) siempre**	for ever
por eso	therefore	**por supuesto**	of course
por fin	at last	**por todas partes**	everywhere
por lo general	in general		

37.6 Según

Según means 'according to', 'depending on':

Según mi tío, no se puede comprar entradas para el partido.	According to my uncle, you can't buy tickets for the match.
Iremos a la playa, según el tiempo.	We'll go to the beach, depending on the weather.

37.7 Sin

Sin means 'without':

Sin mis gafas no veo nada.	Without my glasses I can't see a thing.
A menudo cambiaba de punto de vista sin explicar por qué.	He often changed his mind without explaining why.

37.8 Sobre

Sobre has a number of meanings. In the sense of 'on (top of)', 'over', 'above', there is overlap with **en** and **encima de**:

1 *Over*

Los aviones volaban sobre su casa.	Aeroplanes used to fly over his house.

2 *On*

¡Ponlo sobre la mesa!	Put it on the table!

3 *Around,* with time and numbers:

sobre las ocho	around 8 o'clock
El informe contenía sobre 200 páginas.	The report contained about 200 pages.

4 *About, on*

Se ha escrito mucho sobre el tema de la Unión Europea.	A lot has been written on the subject of the European Union.

5 Expressions with **sobre**

sobremanera	exceedingly	**sobresaliente**	outstanding
sobremesa	after-lunch	**sobre todo**	especially

37.9 Tras

Tras, 'behind', 'after' is the literary equivalent of **detrás de** or **después de**:

Tras una breve pausa, el Rey pronunció su discurso.	After a brief pause, the King gave his speech.

1 Expressions with **tras**

día tras día	day after day	**uno tras otro**	one after another

Exercises

1 Fill the gaps with a suitable preposition:

a Voy _____ hospital _____ ver a mi abuela.

b Los poemas _____ Lorca me fascinan.

c Le han reñido _____ no hacer los deberes.

d Celia está _____ el cine _____ los amigos.

e Vivimos en Málaga _____ hace tres años.

f No cojas esa bici que es _____ mi hermano.

g Creo que esta noche voy _____ ver la televisión.

h He sacado todos estos libros _____ la biblioteca.

i _____ la mañana estoy lleno de energía pero _____ la noche estoy muy cansado.

j Tenemos que comprar un regalo _____ Dani porque hoy es su cumpleaños.

k Este fin de semana podríamos ir _____ acampada.

l Siéntate _____ Tono y Eladio.

m ¡Estoy _____ las narices _____ que seas tan desordenada!

n Creo que va _____ haber tormenta.

o Me encontré _____ Carmela _____ casualidad.

p Los servicios están _____ el pasillo, _____ la derecha.

2 Do the crossword, putting in the correct prepositions:

Horizontales

1 Le vi correr _____ el mercado.

2 Hoy vamos _____ comer tortilla.

3 Salen juntos _____ el verano pasado.

5 Traigo una carta _____ el juez.

8 El mejor ron lo hacen _____ Cuba.

Verticales

1 Vende el mejor café _____ Colombia.

2 _____ ahora no hay noticias de la expedición a la Antártida.

3 Es un ángel, nos estuvo esperando _____ la medianoche.

5 Se pone nerviosa cuando está _____ la policía.

6 Prefiere el agua _____ gas.

Answer in Key to Exercises, p. 361.

38 Conjunctions

What are conjunctions?

Conjunctions are words which link words, phrases and clauses. 'And', 'but' and 'because' are typical conjunctions.

Conjunctions have an important role in communicating meaning. To link two sentences, e.g. 'She shouted' and 'Nobody was listening', we use a conjunction. By turning the two sentences into one, we can express an additional (and perhaps more interesting) meaning concerning the relationship between these two events. If, for example, we use the conjunction 'but', the single linked sentence is: 'She shouted **but** nobody was listening'. The meaning will change again if we use 'because': 'She shouted **because** nobody was listening'.

el perro y el gato

Cansada porque no ha dormido

Un genio aunque no lo parezca

Música mientras trabaja

hijo e hija

Key ideas

Spanish conjunctions work in a similar way to English ones. There are two types of conjunctions:

- **co-ordinating conjunctions,** such as **y** (and) and **pero** (but), so called because they make a simple link between two words or sentences of equal weight.

el perro y el gato	the dog and the cat
bonito pero caro	pretty but expensive
Ni carne ni pescado	Neither meat nor fish

- **subordinating conjunctions**, which introduce a clause that is dependent on a main clause, such as **porque** (because), **aunque (**although) and **cuando** (when):

Le dije que viniera aunque fuera tarde.	I told him to come even if was late.
No hablaba mucho porque prefería escuchar.	She didn't speak much because she preferred to listen.

38.1 Co-ordinating conjunctions

The co-ordinating conjunctions are:

ni	neither, nor
o (u)	or
pero	but
sino	but
y (e)	and

Ni

1 When **ni** follows the verb, a negative word, such as **no** or **nunca**, must precede the verb:

No sé de dónde es ni adónde va. I don't know where she's from nor where she's going.

2 Ni ... ni means 'neither ... nor':

Ni él ni yo tenemos casa propia. Neither he nor I have our own house.
No como ni carne ni pescado. I eat neither meat nor fish.v

O

1 **O** means 'or':

Va a Bilbao el viernes o el sábado. She's going to Bilbao on Friday or Saturday.

2 **O** changes to **u** before a following **o** or **ho**:

siete u ocho six or seven
restaurantes u hoteles restaurants or hotels

3 Note that when **o** is between two numbers it normally carries an accent in order to distinguish it from the number 0:

Le quedan solo 3 ó 4 entradas. He has only 3 or 4 tickets left.

4 **O** ... **o** means 'either ... or':

¡O se va él o me marcho yo! Either he goes or I do!
Podemos o ir a la playa o descansar en casa. We can either go to the beach or rest at home.

Pero and sino

 There are two words for 'but' in Spanish: **pero** and **sino**. The use of these two words frequently gives rise to confusion.

- **Pero** is used to restrict the meaning of the word or phrase which comes before it, but not to exclude or contradict it. **Pero** may be preceded by a positive or a negative statement.

  El dice que es amigo tuyo pero no lo creo. He says he's a friend of yours, but I don't believe it.
  Laura no ha llegado aún, pero no tardará mucho. Laura not hasn't arrived yet but she won't be long.
  No sabe qué hacer, pero su tutor le ayudará a decidir. He doesn't know what to do, but his tutor will help him to decide.

- **Sino** is normally used when the two words or statements that are linked by 'but' are mutually exclusive. **Sino** is preceded by a verb in the negative:

  No fue él quien compuso la página sino ella. It was not him who wrote the page but her.
  Su casa no era pequeña y fea sino grande y hermosa. His house was not small and ugly but big and beautiful.

Y

Y changes to **e** before **i** and **hi**:

Es joven e inteligente.	She's young and intelligent.
verano e invierno	summer and winter
padres e hijos	parents and children

38.2 Subordinating conjunctions

Subordinating conjunctions (i.e. conjunctions that introduce subordinate clauses) which are usually followed by the subjunctive are discussed elsewhere (Part I, 22.3). The most common conjunctions are:

así que	and so	**mientras**	while
aunque	although	**porque**	because
como	since, as	**pues**	because, since, for
conque	so	**puesto que**	since
cuando	when	**que**	that, than, because
de modo/manera que	so	**si**	if
entonces	and so, then	**ya que**	since
luego	and so		

Como

Como meaning 'since', 'as' appears at the beginning of a sentence or clause:

Como quieres aprender español, te voy a mandar a un curso de verano en España.	Since you want to learn Spanish I'm going to send you on a summer course in Spain.
Conduce como un loco.	He drives like a madman.

Note: **como** is *not* used in a temporal sense like the French *comme* (*Comme il est entré ...*, As he entered ...). 'As' in this sense is conveyed in Spanish by **cuando, mientras** or **al** with the infinitive (see Part I, 32.1.3).

Conque

Conque is the equivalent of English 'so', 'as so long as':

No hace falta que sepas de informática, conque sepas usar el teclado basta.

You don't need to know about IT; so long as you know how to use the keyboard it's enough.

Cuando *and* mientras

Cuando and **mientras** are 'time' conjunctions:

Estábamos hablando en la cocina cuando oímos sonar mi móvil.	We were talking in the kitchen when we heard my mobile ring.
Haz tus deberes mientras preparo la comida.	Do your homework while I get the meal ready.

Porque

Porque is a causal conjunction:

Hoy no hay periódicos porque es Navidad.	There are no papers today because it's Christmas.

Note: porque is one word whereas **¿por qué?** meaning 'why?' is composed of two words:

–¿Por qué vas por esta calle?	'Why are you going down this street?'
–Porque se llega antes.	'Because it's quicker.'

Pues

Pues can mean 'for', 'since' or 'because'. More frequently, however, it begins a response, meaning 'well (then)' or 'so'. **Pues** often fills a pause while the speaker hesitates and thinks of an answer:

Pues parece que se está recuperando muy bien. So it looks as if he's recovering well.

Pues … no recuerdo su nombre. Well … I don't remember his name.
–Tú, ¿qué haces aquí? 'What are you doing here?'
–Pues, ya ves, esperándote. 'As you can see, waiting for you.'

Que

1   **Que**, meaning 'that' or 'than' (in comparatives), is one of the most common conjunctions in Spanish:

Dicen que el pueblo vasco es muy antiguo. They say that the Basque people is an ancient one.
Cuando se empieza a aprender una lengua, When one starts to learn a language,
entender es más fácil que hablar. understanding is easier than speaking.

2   **Que** can also mean 'because':

Hoy no salimos, que nieva. We shan't go out today, because it's snowing.

Si

For a full account of the use of **si**, see Part I, 24 and Part II, 24.

Exercises

1   Fill the gaps with one of the following conjunctions: **y, e, o** or **u**:

a No sabíamos qué hacer: si alquilar un local _____ organizar la fiesta en casa.

b Cuando se vieron, Nadal _____ Federer se dieron la mano efusivamente.

c El menú del día incluye pan _____ vino de la casa.

d ¿Qué prefieres, helado _____ horchata?

e Veremos la película hoy _____ mañana.

f Es una anciana seria _____ respetuosa.

g _____ vienes _____ me voy sola.

h _____ entonces nos contaron la historia los dos, padre _____ hijo.

i El técnico llegó _____ instaló el ordenador en un momento.

j ¿Prefieres las rosas _____ los claveles?

k Había siete _____ ocho personas esperando.

l Mariana, ese vestido es cursi _____ infantil.

m Se pelean como el perro _____ el gato.

n Me da igual una cosa _____ otra.

2   Fill the gaps in the following sentences with **cuando, cuándo** or **mientras**. In some cases more than one conjunction can be used:

a Siempre canta _____ se ducha.

b Estaba limpiando la cocina _____ lo oí por la radio.

c Dime _____ vas a llegar para tenerlo todo listo.

d ¿Se puede saber _____ terminarás de hacer ruido?

e No hay que molestarle _____ está en el laboratorio.

f Estaba pensando en otra cosa _____ le escuchaba.

g _____ esté contento, no me preocupo.

h _____ tanto estoy entretenida pintando la casa.

i Dime, ¿_____ terminaste la carrera?

j Aprenderé a conducir _____ tenga 18 años.

k Podemos jugar una partida de ajedrez _____ acaban la comida.

l _____ sea mayor seré catedrática.

m Queremos que lo pase bien _____ sea joven.

3 Complete the sentences using either **por qué** or **porque**:

a Ignacio me irrita _____ siempre llega tarde.

b No entiendo _____ se comporta así.

c ¿_____ no vienes en tren?

d Es difícil explicar _____ pasan las cosas.

e Las tiendas están cerradas _____ hoy es domingo.

f Rafa, ¿_____ no has venido con nosotros?

g ¿_____ no se habrá sentado conmigo hoy?

h La clase se ha suspendido _____ el profesor está enfermo.

i El pescado es caro _____ cada día hay menos en el mar.

j Nos gustaría saber _____ han cambiado los horarios.

k Tengo que hablar con Vd. _____ hay un error en el informe.

l ¿_____ serán tan malos los programas de televisión?

m Nos hemos comprado un ordenador nuevo _____ queremos tener correo electrónico en casa.

39
Diminutives and augmentatives

What are diminutives and augmentatives?

In English, when we want to insist on the smallness or largeness of a person, thing or idea, we usually qualify it by using an adjective: *small, tiny, little, great, large* or *big*. We say 'a small boy', 'a little old lady', 'a great big man', 'a large overdraft', 'my big brother'. Only very occasionally in English do we point out the smallness of something by adding a suffix to the noun, as in *duck > duckling, drop >droplet, hill > hillock, brick > briquette*. When talking to small children we use diminutives like 'birdie' or 'doggie'.

Key ideas

- In Spanish the usual way of pointing out the size of something, whether small or large, is by adding a suffix to the noun. The idea of smaller or greater size is conveyed neatly and appropriately, without the need for a qualifying adjective. **Pequeño** and **grande** may also be used for this purpose:

chico > chiquito	boy > small boy	oferta > ofertón	offer > big offer
vieja > viejecita	old lady > little old lady	hombre > hombrón/hombretón	man > great big man

- Spanish speakers of all ages use diminutives and augmentatives profusely, especially in popular speech, when talking to young and old alike
- Diminutives and augmentatives can show emotion or express a special quality in a person or object, as well as being used to convey the idea of size

39.1 Formation of diminutives and augmentatives

The most common diminutive suffixes

They are:

-ito/a	chica > chiquita	girl > little girl
-illo/a	árbol > arbolillo	tree > small tree
-uelo/a	calle > callejuela	street > alleyway

1 The diminutive suffix is usually preceded by **-c** when added to words of more than one syllable ending in **-n, -r** or **-é**:

montón	pile	**montoncito**	little pile
mujer	woman	**mujercita**	little woman
café	coffee	**cafecito**	small coffee

2 The diminutive suffix is usually preceded by **-ec** when added to words of a single syllable:

flor	flower	**florecita**	little flower
pan	bread	**panecillo**	bread roll
pez	fish	**pececito**	little fish
sol	sun	**solecito**	a little sunshine

3 A change of spelling is sometimes necessary when the suffix is added, to retain the correct sound:

un poco	a little	**un poquito**	a tiny bit
una voz	a voice	**una vocecita**	a little (i.e. quiet) voice

4 Proper names usually have diminutive forms. Spaniards often add a further diminutive to express closeness and affection:

Francisco > Paco > Paquito
Dolores > Lola > Lolita/Lolín
José > Pepe > Pepito/Pepín

Rosario > Charo > Charito
Carmen > Carmiña/Carmencita

The most common augmentatives

They are:

-on/ona	mujer > mujerona	woman > big woman
-azo/a	coche > cochazo	car > big car
-ote/a	muchacho > muchachote	boy > big boy

Exercises

1 Make diminutives of the following:

a	niña	f	luz	k	descanso
b	paloma	g	pie	l	tren
c	perra	h	cordón	m	bombón
d	copa	i	falda	n	canción
e	pájaro	j	poema	o	piscina

2 Give the nouns or adjectives from which the following augmentatives are derived:

a	cobardón	f	bromazo	k	vinazo
b	pobretón	g	guapetón	l	barcaza
c	señorón	h	azulona	m	avionazo
d	solterona	i	pesadote	n	fortunón
e	abejón	j	paellón	o	mujerona

40
Word order

Sentences consist of several parts, each one with a particular function. For example, the sentence 'My teacher explains the subjunctive very well' breaks down into the following parts:

subject	*verb*	*object*	*adverbial phrase*
My teacher	explains	the subjunctive	very well

In English the order of words in a simple sentence is relatively rigid. It would be impossible to re-order the elements of the above sentence by, for example, placing the verb 'explains' first, or placing the subject 'my teacher' last.

In Spanish much more flexibility in the order of words is possible. When translated into Spanish, the parts of the above sentence will normally have the same order as in English:

Mi profesora explica el subjuntivo muy bien.

In the following sentence the order of the components varies from the English:

La nueva edición de Windows acaba de salir al mercado internacional.

The new Windows' edition has just come on to the international market.

but it can vary even more, without change of meaning, depending on the emphasis the speaker wants to place on different components. For example, the subject can come last:

Acaba de salir al mercado internacional la nueva edición de Windows.

Key ideas

- It is impossible to formulate rules for the placing of words in a sentence in Spanish, but there are clear tendencies.

- The position of the words in a sentence, and their repetition, are closely linked to the meaning to be conveyed. In the following sentences:

  ¡El gordo, me ha tocado el gordo!   I've just won the big prize!
  A mí me da igual. ¿Y a ti?   *'I* don't mind. Do *you?'*

  Key ideas are repeated in order to make the maximum impact. In English meaning tends to be communicated by intonation, as in the second example, where 'I' and 'you' are heavily emphasised by the speaker to show the importance of these two words. In Spanish this emphasis is conveyed by repeating the pronoun and placing it before the verb.

40.1 Guidelines for the order of words

The position of the verb

1 The normal rule is for the verb to go after the subject, as in English. There is, however, a tendency in Spanish to place the verb before the subject in short sentences, especially when the speaker wants to emphasise the subject:

Vienen Tomás y sus amigos.   Thomas and his friends are coming.
Ha llamado tu banco.   Your bank called.
Iba yo paseando tranquilamente…   I was walking along minding my own business…

2 The verb is rarely placed at the end of a clause, unless the clause is very short, or consists of short elements such as pronouns. The verb usually appears as the *first* or *second* element in a sentence:

El año pasado trabajó de voluntario en Perú.   Last year he worked as a volunteer in Peru.

3 In questions:

a Direct questions

In direct questions it is usual to invert the order of the words, putting the verb first:

¿Está llorando el bebé?   Is the baby crying?
¿Han vuelto ya José y Paco de Holanda?   Have José and Paco come back from Holland already?

b Indirect questions

In indirect questions the verb precedes the subject:

No sé qué quiere tu novia.   I don't know what your girlfriend wants.
Me preguntó cuándo aprendí a programar.   He asked me when I learnt programming.

4 Impersonal verbs

In verbs such as **gustar, hacer falta** and **doler** (see Part I, 28.1) the indirect object pronoun is often repeated before the verb:

A mí ya no me duele la cabeza.   My head isn't aching any more.
A los chicos les gustaban las fiestas del pueblo.   The children enjoyed the town's festivities.
Me hace falta un descanso.   I need a break.

5 Relative clauses

In relative clauses the verb in the main clause often precedes the subject, so that the relative pronoun can directly follow the noun it refers to:

Son muchas las posibilidades que tenemos para expansionar el mercado.   We have many possibilities to expand the market.
Estaba muy rica la comida francesa que comimos anoche.   The French food we ate last night was very good.

The position of adjectives

1 While adjectives are usually placed after the noun, speakers frequently put them before the noun, for a variety of subjective reasons. For example, you might choose to say **una triste/alegre historia** (a sad/happy story) rather than **una historia triste/alegre**. When **triste** goes before the noun, you are insisting on your emotional reaction to the story.

2 Some adjectives change their meaning according to their position (see Part II, 4.2).

3 Where more than one adjective qualifies a noun, the one which has the most emphasis is placed last:

la realidad social española   Spanish social reality

4 Numbers

Primero and **último** are placed immediately before the noun when accompanied by a cardinal number:

las dos primeras semanas   the first two weeks
los cien últimos días   the last hundred days

5 Otro

Otro normally goes before **mucho, poco** or a number:

Llegaron otras dos personas.   Two other people arrived.
Te voy a dar otros pocos melocotones.   I'll give you a few more peaches.
Las otras cinco mujeres se sentaron sin decir nada. The other five women
                                            sat down without saying a word.

Otros muchos* países se declararon en contra Many other countries stated that they were
de la guerra.   against the war.

*__otro__ may also be placed after **mucho** in this construction: Muchos otros países ...

The position of prepositions

Prepositions never go at the end of a sentence:

Es la persona de la que hablamos.   He's the person we spoke **of**.
Han cancelado el tren en el que íbamos a viajar. They've cancelled the train we were going to
                                            travel **on**.

Expressions

In certain common adverbial expressions the word order is the opposite of English:

ahora mismo	right now	**todavía no**	not yet
aquí mismo	right here	**ya no**	no longer
aquí dentro	in here		

Exercises

1 Here are the answers to some questions. Try to find out what the questions are. Take care with the word order of the questions.

Example: Clara tiene un pastor alemán. *¿Qué clase de perro tiene Clara?*

a No, no bebe nunca San Miguel.

b Quedamos a las cinco en la estación.

c Sí, la preparé ayer.

d Mire, la parada de taxis está en aquella esquina.

e No, la llamé hace cinco minutos pero estaba comunicando.

f No lo creas, en FNAC los libros son baratos.

g Creo que el DVD saldrá el mes que viene.

h Sí, estaremos encantados.

i Se lo ha comido el gato.

2 Translate the following sentences into English:

a Nunca he oído nada tan tonto.

b Otros veinte invitados inesperados aparecieron como por arte de magia.

c ¿Cuánto has dicho que te costó esta casa?

d Ya te dije que a Consuelo no le gusta salir de noche.

e Aquí hace demasiado calor.

f Sara ha conocido a los amigos de los que me hablaste.

g Mi familia siempre me apoya en mis decisiones.

h ¿Cuándo te veremos de nuevo? ¿Cuándo te volveremos a ver?

i Se compró un par de zapatos nuevos.

Part II

More Advanced Knowledge

1

Pronunciation, accents, spelling and punctuation

(See Part I, page 2)

Articles

2.1 The definite article

Remember:

- In Spanish there are four forms of the definite article: **el/la/los/las**. The definite article agrees with the noun in number and gender.
- **a** or **de** when followed by **el** become a single word: **al/del**.
- The definite article is used with nouns in a general sense and to indicate a unique person or thing.

Form of the definite article

1 **El** used with a feminine noun

The masculine article **el** is always used before *feminine* nouns which begin with stressed **a** or **ha**. The gender of the noun remains feminine:

el aula universitaria	the university class/lecture room
el agua limpia	clean water
el águila	eagle
el hambre	hunger

El agua de Madrid es buena para guisar los garbanzos.	The water in Madrid is good for cooking chickpeas.

Note the feminine definite article is used for the plural: **las aulas**, etc.

2 **A El, de El**

The contracted forms **al** and **del** are not used with proper nouns:

la edición del domingo de El País.	the Sunday edition of *El País*.
Fui a El Escorial a ver el monasterio.	I went to El Escorial to see the monastery.

Uses of the definite article

1 Parts of the body

The articles rather than possessive adjectives are normally used with parts of the body (Part I, 9.1). When a reference is made to parts of the body *in the plural* (legs, hands, lips), the definite article is used:

Tiene las piernas largas y torneadas.	She has long, shapely legs.
Le han operado las orejas porque las tenía como Dumbo.	He's had an operation on his ears because they were sticking out.

and the indefinite article is used for parts of the body *in the singular*:

Se ha roto una pierna.	He's broken his leg.

unless we are referring to one of the two specifically:

¿Te duele mucho la pierna?	Does your leg hurt a lot?

2   Age

The definite article is used to connect a person's age with a specific event:

A los 17 años fui a Madrid para buscar trabajo.   At 17 I went to Madrid to look for work.
Había que hacer el servicio militar **a los 21 años.**   You had to do your military service at 21.

3   Time expressions

a   The definite article is used to express the time:

Son **las** ocho y cuarto.   It's eight fifteen.
Nos veremos a **la** una y media.   We'll meet at half-past one.

b   When the noun **año** is omitted before a year the definite article is used:

Las celebraciones **del** 92   The 1992 celebrations

c   The seasons are normally preceded by the article, except after prepositions:

Aquel año **la** primavera fue muy hermosa.   That year spring was very beautiful.
En invierno no solemos salir al campo.   In winter we don't usually go to the country.

4   **Hay**

The article is not used after **hay** (there is, there are) except in the sense of 'there exist(s)':

Hay gritos en la calle.   People are shouting in the street.
¿Qué tiene Santander para el turista?   What can Santander offer the tourist?
Hay el mar, el pescado y unas playas muy limpias.   There's the sea, the fish and very clean beaches.

5   **El de/la de/los de/las de**

The definite article followed by **de** means 'that/those of' or 'the one(s) from/belonging to'. The article agrees in number and gender with the noun it stands for. Note that **el (de)** *does not bear an accent* when used in this sense, as it is an article and not a pronoun:

Perderemos el tren de las doce, pero   We'll miss the twelve o'clock train,
cogeremos **el** de la una.   but we'll catch the one at one o'clock.
Los problemas de la familia real son menos   The royal family's problems are less
importantes que **los** de la economía.   important than those of the economy.
La hija de Juan trabaja en Telefónica; **la** de   Juan's daughter works for Telefónica; Pedro's is
Pedro está en paro.   out of work (lit. 'the one belonging to Pedro').

6   Colours

The definite article is used with colours, except after prepositions:

El azul es mi color preferido.   Blue is my favourite colour.
La pared estaba pintada de azul.   The wall was painted blue.

7   The infinitive

The infinitive, when it acts as a noun, is frequently preceded by the masculine singular article (see Part I, 32.1):

Nos gusta escuchar el trinar de los pájaros.   We like to hear the birds singing.

8   Proper nouns

The article normally precedes a qualified proper noun:

La vieja María   Old Mary
El sargento García   Sergeant Garcia

2.2   The indefinite article

Remember:

In Spanish there are four forms of the indefinite article: **un/una/unos/unas**. The indefinite article agrees with the noun in number and gender.

Form of the indefinite article

1   **Un** used with a feminine noun

The masculine indefinite article **un,** like the definite article, is always used before *feminine* nouns which begin with stressed **a** or **ha.** The gender of the noun remains feminine:

un área	an area
un hacha afilada	a sharp axe
un hambre	a hunger
–¿Tienes hambre?	'Are you hungry?'
–Sí. Tengo un hambre tremenda.	'Yes, I'm starving.'

Note that the feminine indefinite article is used for the plural: **unas armas** (arms).

Uses of the indefinite article

1   The indefinite article is used when an abstract noun is qualified by an adjective:

En toda la casa se oía una música muy dulce.   In the whole house one could hear sweet music.

2   The indefinite article is normally omitted:

a   After **tener**, **llevar** and **ser**:

No tengo ni idea de donde dejé las llaves.   I've no idea where I left the keys.
Tiene mucho complejo porque lleva gafas.   He's very self-conscious because he wears glasses.
Es estudiante de derecho pero   She's a law student but
los fines de semana es camarera.   at the weekends she's a waitress.

b   After **con** and **sin**:

La miraba con cara de pocos amigos.   He looked at her with an unfriendly face.
No quiere quedarse sin leche.   He doesn't want to be left without any milk.

c   Before **cantidad** and **parte**:

Parte de la ciudad se quedó sin luz.   Part of the town was left without electricity.
Aquel día se perdió cantidad de dinero   That day a great deal of money was lost on the
en la Bolsa.   Stock Exchange.

2.3 The neuter article lo

1   **Lo** is a neuter article which, when followed by an adjective or a past participle (see Part II, 33.5) can act as a noun:

Lo más difícil es mantenerse en calma   The most difficult thing is to keep calm
en los momentos de crisis.   in moments of crisis.

2   **Lo** + adjective + **que** + verb is a special construction which expresses the idea of 'the degree to which' the adjective applies. The adjective must agree with the noun that it describes.

No puedes imaginarte lo sosa que era la película.   You can't imagine how boring the film was.

Exercises

1   Cambia las frases con el artículo indeterminado por otras frases con el determinado, siguiendo el ejemplo:

Ejemplo: En *una* de las avenidas vive *una* actriz famosa.
            Pérez Galdós/Victoria Abril
            En la avenida Pérez Galdós vive la actriz Victoria Abril.

a En *una* de las estaciones de Madrid se puede coger *un* tren rápido a Sevilla.
Atocha/AVE

b *Un* amigo de Rafael ha conseguido *un* buen trabajo.
Gonzalo/puesto de director gerente

c Para tomar *una* buena paella lo mejor es ir a *un* restaurante valenciano.
mejor paella/*La Pepica*

d No puedo salir contigo porque tengo *un* examen mañana.
examen de gramática

e Ayer conocí a *una* chica estupenda en *una* fiesta.
Chica de mis sueños/fiesta de Lola

f Le han puesto *una* multa por atacar a *un* policía.
Sargento Roldán

g Este fin de semana me he gastado *unas* tres mil pesetas en *un* club.
Que me quedaban/Club Dorma

2 Lee el párrafo siguiente y haz una lista de los nombres que no tienen artículo determinado en inglés pero sí en español. Traduce estos nombres al español:

Ejemplo: electronics   la electrónica

Electronics has changed everything. Cars, televisions, telephones have all been transformed by the electronic revolution. Performance has been enhanced by computers which are in total control of the engine. Only 10 years ago electronic components made up a small proportion of all parts. As time passes and we enter the digital age, people will forget that not long ago everyday activities like driving were not dominated by technology.

3 Rellena los espacios con los artículos determinados o indeterminados que hagan falta. Ten cuidado porque a veces el artículo va detrás de las preposiciones **a** o **de**:

_____ (1) Festival Internacional de Benicasim (FIB), fue creado por dos hermanos leoneses residentes en Madrid (Miguel y José Morán) en 1995, con _____ (2) intención de reunir a _____ (3) 30 grupos en esta localidad castellonense, todos ellos dentro de _____ (4) panorama más independiente de _____ (5) música que ya estaba teniendo _____ (6) gran éxito en _____ (7) Reino Unido y que en España daba sus primeros coletazos de vida. _____ (8) principales aportaciones a ese primer cartel fueron The Charlatans, Supergrass y _____ (9) Planetas, _____ (10) cuales han estado siempre muy ligados a _____ (11) festival y han actuado varias veces en él. En ese primer FIB hubo _____ (12) asistencia de _____ (13) 8.000 personas y sus conciertos se organizaron en _____ (14) Velódromo de Benicasim.

Source: Adapted from Wikipedia

4 Escribe, con el artículo correspondiente, el nombre general al que pertenecen estos nombres. Ayúdate con expresiones como **una parte de, uno/a de, un/a miembro de**:

Ejemplo: la rodilla/una parte del cuerpo

a el BlackBerry™   **i** el balonmano

b el soldado   **j** el pan

c el dormitorio   **k** la discoteca

d la hija   **l** la televisión

e la ducha   **m** el supermercado

f el diccionario   **n** la gasolina

g la naranja   **o** el paro juvenil

h el juez   **p** Windows™ 7

5   Termina las frases siguientes usando **lo**, siguiendo el ejemplo.

Ejemplo: Me pongo muy nerviosa cuando subo a un avión.
No te imaginas lo nerviosa que me pongo cuando subo a un avión.

a Me costó mucho meterle esa idea en la cabeza.
No te imaginas …

b Va siempre super arreglado.
Es increíble …

c Al profesor de historia no le gusta dar buenas notas.
Parece mentira …

d La boda resultó muy bonita.
Tenías que haber visto …

e Nos quedamos en un hotel cochambroso.
No te puedes imaginar …

f La pobre Eugenia ha estado muy enferma.
Cuéntale a mi hermana …

g Los jóvenes beben mucho hoy en día.
Es mala señal …

6   Traduce al español:

a Coffee is not good for you.

b I'm studying IT.

c Spaniards are patriotic.

d Italian is a beautiful language.

e The restaurant was full of young people.

f The ground was covered with snow.

g My brother is a gardener.

h I haven't got any money.

i I speak Russian every day.

j She doesn't speak English very well.

k Dr González is on the phone.

l She's having her hair cut.

m Get me another drink!

n Thai food.

3 Nouns

Remember:

- All nouns in Spanish are either *masculine or feminine* in gender.
- Nouns ending in **-o** tend to be masculine and nouns ending in **-a** tend to be feminine, but there are important exceptions to this rule.
- Plurals of nouns are formed by adding **-s** to nouns ending in a vowel and **-es** to nouns ending in a consonant.

3.1 Gender

Nouns ending in -ma

Be wary of nouns ending in **-ma** because their gender is not predictable.

1 Common masculine nouns ending in **-ma**:

el clima	climate	**el poema**	poem
el crucigrama	crossword	**el problema**	problem
el diploma	diploma	**el programa**	program(me)
el drama	drama	**el sistema**	system
el panorama	panorama	**el tema**	theme, topic
el pijama	pyjama	**el teorema**	theory

2 Common feminine nouns ending in **-ma**:

la alarma	alarm
la cama	bed
la forma	form
la lágrima	tear
la llama	flame
la paloma	dove

Invariable nouns

Many nouns have no separate masculine or feminine form. Gender is indicated only by the definite article.

1　Nouns ending in **-ista**:

el/la artista	artist	**el/la tenista**	tennis player
el/la socialista	socialist	**el/la telefonista**	telephonist

2　Present participles ending in **-nte**:

el/la amante	lover	**el/la estudiante**	student
el/la cantante	singer	**el/la gerente**	manager

Note that some of these nouns have a feminine form:

el dependiente	**la dependienta**	shop assistant
el infante	**la infanta**	prince/princess

3　A number of other common nouns have the same form for masculine and feminine:

el/la atleta	athlete	**el/la joven**	young person
el/la camarada	comrade	**el/la guía**	guide

Nouns with a fixed gender

A few nouns that refer to people have a fixed gender, regardless of whether the person is male or female:

la persona	person
el personaje	character (in book, play, etc.)
la víctima	victim

Nouns with a distinctive feminine form

Many nouns distinguish between masculine and feminine by a small change in the end of the word (e.g. **profesor/profesora**). Others have a separate feminine form:

masculine	*feminine*	
actor	**actriz**	actor/actress
héroe	**heroína**	hero/heroine
alcalde	**alcaldesa**	mayor/mayoress
rey	**reina**	king/queen

Gender of countries, regions, towns and cities

Countries, regions, towns and cities may be either masculine or feminine. When they end in unstressed **-a**, they are normally feminine; otherwise they are masculine (see Part I, 2.1).

la España del siglo veintiuno	twenty-first-century Spain
el Japón del futuro	the Japan of the future
el País Vasco	the Basque Country
la Córdoba mora	Moorish Cordoba
el Madrid de los años 80	'80s Madrid

Gender differentiating meaning

A number of common nouns have a different meaning according to their gender:

noun	*masculine*	*feminine*
el/la capital	capital (money)	capital (city)
el/la cura	priest	cure
el/la frente	front (military)	forehead
el/la mañana	future	morning
el/la orden	order (harmony, pattern)	order (command; religious)
el/la parte	message, dispatch	part
el/la pendiente	earring	slope
el/la policía	policeman	police force/policewoman

Mar and arte

Mar (sea) is usually masculine, but the feminine form is sometimes found. It is always feminine in:

a   Derivative words and expressions:

la pleamar	high tide
en alta mar	on the high seas

b   The colloquial expression **la mar de** (a lot of):

Tienes una hija la mar de simpática.   You have a really nice daughter.

c   **arte** (art), can be either masculine or feminine in the singular, but it is always feminine in the plural:

el arte musulmán	Moslem art
las artes gráficas	graphic arts

New feminine words

The status of women has undergone rapid change in Spain in recent years, with the result that some words that relate to professional life have acquired feminine forms:

masculine	*feminine*	
el abogado	**la abogada**	lawyer
el catedrático	**la catedrática**	professor
el doctor	**la doctora**	doctor
el ingeniero	**la ingeniera**	engineer
el jefe	**la jefa**	boss
el ministro	**la ministra**	minister

Gender of foreign nouns

Spanish has always taken nouns from foreign languages although not necessarily with the same meaning, e.g. **el chalet** is a detached house or bungalow with a garden around it; **la cocina office** is a modern fitted kitchen.

The development of new technologies has increased the number of nouns imported from English.

El (teléfono) móvil	mobile
El módem	
El joystick	

If the noun refers to a particular person, its gender will depend on who this person is. If unclear, the gender will be masculine.

Lisbeth Salander es una hacker muy famosa gracias a las novelas de Larsson.	Lisbeth Salander is a famous hacker, thanks to the novels of Larsson.
Los hackers pueden crear grandes problemas internacionales.	Hackers can create big international problems.

El/La Internet. This word does not normally have an article after prepositions.

(For more a detailed explanation of the gender of foreign nouns see: Butt & Benjamin, 5th edition, 2011, 12-13 and 562.)

3.2   Number

Plural words that are masculine and feminine in meaning

A number of words are used in the masculine plural but refer to both genders:

los hermanos	brother(s)/brother(s) and sister(s)
los padres	parents/fathers

los reyes	kings/king and queen
los suegros	fathers-in-law/mothers- and fathers-in-law
los hijos	sons/sons and daughters

Words that have the same form for singular and plural

Words ending in unstressed **-s**:

el/los atlas	atlas/atlases
la/las crisis	crisis/crises
el/los análisis	analysis/analyses
el/los lunes/martes, etc.	Monday/s, Tuesday/s, etc. (and the other days of the week ending in **s**)

Proper nouns:

los Carazo	the Carazos/Carazo family
los Renault	Renault cars

Words ending in a stressed vowel

These words add **s**:

el café	los cafés	coffee/s
el champú	los champús	shampoo/s
el menú	los menús	menu/s
el papá	los papás	daddy/-ies/mummies and daddies
el sofá	los sofás	sofa/s

Words of foreign derivation

Words of foreign derivation normally add **s**:

el coñac	los coñacs	brandy/-ies
el club	los clubs	club/s
el póster	los pósters	poster/s

Plural nouns

Certain common nouns are found, in specific meanings, only in the plural:

las afueras	outskirts
los bienes	property, goods
las tinieblas	darkness
las vacaciones	holiday(s)
los víveres	provisions

Words that mean the same whether used in the singular or the plural

la escalera/las escaleras	stairs
la nariz/las narices	nose
el pantalón/los pantalones	trousers

Compound nouns

1 Compound nouns are invariable when the second element is already plural:

el/los rompecabezas	puzzle/s
el/los limpiaparabrisas	windscreen wiper/s
el/los paraguas	umbrella/s

2 A normal plural is formed when the second element is not plural:

| la coliflor | las coliflores | cauliflower/s |
| la bocacalle | las bocacalles | (street) turnings, intersections |

3 Compound nouns are increasingly written as two separate words. In these cases the first word only is made plural:

| el hombre rana | los hombres rana | frogman/men |
| la cuestión clave | las cuestiones clave | key question/s |

Exercises

1 Indica el género de los nombres siguientes, masculino, femenino o los dos géneros:

1	problema	10	atleta	19	déficit	28	intestinos
2	tesis	11	gimnasta	20	ballet	29	cabra
3	lágrima	12	hincha	21	rapapolvo	30	masía
4	guía	13	racista	22	ikurriña	31	corral
5	personaje	14	esperanza	23	tragaluz	32	pechera
6	ángel	15	duque	24	bombón	33	uva
7	demócrata	16	pereza	25	armónica	34	ajedrez
8	dependiente	17	cometa	26	Baleares	35	puesta de sol
9	bailarín	18	rubí	27	pico		

2 Haz cuatro listas de los nombres siguientes según: (a) se refieran a nombres que incluyan los géneros masculino o femenino sin distinción, (b) si las formas masculina y femenina se expresan sólo en el artículo, (c) si las formas masculina y femenina se expresan por medio de dos palabras distintas, (d) se refieran a nombres que cambian sólo la terminación:

Ejemplos:

	lista (a)		**lista (b)**	**lista (c)**		**lista (d)**	
	una rata		un/una policía	un conde		un ingeniero	
ministro	ingeniero	testigo	delincuente	guía	duque
rey	personaje	piloto	cangrejo	príncipe	persona
dependiente	cantante	pintor	rana	modelo	gato
toro	franquista	escocés	héroe	varón	bebé
mendigo	pantera	corresponsal	deportista	madrina	yerno
cirujano	delfín				

3 Indica el nombre abstracto relacionado con las siguientes ocupaciones:

Ejemplos: *estudiante* *estudio*
  economista *economía*

vendedor	artista
filósofo	industrial
actor	diseñador
agente	twitero
corresponsal	delincuente

médico	músico
concertista	florista
cocinero	burócrata
académico	político
director	saxofonista

4 Escribe un texto que contenga los nombres de la lista a continuación. Una vez escrito repítelo usando los mismos nombres en plural. Ten cuidado con las concordancias.

> padre, escocés, problema, mapa, abogada, héroe, vacaciones, cuestión clave, escalera, accidente, coñac, mañana.

4

Adjectives

Remember:

- Spanish adjectives agree with the noun in *number* and *gender*.
- They are normally placed *after* the noun.
- Some common adjectives (e.g. **bueno, malo**) are shortened before masculine singular nouns.

Adjectives are important words which add information about a noun, such as colour, quantity, quality, size and value. It could be said that our ability to choose gives us freedom to be creative and imaginative. Note the difference between:

Era simplemente una silla.	It was just a chair.

and

Era una silla decimonónica, oscura y misteriosa, evocadora de miles de doncellas suspirantes y caballeros enamorados.	It was a nineteenth-century chair, dark and mysterious, evocative of thousands of sighing maidens and lovesick gentlemen.

4.1 Form of adjectives

1 Spanish habitually creates adjectives to indicate the town of origin of a person or thing. Some of the more common adjectives of this type are listed below. Note that the adjective always begins with lower-case letter:

town	*adjective*	*town*	*adjective*
Barcelona	**barcelonés**	Salamanca	**salmantino**
Granada	**granadino**	Sevilla	**sevillano**
Londres	**londinense**	Valencia	**valenciano**
Madrid	**madrileño**	Zaragoza	**zaragozano**
Málaga	**malagueño**	Buenos Aires	**bonaerense**
Nueva York	**neoyorquino**		

2 Adjectives are commonly created from nouns as an alternative to the construction **de** + noun, e.g. **el mundo de la educación** becomes **el mundo educativo***:*

de + *noun*	*adjective*	
una compañía de seguros	una compañía aseguradora	an insurance company
la vida de familia	la vida familiar	family life
un grupo de bancos	un grupo bancario	a banking group
una crisis de energía	una crisis energética	an energy crisis
la industria de hoteles	la industria hotelera	the hotel industry
una llamada de teléfono	una llamada telefónica	a telephone call

3 Many adjectives ending in **-a** (frequently **-ista**) have the same form for masculine and feminine singular and for masculine and feminine plural:

singular	*plural*	
optimista	**optimistas**	optimistic
pesimista	**pesimistas**	pessimistic
realista	**realistas**	realistic
socialista	**socialistas**	socialist
suicida	**suicidas**	suicidal

4 Adjectives denoting colour

a For some colours, such as **violeta** (violet), **naranja** (orange) and **rosa** (pink), the noun is used like an adjective, but remains invariable. When describing the colour of an object the phrase **color** or **(de) color** plus the noun for the colour is often used.

uñas (de color) violeta	violet fingernails
novelas rosa	sentimental novels
tonalidades fresa	strawberry-coloured tones

b Other colours follow the conventional rules for their form, but note that their meaning may change in translation:

un chiste verde	a dirty joke
un ojo morado	a black eye

5 **Santo** is shortened to **San** before proper names except those beginning with **Do-** or **To-**:

La noche de San Juan es la más corta del año.	San Juan's (Midsummer) night is the shortest of the year.
Las Fallas terminan el día de San José.	The Fallas finish on St Joseph's Day.
Santo Domingo de Silos es una iglesia románica preciosa.	Santo Domingo de Silos is a fine Romanesque church.
Santo Tomás es el patrón de los estudiantes.	St Thomas is the patron saint of students.

6 When two or more nouns of different gender are linked, the adjective is always masculine:

Juan y Lola están casados.	Juan and Lola are married.
Sus hijos, Manolo y Eugenia, son los dos guapísimos.	Their son and daughter, Manolo and Eugenia, are both very good-looking.

7 Where a plural noun is qualified by two or more adjectives, each referring to just one thing, the adjectives are singular:

Las lenguas inglesa y española.　　　　　　　The English and Spanish languages.

4.2　Position of adjectives

1 Some adjectives change their meaning according to their position:

	before the noun	*after the noun*
antiguo	former	old
gran(de)	great, big	big
mismo	same	-self, very
nuevo	new (another, more)	brand-new
pobre	poor (unfortunate)	poor (not rich)
viejo	old (long-standing)	old (not young)

Mi antiguo novio.	My ex-boyfriend.
En ese pueblo el centro es muy antiguo pero las afueras están llenas de edificios nuevos.	In this town the centre is very old but the outskirts are full of new buildings.
El gran pintor, Picasso, en realidad era un poco bajito.	The great painter, Picasso, was in fact rather a small man.
El gran diccionario de María Moliner consiste en dos volúmenes grandes.	Maria Moliner's great dictionary consists of two large volumes.
Siempre cuenta la misma historia por las mismas fechas.	He always tells the same story on the same occasions.
El Rey mismo le dio la medalla.	The King himself gave him the medal.
Nuevos avances en la ciencia.	New (i.e. more) scientific progress.
Compró un coche nuevo para ir de vacaciones a Galicia.	He bought a new car to go on holiday to Galicia.
¡Pobre Manolo! ¡Tan rico y tan desgraciado!	Poor (old) Manolo! So rich yet so unhappy!
El Albaicín es un barrio pobre pero bonito y muy visitado.	The Albaicin is a poor quarter, but it is pretty and much visited.
Son viejos amigos, desde los tiempos de la universidad.	They are old friends from their university days.
Una mujer vieja pero todavía hermosa.	An old, but still beautiful, woman.

2 Where an adjective is placed before more than one noun it usually agrees in gender and number with the first noun:

Te acuso de haberme engañado con falsas palabras y hechos.	I accuse you of having deceived me with false words and deeds.

4.3　Meaning of adjectives

1 Use of the definite articles **el/la/los/las/lo** with an adjective:

a The masculine singular adjective is often preceded by **lo** to make a kind of abstract noun:

Lo importante sería continuar aprendiendo.	The important thing is to carry on learning.
Lo bueno es que no lo hayamos perdido todo.	The good thing is that we haven't lost everything.

b The definite article may be placed before a following adjective standing on its own. In this construction, the noun which the adjective describes is implied and the adjective must agree with that noun.

Mi hija mayor es la guapa de la familia y la pequeña la simpática.	My eldest daughter is the best-looking person in our family and my youngest daughter is the nicest (one).

c The definite article is frequently used with the masculine and feminine plural adjective to refer to a group or class:

los verdes	the Greens
los blancos	the whites
las andaluzas	(the) Andalusian women
los carcas	narrow-minded people
las feministas	(the) feminists

2 'Negative' adjectives with **poco, no,** and **sin**

'Negative' adjectives can be made by placing **poco, no** or **sin** before certain words:

poco escrupuloso/sin escrúpulos	unprincipled
poco inteligente/sin inteligencia	unintelligent
no esencial	inessential
no leído	unread
no registrado	unrecorded
sin provocación	unprovoked
sin gas	still (water)
sin formatear	unformatted
sin contestar	unanswered
sin alcohol	alcohol-free
sin refinar	unrefined

3 Translation of the English adjective ending in *-ing*

The *-ing* form in English is often used adjectivally, as in 'Sleeping Beauty'. In Spanish the gerund *never* acts as an adjective; *-ing* is usually rendered by a relative clause or an adjective (see Part I, 34.3).

la Bella Durmiente	Sleeping Beauty
la vaca que ríe	the laughing cow
una tarde encantadora	an enchanting evening
la clase trabajadora	the working class

4 Some adjectives ending in *-ing* are rendered in Spanish by the past participle, e.g. **sentado** (sitting [down]), **echado/tumbado** (lying [down]), **arrodillado** (kneeling [down]):

Toro Sentado	Sitting Bull
A mi gato le encanta estar tumbado al sol.	My cat likes lying in the sun.
Te lo pido arrodillado.	I beg you on bended knee.

Exercises

1 Construye frases uniendo un sustantivo de la columna **A** con un adjetivo adecuado de la columna **B**:

A	B
león	oscura
verano	afilado
flor	fuerte
noche	guapa
idioma	roja
edificio	feroz
chica	alto
lápiz	alegre
cerveza	extranjero
fiesta	cálido

2 Escribe un adjetivo que signifique lo mismo que la frase que está entre paréntesis:

a Pasamos el fin de semana en una casa _____ (de la costa).

b La industria _____ (de hoteles) es una de las más importantes para la economía española.

c Tus razones son _____ (que no se pueden comprender).

d Esto es un problema _____ (que no se puede remediar).

e En los años 90 pasamos una vida _____ (de estudiantes) maravillosa.

f La casa se ha quedado _____ (que no se puede vender).

g Era un chico _____ (sin mucha inteligencia).

h Salió a la calle desaliñado y _____ (que no se había afeitado).

3 En este párrafo faltan los adjetivos. Colócalos, usando los del recuadro:

profunda	del cielo	encinta	políticas
ateo	femenino	numerosos	apocalípticas
concurrida	masón		

Severo del Valle era _____ (1) y _____ (2) pero tenía ambiciones _____ (3) y no podía darse el lujo de faltar a la misa más _____ (4) cada domingo y fiesta de guardar, para que todos pudieran verlo. Su esposa Nívea prefería entenderse con Dios sin intermediarios, tenía _____ (5) desconfianza de las sotanas y se aburría con las descripciones _____ (6) el purgatorio y el infierno, pero acompañaba a su marido en sus ambiciones, en la esperanza de que si él ocupaba un puesto en el Congreso, ella podría obtener el voto _____ (7) por el cual luchaba desde hacía diez años, sin que sus _____ (8) embarazos lograran desanimarla. Ese Jueves Santo el padre Restrepo había llevado a los oyentes al límite de su resistencia con sus visiones _____ (9) y Nívea empezó a sentir mareos. Se preguntó si no no estaría nuevamente _____ (10).

Source: Isabel Allende, La casa de los espíritus

4 Llena los espacios vacíos con los adjetivos que encontrarás en el cuadro. ¡Ojo! No se usan todos los adjetivos.

> deprimentes inoportuno maldito aburrido helada trasera imprevisto ligerita desvelado inesperado necio tranquila cotilla mala estropeados agotado destartalado encendidas desesperado aburrido pequeño inquietantes rápida cansado agotada desprestigiado culpable siguiente viejo fríos templado

Me preparé para tener una noche (1) _____ . Hacía tiempo que no estaba tan (2) _____ y además el (3) _____ teléfono no funcionaba y no podía llamar a nadie para salir. Decidí ponerme a ver las noticias en la televisión, pero resultaron muy (4) _____ y pensé que lo mejor sería darme un baño (5) _____ pero no pude porque el agua estaba (6) _____ . ¿Y si saliera a dar un (7) _____ paseo? Después de todo no era muy tarde. De pronto oí un ruido (8) _____ que parecía venir de la puerta (9) _____ . Era el vecino de arriba, que siempre me pareció un poco (10) _____ y (11)_____ , que venía a decirme que me había dejado (12)_____ las luces del coche. Me sentí un poco (13) _____ por haber pensado mal de él. Estaba seguro de que la batería estaría (14) _____ y, como el coche ya estaba (15)_____ y (16)_____ , no podría ponerlo en marcha por la mañana. Bajé corriendo y apagué las luces. Creí que lo mejor sería hacerme una cena (17) _____ , darme una ducha (18) _____ y meterme en la cama ya que al día (19) _____ , sin coche, iba a costarme mucho llegar al despacho. Tardé mucho en dormirme porque estaba (20) _____ y luego, durante la noche, soñé con baños (21) _____ , ruidos (22)_____ , coches (23) _____ . Cuando sonó el despertador estaba aún más (24) _____ que cuando me acosté.

5 Siguiendo las reglas que has aprendido, rellena los huecos de la historia con adjetivos de tu elección:

Esta iba a ser una noche _____ . Hacía _____ tiempo que no estaba tan _____ y además el _____ teléfono no funcionaba. Decidió ponerse a ver un programa _____ en la televisión, pero estaba muy _____ y los programas _____ acababan por aburrirle. Pensó que lo mejor sería darse un baño _____ pero el agua estaba _____ . ¿Y si saliera a dar un _____ paseo? Después de todo no era muy tarde. De pronto oyó un ruido _____ que parecía venir de la puerta _____ . El vecino de _____ venía a decirle que se había dejado _____ las luces del coche.

6 Traduce al español:

a a person from Madrid   **f** the Queen herself

b my old friend   **g** Happy Christmas!

c an amusing story   **h** the French

d poor George!   **i** smiling faces

e the reds   **j** the last few days

5
Comparison

Remember:

- When we want to make a comparison in Spanish we use **más que** and **menos que.**
- For comparisons of equality (as … as) we use **tan(to) … como.**
- The superlative (the most/least) is formed by placing the definite article before the comparative adjective (**el más hermoso**, etc.) or by adding the ending **-ísimo/a.**

5.1 Más and menos followed by a number

When a number follows **más** or **menos** (in the sense of 'over' or 'under'), **de** must be used instead of **que**:

Más de veinte amigos fueron a la fiesta de su cumpleaños.	More than twenty friends went to his birthday party.
Le han tocado más de veinte millones en la lotería.	He's won more than twenty million on the lottery.

5.2 Mayor/menor and más grande/más pequeño

Mayor and **menor** must be used to refer to *age* (older/younger).

Más grande and **más pequeño** can be used as an alternative to **mayor** and **menor** in all meanings except age:

Juan es mayor que Felipe.	Juan is older than Felipe.
Su hermano menor es pelirrojo.	Her younger brother has red hair.
Su casa es más pequeña que la mía.	His house is smaller than mine.
Su capacidad de solucionar problemas es mayor que la tuya.	Her problem-solving ability is greater than yours.
El Estadio Bernabeu en Madrid es más grande que Wembley.	The Bernabeu Stadium in Madrid is bigger than Wembley.

5.3 Cuanto más/menos … (tanto) más/menos

The English comparative construction (the more/less … the more/less) is rendered in Spanish by **cuanto más/menos … (tanto) más/menos**.

Note that

a   **tanto** can be omitted in the second half of the construction

b **cuanto** and **tanto** agree with a following noun:

Cuantos más dulces le das, (tantos) más quiere.	The more sweets you give him, the more he wants.
Cuanto menos trabajaba, menos ganas tenía de trabajar.	The less he worked, the less he wanted to work.
Cuanto más rápido, mejor.	The quicker the better.
Cuanto más le conozco, más me gusta.	The more I know him, the better I like him.

5.4 Más/menos del que ...

When **más/menos que** is followed by a clause with a verb in it **que** is replaced by **del que, de la que, de los que** or **de las que**, depending on the number and gender of the preceding noun; **de lo que** is used if you are referring back to the whole preceding phrase rather than to a specific noun:

Gastó más dinero del que quería.	He spent more money than he wanted to.
Tiene menos amigas de las que cree.	She has less friends than (s)he thinks.
Es menos tonto de lo que parece.	He's less stupid than he looks.

5.5 -ísimo

A number of common adjectives have an irregular form when the suffix **-ísimo** is added:

amable	**amabilísimo**	grande	**máximo** (or **grandísimo**)
antiguo	**antiquísimo**	joven	**jovencísimo**
bueno	**óptimo** (or **buenísimo**)	malo	**pésimo** (or **malísimo**)
fácil	**facilísimo**	pequeño	**mínimo** (or **pequeñísimo**)

Dicen que el examen va a ser difícil, pero a mi parecer será facilísimo!	They say the exam is going to be tough, but I think it will be extremely easy!
En Toledo compramos una mesa antiquísima.	In Toledo we bought a very old table.

5.6 Ways of expressing comparison

Certain expressions are used typically to express comparison, such as:

es/sería mejor que	it is/would be better to
prefiero	I prefer/like better
me/te/le gusta más	I/you/he/she like(s) better/best
cada vez más	more and more
cada vez menos	less and less
tanto ... como	both ... and, as much ... as

¿Vamos al teatro o crees que sería mejor que nos quedáramos en casa?	Shall we go to the theatre, or would it be better to stay at home?
Prefiero el té al café.	I like tea better than coffee.
Le gusta más comprar la verdura en el mercado porque dice que es más fresca y más barata.	She prefers to buy vegetables at the market because she says they're fresher and cheaper.
Las aceitunas españolas me gustan más que las italianas.	I like Spanish olives better than Italian ones.
Parece que la gente es cada vez más rica.	It seems as though people are getting richer and richer.
Cada vez vas menos a los toros.	You go to bullfights less and less.
Se bebe tanto vino blanco como tinto.	People drink as much white wine as red.

5.7 Useful phrases

a lo mejor	probably	**colegio mayor**	university hall of residence
al por mayor	wholesale	**mayor de edad**	grown-up
al por menor	retail	**menor de edad**	under age
calle mayor	high street	**una persona mayor**	an elderly person

Exercises

1 Construye frases con comparativos o superlativos entre las cuatro palabras:

Ejemplo: la luna   la Tierra   el sol   Marte

La Tierra es más grande que la luna.
Marte es menos romántico que la luna.
El sol es el más caliente de los cuatro astros.

a	España	Suiza	Inglaterra	Italia
b	fútbol	ciclismo	tenis	baloncesto
c	tortuga	tigre	ratón	gato
d	filosofía	historia	ciencias	lenguas
e	madera	cobre	papel	plástico
f	melocotón	naranja	aceituna	manzana
g	cine	teatro	discoteca	concierto
h	Valencia	Madrid	Málaga	Vigo

2 Rellena los espacios en blanco en las frases siguientes con las palabras de la lista:

bien	suerte	ilusiones	amigos
rápidamente	placer	derechos	

a No conozco a nadie con tantas _____ como Daniel.

b Mis exámenes no salieron tan _____ como había esperado.

c Alberto tiene tantos _____ como enemigos.

d Los cambios no se hacen tan _____ como piensas.

e El viaje me trajo tanto _____ como el del año pasado.

f Los jóvenes de ayer no tenían tantos _____ como los de hoy.

g Nadie tiene tanta _____ como él.

3 Rellena los espacios con **del que, de la que, de lo que, de los que** o **de las que,** según convenga:

a Este trabajo es más difícil _____ creía.

b Gané menos dinero _____ me habían prometido.

c Tengo más entradas para el cine _____ necesito.

d Esta chica es más joven _____ me había imaginado.

e Compré menos ropa _____ quería.

f Tengo menos libros _____ quisiera.

4 En español se dice que **las comparaciones son odiosas,** pero eso no es necesariamente verdad. ¿Podrías añadir algo a estas frases de manera que resulten más equilibradas?

Ejemplos: Los ingleses son más fríos que los españoles, ... *pero son más educados*
Los españoles son muy generosos ... *pero también pueden ser más irresponsables.*

a La comida vegetariana es más sana ... pero

b Los africanos no son tan ricos como los europeos ... pero

c Los sueldos hoy en día son más altos ... pero

d Prefiero vivir en un último piso ... pero

e Dicen que las rubias se divierten más que las morenas ... pero

f Está muy bien tener muchos amigos ... pero

g Tiene un novio guapísimo ... pero

h En los países fríos la gente trabaja más ... pero

5 A los españoles les gusta mucho utilizar el superlativo **-ísimo.** Traduce las siguientes frases al español utilizándolo:

a His sons are very polite.

b He bought her a very expensive bracelet.

c Their house was immaculate.

d He had a very serious accident.

e Italian food is really tasty.

f The baby cried because he was very tired.

g My parents were really angry because I came back very late.

6

Numerals

Remember:

- Cardinal numbers are for counting things (**el número tres de la clase**).
- Ordinal numbers are for ordering things (**el primero de la clase**).
- Spanish places **y** between tens and units and not between hundreds and tens (**ciento cincuenta y nueve** = one hundred and fifty-nine).
- **Primero** and **tercero** drop the final **o** before a masculine singular noun.

6.1 Dimensions

When measuring things the following structure is used: **tener** plus dimension plus **de** plus adjective.

La piscina **tiene** 20 metros **de** largo,
15 metros **de** ancho, y 2 metros **de** profundo.

The swimming pool is 20 metres long
and 15 metres wide, and 2 metres deep.

Note: the adjective in this construction is always masculine regardless of the gender of the noun.

6.2 Figures and calculations

1 'Half' is normally **la mitad**, except in counting precisely, where it is **medio**, and when telling the time, where it is **media**:

Había hecho la mitad del viaje.
Medio millón.
Son las dos y media.

He'd completed half the journey.
Half a million.
It is half past two.

2 To express a fraction use **medio** for 1/2 and **tercio** for 1/3; for fractions from 1/4 to 1/10 use the ordinal numbers. After a tenth add **-avo** to the cardinal number:

un tercio	a third	**un décimo**	a tenth
un quinto	a fifth	**un onceavo**	an eleventh
un octavo	an eighth		

An alternative way of expressing fractions is as follows: **la mitad, la tercera parte** *(1/3)*, **la cuarta parte** *(1/4)*, **las tres cuartas partes** *(3/4)* etc.

La cuarta parte de la población del mundo
pasa hambre.

A quarter of the world population
is hungry.

3 Percentages (**porcentajes**) are preceded by either **el** or **un**; 'per cent' is either **por cien** or **por ciento**:

Dice que el/un 90% (noventa por cien[to])
de los encuestados cree en Dios.

He says that 90% of those interviewed
believe in God.

4 Note that in Spanish: – a point is used between thousands

– a comma is used for the decimal point:

a 30.347 (**treinta mil trescientos cuarenta y siete**) (thirty thousand three hundred and forty-seven)

b 15,69 metros (**quince coma sesenta y nueve metros**) (fifteen point six nine metres)

5 Simple calculations are expressed in Spanish as follows:

$4 + 6 = 10$	cuatro y (or más) seis, diez	four plus six is ten
$10 - 5 = 5$	diez menos cinco, cinco	ten take away five is five
$7 \times 3 = 21$	siete por tres, veintiuno	seven threes are twenty-one
$45 \div 5 = 9$	cuarenta y cinco dividido por cinco, nueve	forty-five divided by five is nine

Exercises

1 Lee en voz alta las siguientes cifras:

a $20 - 7 = 13$ **f** $1000 \div 4 = 250$ **k** Bilbao 98 23 45

b $100 \div 20 = 5$ **g** $8 \times 12 = 96$ **l** Jaén 13 67 76

c $21 \times 10 = 210$ **h** $16 + 11 = 27$ **m** 16 de mayo de 1616

d $1000 - 5 = 995$ **i** $1/2 + 1/4 = 3/4$ **n** 46, 78%

e $7 + 45 = 52$ **j** 23 de enero de 2001   **o** 12.309

2 Calcula, y escribe el resultado en palabras:

a cien menos noventa, _____   **e** ochenta y ocho dividido por cuatro, _____

b veinte por cinco, _____   **f** cincuenta menos veintinueve, _____

c doscientos dividido por diez, _____   **g** mil uno y siete, _____

d cien más ocho, _____   **h** doscientos por tres, _____

3 Completa con números ordinales:

a He estado cuatro años en la Universidad de Granada. El año que viene voy a pasas mi _____ año en la Universidad de Cambridge.

b Estamos en el sexto piso; tus amigos viven en el próximo, el _____ .

c De _____ quiero ensalada mixta. Después, de _____ prefiero pollo.

d He estado en Rusia tres veces. El año que viene iré por _____ vez.

e Cada billete de lotería se divide en diez participaciones; se llaman _____ .

4 Lee en voz alta el siguiente texto:

A grandes problemas, grandes soluciones

Hacía ya cuatro años que Rodrigo y su pandilla de amigos, Jorge, Pau, Isabel y Marta habían terminado sus estudios universitarios y hecho el curso especial para acceso a la enseñanza, pero no habían podido encontrar ni trabajo ni vivienda. Las escuelas en la ciudad no tenían vacantes y los bancos no daban hipotecas para pisos que de todas formas eran carísimos.

Después de mucho pensar tuvieron una idea original. Las escuelas rurales estaban en crisis y los precios de las casas de pueblo eran bastante razonables.

–Si encontramos una casa en un pueblo bastante grande para todos, y nos reunimos para pagar la entrada, quizás podamos solucionar el problema– dijo Jorge.

Encontraron una casa con seis habitaciones que valía 274,550 euros. Entre todos, pidiendo ayuda a sus familias y vendiendo algunos objetos de valor consiguieron reunir 123,410 euros. Con esa entrada y el aval de sus padres, el banco les ofreció una hipoteca de 151,140 euros a pagar en 30 años. Esta hipoteca, al 2,5%, resultaba en un pago mensual de 597 euros los que, divididos por cinco, eran unos 120 euros al mes para cada uno.

La casa necesitaba algunas mejoras para las que un constructor les dio un presupuesto de 27,300 euros. Ellos decidieron hacer el trabajo ellos mismos bajo la dirección de un amigo arquitecto, ahorrándose con ello 19.350 euros.

Todos, menos Pau, han encontrado trabajo en escuelas de pueblos cercanos. Pau se ha dedicado a cultivar el jardín y proveer verduras de todo tipo para la casa. La vida comunitaria ha sido un reto pero ellos están seguros de haber encontrado una buena solución.

5 Traduce al español:

a King Philip II

b the 19th century

c the third Millennium

d Pope John XXIII

e the 25th anniversary of the association

f the 400th anniversary of Velázquez's birth

g the eighth floor

h in seventh heaven

i the Third Man

j Queen Elizabeth I

k the first flowers of spring

l Henry VIII

m 4th July

n my eighteenth birthday

7

Personal pronouns

(See Part I, page 39)

8 Demonstrative adjectives and pronouns

Remember:

• There are **two** ways of saying 'that'/'those' in Spanish: **ese, esa, eso, esos, esas** and **aquel, aquella, aquello. aquellos** and **aquellas**.

8.1 The former/the latter

Este and **aquel** have the meaning of 'the latter' and 'the former':

De los dos estilos, el cubismo y el impresionismo, **este** comenzó antes que **aquel.**

Of the two styles, Cubism and Impressionism, the latter began before the former.

8.2 Esto/eso/aquello de meaning 'this/that business/question, of'

No me gusta esto de los toros.
Me han contado aquello de Rosa.
Considera eso de la moneda única…

I don't like this bullfighting business.
I've been told all that stuff about Rosa.
Take that matter of the single currency.

8.3 Position of the demonstrative adjective after the noun

The normal position of the demonstrative adjective is before the noun but it may be placed after the noun, especially in speech. In this case the meaning is usually pejorative:

El chaval este se las sabe todas.
Cuidado. Ya viene el tonto ese.

This guy knows it all.
Careful. That idiot is coming now.

8.4 Translation of 'those who', 'those of us who'

1. **Los que** and **las que** (and *not* **aquellos que**) are used to translate 'those who':

Los que suspenden los exámenes tienen otra oportunidad de presentarse en septiembre.
Los que visitan España por primera vez tienen que ir a Granada a ver la Alhambra.

Those who fail their examinations have another chance to take them in September.
Those who visit Spain for the first time must go to Granada to see the Alhambra.

2   **Los/las que** + verb in the first person plural renders the idea 'those of us who':

Los que sabíamos que iba a salir un nuevo modelo de coche eléctrico, preferimos esperarlo.

Those of us who knew that a new model of electric car was coming out preferred to wait for it.

Exercises

1   Completa con la forma que creas más adecuada del adjetivo o pronombre demostrativo. Hay varias posibilidades en algunos casos:

a Mira _____ cuadro; es de Velázquez.

b No quiero saber nada de _____ de los fondos robados.

c Tiene dos tíos, Roberto y Alfredo. _____ murió hace dos años; _____ todavía vive.

d La mujer _____ cree que el mundo la ignora.

e Toma _____ pan. Está hecho en casa.

f _____ verano vamos a Grecia.

g ¿De quién es _____ cámara? La encontramos en la biblioteca.

h Me gusta más _____ pintura que _____.

2   Rellena los espacios vacíos con los pronombres o adjetivos en el recuadro. Hay más adjetivos/pronombres de los que necesitas.

| los que   esa   aquel   ese   Ese   este   éstos   esta |
| aquellos   los que   aquella   las que   este   estos |

En la clase de D. Julián los alumnos siempre están alborotando. D. Julián esta a punto de jubilarse y además ve poco y los chavales se aprovechan.

–A ver, ¿quién ha hecho (1) _____ ruido?

–¿Qué ruido, D. Julián?

–(2) _____, como si alguien hubiera tirado una pelota.

–D. Julián, ¡ha sido (3) _____!

–(4) _____ tiene un nombre. ¿Quién?

–D. Julián, ¡yo no he sido!

–Y tú ¿quién eres?

–Yo soy Carmelo, pero no he sido yo, ha sido (5) _____, la nueva.

–¡Basta ya! José Maria, sube aquí a la tarima conmigo y dime los nombres de (6) _____ están armando jaleo.

–José María no ha venido hoy, D. Julián. Dicen (7) _____ que tiene la gripe.

–Bueno, si José María no está, que venga Raimundita. El caso es acabar con (8) _____ alboroto. (9) _____ griten, tiren cosas, se levanten etc. etc., tendrán que ir al despacho del director. ¡Hay que ver! (10) _____ chicos. Cada día están peor.

–No se enfade, D. Julián, que le puede dar algo.

3   Traduce al español:

a This computer works better than that one.

b I'd like to clear up that matter of the broken window once and for all.

c Of the two arguments, I favour the latter.

d All those who wish to help with the party, come with me.

e I don't like that building over there.

f Those people never stop complaining.

g I've thought a lot about that matter.

h Those of us who supported the government were disappointed.

i Those photos are good, but these are better.

j Don't say that! It isn't true.

9
Possessive adjectives and pronouns

Remember:

- Possessives **mi, tu,** etc., are used to show possession and relationships between people and things/other people.
- Possessives agree in gender and number with the *thing possessed.*

9.1 The second form of the possessive adjective

The possessive adjective has a second form, as follows:

singular	plural	
mío/mía	míos/mías	of mine
tuyo/tuya	tuyos/tuyas	of yours (familiar)
suyo/suya	suyos/suyas	of his/hers/its; of yours (formal)
nuestro/nuestra	nuestros/nuestras	of ours
vuestro/vuestra	vuestros/vuestras	of yours (familiar)
suyo/suya	suyos/suyas	of theirs; of yours (formal)

Notes

1. This form of the possessive adjective is used far less than the first form (see Part I, 9.1).

2. The second form of the possessive adjective is the same as that of the possessive pronoun, but the definite article is omitted.

3. Like the first form of the possessive adjective this form must also agree in gender and number with the thing possessed.

4. the second form always *follows the noun,* and in English means 'of mine', 'of his', etc.:

un amigo mío	a friend of mine
una hermana suya	a sister of his/hers/theirs/yours
Tengo algunas revistas tuyas.	I've got a few magazines of yours.

In these examples it can be seen that **mío, suya** and **tuyas** agree in number and gender with the 'thing(s) possessed' and not with the possessor.

9.2 Use of the definite article with the possessive pronoun

The possessive pronoun is normally preceded by the definite article, except after the verb **ser:**

Aunque mi televisión es más grande que la tuya, la mía no tiene alta definición.
Although my TV is bigger than yours, mine doesn't have high definition.

Este MP3 es tuyo y no mío, creo.
This MP3 is yours, not mine, I believe.

9.3 Neuter lo with the possessive pronoun

The neuter article **lo** is used with the possessive pronoun to indicate a general state of affairs:

No sé nada de lo suyo.
I know nothing about his affairs.

Lo nuestro no puede resolverse.
This business of ours cannot be resolved.

9.4 Useful phrases

salirse con la suya — to get one's own way
Muy señor mío — Dear Sir
en torno mío — around me
a pesar mío/suyo — in spite of me/him (her/their)

Exercises

1 Rellena los espacios con el adjetivo posesivo más adecuado:

Le dije que recogiera _____ (1) ropa que estaba toda por el suelo, y también que no estaba dispuesta a compartir _____ (2) piso con una persona tan desordenada como ella. Además cada vez que venían _____ (3) amigas dejaban _____ (4) CDs fuera de las fundas todos mezclados. En fin que Clara se ha convertido en _____ (5) pesadilla particular. Si tú la tuvieras en _____ (6) casa seguro que la habrías echado a la calle hace tiempo.

2 Coloca el adjetivo o pronombre posesivo más adecuado:

Ejemplo: Mi inglés es bueno, pero _____ es mejor. (tú)
Mi inglés es bueno, pero el tuyo es mejor.

a Tu trabajo es interesante; (_____) es aburrido. (yo)

b Aquel amigo (_____) no conoce Madrid. (tú)

c Mi hija sabe de cine más que (_____) mujer. (yo)

d Mariluz, si no tienes bastante leche, coge de (_____). (nosotros)

e Amigos, (_____) cena está preparada. (nosotros)

f Javier, tienes que saber que mis amigos son menos tolerantes que (_____) (tú)

g Tus ideas y (_____) no se parecen nada. (yo)

h Cariño, lo que es mío es también (_____). (tu)

i Este tío (_____) nunca se pone de acuerdo con nadie. (vosotros)

j Déjeme (_____) dirección. (usted)

10

Relative clauses

Remember:

- Relative pronouns refer back to an antecedent.
- Relatives introduce subordinate clauses.
- The relative pronoun is *never omitted* in Spanish, as it is in English.
- When a relative pronoun is used with a preposition in Spanish, the preposition always *precedes* it.
- Always place the relative as close as possible to its antecedent.

In addition to the relative pronouns introduced in Part I, there are two further important relatives, the pronoun, **el cual** and the adjective, **cuyo.**

el cual, la cual, los cuales, las cuales, lo cual	whom, which, that
cuyo, cuya, cuyos, cuyas	whose

10.1 El cual, la cual, los cuales, las cuales

This pronoun has the same meaning as **el que**, **la que**, etc., and is used mainly after prepositions. This relative is used principally in more formal contexts, and is rarely spoken:

Su madre posee joyas por las cuales se pagaría una fortuna.

His mother owns jewellery for which you'd pay a fortune.

Hay una teoría según la cual la producción de comida será insuficiente dentro de unos años.

There's a theory according to which food production will be insufficient within a few years.

La catedral de Valencia, delante de la cual tiene lugar 'El tribunal de las aguas', contiene una gran mezcla de estilos artísticos.

Valencia Cathedral, in front of which the 'Water Tribunal' takes place, contains a rich mixture of artistic styles.

10.2 Cuyo

Cuyo (whose) agrees in number and gender with the following noun and can refer to either persons or things:

El médico, **cuyo** nombre no recordaba, me saludó calurosamente.

The doctor, whose name I did not remember, greeted me warmly.

Todos los estudiantes cuya gramática necesite un repaso, tendrán una clase extra los viernes.

All those students whose grammar needs revision will have extra tuition on Fridays.

La fábrica, **cuyos** obreros se habían puesto en huelga, estaba cerrada.

The factory, whose workers had gone on strike, was closed.

10.3 Restrictive and non-restrictive clauses

It is sometimes useful to distinguish between two types of relative clause.

Compare these two sentences:

a   Mi primo que trabaja en Zaragoza   My cousin who works in Zaragoza is
    vuelve mañana.   returning tomorrow.

b   Mi primo, quien trabaja en Zaragoza,   My cousin, who works in Zaragoza, is
    vuelve mañana.   returning tomorrow.

In all the information given is essential to the meaning of the sentence. Subordinate clauses of type **a** are called 'restrictive', because they restrict or limit the noun. In sentence **b** the information given is additional, as a kind of aside, and is not essential to the meaning: the commas at the beginning and end of the clause act like brackets. Subordinate clauses of type **b** are called 'non-restrictive', because they do not define the noun that comes before, but give you extra information about it. In this type of clause *there is usually a comma before the relative pronoun.*

There is a particular area where the distinction between restrictive and non-restrictive pronouns is useful: **Quien**, **el que** and **el cual** cannot be used as a subject or object pronoun in restrictive clauses. In the example **Mi primo que trabaja en Zaragoza vuelve mañana** the only relative pronoun that can be used is **que**.

10.4 Special construction with 'to be' plus a relative

'He who', 'she who', 'the ones who/which', etc., are normally translated by **el que, la que, los que, las que**. For people **quien(es)** can also be used. There is a special construction in Spanish involving the use of the relative after **ser**, to translate ideas such as:

'They were the ones that ...'

'It is you who ...

In this construction the personal pronoun is often included because there is a special emphasis on the subject of the sentence:

Eres tú **el que** va a llevar la bandera.   You are the one who must carry the flag.
Estas personas son **las que** vimos en la corrida. Those are the people we saw at the bullfight.
Soy yo **quien** es el responsable.   I am the person who is responsible.
Fue él **quien** trajo el DVD.   He was the one who brought the DVD.
Son estos zapatos **los que** costaron un dineral.   Those are the shoes that cost a lot.

Notes

1   When there is a preposition in the first half of the sentence it is usually repeated before the relative:

Era **por eso por lo que** decidimos ir   That was why (i.e. it was for that reason that) we
de vacaciones a Italia.   decided to go to Italy on holiday.
Es a ti a quien he venido a ver.   It's you (whom) I've come to see.

2   **Donde** is often used in this type of construction, when place is indicated:

Cerca del mar **es donde** me gustaría vivir   Near the sea is where I would like to live
si pudiera.   if I could.

3   Note the construction with **entonces cuando** for past time:

Fue **entonces cuando** terminó la guerra.   It was then that the war finished.

4   The expression **hay quien(es)** (there are those who) and **no hay quien** (there is nobody who) are often used in this type of sentence:

Hay quienes creen que el gobierno   There are those who believe that the government
va a reducir los impuestos.   is going to lower taxes.
No hay quien se atreva a decirle nada.   Nobody (i.e. there is nobody who) dares to say
                                                    anything to her.

10.5 Relative pronouns replaced by adverbs

The adverbs **(en) donde** and **cuanto** are often used in place of relatives:

La casa **(en) donde** vivió García Lorca
la han convertido en un museo.
(*en donde* is an alternative for *en la que*)

They've turned the house where García Lorca
used to live into a museum.

Todo **cuanto** leo en los periódicos me
convence que la Unión Europea es
un proyecto muy complicado.
(*todo cuanto* is an alternative for *todo lo que*)

Everything I read in the newspapers convinces
me that the European Union is a very complicated
project.

Exercises

1 Llena los espacios con un relativo adecuado:

a Han reformado el bar en _____ solíamos comer.

b Esa película _____ actriz ganó un Oscar el año pasado, me ha encantado.

c En un lugar de La Mancha, de _____ nombre no quiero acordarme...

d Esa es la tienda en _____ compré mi iPod.

e Es Concha _____ se va a encargar de la comida.

f Es por eso por _____ me da miedo nadar en el mar.

g Aquellos _____ carnets de conducir tengan mas de tres puntos, no podrán seguir con-
duciendo.

h Las mujeres _____ edad sobrepase los 40 años, podrán tener problemas a la hora de
concebir.

i Todo _____ he aprendido en estos años, me ha transformado en otra persona.

j Fue entonces _____ comprendimos que había que apretarse el cinturón.

k Javier ha comprado una casa en _____ hay piscina y jardín.

2 Traduce al español:

a All we know is that they are coming tomorrow.

b There are those who save and there are those who spend.

c That is where we used to live before.

d Ramón, whose mother was a nurse, is now a professor of medicine.

e That's the reason why I asked the question.

f Carmiña is the one who can give you the right information.

g Sofía, whose children go to a private school, is poorer than you think.

h All I can say is that I'll try to help you.

i Raimundo, who is the chef at the Ritz, is throwing a party.

j I was in Mexico the year that the earthquake happened.

11

Interrogatives and exclamations

Remember:

- Words which introduce questions and exclamations *always* bear an accent.
- Questions are preceded by an inverted question mark and exclamations by an inverted exclamation mark.

11.1 Indirect questions and exclamations

1 Indirect questions and exclamations are used when we want to report on something which has been asked. If the direct question was 'What did you mean?' the indirect question might be ' We asked him what he meant.'

Indirect question words always bear an accent, but, unlike direct questions, they are *not* preceded by an inverted question mark. (This sometimes makes them more difficult to recognise.)

No sé cuántas veces has olvidado el móvil.	I don't know how many times you've forgotten your mobile.
Siempre me he preguntado por qué los españoles cenan tan tarde.	I've always wondered why Spaniards dine so late.
Estaban hablando de cómo podrían salir sin ser vistos.	They were talking about how they could go out without being seen.

2 **Qué** and **lo que**

In indirect questions **lo que** may replace **qué**.

No sé qué/lo que vamos a hacer esta noche.	I don't know what we are going to do tonight.
Pregúntale qué/lo que dijo el técnico.	Ask him what the technician said.
No le hacía falta mi consejo porque sabía qué/lo que hacer.	She didn't need my advice because she knew what to do.

11.2 Más and tan in exclamations

In exclamations beginning with **qué**, it is usual for a following adjective to be preceded by **tan** or **más**.

¡Qué película más aburrida!	What a boring film!
¡Qué señora tan elegante!	What an elegant woman!

11.3 Quién plus the imperfect subjunctive

Exclamatory **quién** followed by the imperfect subjunctive has the meaning 'if only...'

¡Quién supiera la verdad del caso!	If only one/I knew the truth of the matter!
¡Quién pudiera ser joven otra vez!	I wish I could be young again!

Exercises

1 Rellena los espacios con un pronombre interrogativo o exclamativo adecuado:

a No me preguntes _____ me siento, porque hoy lo veo todo muy negro.

b Tu jefe no se da cuenta de _____ horas trabajas.

c Estaban asustados y no sabían _____ hacer.

d ¡ _____ tuviera otra oportunidad!

e No pude explicarme _____ perdimos el partido.

f Dime ¿_____ prefieres, té o café?

g ¡ _____ piso tan grande! ¿_____ os ha costado?

h No sabemos _____ llegamos al aeropuerto.

i ¿Ha considerado _____ servicios le ofrece su banco?

j ¡ _____ nenes tan monos!

2 Traduce al español:

a Do you know where you are going?

b Which singers do you like best?

c Which of the two do you prefer?

d Ask the man how to get to the main square.

e What a great party!

f What is the magazine you are reading?

g Whose wallet is that on the table?

h We don't know what they are doing.

i What is the use of talking to you if you don't listen to me?

j Who did you give the camera to?

12
Indefinites

Remember:

● Adjectives and pronouns are indefinite when they do not refer to a particular person or thing.

● In Spanish words like **alguno, alguien, cualquier, otro** and **todo** are indefinites.

12.1 Alguno

Note the following two special uses of **alguno/a**:

1 In a negative sentence, when **alguno** is placed after the noun it means 'no', 'not a' (having the same meaning as **ninguno**):

Aquel libro no tiene interés alguno.   That book is of no interest (at all).
No tenemos conocimiento alguno de matemáticas.   We have no knowledge of mathematics at all.

2 **Alguno/a que otro/a**

The phrase **alguno/a que otro/a** means 'the occasional', 'a few':

Juan es el único que la hace reír,   Juan is the only one who can
y hasta decir   make her laugh, and
algún que otro chiste.   even get her to tell a joke or two.

12.2 Cualquiera used pejoratively

Cualquiera is usually shortened to **cualquier** and placed before the noun, but it can also follow it, in which case it is not shortened and the meaning can be more pejorative, e.g. 'any old'. In some cases it is used as a pronoun with a clear pejorative meaning.

Aquel problema lo puede resolver un hombre   That problem can be solved by any one at all.
cualquiera.
Ese tipo es un cualquiera.   That guy is a so and so.

12.3 Word order with otro (see Part I, 40.1)

12.4 Todo(s) cuanto(s)

In written Spanish 'all who/that/which' is frequently conveyed by **todos/as cuantos/as**, or simply **cuantos/as**. The neuter form is **todo cuanto** (or **cuanto**):

Todos cuantos fueron al parque   All (those) who went to the park
lo pasaron bien.   enjoyed themselves.

La vieja dio (todo) cuanto tenía a un refugio para gatos.		The old woman gave everything she had to a cat refuge.	

12.5 Useful phrases

así y todo	even so	**en parte alguna**	nowhere
de todos modos	in any case	**en todas partes**	everywhere
en cualquier caso	in any case	**en todo momento**	all the time
en modo alguno	not at all	**todo el mundo**	everybody

Exercises

1 Rellena los espacios con un indefinido adecuado:

a Iban al mismo bar _____ los lunes.

b La canción se repetía monótonamente, una y _____ vez.

c _____ mis parientes viven en el barrio de Gràcia salvo mi tío Paco, que vive en _____ barrio.

d Su casa está enfrente, al _____ lado de la calle Silvela.

e El chico se comportó muy mal pero, así y _____, no le castigaron.

f Se conocieron _____ tiempo atrás.

g Tengo mucho calor. Quisiera beber _____ frío, por favor.

h _____ de estos documentos no valen nada.

i _____ libro que investigue la historia de España me interesa.

j Muchos restaurantes se cierran _____ el mes de agosto.

2 Traduce al español:

a He could arrive at any moment.

b He has another sister.

c The decision was approved by all those present at the meeting.

d A few people were there before eight o'clock; three others arrived later.

e The keys were nowhere to be found.

f He has family everywhere, but mostly in Argentina.

g All teachers need their holidays.

13 Verbs

(See Part I page 72)

14 Present tense

Remember:

The present tense is used:

- to describe a state of affairs which exists at the time of speaking
- to describe a habit
- for statements generally held to be true
- for future intention

In addition to the uses listed in Part I, the simple present is also used in the following contexts:

14.1 To convey a past action more vividly

This use is sometimes known as the 'historic present':

El 12 de octubre de 1492 Cristóbal Colón llega a una isla del archipiélago de Las Antillas.	On 12th October 1492, Christopher Columbus arrives at an archipelago in the Caribbean.
No llega a la India como él esperaba, sino al continente americano.	He doesn't reach India as he expected, but the continent of America.
Anoche vuelve a casa a las tres de la madrugada, enciende las luces y pone la música en el salón …	Last night he returned home at three in the morning, turned on the lights and put music on in the lounge …

14.2 To make a link with the past in time expressions

In English we normally use the perfect tense in these expressions (see Part II, 17.2):

Te esperamos desde hace tres horas.	We've been waiting for you for three hours.
Lleva mucho tiempo estudiando música.	He's been studying music for a long time.
Hace diez años que no la veo.	I haven't seen her for ten years.

14.3 As a kind of imperative

Juan, ¿me traes los cigarrillos?	Juan, bring me the cigarettes, will you?
Me haces el favor de escuchar.	Will you please listen to me.
Ve al quinto piso y le dices a doña Rosa que si te puede prestar el periódico de hoy.	Go to the fifth floor and ask Doña Rosa if she can lend you today's paper.

In the above examples we could equally well use the imperatives **tráeme**, **hazme** and **dile**.

14.4 With por poco (almost), translated by a past tense in English

Estaba tan cansada que por poco me duermo.
en clase.
No me baño en el mar porque el año pasado por poco me ahogo.

I was so tired that I almost fell asleep in the lecture.
I don't swim in the sea because last year I almost drowned.

Exercises

1 Pon la forma correcta del verbo en presente:

a Te _____ (yo decir) que vas a conseguir el empleo.

b Clara se _____ (poner) nerviosa siempre que se examina.

c ¡Eso no _____ (tener) nada que ver conmigo!

d No _____ (yo conocer) a tu hijo.

e Me _____ (doler) mucho la cabeza.

f Desde hace ya algun tiempo, las iglesisas se _____ (estar) vaciando.

g Andrés, _____ (tener) que renovar el anti-virus antes de que caduque.

h Todos los años _____ (subir) de precio los combustibles.

i Miguel siempre _____ (contar) chistes divertidos.

j (Ir) (yo) _____ a clase de salsa una vez a la semana.

2 Esta narrativa fue escrita por un periodista que pudiera haberla escrito en tiempo 'histórico'. Escríbela en presente:

La policía llegó al bar a medianoche. Los agentes hablaron con el dueño, quien les explicó cómo mejor coger a los criminales. Entraron por la puerta de atrás e interrumpieron el reparto de armas y objetos robados. Los criminales intentaron huir por todos lados, pero los detuvieron a todos sin que nadie pudiera escapar. Luego fueron a la comisaría y con eso se terminó la redada.

3 Traduce al español:

a I've been waiting here for you for five hours.

b We've been living in Barcelona for 20 years.

c They've had their SEAT Marbella since 1985.

d How long have you been staying in Bilbao?

e It's been a long time since we last saw each other.

f I liked Paris so much that I almost bought a house there.

15 Future tense

Remember:

- The future is used for *predicting or giving information about what is going to happen.*
- There are three ways of expressing the future: (i) the future simple (formed by adding an ending to the infinitive (**hablar + é = hablaré**); (ii) using **ir a** plus the infinitive when declaring a future intention; (iii) using the present tense.

15.1 Supposition, probability, sympathy or disappointment :

Serán las nueve.	It must be around nine o'clock.
No sé cuántos años tiene Lucía pero tendrá unos 20.	I don't know how old Lucía is but she's about 20.
Creo que el bebé será chica.	I believe the baby will be a girl.
– Mi ordenador no funciona.	'My computer is not working.'
– Tendrá un virus.	'It must have a virus.'
– Diego y Patti van a tener un bebé.	'Diego and Patti are going to have a baby.'
– Estarán contentos.	'They must be happy.'
– Me han suspendido las matemáticas.	'I have failed Maths.'
– ¡Estarás orgulloso!	'You must be proud!'

15.2 Haber de

Haber de meaning 'to be to', 'to have to' has a future sense, and can also imply obligation (see Part I, 27.3):

Han de llegar dentro de 20 minutos.	They are (due) to arrive in 20 minutes.
Has de saberlo en seguida.	You have to know immediately.
Antes he de pedir permiso a mi jefe.	I've got to ask my boss first.

15.3 Querer meaning 'will'

The verb **querer**, and not the future, usually expresses the idea of 'will' in English, in the sense of 'willing to':

¿Quieres darme el pan?	Will you pass me the bread?
No quiere ir al cine esta noche.	He won't go to the cinema tonight.

Exercises

1 Rellena los espacios con la forma correcta del futuro de uno de los verbos del recuadro:

tener	traer	ir	poder	salir
hacer	llegar	cerrar	decir	estar

a Ahora no puedo darte la respuesta pero te la _____ mañana.

b El tren lleva retraso. No sé si _____ antes de medianoche.

c Pablo, ¿cuándo _____ tiempo para ayudarme con los deberes?

d Mañana _____ buen tiempo, según el pronóstico.

e Carla y Jaime _____ contentos con su piso nuevo.

f Mis amigos _____ bebidas y comida a la fiesta.

g ¿Cómo _____ a la fiesta? ¿En taxi o en autobús?

h ¿A qué hora _____ los bancos hoy?

i No _____ estar con vosotros antes de las cinco.

j Martín no _____ del hospital hasta Navidades.

2 **Estas frases** se refieren a sucesos que ocurrirán en el futuro. Escribe la frase entera utilizando un futuro:

Ejemplo: La huelga (comenzar) mañana.   *La huelga comenzará mañana.*

a Los Juegos Olímpicos _____ (tener) lugar en Brasil en el 2016.

b La factoría de automóviles _____ (cerrar) en septiembre.

c _____ (Yo aprobar) los exámenes en junio.

d Este verano iremos a un festival de música en Albacete. ¿ _____ (Vosotras poder) venir?

e El rey Juan Carlos _____ (abrir) la nueva sesión de Las Cortes.

f La semana que viene _____ (poner) una película francesa en el cine.

g Los precios _____ (subir) en abril.

h El Presidente del gobierno español _____ (reunirse) en Bruselas con otros dirigentes.

i (Nosotros ir) al teatro esta noche.

j ¿ _____ (tu quedarse) con nosotros?

3 Contesta las preguntas usando el futuro de probabilidad, siguiendo el ejemplo:

Ejemplo: ¿Cuántos años tiene?   *Tendrá 17.*

a ¿Qué hora es en Australia? _____ las 8.30.

b ¿Qué hace Emilio? _____ haciendo los deberes.

c ¿Cuánto cuestan aquellos zapatos? _____ unos 250 euros.

d ¿Dónde está Sara? En esta época del año _____ en Madrid.

e ¿Cuándo llega el correo? _____ alrededor de las 11.

f ¿Cuánto ganan los profesores? No mucho, _____ unos 2000 euros al mes.

16 Conditional tense

Remember:

The conditional is used:

- to express oneself politely
- to describe events which could happen if the conditions are met
- to express the future in the past, in reported speech.

16.1 Uses of the conditional

1 To express a **supposition** or **probability** concerning the past:

En aquella época tendría 80 años por lo menos.
Sería alrededor de la medianoche cuando
Rafa volvió de París.

At that time he must/would have been at least 80.
It must/would have been about midnight when
Rafa returned from Paris.

2 Frequently with modal verbs (see Part I, 27):

Por favor, ¿podrías ayudarme?
Debería haber comido poco porque
estaba delgadísima.

Could you help me, please?
She must have eaten very little because
she was extremely slim.

Exercises

1 Transforma las frases siguientes a pasado:

Ejemplo: Dice que los bancos cerrarán a la una.   *Dijo que los bancos cerrarían a la una.*

a Nos ha asegurado que mañana entregará el trabajo.

b Dicen que no podrán ayudarnos hasta mañana.

c Está claro que aumentará la influencia de la tecnología en la vida diaria.

d La presentadora anuncia que habrá una huelga de controladores de vuelo el día ocho de mayo.

e Estoy seguro de que los clientes estarán encantados.

2 Completa las frases de **a** a **i** con una de las frases de *1* a *9*:

Ejemplo: Si tuviera una casa en la costa, *me bañaría en el mar todos los días.*

a Si fuera rico ....

b .... aunque el jefe intentase impedirlo.

c Si tuviésemos un coche rápido ....

d Si estuvieras en Sevilla ....

e .... aunque me llevaran a la cárcel.

f Si vivieses en Nueva York ....

g Si hicieras un curso de italiano ....

h Aunque me quitaran el pasaporte ....

i Si nadie viniera a clase ....

1 ... aprenderías a bailar sevillanas.

2 ... no trabajaría.

3 ... necesitarías más dinero que aquí.

4 ... volvería a mi país.

5 ... llegaríamos enseguida.

6 Me retiraría ...

7 ... hablarías la lengua mucho mejor.

8 me preocuparía mucho.

9 Protestaría ...

3 Las siguientes frases en imperativo suenan demasiado directas y poco educadas. Mejóralas usando el condicional, eligiendo una de las dos formas dadas en el ejemplo:

Ejemplo: ¡Dame el diccionario!

¿Podrías darme el diccionario?/¿Querrías hacerme el favor de darme el diccionario?

a ¡Pon la mesa!

b No subas la escalera corriendo.

c Esperadme un momento.

d ¡Antes de salir quita tus libros de la mesa!

e Lleva el abrigo a la tintorería.

f Traiga una zarzuela de pescado y un pollo al ajillo.

g ¡No pongas los pies en el sillón!

h Explicad al policía que fue un accidente.

i Coged el mapa por si os perdéis.

j Dile a tu madre que tienes novio.

17

Perfect tense

Remember:

- The perfect tense is used to describe past actions from the point of view of the present.
- The Spanish perfect is used to describe the very recent past, as long as it is relevant to the present.

17.1 Perfect/preterite contrast

The perfect tense, which is used to connect past and present time, contrasts with the preterite tense, which is used for actions which are wholly confined to the past.

Compare:

Le ha tocado la lotería.	He has won the lottery.
Le tocó la lotería en 1993.	He won the lottery in 1993.

Similarly:

¿Has traído los regalos?	Have you brought the presents? (just now)
La semana pasada trajo los regalos.	He brought the presents last week.

17.2 English perfect = Spanish present

The English perfect tense is usually rendered by the Spanish present tense in time expressions containing 'for' and 'since':

Reside en Madrid desde 1990.	He has lived in Madrid since 1990.
Hace mucho tiempo que no le veo (*or* no le he visto).	I haven't seen him for a long time.
Llevan 50 años viviendo en la misma calle.	They've lived in the same street for 50 years.
Estamos esperando aquí desde hace media hora.	We've been waiting here for half an hour.

17.3 Acabar de

Acabar de followed by the infinitive means 'to have just', which is followed by the past participle in English:

Acaba de salir.	She has just gone out.
Acabamos de verle en la calle.	We've just seen him in the street.

17.4 Tener as an auxiliary verb

Tener is occasionally used instead of **haber** as the auxiliary for the perfect tense with transitive verbs, stressing the completion of the verbal action. The past participle agrees with the direct object in number and gender:

Ya tengo hecho mi trabajo.	I've done my work now.
Angela tiene puestas sus intenciones en un trabajo en TVE.	Angela has her mind set on a job in Spanish TV.
¿Lo tienes todo preparado?	Have you got it all ready?

Exercises

1 Elige la forma del verbo que convenga en cada frase, el pretérito perfecto o el pretérito indefinido:

a Anoche Carlos _____ (llegar) con su amiga.

b ¿Ya _____ (anunciar) las bases del concurso?

c El año pasado _____ (yo viajar) a Córdoba para ver la Mezquita.

d No sé dónde está Alfredo. Creo que _____ (marcharse) a Madrid a buscar trabajo.

e Últimamente _____ (yo leer) muchos libros.

f Esta mañana Pablo _____ (levantarse) temprano para ir de acampada.

g Hoy hace un año que _____ (nosotros casarse), Andrea.

h Todavía no _____ (yo poder) terminar el projecto.

i Ayer a la una _____ (anunciarse) el nuevo decreto de extranjería.

j Esta mañana _____ (tener) que llamar a un fontanero con urgencia.

k ¿(tu) _____ (ver) a Juan? –Si, anteayer _____ (yo encontrarse) con él en la calle.

l Ya _____ (estrenarse) la nueva película de Almodóvar.

m En 1898 España _____ (perder) su última colonia, Cuba.

n Todavía no _____ (ellos abrir) el teatro, a causa del incendio.

o Este verano _____ (hacer) muchísimo calor.

2 Llena los espacios con un verbo del recuadro en préterito perfecto:

trabajar	decir	poner	conocer	abrir
resolver	ver	escribir	quedar	llover

a ¿Por qué te _____ este vestido? No te sienta bien.

b Esta mañana _____ mucho y todavía hace mal tiempo.

c En toda mi vida (yo) no _____ un cuadro tan maravilloso.

d ¡Qué bonita _____ la cocina después de la reforma!

e Todavía no _____ el nuevo polideportivo.

f Nunca _____ yo a un hombre tan tacaño.

g El Gobierno ya _____ el problema de los inmigrantes ilegales.

h Tomás, ¿le _____ al jefe que te marchas mañana?

i Van a terminar las obras pronto porque los obreros _____ muchísimo.

j Alicia no _____ el informe, así que va a tener que trabajar toda la noche.

3 Rellena los espacios con la forma correcta del pretérito perfecto:

No sé por qué Xavier _____ (enfadarse) (1) tanto. Le _____ (decir) (2) que tenía que terminar el ensayo y no _____ (poder) (3) hacerlo porque aún no me _____ (devolver) (4) el libro que necesito. Me _____ (decir) (5) por teléfono que no _____ (conocer) (6) nunca a una persona tan pesada como yo. Claro, yo también me _____ (enfadar) (7) con él. Es una pena porque siempre _____ (ser) (8) muy buenos amigos y lo _____ (pasar) (9) muy bien juntos. No sé cómo _____ (poder) (10) decirme eso. _____ (tener) (11) mi libro más de un año y yo ni siquiera se lo _____ (recordar) (12) hasta que me _____ (hacer) (13) falta a mí. ¡Qué le vamos a hacer! ¡ Son cosas de la vida!

4 Traduce al español:

a I've been going to the gym regularly.

b We've been waiting for your father since two o'clock.

c The postman has rung twice.

d This year we have been to two gigs and a music festival.

e The boss has been working on the project since yesterday.

f They've just bought a new car.

g My friends haven't seen the film yet.

h How many years have you been playing the drums?

i How long is it since you last ate?

j How many times have I told you not to come back after midnight?

18
Preterite tense

Remember:

The preterite tense is used:

- for actions in the past
- to recount a completed action
- to narrate a sequence of single events: this happened, then that, then that, etc.
- for completed actions which took place over a long period.

18.1 Irregular forms

A large number of verbs contain changes in spelling in the preterite. The most common of these verbs are:

1   Certain **-ir** verbs, such as **pedir** and **dormir**, which change their stem from **e** to **i** or **o** to **u** in the third persons singular and plural: **pedí/pidió/pidieron** (I/(s)he/they asked); **dormí/durmió/durmieron** (I/(s) he/they slept).

2   Certain **-er** and **-ir** verbs, such as **leer** and **caer** and **destruir**, which insert **y** rather than **i** in the third persons of the preterite: **leí/leyó/leyeron** (I/(s)he/they read); **caí/cayó/cayeron** (I/(s)he/they fell); **destruí, destruyó, destruyeron** (I/(s)he/they destroyed):

3   Verbs which change the end of the first person singular of the preterite *only*:

      c > qu buscar: **busqué**, buscaste, etc. (I/you looked for)

      g > gu llegar: **llegué**, llegaste, etc. (I/you arrived)

      z > c   empezar: **empecé**, empezaste, etc. (I/you began)

(See Part I, 26.2.)

18.2 Saber, conocer and querer in the preterite

Some important verbs undergo a change of meaning when they are used in the preterite.
Saber has the meaning of 'to learn', 'to hear about':

Cuando supe la noticia fui a ver a mi madre en seguida.	When I learned the news I went to see my mother at once.

Conocer has the meaning 'to meet (for the first time)':

Se conocieron en París en 1937.	They met in Paris in 1937.

Querer, in the negative, means 'to refuse to':

Intenté convencerle para que escribiera un artículo en mi revista pero no quiso.	I tried to persuade him to write an article for my magazine but he refused.

(No quería in the previous example would have meant that there was still a possibility for agreement. The preterite expresses a final decision.)

Exercises

1 Contesta las preguntas usando el verbo que se emplea en la pregunta:

a ¿Cuántos años hace que terminasteis vuestros estudios?

b ¿Cuándo dijo que iríamos a cenar juntos?

c ¿Cuánto dinero te costó tu iPod?

d ¿Qué le dijiste a María que está tan triste?

e ¿Cómo se entrenaron para el triathlon?

2 Llena los espacios con verbos adecuados del recuadro:

darse cuenta	ir	poner	levantarse	hacerse	volver	pasar
quedarse	aparecer	empezar	bajar	verse	saludar	

_____ (1) (el) la camisa y por un momento _____ (2) la pistola, luego _____ (3) la camisa y la pistola _____ (4) a esconderse. Alguien _____ (5) con la mano desde la carretera. Cien pájaros _____ (6) a dar vueltas alrededor de un poste de luz hasta que _____ (7) de noche y ya no _____ (8) nada.
_____ (9) las luces largas y (ellos) _____ (10) de que más adelante tampoco se veía nada. (ellos) _____ (11) por delante de un coche de policía. Ellos _____ (12) deprisa, los policías _____ (13) quietos.

Soure: Ray Loriga: *La pistola de mi hermano*; Plaza & Janés; 2000; p. 87

3 Elige una excusa o razón de la lista B para las situaciones de la lista A, colocando el verbo en infinitivo en la forma correcta del indefinido:

Lista A

a Lo siento mucho pero he llegado tarde porque …

b Señorita, no he hecho los deberes porque …

c No sabes cuánto lo siento pero no te puedo devolver tu libro porque …

d Tengo que llamar al fontanero porque anoche …

e Tiene resaca porque ayer …

f No te puedo prestar mi coche porque …

g Te he comprado rosas porque …

h Camarero, …

i Siento tener que decírtelo pero ayer …

j Hemos de informarles que la semana pasada …

Lista B

k hace tres días me _____ (robar) todo lo que tenía en casa.

l _____ (haber) un golpe de estado en Moldavia.

m el tren _____ (retrasarse) más de una hora.

n _____ (estropearse) hace más de un mes.

o le _____ (pedir) gambas, y me _____ (traer) un filete.

p me _____ (decir) que te gustan.

q _____ (ver) a tu novia con otro chico.

r _____ (inundarse) el cuarto de baño.

s _____ (salir) de fiesta con sus amigotes.

t _____ (ponerme) enfermo.

4 Traduce al español:

a Last week I went with my friends to see Almodóvar's film *All about my Mother.*

b What did your friends say about the film? Did they like it?

c She met him in Gerona.

d They tried and tried to find out who killed her, but they never did.

e I arrived at the office at 3 p.m. and began working straight away.

f When I learned that he had come back I contacted my lawyer at once.

g Last night Clara and Emilia brought some photos of their holiday in Morocco.

h The police arrested two terrorists on the border.

i How did you cope when your car was stolen?

j The news of her accident shocked me. I could not believe it.

19 Imperfect tense

Remember:

The imperfect tense is used in four ways:

- for past actions, when the beginning and the end of the action are not clearly defined
- to indicate habits or repeated events in the past
- for descriptions in the past
- to say what was happening when a particular event occurred.

Note: The imperfect is often equivalent to the English 'was ... ing', 'used to (+ infinitive)' or 'would (+ infinitive)'.

19.1 Uses of the imperfect tense

1 The imperfect is employed in time expressions, where in English a pluperfect tense would be used:

Esperábamos muy ilusionados la publicación de su siguiente novela.	We had been waiting excitedly for the publication of her next novel.
Hacía mucho tiempo que sabía que esa pareja terminaría bien.	I had known for a long time that those two would end up OK.

2 The imperfect sometimes replaces the present tense to express a polite request:

¿Se dirigía Vd a mí?	Are/Were you talking to me?
¿Esperaba Vd. un taxi, señorita?	Are/Were you waiting for a taxi, Miss?

3 In journalism the imperfect is sometimes used instead of the preterite to recount dramatic events:

A mediados de noviembre se descubría la conspiración.	The conspiracy was discovered in the middle of November.
En medio de un gran bullicio popular se declaraba la Segunda República.	The Second Republic was declared amidst great popular excitement.
En el último minuto el Deportivo de La Coruña marcaba el gol definitivo.	In the last minute Deportivo La Coruña scored the deciding goal.

4 The imperfect sometimes replaces the conditional in speech:

Cris dijo que ya no limpiaba más la casa.	Cris said that she wouldn't clean the house any more.
Le dije a la pandilla que yo me ocupaba de encontrar un grupo de música para la fiesta.	I said to the group that I would see to finding a band for the party.

Exercises

1 Completa las frases, usando el imperfecto:

a Ayer fui al médico porque …

b Hace un momento el camarero …

c Cuando entramos en la sala de estar …

d Siempre me gustaba hablar con Pepe porque …

e Después de cenar siempre …

f Ahora viajo en autobús pero antes …

g Cuando estábamos de vacaciones en Argentina …

h Entrábamos en casa del abuelo por una puerta pequeña que …

i No salían porque …

j Cuando mis colegas estaban en Colombia …

2 Después de un viaje se puede describir lo que se ha visto usando el presente o el pasado. Cambia la siguiente descripción de un viaje a Lanzarote, sustituyendo los tiempos en presente por pretérito imperfecto:

> La isla *es* preciosa y como *es* tan pequeña se *puede* recorrer en un día. *Parece* imposible que una tierra tan seca *pueda* ser hermosa pero lo es. Los volcanes *producen* una impresión de sorpresa porque *dan* la tierra colores rosas y violetas que no se *encuentran* en otras partes. En realidad lo que más me *impresiona* es el esmero que la gente *pone* para cuidar la isla. Las construcciones *están* en armonía con el paisaje y todo *está* limpísimo. Además *están* las construcciones de César Manrique. *Hay* móviles en las carreteras y un auditorio dentro de una cueva. La casa del artista *recoge* el espíritu del arte moderno pero *está* construida dentro de la roca y *utiliza* la luz y los materiales de una forma tan cuidada que *parece* estar hecha por la naturaleza. Una de las cosas que más me *gusta* de la isla *es* ver lo mucho que la gente joven *disfruta* con todo. Seguro que después de ver las obras artísticas de Lanzarote ya no *piensan* que los museos *son* aburridos.

3 Imagina que pasaste un mes en Salamanca como estudiante. Escribe un párrafo de 100 palabras contando lo que hacías cada día. Utiliza por lo menos diez verbos en imperfecto. Puedes comenzar así: *Todos los días me despertaba a eso de las 7.30 y desayunaba en el comedor de la casa en que me alojaba* …

4 Traduce al español:

a When I was in Spain I liked going to tapas bars before the evening meal.

b She had known what was going to happen for a long time.

c We played cards while we were waiting for the match to start.

d When autumn came we would often walk in the wood.

e While we were chatting in the sitting room my mother was working on the computer.

f I was so tired that I had to go to bed early.

g We didn't feel like going out even though the sun was shining.

h He never played the piano when he was young.

i Paco, what were you doing when I saw you yesterday?

j Angela used to swim in the sea every day.

The preterite and imperfect tenses contrasted

Remember:

- The **preterite** is used to recount completed actions in the past, whether single actions or in a sequence. The action is completely finished, the beginning and ending of the time period being clearly defined.

- The **imperfect** is used when the beginning and the end of the action are not clearly defined, for description and for habits or repeated events in the past.

- These two past tenses are frequently contrasted in the same sentence, to describe something in the 'background' (imperfect) as opposed to specific events (preterite).

There follow two versions of the same story about a young man, Carlos, who took up parachuting in order to impress a girl. The short version uses only preterite tenses, sticking to the sequence of facts.

> El sábado pasado Carlos **pensó** en hacer algo diferente. **Se enteró** del interés de Lucía en el paracaidismo y **decidió** tirarse él mismo. **Subió** al avión y **se tiró**. Al principio no tuvo mucha suerte porque no **se** le **abrió** el paracaídas pero todo **terminó** bien al final porque el segundo paracaídas **se abrió** a tiempo y **aterrizó** sano y salvo. Lucía **corrió** hacia él y Carlos **se dio cuenta de** que el salto **valió** la pena.

In this first version you can see that the actions happened *one after the other, each one at a specific moment in time.*

Carlos pensó en hacer algo.

Decidió tirarse en paracaídas.

Cuando se tiró no tuvo suerte porque el paracaídas no se abrió.

Por fin el segundo paracaídas se abrió y todo salió bien.

Carlos, que estaba enamoradísimo de Lucía,

pensó en hacer algo para impresionarla.

Como sabía que a Lucía le gustaban los paracaidistas.

decidió tirarse aunque tenía mucho miedo.

Cuando se tiró no tuvo suerte porque el paracaídas no se abrió.

El Pobre Carlos Pensaba en su familia, en lo mucho que quería a su Perro Tobi.

Por fin, el segundo paracaídas se abrió y todo salió bien.

Mientras Lucía le felicitaba Carlos pensó que el salto valió la pena.

The longer version gives us much more than the concrete facts. We are told the background to the story so that we may have a better understanding of what really went on. For this context we need to use imperfect tenses.

El sábado pasado Carlos, **un estudiante que estaba enamoradísimo de Lucía, que era una chica muy maja**, pensó en hacer algo diferente para impresionarla. Cuando se enteró de que a **Lucía le gustaba mucho el paracaidismo**, decidió tirarse él mismo para demostrarle **que era un hombre valiente y decidido**.

El sábado Carlos subió al avión **del que se iba a tirar. Tenía bastante miedo. Una vez en el aire la tierra estaba lejísimos y sus ganas de demostrar su valentía empezaban a desaparecer.** Se tiró. Al principio no tuvo mucha suerte porque no se le abrió el paracaídas. ¡Imaginaos el susto tan tremendo! **El pobre Carlos rezaba, se acordaba de la comida tan estupenda que hacía su madre, de lo mucho que quería a su perro Tobi y lo mucho que lo echaba de menos ... curiosamente de Lucía no se acordaba para nada.**

Pero todo terminó bien. **Ya cuando estaba a punto de estrellarse contra el suelo** el segundo paracaídas se abrió milagrosamente y Carlos aterrizó sano y salvo. Lucía, **que estaba asustadísima**, corrió hacia él y Carlos se dio cuenta de que el salto valió la pena.

In the second version the imperfect tense is used for information describing **feelings, qualities** or **situations** which go beyond the strict facts of the parachute jump, such as Carlos's passion for Lucía, his desire to be brave, and his love for his dog. In some cases the two tenses are contrasted in the same sentence: the preterite recounts the action while the imperfect tense gives the background, as when Carlos decided (**decidió**), at one particular moment in the past, to jump in order to show that he was (**era**) brave and resolute, as a person.

Exercises

1   Los dos textos a continuación podrían admitir los dos tiempos, el indefinido y el imperfecto. Escoge cuál de los dos tiempos es más adecuado para cada texto. Razona tu respuesta y por último rellena los espacios en blanco con el verbo que corresponda:

Una guerra en el olvido

Texto A

España recuerda a menudo los hechos que _____ (1) (desencadenar) tres años de guerra civil y cuarenta de dictadura militar. El 18 de julio de 1936 un grupo de oficiales _____ (2) (sublevarse) y _____ (3) (pronunciarse) contra el régimen democrático de la Segunda República. La situación social en España _____ (4) (ser) muy conflictiva. En pocos días, el país _____ (5) (quedar) dividido, militar, geográfica y políticamente. El lado nacional _____ (6) (enfrentarse) al republicano. _____ (7) (ser) la primera guerra moderna con bombardeos aéreos y propaganda. Un millón de personas _____ (8) (morir) en este período de tiempo. El país _____ (9) (quedar) en la ruina y _____ (10) (empezar) una dictadura que _____ (11) (durar) cuarenta años.

Texto B

Mi abuela a veces me cuenta lo mal que lo _____ (1) (pasar) durante la guerra. Dice que la gente no _____ (2) (tener) comida y casi todos _____ (3) (tener) un familiar en el frente lo que les _____ (4) (preocupar) mucho. Mi abuela _____ (5) (vivir) entonces en Madrid que _____ (6) (ser) bombardeado por los nacionales. Las sirenas _____ (7) (sonar) de día y de noche y todos _____ (8) (ir) corriendo a los refugios. Yo creo que aunque la mayoría de los españoles _____ (9) (sufrir) mucho entonces, los jóvenes ahora parece que prefieren olvidar aquella tragedia.

2   Escribe un cuento, bien uno que te guste o uno de tu invención, contrastando el pretérito indefinido y el imperfecto. No te olvides de empezar con la frase 'Érase una vez ...'.

3   **Llena los espacios en blanco utilizando el indefinido o el imperfecto de los verbos entre paréntesis:**

Tres artistas españoles

Durante el siglo XX _____ (1) (haber) tres artistas en España cuyo trabajo se ha identificado con tres lugares diferentes.

Antoni Gaudí _____ (2) (nacer) en Reús en 1852 y _____ (3) (dedicar) su vida a la arquitectura. Durante finales del siglo XIX, Cataluña _____ (4) (pasar) por un período de expansión. Las clases burguesas acomodadas _____ (5) (estar) interesadas en invertir parte de su riqueza en el embellecimiento de su ciudad y Gaudí _____ (6) (decidir) colaborar con este sentimiento. Ayudado por ricos mecenas catalanes como la familia Güell, _____ (7) (construir) edificios originales y hermosos que _____ (8) (inspirarse) en el paisaje y la historia de la ciudad. Gaudí no _____ (9) (poder) terminar su última obra, el templo de la Sagrada Familia, pero lo que nos _____ (10) (dejar) nos habla de un hombre que _____ (11) (tener) una gran fe religiosa, que _____ (12) (querer) hacer una construcción capaz de reflejar su amor a su ciudad y su respeto por la religión.

Federico García Lorca _____ (13) (ser) un poeta y dramaturgo que _____ (14) (nacer) en Granada a principios del siglo XX. Sus obras _____ (15) (inspirarse) en los habitantes de su ciudad, gitanos y campesinos, en su belleza, en sus tragedias y en su pasión. En 'Poema del Cante Jondo', Lorca _____ (16) (describir) lo que generalmente se llama 'el duende' algo así como el alma gitana que el _____ (17) (conocer) de observar a los habitantes de barrios como 'El Albaicín' o 'El Sacromonte' de Granada. Cuando _____ (18) (declararse) la Guerra Civil, Lorca no _____ (19) (querer) salir del país como le _____ (20) (aconsejar) sus amigos y _____ (21) (regresar) a Granada desde Madrid. Esto _____ (22) (resultar) en el arresto y la muerte del poeta a manos de un grupo de nacionales. Este hecho _____ (23) (condenarse) internacionalmente, pero no _____ (24) (cambiar) el hecho de que García Lorca haya quedado unido a Granada para siempre.

El tercero es un artista menos conocido. Se trata de César Manrique, un pintor y arquitecto que _____ (25) (nacer) en Lanzarote. Manrique _____ (26) (vivir) en Madrid y en Nueva York pero a la edad de 54 años _____ (27) (decidir) volver a su isla y trabajar en ella. Manrique _____ (28) (pensar) que Lanzarote, una isla volcánica, seca y pobre, _____ (29) (tener) una belleza singular y _____ (30) (pensar) en descubrir esa belleza a los demás. Él _____ (31) (creer) que si pudiera hacer que la gente viera Lanzarote con sus ojos, verían esa belleza también. Los resultados de esa teoría _____ (32) (ser) sorprendentes: la vegetación de un clima árido, y las rocas negras en lucha constante con un océano bravío _____ (33) (dar) como resultado unos visitantes respetuosos y una isla singular, todo ello gracias a la obra de César Manrique.

4   Traduce al español:

a A friend of my sister's, whom I did not know, came in and began to talk in a loud voice.

b He told me that every summer the people held a fiesta in their village.

c It was then that I realised that the car was travelling too fast.

d When we learned that our teacher was sick we sent her a bunch of roses.

e It was about to strike 12 when she remembered something important and got up.

f When he met my mother he was working as a waiter, a job that he took very seriously.

g There was a time when they would dance the tango every day.

h When I came back from Peru I discovered that nobody knew anything about the crisis.

i It was a summer night. In the square the band struck up and the celebrations began.

j My return home from school was always the same: I would forget my homework and my clothes would be dirty from fighting with the other boys. My mother used to laugh but my father would always tell me off.

5   Traduce al español el siguiente texto poniendo especial cuidado en la traducción de los verbos:

Achievements – and consequences – of GAL

What did the democratic politicians who, actively or passively, approved of GAL, hope to achieve from its operations? Did they achieve their goals, and, if so, what was the cost to Spanish democracy? I think we can say that the goals of the dirty war were threefold: keeping the military and police onside with democracy; hitting ETA hard; and, above all, pressuring France to crack down on the terrorists in their 'French sanctuary'.

We have seen that the Socialists were under immense pressure from the security forces to take a harder line against ETA. Andrés Cassinello, a senior general whose cynicism about democracy was notorious, said that GAL was 'an imaginative campaign, successfully conducted'. We can take it that his views were widely shared among his comrades-in-arms, and that the widespread tacit assumption that the dirty war had government approval did provide a kind of safety valve for the angry frustrations of the military and police. It is a sad reflection, however, on the leadership of a great democratic party like PSOE, that it preferred to appease the Francoists within the security forces, rather than to purge them.

Source; Paddy Woodworth, 'The war against terrorism: the Spanish experience from ETA to al-Qaeda' *International Journal of Iberian Studies* 17.3.

21 Compound tenses

Remember:

In compound perfect tenses:

- there is always an auxiliary verb, **haber**, plus the past participle
- the past participle is *invariable*
- **haber** should *never* be split from the past participle.

21.1 Past anterior

This tense has the same meaning as the pluperfect tense and its use in modern Spanish is almost exclusively literary. It is used only in time clauses, after conjunctions such as **después de que, cuando, apenas and en cuanto** to indicate an event which occurred before another past event. The verb in the main clause must be in the preterite.

The past anterior is formed from the preterite tense of **haber** and the past participle:

hube
hubiste
hubo $\Big\}$ hablado/comido/vivido
hubimos
hubisteis
hubieron

Apenas hube visto su cara en la televisión, recordé nuestro encuentro en Mallorca.

No sooner had I seen his face on the television than I remembered our meeting in Mallorca.

Note that the preterite tense often replaces the past anterior. The above example would then become:

En cuanto vi su cara en la televisión …

21.2 Pluperfect replaced by imperfect subjunctive

In literary Spanish, the **-ra** form of the imperfect subjunctive occasionally replaces the pluperfect tense:

No le gustó el regalo que le diera (i.e. había dado).   She did not like the present I had given her.

21.3 Supposition or probability

The future perfect and conditional perfect tenses are used for *supposition* or *probability* (see also the future and conditional tenses, Part II, 15.1 and 16.1):

Seguro que para ahora ya se habrá enterado.   Most probably she will have heard by now.
Si fuera verdad ya me habría enterado.   If it was true, I should have known already.

21.4 If-clauses

Note that the compound tenses are frequently used in one type of conditional sentence (see If-clauses, Part I, 24.3), according to the pattern *pluperfect subjunctive* (**si**-clause) *conditional perfect* (main clause):

Si hubiera sido rico me habría comprado   If I had been rich I would have bought
una casa en el centro de Barcelona.   a house in the centre of Barcelona.

Exercises

1   Construye frases según el ejemplo:

Ejemplo: Yo ir a la agencia/vender todas las entradas para el concierto

Cuando fui a la agencia habían vendido todas las entradas para el concierto.

a Nosotros llegar a Honduras/la huelga de pilotos terminar.

b El general Franco morir/después de estar en el poder 36 años.

c Yo empezar a fumar/el Gobierno aún no prohibir la publicidad del tabaco.

d Lola empezar en este colegio/ no hacerse ningún tatuaje.

e Yo entrar en casa/mis hermanos ya poner la mesa.

2   Inventa una frase usando el futuro perfecto de probabilidad, según el ejemplo.

Ejemplo: Ana no está. *Habrá decidido no ir al cine con nosotros.*

a Mis vecinos han puesto placas solares.

b Jorge se ha levantado temprano.

c Clara está cansadísima.

d El abuelo se ha comprado un coche eléctrico.

e No contestan el teléfono.

3   Traduce al español:

a They'll have answered your job application by now.

b If you had gone to the match you'd have seen Laura.

c What would your boss have said if he had known?

d When she had washed her hair she turned on the television.

e Don't worry! He'll have forgotten about the appointment.

f As soon as they had sat down the waiter brought the menu.

g She had been waiting for Broadband to arrive in her town and eventually it did.

22 The subjunctive

Remember:

- The subjunctive is a mood, not a tense
- It is associated with actions that are, in the mind of the speaker, (im)possible, desirable, unreal, uncertain or necessary
- It is used after time conjunctions (such as **cuando**) with a future sense
- It is obligatory after some conjunctions, e.g. **como si** and **para que**
- There are four tenses of the subjunctive: present, perfect, imperfect and pluperfect

Part II aims to build on the explanations of the use of the subjunctive given in Part I in order to consolidate the understanding of this mood and to extend the range of contexts in which it is used. The lists of verbs and expressions given below are not exhaustive. They have been chosen because of the frequency of their use.

22.1 The subjunctive in que clauses

1 *Doubt, uncertainty, possibility, probability*

Where there is a notion of *doubt* or *uncertainty* in the main clause this indicates that a subjunctive will follow. There is a very wide range of verbs and phrases which imply *possibility, probability* and *doubt,* among them the following:

dudar	to doubt
es dudoso que	it is doubtful that
es (im)posible que	it is (im)possible that
es probable que	it is probable that
existe la posibilidad/probabilidad de que	it is possible/probable that
lo más probable es que	the most likely thing is that
parece poco probable que	it seems unlikely that
puede (ser) que	it may be that

Dudo que consiga el empleo si no se prepara bien.	I doubt that he'll get the job if he doesn't prepare himself properly.
Puede que vayamos al concierto mañana.	Maybe we'll go to the concert tomorrow.

Note: parece que (it seems that), although it might imply doubt, is normally followed by the indicative:

Parece que los Pérez van a mudarse de casa.	It seems that the Perez family are going to move house.

2

Emotional attitude

There are many verbs and expressions used with the subjunctive *which imply an emotional attitude*. They include:

alegrarse de que	to be pleased that
a mí me es igual/me da igual que	it's all the same to me that
desear	to want, wish
es bueno que	it's good that
esperar	to hope
es una pena que	it's a shame that
estoy harto de que	I'm fed up with the fact that
me extraña que	it surprises me that
me gusta/encanta que	I'm pleased that
me molesta que	I'm annoyed that
qué lástima que	what a pity that
querer	to want, wish
temer	to fear
tener miedo de que	to be afraid that

A María le encanta que sus hijos vayan a estudiar a Salamanca.	Maria is delighted that her children are going to study in Salamanca.
Teníamos miedo de que en aquella casa de campo hubiera ratones.	We were afraid that that country house had mice.
Con el frío que hace no me extraña que haya comenzado a nevar.	It's so cold that I'm not surprised it's started snowing.
No es bueno que los jóvenes beban tanto.	It's not a good thing for young people to drink so much.
¡Qué lástima que no vengas conmigo de vacaciones!	What a pity you are not coming on holiday with me!
Tiene miedo de que la situación económica empeore.	He's afraid the economic situation will get worse.
Nos extraña que no se haya puesto en contacto con nosotros.	We are surprised that she hasn't got in touch with us.
Estoy harta de que me hagan trabajar tanto.	I'm fed up that they make me work so hard.

Influence, requests, necessity

The subjunctive normally follows verbs and expressions:

- which imply the *desire to influence others*, e.g. by giving an opinion or judgement
- which *make requests* and
- which *state necessity*

a **Influence**

aconsejar	to advise	**impedir**	to prevent
conseguir	to manage, get (someone to do)	**lograr**	to manage, get (to do)
decir	to tell (to do)	**mandar**	to order
dejar	to allow	**permitir**	to allow
es importante que	it is important that	**preferir**	to prefer
es lógico que	it is natural that	**prohibir**	to forbid
exigir	to demand	**recomendar**	to recommend
hacer que	to make (someone do)	**sería mejor que**	it would be better to

Conseguí que me ayudara con las faenas domésticas.	I got him to help me with the housework.
El buen tiempo hizo que saliéramos mucho.	We went out a lot because of the good weather. (i.e. The good weather made us go out a lot.)
Cuando un estudiante aprende una lengua, es importante que pase un poco de tiempo estudiándola todos los días.	When a student is learning a language, it is important to spend a little time working on it every day.

Si no vas a seguir viviendo en esta ciudad sería mejor que alquilaras un piso.	If you are not going to carry on living in this town it would be better for you to rent a flat.
Es importante que protejamos el medio ambiente con leyes severas.	It's important that we protect the environment with strict laws.
Su enfermedad no le permite/deja que las cosas sigan como antes.	His illness doesn't allow things to carry on as before.

b *Requests*

pedir	to ask for, request
rogar	to ask, request

Le pedimos que llevara el paquete a Correos.	We asked him to take the parcel to the Post Office.
Rogó que no siguiéramos hablando de ese tema.	She requested that we should not continue talking about that subject.

c *Necessity*

es necesario que	it is necessary that
hace falta que	it is necessary that
es preciso que	it is necessary that
es imprescindible que	it is essential that
es importante que	it is important that

No es necesario que vengas de compras conmigo.	You don't have to come shopping with me.
Hace falta que alguien permanezca aquí.	Somebody has to stay here.
Es imprescindible que asistas a las clases de matemáticas.	It's essential that you attend the maths classes.
Es preciso que batalles con el subjuntivo hasta que lo hayas aprendido.	It's vital that you struggle with the subjunctive until you have learned it.

4 **Saying, thinking and knowing in the negative**

The subjunctive is used with a verb or expression of *saying, thinking, knowing* and *perceiving in the negative*. These same verbs and expressions always take the indicative when used in the affirmative. Thus the statement **Es verdad que *ha* venido** becomes **No es verdad que *haya* venido** when the verb in the main clause is negated.

Examples of common verbs and expressions are:

no creo que	I do not believe that	**no parece que**	it does not seem that
no digo que	I do not say that	**no pienso que**	I do not think that
no es cierto que	it is not true/certain that	**no recuerdo que**	I do not remember that
no es verdad que	it is not true that	**no sé que**	I do not know that
no me imagino que	I do not imagine that	**no significa que**	it does not mean that

No digo que tengas que escucharme.	I don't say that you have to listen to me.
Los resultados de la encuesta no significan que los socialistas vayan a perder las elecciones.	The results of the poll do not mean that the socialists are going to lose the elections.
No cree que los precios hayan subido mucho.	He doesn't think prices have gone up much.
No parece que esté de mal humor.	He doesn't appear to be in a bad mood.

5 **No es que** *and* **no es porque** *followed by the subjunctive:*

No entiendo los cambios económicos, y no es que yo sea tonto.	I don't understand the economic changes, and it's not that I'm stupid.
Le ayudé pero no porque lo necesitara.	I helped him, but not because he needed it.
Si te digo que estás muy elegante no es porque quiera adularte.	If I tell you that you look very smart it is not because I want to flatter you.

Note: **no creer que** when used in the negative imperative or the interrogative is followed by the indicative:

No creas que el Real Madrid ganará el partido tan fácilmente.
Don't think Real Madrid will win the match that easily.

¿Crees que caerá el gobierno?
Do you think the government will fall?

¿No crees que tengo razón?
Don't you think I'm right?

6   *Indefinite and negative antecedents in que clauses:*

A further important area in which the subjunctive idea of uncertainty can be seen is the *indefinite antecedent*. The subjunctive must be used when referring back to a person, object, place, etc., *the identity of which is uncertain or unknown.*

a   The indefinite antecedent may be a person or a thing. In the statement **Busco a una persona que me *pueda* ayudar** (I am looking for a person who can help me), the antecedent is **una persona** and the subjunctive is used because the speaker does not know the identity of the person. If the identity of the person had been known the indicative would have been used, as in the statement **Juan es el único que me puede ayudar** (Juan is the only one who can help me):

Dame algo que me guste.
Give me something I like (the speaker does not know what that 'something' may be).

¿Hay por aquí un hotel que tenga piscina?
Is there a hotel with a swimming pool here? (the identity of such a hotel is not known; it may not even exist).

¿Tiene otro bolso que sea más barato?
Have you any cheaper bags?

b   The subjunctive is also used when the antecedent is negative:

No conozco a nadie que sepa francés.
I don't know anyone who knows French.

No soy una mujer que anhele tener hijos.
I'm not the kind of woman who longs to have children.

No hace nada que me moleste.
She doesn't do anything that upsets me.

c   The subjunctive is frequently used after the indefinite **lo que** (anything):

Haz lo que quieras.
Do anything you like.

d   **-quiera** expressions

Pronouns and adverbs in English which end in *-ever* are rendered by **-quiera** in Spanish and are usually followed by the subjunctive:

cualquiera	whichever	**dondequiera**	wherever
cuando quiera*	whenever	**quienquiera**	whoever

***cuando quiera que** is usually replaced by **cuando** in contemporary Spanish:

Dondequiera que vaya se siente feliz.
She is happy, wherever she goes.

Vuelve cuando quieras.
Come back whenever you like.

A cualquiera que llame le dices que estoy ocupada.
Tell anybody who rings that I'm busy.

e   **Por (mucho) que/por (más) que**

The English idea of 'however' is rendered by **por ... que** followed by the subjunctive:

Por muy simpáticos que fueran, yo no acababa de fiarme de ellos...
However nice they were, I couldn't trust them.

Por mucho que le grites no te entiende porque no habla español.
However much you shout at him, he doesn't undertand you because he doesn't speak Spanish.

7   *El (hecho) de que*

The phrase **el (hecho) de que** (the fact that ...) is often used with the subjunctive, even though it refers to a fact. The subjunctive occurs more usually when this phrase precedes the main verb:

El que haya pagado hoy la cena no significa que sea generoso.	The fact that he paid for the meal doesn't mean he's generous.
El (hecho de) que no le conozca mucho es muy importante.	The fact that I do not know him well is very important.
No se le puede calificar de inteligente por el simple hecho de que haya ido a un colegio privado.	He cannot be considered intelligent just because he went to private school.

22.2 The subjunctive after conjunctions

1 Conjunctions of time when referring to the future are followed by the subjunctive. The most common of these conjunctions are:

antes de que	before	**hasta que**	until
cuando	when	**mientras**	while
después de que	after	**una vez que**	once
en cuanto	as soon as		

Es mejor que hables con alguien de tus cosas antes de que empieces a sentirte deprimido	It's better that you talk to somebody about your worries before you start feeling depressed.
En cuanto lleguemos a Gerona buscaremos un piso.	As soon as we arrive in Gerona we'll look for a flat.
Mientras no te pongas en contacto con un abogado no resolverás nada.	While you don't get in touch with a lawyer you won't resolve anything.
Voy a seguir buscando hasta que aparezca el monedero.	I'm going to carry on looking until my purse turns up.

2 Conjunctions of purpose are followed by the subjunctive. Most such expressions are the equivalent of **para que**:

a fin de que	
de forma que	
de manera que	in order that/so that
de modo que	
para que	

Te he comprado estas vitaminas para que te pongas fuerte.	I've bought you these vitamins so that you can get really strong.
La tienda está abierta hasta la medianoche para que la gente pueda hacer compras por la noche.	The shop is open until midnight so that people can shop late.
Comieron rápido, a fin de que pudieran salir lo más pronto posible.	They ate quickly so that they could go out as soon as possible.

3 Conjunctions which indicate condition and limitation require the subjunctive; note however that conjunctions indicating concession may be used with either the subjunctive or the indicative:

concession:	**aunque**	although
	aun cuando	even if, even though
	a pesar de que	despite
condition:	**a condición de que**	on condition that
	con tal que	provided that
	(en) caso de que	in case
	siempre que	provided that
limitation:	**a menos que**	unless
	a no ser que	unless
	excepto que	unless
	salvo que	unless
	sin que	without

Aunque sea un chico rico no le voy a hacer caso.	He may be a rich boy but I'm not going to take any notice of him.
Te invito a la fiesta con tal de que te portes bien.	I'll invite you to the party provided you behave yourself.
Hemos decidido aprobar el proyecto a menos que no estés de acuerdo.	We've decided to approve the project unless you disagree.
Se escaparon por los Pirineos sin que el enemigo se diera cuenta.	They escaped over the Pyrenees without the enemy realising.

4 **Como si**

Como si (as if) invariably takes the subjunctive:

Huyó de la ciudad como si fuera un criminal.	He fled the town as if he were a criminal.
Hablaba en voz baja, como si estuviéramos en la iglesia.	He spoke quietly, as if we were in church.

22.3 The subjunctive in main clauses

The subjunctive is used in main clauses to express uncertainty, wishes and commands (see Part I, 23.3) with:

1 **Quizás, tal vez, acaso**, all of which mean 'perhaps', provided that there is a good degree of doubt involved:

Tal vez pueda quedarse unos días más.	Perhaps he will be able to stay a few more days.
Posiblemente tenga que cambiar mi proveedor habitual.	I may have to change my usual provider.
Tal vez veamos el eclipse desde el balcón.	Perhaps we'll see the eclipse from the balcony.

Note: a lo mejor (probably) is followed by the indicative:

A lo mejor termino este trabajo enseguida.	Maybe I will finish this job very quickly.

2 **Ojalá (que)** (if only, I wish) to express a strong wish:

¡Ojalá se ponga buena la niña!	I do hope the little girl gets better!
¡Ojalá deje de llover!	I wish it would stop raining!

3 **Que...** used for a command or strong wish:

¡Que aproveche(n)!	Enjoy your meal!
¡Que lo pases bien!	Have a good time!
¡Que te mejores!	Get well soon!
¡Que tengas suerte!	Good luck!

Sometimes **que** may be left out but the sense of the wish remains:

¡(Que) Viva España!	Long live Spain!
¡(Que) Vivan los novios!	Long live the bride and groom!

22.4 Further notes about the use of the subjunctive

1 The sequence of tenses with the subjunctive

Where the subordinate clause contains a subjunctive, the subjunctive verb usually conforms to a predictable 'sequence' of tenses. Thus, when the main clause contains a *present, future* or *perfect* tense or an *imperative*, the verb in the subordinate clause will be in either the *present* or the *perfect subjunctive*:

Me alegro de que Fernando tenga/haya tenido tanta suerte.	I'm glad that Fernando has/ has had such good luck.
Espero que me traiga/haya traído el vestido rojo.	I hope she brings/has brought me the red dress.

Similarly, when the main clause contains an *imperfect, preterite, conditional* or *pluperfect* tense the verb in the subordinate clause will be in either the *imperfect* or the *pluperfect* subjunctive:

Me alegré de que Fernando tuviera/hubiera tenido tanta suerte.	I was glad that Fernando had/had had such good luck.
Marga esperaba que no se dieran cuenta de lo poco que sabía.	Marga hoped nobody would notice how little she knew.

2   The same subject in both clauses

The subjunctive construction is not used when the subject of the main verb is the same as the subject of the subordinate clause:

Querría salir a dar un paseo.	I would like to go for a walk.
Fueron al cine para ver la última versión de *Orgullo y Prejuicio*.	They went to the cinema to see the latest version of *Pride and Prejudice*.

3   Verbs with either the subjunctive or the infinitive

With certain verbs an infinitive construction can be used as an alternative to a subjunctive one, even if the subjects are not the same. The most common of these verbs are:

impedir	mandar	permitir	prohibir	recomendar

Les mandó que tuvieran cuidado por aquel barrio tan peligroso.

OR Les mandó tener cuidado por aquel barrio tan peligroso.	He told them to be careful in such a dangerous neighbourhood.
Mi padre no me deja que salga. OR Mi padre no me deja salir.	My father won't allow me to go out.

4   Indicative and subjunctive contrasted

The broad difference in meaning between the indicative, for factual statements, and the subjunctive, for uncertainty or lack of reality, can be seen in the following pairs of sentences. The choice of mood reflects this difference of meaning.

a   **Quizás**

Quizás, and most other words meaning 'perhaps', can be followed either by the indicative or the subjunctive, depending on the degree of certainty:

Quizás saldrá el sol mañana.	Perhaps the sun will shine tomorrow (it is likely it will).
Quizás salga el sol mañana.	Perhaps the sun will shine tomorrow (it is less certain).

b   Verbs of emotion and influence

Some verbs are followed by the indicative or subjunctive depending on their meaning, for example, **temer** and **decir**.

When **temer** is used in its 'weak' sense, the sense of fear is minimal, and so the indicative is used:

Me temo que el libro está agotado.	I am afraid the book is sold out.

When there is a genuine sense of fear the subjunctive is used:

Temo que vayas a tener un accidente si sigues conduciendo de esa manera.	I fear that you'll have an accident if you continue driving like that.

When **decir** is used in the sense of giving information, the indicative is used:

Le dije que había llegado un paquete para ella.	I told her a parcel had arrived for her.

When **decir** implies influence, akin to a prohibition, the subjunctive is required:

Te digo que no vayas descalzo por la casa.	I'm telling you not to walk barefoot around the house.

22.5 Common idioms with the subjunctive

digan lo que digan	whatever they may say	**venga lo que**	come what may
o sea	in other words	**venga/viniere**	
que yo sepa	as far as I know	**¡venga!**	come on!
que yo recuerde	as far as I remember	**¡vaya por Dios!**	oh, dear!
sea como sea/fuere	be that as it may		

Exercises

1   Subraya el verbo adecuado:

a Les rogué que me **mandaron/mandaran** el presupuesto del proyecto.

b Creo que Olga **ha aprobado/haya aprobado** el examen de física.

c Es bueno que los sindicatos se **ponen/pongan** de acuerdo con el Gobierno.

d Me parece que no **hay/haya** bastantes médicos en los países subdesarrollados.

e Buscamos un garaje donde **podemos/podamos** guardar el coche.

f Carolina siempre llegaba a la oficina a una hora que le **permitía/permitiera** organizarse.

g Antes de que **llegan/lleguen** los demás, vamos a tomar un café.

h Me habló como si **estaba/estuviera** ofendido.

i Le pregunté qué **sabía/supiera** del caso de los inmigrantes detenidos.

j Pablo le dijo a su padre que **quería/quisiera** viajar a los países de Oriente Medio.

2   Completa las frases con la forma correcta del verbo:

a Iremos al parque después de que _____ (vosotros terminar) de comer.

b No comenzaremos la cena hasta que _____ (llegar) Juan.

c No hay que perder tiempo. En cuanto _____ (oír) la sirena, nos vamos.

d Cuando _____ (amanecer) verás lo bonita que es la playa.

e Vamos a cambiar la televisión antes de que _____ (empezar) la digital.

f Mientras _____ (yo estar) en España los vecinos se ocuparán de cuidar mi casa.

3   Rellena los espacios con los verbos del recuadro en subjuntivo, usando el tiempo adecuado.

ayudar	llegar	haber	mantener	llamar	
caer	tener	estar	pasar	ofrecer	conseguir

a Es posible que el euro _____ más con relación a la libra esterlina.

b Le encantó que sus amigos le _____ cuando tenía problemas financieros.

c Te deseo que _____ unas felices vacaciones.

d A Enrique le extrañó que (ellos) _____ a la puerta a esas horas de la noche.

e ¡Quizás Marta _____ que le _____ el empleo!

f El atasco en la carretera impidió que _____ a tiempo.

g Parecía poco probable que _____ nuevas elecciones.

h Durante la huelga hacía falta que el gobierno _____ los servicios mínimos.

i No puedo responderle hasta que el jefe no _____ de acuerdo.

j Busco un piso que _____ cuatro dormitorios y dos cuartos de baño.

4   Contesta a un anuncio para un trabajo de secretaria/o bilingüe en la sección 'Ofertas de trabajo' del periódico. Escribe una carta a la empresa pidiendo más información y explicando las cualidades que puedes aportar al empleo. Utiliza por lo menos cinco verbos en subjuntivo utilizando, por ejemplo, los verbos o expresiones **querer, desear, rogar, esperar, es posible que, es importante que, cuando,** etc. La carta puede comenzar así:

Muy Sres míos:
Les ruego hagan el favor de considerar esta carta para el puesto de ...

5 Rellena los espacios vacíos de las siguientes frases con una de las formas verbales que se dan a continuación.

a La elección de los juguetes para los niños es importante, pero lo es más que los padres _____ y _____ si son apropiados para ellos.

valoren/decidan; valoraran/decidieran; hubieran valorado/hubieran decidido

b En 1972, la alternativa de que Franco _____ originar una nueva dinastía real, cobró fuerza al casar a su nieta con un príncipe.

pudiese; pueda; hubiera podido; haya podido

c Andrés está alarmado ante la posibilidad de que le _____ del periódico.

despidieran; despidiesen; hubiesen despedido; despidan

d Aunque _____ un invento actual, la lotería nacional fue introducida en España en el siglo XVIII.

pareciera; hubiera parecido; parezca; pareciesen

e Los que no _____ entradas, recuerden que la representación estará en cartel durante todo el mes.

consigan; consiga; consiguieran; hubiera conseguido

f Quién _____ conocer la obra del fotógrafo Robert Capa, ahora podrá hacerlo gracias a la aparición de un libro sobre él.

hubiera querido; quisiese; haya querido; quiera

g En lo que sí coincide toda la familia, es en que la comida del aniversario _____ lugar en el restaurante 'Los olivos'

hubiesen tenido; tenga; tuviera; tengan

h Para conseguir un dulce que no se _____ pronto, se organizó un concurso que ganó un pastelero barcelonés llamado Pablo Turrón.

estropearan; estropee; hubiera estropeado; estropease

i No estoy segura de la reacción de mi ex marido cuando se _____ mi autobiografía.

publique; publicasen; haya publicado; publicara

j Hoy ya no existe ningún país occidental que no _____ en tela de juicio las decisiones de su gobierno.

haya puesto; ponga; pusiera; hubieran puesto

k Creo que si no se _____ a los musulmanes de España en el 1492, quizá el Islam habría tomado una dirección diferente.

hayan expulsado, expulsara; expulsase; hubiera expulsado

l A finales del siglo XVIII, el Sr Twinings esperaba que su hijo se _____ cargo de su flamante negocio de importación de té, y eso fue lo que sucedió.

hiciera; hayan hecho, hagan; hicieran

m _____ quien _____ el que _____, no estoy para nadie.

fuera/fuera/llamase; sea/sea/llame; esté/esté/llamara

n Me dijo que _____ quien _____ el que _____, no estaba para nadie.

fuera/fuese/llamara; haya sido/haya sido/llamase; fuese/fuese/haya llamado; estuviera/estuviese/hubiera llamado.

o Le pedimos al director español de un proyecto arqueológico en Siria, que nos _____ la vida diaria de su equipo en la cuna de la civilización.

describa; describiese; hayan descrito; hubiera descrito.

p Juana albergaba esperanzas de que su antiguo novio _____ con ella.

hubiera vuelto; haya vuelto; volviera; vuelva.

q Aunque te _____, vamos a tener que apretarnos el cinturón en cuestiones de gasto.

duela; haya dolido; dolieran; doliese

r Si la fecha límite _____ y el trabajo no _____, tendrías que darle una buena explicación a tu jefe.

llegara/haya terminado; llegue/hubiera terminado; haya llegado/haya terminado; llegara/estuviera terminado.

s Los países ricos ofrecen más ayuda a los pobres para que _____ salir de su actual situación.

lograran; hubieran logrado; hayan logrado; logren

6 Rellena los espacios en blanco con la forma correcta del verbo entre paréntesis.

Los jóvenes y la tele

Pobres niños, pobres adolescentes. Por lo visto _____ (1) (vivir) solos en sus casas, sin más compañía que los televisores. No hay nadie junto a ellos que _____ (2) (poder) comentar las imágenes que _____ (3) (ver), para desmentirlas, para reírse juntos de sus exageraciones, para zapear en busca de mejores entretenimientos, o para apagar la tele. Los padres no _____ (4) (tener) tiempo, no _____ (5) (poder) estar constantemente encima de los chicos, no hay quien los _____ (6) (controlar). Lo mejor es que _____ (7) (ser) las cadenas las que _____ (8) (suprimir) todo lo que _____ (9) (resultar) incitante o excitante para la población juvenil, de modo que los padres _____ (10) (descansar) tranquilos. ... Esta solución me _____ (11) (recordar) la de esos santos progenitores que viven desesperados por la ruta del bakalao*, reclamando que el Gobierno _____ (12) (clausurar) o al menos _____ (13) (imponer) horarios draconianos a tanto antro de perdición. ¡Hombre, precisamente ellos, que _____ (14) (admitir) no ser capaces de mantener en el buen camino a sus propios hijos, deberían comprender mejor que nadie que el Ministerio del Interior nunca _____ (15) (ser) capaz de controlar a los de todo el país! Quien _____ (16) (querer) ser padre, que _____ (17) (empezar) por su casa y no _____ (18) (escurrir) el bulto reclamando paternalismos autoritarios para las casas de los demás.

No es que a mí me _____ (19) (gustar) los programas de la tele, más bien lo contrario. Incluso creo que en mi disgusto _____ (20) (ser) más radical que las asociaciones de telecensores, porque hasta los espacios que ellos _____ (21) (recomendar) me parecen también horrendos. Y _____ (22) (preferir) sufrir en mi carne mortal los efectos del kárate que ver una película sobre artes marciales. Pero me _____ (23) (negar) a creer que _____ (24) (ser) los ejemplos de la pequeña pantalla causa principal de nuestros males. No, la auténtica basura no _____ (25) (provenir) de los programas televisados, sino del miedo, la represión supersticiosa y la ignorancia que _____ (26) (presidir) tantas vidas.

La ruta del bakalao: se refiere a las discotecas de la región de Valencia en las que los jóvenes bailan el bakalao y toman droga.

Source: F. Savater, *El País Semanal* (adapted)

23

Continuous forms of the verb

Remember:

- The continuous form is used when you want to express the *duration* of actions which are/were/ will be, etc., in progress.
- Continuous tenses are formed from the verb estar followed by the gerund.
- **estar, ir, ser, tener, venir** and **volver** are not normally used in the continuous form.

23.1 Uses of the continuous form

1 The continuous form is found mostly in the present and imperfect tenses but it may also be used with the infinitive and with other tenses and moods:

No creo que Jorge pueda estar durmiendo a estas horas.	I don't believe that Jorge can be asleep at this time.
¿Le molesta que estemos hablando de fútbol?	Do you mind us talking about football?
¿Qué estuviste leyendo anoche antes de dormirte?	What were you reading last night before you went to sleep?
Se acordaba de que sus amigos le estarían esperando en la estación.	He remembered that his friends would be waiting for him at the station.

2 The verbs **ir, venir, seguir, continuar, andar** and **llevar** are followed by the gerund to indicate the idea of duration (see Part I, 34.2).

Mira por dónde vas poniendo los pies.	Look where you are putting your feet.
Seguiré buscándolo hasta que aparezca.	I'll carry on looking for it until it turns up.
La situación económica sigue siendo desalentadora.	The economic situation continues to be discouraging.
Mi profesor lleva 20 años enseñando en la misma escuela.	My teacher has been teaching at the same school for 20 years.

Exercise

1 Completa las frases siguientes con la forma más adecuada del verbo:

a Cuando Montse llegó yo _____ (estudiar) en la biblioteca.

b Mientras los chicos _____ (fregar) los platos, las chicas _____ (tomar) café.

c El reloj dio la una mientras _____ (nosotros comer) en el restaurante.

d Juan _____ (volver) del partido cuando llamaste.

e Ayer Carlos y yo _____ (estar) hablando durante cuatro horas.

f Todavía no ha conseguido trabajo pero _____ (hacer) un curso para mejorar su técnica en las entrevistas.

g _____ (ir) anocheciendo poco a poco mientras (ellos) _____ (bailar).

h Todos _____ (nosotros tener) sed porque hacía muchísimo calor.

i Cuando Alberto se jubiló en 1999 _____ (llevar) 25 años trabajando allí.

2 Imagina que eres comentarista de radio y que estás haciendo un reportaje sobre un partido de fútbol o sobre la visita del jefe de estado de otro país. Escribe el reportaje tal y como lo hubieras dicho, intentando utilizar frecuentemente la forma continua del verbo.

3 Traduce al español:

a We've been walking for two hours.

b The children were playing in the garden when Martín came back home.

c Last night we were discussing the election until 3 a.m.

d Yesterday I carried on calling her in case she needed me.

e I was watching him for a few seconds.

f When we saw her last she was coming back from Valencia.

g She went on crying and I did not know what to say.

h What are they doing in the summer?

If-clauses

Remember:

There are three main patterns for expressing *if*-clauses in Spanish:

if-clause	main clause
si + present indicative	present indicative/future indicative/imperative
Si viene	**salgo/saldré/sal**
si + imperfect subjunctive	conditional
Si viniera	**saldría**
si + pluperfect subjunctive	conditional perfect
Si hubiera venido	**habría salido**

24.1 Special uses relating to si and conditional clauses

hubiera for habría

In the main clause of conditional sentences which are 'contrary to fact', the pluperfect subjunctive form **hubiera** is frequently used as an alternative to the conditional perfect form, **habría**:

Si Daniel no me hubiera explicado como funcionaba el iPad, no hubiera/habría sido capaz de usarlo.	If Daniel hadn't explained to me how the iPad worked, I wouldn't have been able to use it.
Si no hubiera sido por mis amigos, me hubiera/habría sentido muy solo.	If it hadn't been for my friends I'd have felt very lonely.

Si meaning when(ever)

Si is often used for *reporting* a statement of fact in the past, in the sense of 'when(ever)' and could be replaced by **cuando**. In this case the indicative mood is always used:

Si (Cuando) llovía no salíamos	If (i.e. whenever) it rained we didn't go out.
Si (Cuando) veíamos a Minerva siempre hablábamos con ella.	If we saw Minerva we always spoke to her.

Si meaning whether

Si meaning 'whether' after such verbs as **preguntar** and **saber** is followed by the indicative:

Le preguntaré si estará en Barcelona la semana que viene.	I'll ask him whether he'll be in Barcelona next week.
No sabemos si ha ganado Alberto o no.	We don't know whether Alberto has won or not.

Equivalents of si

a   de + the infinitive

de + the infinitive can replace **si** + a verb, provided the subject of the de *if*-clause and the main clause are the same:

De haber sabido tu dirección te habría visitado.	If I'd known your address I'd have visited you.
De saber que iban a venir tus amigos hubiera comprado más vino.	If I'd known your friends were coming I'd have bought more wine.

b   como

Como may replace **si**, especially for warnings and threats. In this meaning it is always followed by the subjunctive:

Como no me dejes pagar la cena, no vuelvo a salir contigo.	If you don't let me pay for dinner, I will not go out with you again.
Como no dejes de trabajar tanto, te va a dar un ataque al corazón.	If you don't stop working so hard you will have a heart attack.

c   en caso de que

En caso de que, meaning 'if', 'in case', with a future idea is always followed by the subjunctive:

En caso de que no haya bastantes sillas traeremos más de mi casa.	If there aren't enough chairs we'll get some more from my house.
En caso de que mi coche no funcione cogeremos el tuyo.	If my car doesn't start we'll take yours.

A number of conjunctions followed by the subjunctive also express conditions:

a   como si (as if) (see Part II, 22.2.4):

Me miraba como si hubiera visto un fantasma.	She looked at me as if she had seen a ghost.
Nos trató como si fuéramos reyes.	He treated us like kings.

b   con tal que, siempre que, a condición de que (provided that) (see Part II, 22.2.3):

Puedes tomar prestada mi bici con tal que/a condición de que me la devuelvas esta noche.	You can borrow my bike provided you give it back to me tonight.
Siempre que no le digas nada a mi padre te dejo coger el coche.	Provided you don't tell my father, I'll let you take the car.

Si for emphasis

Colloquially **si** sometimes precedes an exclamation or emphasises a point:

¡Si no le he hecho nada!	I've not done anything to him!
No le riñas, si es que es muy tímido.	Don't tell him off. Can't you see he's very shy?

Exercises

1   Decide si el verbo en infinitivo debe ir en subjuntivo o en indicativo:

a Cuando era más joven si _____ (comer) paella nunca le sentaba mal.

b Si me _____ (tú dejar) en paz, terminaría la novela.

c Si _____ (haber) sido judío en los tiempos de la Inquisición te _____ (haber) perseguido.

d Josefina y David me han dicho que si _____ (venir) un 'tablao' flamenco, iríamos a verles.

e Hace años si una mujer _____ (ser) independiente se la consideraba un bicho raro.

f El jefe le explicó que si no _____ (estar) contenta con su trabajo, podía trasladarse a otra oficina.

g En 1939 si _____ (ganar) los republicanos no se habrían exiliado tantos intelectuales.

h En los tiempos de mi abuela, si un chico _____ (querer) salir con una chica, tenía que pedir permiso a sus padres.

i Si yo _____ (saber) montar a caballo, iría al campo contigo.

j Si _____ (ellos poder) terminar la comida antes, habríamos ido al cine.

2 Completa las frases siguientes usando la forma correcta de los verbos en infinitivo.

a Iremos al cine en caso de que no _____ (haber) nada interesante en la tele.

b Carmelo se comporta como si _____ (ser) millonario.

c Una productora americana le ha dado carta blanca a Almodóvar a condición de que _____ (hacer) su próxima película en Hollywood.

d Como no _____ (dejar) de hacer ruido voy a volverme loco.

e En caso de que no me _____ (admitir) en la universidad me iré a trabajar a un banco.

f Ramón puede hacerme muchos favores siempre que se lo _____ (pedir) con educación.

g Me siento como si _____ (tener) gripe.

h Como _____ (seguir) sin estudiar te van a suspender todo.

i Tomaré una copa con tal de que me _____ (dejar) pagar a mí la próxima.

j Se comporta como si lo único importante _____ (ser) el dinero.

25

The imperative

Remember:

- The imperative in Spanish has both positive and negative forms.
- Spanish speakers tend to use imperatives more than English speakers.
- We have to differentiate between *familiar* and *formal* modes of address, and *positive* and *negative* forms.
- All imperative forms, except **tú** and **vosotros**, are taken from the relevant person of the *present subjunctive*.
- The positive imperatives of **tú** and **vosotros** have their own independent forms.

25.1 First person plural imperative

1 The imperative form for the first person plural is the same as the first person plural of the present subjunctive, for both the positive and the negative. This is translated into English by 'let's/let us' (+ infinitive) and 'let us /let's not' (+ infinitive).

Hablemos.	Let's talk.
No entremos.	Let's not go in.
Hagámoslo ahora mismo.	Let's do it right now.

2 In reflexive verbs the final **-s** of the **nosotros** form of the verb is omitted:

Vámonos.	Let's go.
Levantémonos.	Let's get up.
Divirtámonos.	Let's have a good time.

3 The first person plural imperative form is hardly used in colloquial language, where **vamos a** plus the infinitive is normal:

¡Vamos a bailar!	Let's dance!
Vamos a ver lo que hacen.	Let's go and see what they're doing.

25.2 Imperative que

The subjunctive form can be used with any person of the verb to express a wish or command. This form is often preceded by **que** (see Part II, 22.3.3):

Que espere un momento.	Tell him to wait a minute.
Que entren todos.	Let them all come in.
¡(Que) viva la Constitución!	Long live the Constitution!
¡Que gane el mejor!	Let the best man win!

| ¡Que hable! ¡Que hable! | Speech! Speech! |
| ¡Que suene la música! | Let the music play! |

25.3 Infinitives used for commands (see Part II, 32.2)

On public notices and in popular speech the infinitive is often used as a substitute for the imperative:

Peligro. No tocar.	Danger, don't touch.
¡Callaros! (for ¡Callaos!)	Be quiet!
No pasar. Propiedad particular.	No entry. Private property.

25.4 The second-person plural in Latin-American Spanish

The **vosotros** form (**hablad**, etc.) of the familiar plural imperative is not used in Latin-American Spanish. The **ustedes** form is used for both the formal and familiar imperative.

Exercises

1 Transforma la frase en imperativo, usando (i) *tú*, (ii) *usted*, sustituyendo el objeto directo por un pronombre siguiendo el ejemplo:

Ejemplo: Limpiar las ventanas. > *límpialas/límpielas*

a Poner la mesa.　　　　　　**f** Hacer los ejercicios.

b Comer el pan.　　　　　　　**g** Leer la revista.

c Sacar las fotos.　　　　　　**h** Darle el regalo.

d Decirme las noticias.　　　　**i** No pagarle el dinero.

e No coger el autobús.　　　　**j** Apagar la luz.

2 A continuación vas a leer la receta para hacer una buena paella. Coloca los verbos entre paréntesis en la forma correcta del imperativo, usando (i) *tú*, (ii) *usted*:

_____ (1) (Colocar) la paella sobre el fuego preferentemente de madera de naranjo. _____ (2) (Añadir) el aceite y cuando esté caliente _____ (3) (poner) el pollo troceado y _____ (4) (freírlo) hasta que esté dorado. A continuación _____ (5) (verter) los tomates y la verdura troceados y el pimentón. No _____ (6) (permitir) que se queme el pimentón porque tomará mal sabor. Cuando esté todo frito _____ (7) (añadir) el agua y _____ (8) (hervirla) con los otros ingredientes. El fuego debe ser moderado. Cuando haya hervido todo _____ (9) (echar) el arroz. _____ (10) (Hacer) una línea de extremo a extremo de la paella y _____ (11) (procurar) que sobresalga un poco de la superficie del agua como una pequeña cordillera. Entonces _____ (12) (remover) el arroz y _____ (13) (repartirlo) por toda la paella. _____ (14) (Hacer) hervir el agua fuertemente, _____ (15) (añadir) la sal y el azafrán y entonces _____ (16) (bajar) el fuego y _____ (17) (dejar) hervir el arroz suavemente. Cuando el arroz esté casi cocido _____ (18) (colocar) las gambas y los langostinos y _____ (19) (reducir) el fuego. Una vez cocida la paella, _____ (20) (dejarla) que repose sobre el fuego apagado unos 15 minutos. Así los sabores se mezclan y el plato sabe mejor. Antes de servir, _____ (21) (coger) una rama grande de romero y _____ (22) (tocar) con ella la superficie de la paella varias veces. ¡ _____ (23) (vosotros disfrutarla)!

3 El texto siguiente da algunos consejos para comprar un móvil. Pon los verbos en infinitivo en la forma correcta del imperativo utilizando usted:

Antes de comprar un móvil nuevo sería buena idea tener en cuenta estos consejos:

(1) _____ (Fijarse) si el precio está dentro de sus posibilidades.

(2) _____ (Leer) algún catálogo o _____ (preguntar) características del móvil a comprar.

(3) _____ (Comparar) siempre más de dos o tres móviles de diferentes marcas con el mismo precio y _____ (ver) sus diferencias.

(4) _____ (Recordar) que hay móviles de todo tipo, elegantes, sencillos, con muchas funciones, etc.

(5) Si no está seguro de cuál quiere, _____ (regresar) a su casa con las características de los que haya visto. _____ (Imaginar) lo que pueden hacer o no hacer cuando lo tenga en sus manos y cuál se acerca más a su relación calidad – precio.

(6) No _____ (comprar) por impulso o porque simplemente esté de moda. Otro puede no estarlo pero tener exactamente las funciones que Vd. necesita.

(7) _____ (Descubrir) qué compañía ofrece mejores servicios y mejor precio en tarifas.

(8) _____ (Pensar) que un móvil no es solo un gasto, sino un utensilio de comunicación necesario en la actualidad. _____ (Administrarlo) bien para que le cueste lo menos possible.

4 Traduce al español.

a Let's go out now.

b Don't give me your answer yet, Carlos.

c Collect the bottles and put them in the recycling box, boys.

d Let's not wait until tomorrow.

e Tell him what happened.

f Waiter, bring me some more water, please.

g Please don't feed the ducks.

h Don't ring me until 7 p.m., Rosa.

i Keep still, children!

j Switch the light on, it's getting dark.

26

Spelling changes in Verbs

(See Part I page 127)

Modal verbs

Remember:

- Modal verbs are auxiliary verbs followed by an infinitive.
- Modal verbs colour the relationship between the subject of the sentence and the infinitive.

27.1 Querer, saber and soler as modal verbs

1.   **Querer** in the sense of 'to want' functions as a modal auxiliary. The forms **querría** and **quisiera** (I would like) indicate politeness:

¿Quieres compartir este bocadillo conmigo?	Do you want/Would you like to share this sandwich with me?
Quisiéramos hablar con el director.	We would like to speak to the director.

2.   **Saber** is used as a modal verb in the sense of 'to have the ability to', 'to know how to':

Sabe cocinar mejor que su madre	He can cook better than his mother.

3.   **Soler** means 'to be accustomed to':

En la primavera las cigüeñas suelen construir sus nidos en las torres de las iglesias.	In spring the storks usually build their nests on church steeples.

Note: This verb is not conjugated in the preterite because of its meaning.

27.2 Translation of 'could' and 'could have'

Could

 The imperfect (**podía**, etc.) and conditional tenses (**podría**, etc.) of **poder** can both be translated into English by 'could', meaning respectively 'was /were able to' and 'would be able to'. It is therefore important to think about which is the correct meaning in the context:

Si tuviéramos dinero podríamos alquilar un coche para ir a Soria.	If we had time we could (would be able to) hire a car and go to Soria.
No podía saber que estaba haciendo trampas.	He could not (was not able to) know that she was cheating.

Could have

There are two ways of translating 'could have' into Spanish.

In a past sense:

Either: the imperfect of **poder** + perfect infinitive
Or: the pluperfect of **poder** + infinitive

Podía haberlo hecho/Había podido hacerlo.   He could have done (had been able to do) it.

In a conditional sense:

Either: the conditional of **poder** + perfect infinitive
Or: the conditional perfect of **poder** + infinitive

Podría haberlo hecho/Habría podido hacerlo.   He could have done (would have been able to do) it.

Note: hubieras can replace **habrías** in the last example: **hubieras podido hacerlo**.

27.3 Translation of 'should' and 'should have'

Should

The conditional **debería**, and occasionally the imperfect subjunctive **debiera**, mean 'should', in the sense of a strong moral or social obligation:

Deberías informar a la policía enseguida.   You should inform the police at once.

Should have

Debería, and occasionally **debiera**, are also used with the perfect infinitive to convey the idea of 'should have':

Deberías haber informado a la policía enseguida.   You should have informed the police at once.

An alternative construction is possible, by using the conditional perfect of **deber** + the infinitive:

Habrías debido informar a la policía enseguida.

Note: **hubieras** can replace **habrías** in the above example.

Exercises

1   Completa las frases con un tiempo adecuado de *deber, poder, querer o saber:*

a No _____ tocar el piano bien aunque tengo un buen profesor.

b Si no le hubieras regalado tu coche a Manuel, no _____ ir de gira por EE. UU.

c ¿ _____ pasarme el pan?

d ¿Se _____ fumar antes en los cines españoles?

e Según la iglesia católica tradicional, todos los católicos _____ ir a misa los domingos.

f Hace mucho frío. _____ (usted) ponerse el abrigo.

g ¿ _____ Vd. decirnos si hay una tienda de Vodafone por aquí cerca?

h Cuando ocurrió el accidente usted _____ haberme llamado enseguida.

i No sé si _____ llevarte porque no tengo mi coche.

j Si queremos llegar a tiempo _____ coger el autobús de las seis y media.

2   Traduce al español:

a Angel must have gone before they arrived.

b I'd like to learn French.

c We used to go to France every year but now we travel further afield.

d I know how to play golf, but I am not very good at it.

e We should always wear seat belts.

f I could have been a competitor.

g At your age you should have known better.

h At that time we could not see that democracy was going to win.

28 Gustar-type and impersonal verbs

Remember:

There are several ways of expressing an 'impersonal' idea in Spanish:

- By using **gustar**-type verbs
- By using an impersonal verb where the subject of the verb is normally in the third person ('it' in English)
- Where the subject is the impersonal reflexive pronoun **se** ('one, 'you' or 'they' in English)

28.1 Gustar-type verbs in the reflexive

The **gustar** construction occurs in reflexive form with a number of verbs:

antojarse	to feel like
ocurrirse	to occur to oneself
caerse	to fall, to drop
olvidarse	to forget

No se le antojó ir a la fiesta.	She did not feel like going to the party.
Se me cayó la cartera.	I dropped my wallet.
Se me ocurrió de repente llamarle por teléfono.	It suddenly occurred to me to ring him.
Se le olvidó la dirección de la casa.	He forgot the address of the house.

This construction can work in a similar way with verbs which do not have a direct object:

Nos entretuvimos charlando y se nos hizo tarde.	We were so busy chatting that we did not realise the time (lit. 'it [the time] got late').

28.2 Impersonal verbs

Most of these verbs are associated with the weather. The most common ones are:

amanecer	to dawn
anochecer	to get dark
atardecer	to get dark, to get late
helar	to freeze
granizar	to hail
llover	to rain
nevar	to snow
hacer buen/mal tiempo	to be good/bad weather
relampaguear	to flash (of lightning)
tronar	to thunder

Anochece muy pronto.	It is getting dark very early.
Hiela rápidamente.	It is freezing quickly.
Amanecía cuando nos despertamos.	Dawn was breaking when we woke up.

Exercises

1 Escoge un verbo adecuado del recuadro para llenar los espacios. Utiliza la forma correcta del verbo:

tocar	sobrar	encantar	doler	costar
molestar	gustar	olvidarse	ocurrirse	hacer falta

a Ayer fuimos al mercado para comprar un melón pero ninguno nos _____.

b Ayer me corté el dedo. Hoy ya no me _____.

c Anoche les _____ mucho que los vecinos tuvieran una fiesta hasta las cuatro de la madrugada.

d Se _____ que llegaremos tarde si no nos damos prisa.

e ¿A quién le _____ pagar la ronda?

f Leí la novela nueva de Rosa Montero la semana pasada y me _____.

g Nos _____ tiempo para pasear por el pueblo.

h ¡Le _____ mucho subir la escalera hoy, doña Milagros!

i Presté el diccionario a Enrique y se _____ pedirle que lo devolviera.

j _____ dos limones para preparar la comida.

2 Haz una lista de las cuatro cosas que más te gusten, y otra de las que menos te gusten. Haz lo mismo sobre uno de tus amigos. Los ejemplos te darán algunas ideas:

Ejemplo: (yo) Me gustan los viernes porque salgo por la noche.
(amigo) No le gusta conducir porque tuvo un accidente el año pasado.

3 Traduce al español:

a Yesterday my sister showed me her new bracelet but I didn't like it.

b We took a lot of trouble arranging the exhibition.

c The doctor gave me an injection but it didn't hurt.

d We would like to visit Santiago next year.

e It annoyed me that he never stopped complaining.

f He dropped his book.

g It didn't suit us to travel to Cuba in the winter.

h Those jeans really suit you, Gonzalo.

i My friends don't like spending time in bars.

j My little sister has a bad headache.

k D. Alberto, my marks are missing.

l What you need is a good holiday.

m I'm not very interested in television.

n Chris gets offended if I speak Spanish.

o Carlos likes salads but I don't.

p Do you mind if I close the window? No, not at all.

q There was a lot of food left over after the party.

r It was very difficult for them to find the road.

s I'm surprised you didn't know that they got married last year.

29

Ser and estar

Remember:

- There are two verbs meaning 'to be' in Spanish, **ser** and **estar**.
- **Ser** indicates the identity or nature of a person or thing, such as physical features, occupation and nationality.
- **Estar** refers mainly to a temporary state of affairs, such as a mood, and to the location of a person or thing.

29.1 Ser

1   **Ser** is used when giving information about *where or when an event is taking place:*

¿Sabes dónde es la boda?	Do you know where the wedding is (taking place)?
Es en la Iglesia San Pablo.	In St Paul's.
La reunión será el día dos de febrero.	The meeting will be on 2nd February.

2   **Ser** is used in *passive* sentences. It should be noted that although passive constructions are used frequently in journalism, they are almost never used in the spoken language (see Part II, 30.1 for alternatives to the passive).

Passive sentences contain the verb 'to be', followed by a past participle, e.g. 'The government will be criticised by the press', 'War was declared by General Franco'. In this type of sentence there is an agent, real or implied, who is carrying out the action ('the press' and 'General Franco' in the examples above). The agent is preceded by the preposition **por**:

La novela Don Quijote fue escrita por Cervantes.	The novel *Don Quixote* was written by Cervantes.
La solución del conflicto debe ser alcanzada por medio de negociaciones.	The conflict must be resolved through negotiation.
El político era acusado por el pueblo de ser ladrón.	The politician was accused of being a thief by the people.
Las nuevas tecnologías son renovadas constantemente.	New technologies are updated constantly.

29.2 Estar

1   **Estar** can be used with adjectives, where one would normally expect **ser**, to indicate a break with the norm or a change in appearance:

¡Qué viejo está!	How old he looks! (compared with 'how old he is!')
¡Estás muy contenta hoy, Gloria!	You're very happy today, Gloria! (i.e. she looks unusually happy for her)

The verb **ser** could be used with the two adjectives above, **viejo** and **contenta**, but the use of **ser** would emphasise the intrinsic characteristic and not the immediate impression: Gloria may be (**ser**) a happy person anyway, but the speaker is interested in how she is/appears (**estar**) at the moment.

2   **Estar** is also used with the past participle, but in contrast to the use of **ser** with the passive described above, this construction does not express an action, but *the state which results from an action*.

The difference between the use of **ser** and **estar** with a past participle might best be demonstrated by the following examples:

El libro estaba escrito en inglés.	The book was written in English.
El libro fue escrito por Charles Dickens.	The book was written by Charles Dickens.

In the first case a state of 'being written' is described, which has resulted from the action of 'writing'; in the second the action itself is being described:

La ventana está rota.	The window is broken. (i.e. it had already been broken)
Estamos encantados.	We're delighted (lit. 'in a delighted state').
Estaba muy impresionado por la exposición.	I was very impressed by the exhibition.
No están convencidos de que vayan a ganar.	They are not sure that they are going to win.
El crimen ha estado siempre relacionado con el paro.	Crime has always been linked with unemployment.

29.3 Useful expressions with estar

¿A cuánto estamos?	What is the date?
Estamos a 2 de marzo.	It's 2nd March.
Estamos a jueves.	It's Thursday.
estar muerto	to be dead
estar para/a punto de (+ infinitive)	to be about to
estar por	to remain to be done

Exercises

1   María se está probando un vestido y no se decide a comprarlo. Completa sus pensamientos utilizando la forma correcta del verbo *ser* o *estar*:

_____ (1) bonito y me _____ (2) muy bien, pero no _____ (3) de buena calidad y además _____ (4) un poco caro para _____ (5) un vestidito de verano. Las faldas tan largas no _____ (6) de moda ahora, pero eso no _____ (7) demasiado importante porque no _____ (8) bien llevar faldas muy cortas a la oficina. _____ (9) difícil decidirse. Lo peor _____ (10) el color, creo que el amarillo _____ (11) un color raro, hay que _____ (12) muy morena para que favorezca.

2   Sustituye las palabras **en negrita** de las siguientes frases por ser o estar según convenga de acuerdo con el sentido de la frase.

a ¿Cuándo **podré ver** al doctor?

b A Iñaki y a Lourdes les cuesta mucho **ponerse** de acuerdo sobre dónde ir de vacaciones.

c Todavía no he **ido a** Buenos Aires.

d Los ingleses al principio **parecen** muy antipáticos, pero cuando se les conoce bien **resultan** encantadores.

e El crimen **tuvo lugar** en la calle del Pez de Madrid.

f Todos los que terminaron conmigo la carrera **han encontrado trabajo** en buenas compañías españolas y **trabajan de** gerentes.

g Andrés, últimamente, **se encuentra** en plena forma física.

h Conchita dice que su marido **se pasó** toda la semana de mal humor.

i Si **se ve** delgada coquetea, pero cuando **se siente** gorda **se queda** siempre en casa.

j El chal del bebé **parecía** de ganchillo.

3 Lee el siguiente texto y escoge para cada espacio en blanco la opción que consideres correcta.

El mito de Carmen en el cine

La historia de Carmen (1) _____ conocida en todo el mundo hasta el punto de poderse decir que (2) _____ uno de los mitos modernos más populares. (3) _____ por esta razón que diferentes versiones de su historia aparecen regularmente y no sólo en el cine sino también en el arte, la literatura y la música.

Carmen, por otra parte, (4) _____ ligada a un país concreto, aún más, a una parte muy concreta de ese país y a una visión extraña, violenta y pintoresca de lo que (5) _____ ese territorio. Esta (6) _____ la visión de escritores, pintores y viajeros que (7) _____ de varios países de Europa y pensaban que los gitanos andaluces (8) _____ románticos, libres y por lo tanto atractivos.

La pantalla cinematográfica (9) _____ indiscutiblemente un marco idóneo para representar esta historia de toreros, gitanos y amores apasionados y a lo largo de la historia del cine, Carmen (10) _____ representada por las mejores actrices desde Geraldine Farrar en 1915 a Paz Vega en 2003 pasando por estrellas como Marlene Dietrich y Rita Hayworth que (11) _____ Cármenes inolvidables.

(1) Está; es; fue; era

(2) Estaba; ha sido; era; es

(3) Es; fuese; estuvo; está

(4) Ha sido; había estado; estuvo; está

(5) Era; fue; es; fuera

(6) Habría sido; sería; fue; es

(7) Estuvieron; fueron; eran; serían

(8) Son; están; eran; estaban

(9) Es; ha sido; sería; fue

(10) Es; fue; sería; estuvo; ha sido

(11) Serían; eran; estuvieron; fueron

4 Rellena los espacios en blanco con ser o *estar* utilizando el tiempo adecuado:

Así _____ los españoles

En una encuesta reciente, se descubrió que, en el fondo, los españoles _____ (1) contentos. Estos días los españoles _____ (2) redescubriendo los valores del pasado, sobre todo el hogar y la familia. El mayor hallazgo _____ (3) que existe el calor de la familia.

A pesar de esto, la sociedad española ya no _____ (4) tan tradicional como _____ (5). _____ (6) cada vez más tolerantes. _____ (7) demócratas, ecologistas y valoran la libertad personal. Hace 40 años las mujeres sólo estudiaban si _____ (8) garantizado el estudio de los hijos varones. Ahora los colegios _____ (9) llenos de alumnas.

Pero no todo _____ (10) bien. En el pasado, la delincuencia _____ (11) menos frecuente. Hoy en día más españoles _____ (12) dispuestos a comprar lo robado, a no comprar billetes de tren y a evadir impuestos.

Nuestro país sigue _____ (13) el país de la diversión y el turismo. Según la encuesta, los españoles _____ (14) más alegres y abiertos que los demás habitantes de la Unión Europea. España _____ (15) el lugar ideal para jubilarse.

5 Completa el texto siguiente con la forma apropiada del verbo *ser* o *estar*:

Cuando uno _____ (1) solo y además en el extranjero, se fija mucho en el cubo de basura, porque puede llegar a _____ (2) lo único con lo que se mantiene una relación constante. Cada bolsa negra de plástico produce el efecto de la absoluta limpieza y la infinita posibilidad. Cuando se saca por la noche, _____ (3) ya la inauguración o promesa del nuevo día: _____ (4) todo por suceder. Esa bolsa, ese cubo, _____ (5) los únicos testigos de lo que ocurre en la vida de un hombre solo, lo que ha decidido no _____ (6), el negativo de lo que ha comido, de lo que ha bebido, de lo que ha fumado, de lo que ha comprado, y de lo que ha producido. Al término de ese día la bolsa, el cubo _____ (7) llenos y _____ (8) confusos, pero se los ha visto crecer y transformarse de forma que la indiscriminada mezcla _____ (9) el orden y la explicación del hombre. La bolsa y el cubo _____ (10) la prueba de que ese día ha existido.

Javier Marías, Todas las almas

6 Leonardo y Concha discuten sobre su vida matrimonial. Rellena los espacios en blanco con *ser* o *estar,* utilizando un tiempo adecuado. ¿Crees que uno de los dos tiene razón?

Leonardo: ¡ _____ (1) a punto de volverme loco! ¡Nunca _____ (2) en casa!

Concha: Ya sabes que no _____ (3) mujer para estar en casa. Cuando hace sol necesito _____ (4) fuera.

Leonardo: Claro, y yo _____ (5) todo el día trabajando y cuando vuelvo a casa me gusta que la comida _____ (6) preparada.

Concha: Leonardo, los tiempos han cambiado y las mujeres ya no _____ (7) esclavas del matrimonio. Antes sí lo _____ (8). Ahora ya no nos dais miedo.

Leonardo: Lo que os pasa a las mujeres _____ (9) que _____ (10) muy poco disciplinadas.

Concha: _____ (11) disciplinadas para las cosas que _____ (12) importantes como _____ (13) con los niños, _____ (14) cariñosas, _____ (15) guapas ... Mira, hoy por la mañana voy a _____ (16) con los niños en el parque y por la tarde, si _____ (17) buenos les llevaré al cine. Cuando llegues del trabajo, si no _____ (18) muy cansado podrías empezar a preparar la cena ...

Leonardo: ¡Esto _____ (19) el colmo! ¡Si mi abuelo levantara la cabeza!

30

Active and passive

Remember:

- In Spanish the passive is formed using **ser** *plus the past participle,* which must agree in number and gender with the subject of the sentence.
- The agent of the action which has been carried out is normally preceded by the preposition **por**.

30.1 Different ways of expressing the passive

The use of the passive is on the increase in written Spanish, especially in journalism. Spaniards, however, tend not to use passive constructions in speech. There are several alternative ways of expressing the passive.

Third person plural with an active verb

This construction is used when the agent is known but not stated:

Le mandaron a París.	He was sent to Paris./ They sent him to Paris.
Me han dado un coche nuevo.	I was given a new car./They gave me a new car.

Duplication of the direct object

The direct object can be placed first and duplicated as a pronoun before the verb:

Aquel piso lo vendió mi padre.	That flat was sold by my father.
Estas novelas las escribió Galdós.	These novels were written by Galdós.

Use of **se** with the passive

a   **Se** with things and ideas

Se can be used to express the passive without an agent. The verb can be either singular or plural.

Aquí se venden limones.	Lemons (are) sold here.
Se precisa un buen nivel de conocimientos de informática.	A good level of computer expertise (is) required.
Los estudios que se han realizado sobre este tema son inútiles.	The studies of this topic that have been carried out are useless.
No sé cómo se hizo esa película.	I don't know how that film was made.
Se construyeron estos pisos en 1990.	These flats were built in 1990.

b   Impersonal **se**

Se can be used impersonally, followed by a singular verb.
(i) **Se** as the apparent subject of the sentence:

Se habla español.	Spanish is spoken.
Se vende coches.	Cars (are) sold/We sell cars.

In these examples **se** could be considered the subject of the sentence. In the first example the construction is like French *on:* 'We/One speaks Spanish'. The construction in the second example is quite commonplace, although many linguists consider it to be incorrect. Here **se** is clearly the subject of the sentence.

(ii) a number of common verbs are used in the impersonal construction:

se cree, se dice, se espera, se tiene que, se permite, se puede, se sabe:

Se cree que hay vida en el planeta Marte.	It is believed that there is life on Mars.
No se dice así en español.	It isn't said/We don't say it like that in Spanish.
¿Se puede confirmar la cita?	Can the appointment be confirmed?
No se sabe qué va a ocurrir.	It isn't known/We don't know what will happen.

c   Se with people

(i) Be aware of the difference between passive **se** with people and reflexive **se**.

Passive **se**: with people the impersonal construction must be used; **se** behaves like a pronoun which is the subject of the sentence, and personal **a** (see Part I, 16.3.1.1) is placed before the object, as follows:

se +	singular verb +	personal **a** before the direct object
Se	propuso	**a** Ramírez como el nuevo entrenador

Ramírez was proposed as the new coach.

Reflexive **se**: the reflexive construction functions differently:

Ramírez	se propuso	como el nuevo entrenador.

Ramírez proposed himself as the new coach.

(ii) Passive **se** with object pronouns

When the object is a pronoun it is placed before the verb in the usual way:

Se le llevó a la cárcel.	He was taken to jail.

(iii) Repetition of the object before the verb

If you wish to emphasise the person it is possible to repeat the object as a pronoun before the verb.

Direct object:

A González se le llevó a la cárcel.	Gonzalez was taken to jail.

Indirect object:

Se me aconseja que deje de fumar.	I've been advised to stop smoking.
Se le dio el regalo ayer.	She was given the present yesterday.

Uno/una

Uno/una can mean 'one', 'people','they', 'we' (in the sense of French *on*), and even 'I', in popular speech.

a   As the equivalent of impersonal **se**

Uno tiene sus ideas.	I've got my own views.
Una tiene que saber lo que quiere.	One has to know what one wants.
Uno no sabe por dónde ir.	You don't know which way to go.

b   Uno has to be used as an impersonal subject when the verb is already reflexive, since **se** cannot be used twice:

Uno no se puede creer todo lo que oye.	You can't believe everything you hear.

30.2 Conversion from English passive voice to Spanish active voice

In order to turn a passive sentence into an active one or vice versa we need to look at the components of the sentence to ensure an exact equivalence. For example, to change the sentence 'The chocolates were bought by Ángel' into the active voice we turn the agent, Ángel, into subject of the active sentence, discarding the preposition *by*. The verb is then an active one, keeping the same tense, with the new subject. The subject of the passive sentence, 'los bombones', becomes the object:

Subject	*passive verb*	*agent*
Los bombones	**fueron comprados**	**por Ángel**
Subject	*active verb*	*object*
Ángel	**compró**	**los bombones**

If the agent is missing in the passive, the construction explained in c) (i) above is used:

Se compraron los bombones.   The chocolates were bought.

Note: in some regions **se** is used with the verb in the third person singular: **Se *compró* los bombones.**

Although the use of this construction is widespread it is generally considered to be incorrect by grammarians. Similarly:

No se respeta(n) mucho las reglas del   Traffic rules are not well
tráfico en ciertos países.   respected in certain countries.

Exercises

1 En la oficina del Banco de Santander existen muchas reglas para los empleados y los clientes. Rellena los espacios con la forma correcta del infinitivo entre paréntesis:

Ante todo en esta oficina no ＿＿ (1) (permitir) fumar ni tampoco ＿＿ (2) (poder) cantar o hacer ruidos innecesarios. ＿＿ (3) (esperar) de los empleados que ＿＿ (4) (dirigirse) a los clientes con educación y a los clientes que ＿＿ (5) (comportarse) debidamente. No ＿＿ (6) (atender) a aquellos que lleguen cinco minutos antes de cerrar. Todo cliente ＿＿ (7) (ser) aconsejado por un empleado cualificado e informado sobre las facilidades que ＿＿ (8) (ofrecer) en el banco. Garantizamos que sus necesidades financieras ＿＿ (9) (ser) analizadas minuciosamente.

2 Transforma las frases en voz pasiva por frases en activa según el ejemplo:

Ejemplo: *La rendición de Breda fue pintada por Velázquez .*
La rendición de Breda la pintó Velázquez.

a El teléfono fue inventado por Alexander Graham Bell.

b La película *Tacones lejanos* fue dirigida por Pedro Almodóvar.

c El Museo Guggenheim fue construido por un arquitecto estadounidense.

d Méjico fue conquistado por Hernán Cortés en 1519.

e El banco Argentaria fue privatizado en los años 90.

3 Transforma las frases según el ejemplo:

Ejemplo: Las tasas de interés fueron reducidas. *Se redujeron las tasas de interés.*

a Los edificios fueron vendidos en septiembre.

b Este laboratorio es donde son analizados los residuos químicos.

c La sede del banco ha sido establecida en San Sebastián.

d En Galicia mucho bosque fue destruido en los años 80.

e Los documentos serán traducidos dentro de poco.

4 Traduce al español:

a The decision was taken by the Prime Minister.

b She was asked if she had anything to say.

c One never knows, does one?

d Waiters required.

e Second-hand cars can be bought here.

f She was taken to see her grandmother in hospital.

g Spanish olive oil is sold throughout Europe.

h It was said that his father was French.

i It was so noisy that they couldn't be heard.

j Interest rates were lowered yesterday

31

Pronominal verbs

Remember:

- Pronominal verbs, e.g. **levantarse**, are always accompanied by a reflexive pronoun.
- In their *reflexive* meaning pronominal verbs 'reflect back' on to the subject of the verb, and reflexive pronouns are the equivalent of the English 'myself', 'yourself', etc.
- Pronominal verbs can also express a 'reciprocal' meaning ('each other', 'one another').

31.1 The reflexive pronoun

The reflexive pronoun can be either a direct or an indirect object:

Se afeitó rápidamente.	He shaved quickly.
Me quité el abrigo.	I took off my coat.

31.2 Reciprocal use of pronominal verbs

Pronominal verbs can have a 'reciprocal' meaning ('each other', 'one another') as well as a reflexive one. **Se comunican** can mean either 'they get in touch with themselves' (reflexive) or 'they get in touch with each other' (reciprocal). To avoid ambiguity, Spanish often adds a phrase, either **a sí mismos** (reflexive) or **el uno al otro/los unos a los otros** (reciprocal):

Se felicitan a sí mismos.	They congratulate themselves.
Se felicitan el uno al otro.	They congratulate one another.
Sólo se preocupan de sí mismos.	They are only concerned about themselves.
Sólo se preocupan el uno del otro.	They are only concerned about each other.

31.3 Non-reflexive meanings of pronominal verbs

Pronominal verbs *often do not have a reflexive or reciprocal meaning* but reinforce the involvement of the subject in the verbal action, and/or change the meaning of the verb.

1. The reflexive pronoun is often added to transitive verbs to emphasise the whole action (of eating, drinking, etc.):

Compra los viernes.	He goes shopping on Fridays.
Se compra el periódico los viernes.	He buys the paper on Fridays.
Bebió un vaso de agua.	He drank a glass of water.
Se lo bebió de un trago.	He drank it all in one go.
Cargaron el camión.	They loaded the lorry.
Se cargaron el camión en media hora.	They loaded the lorry in half an hour.

Espero el autobús en la parada.	I wait for the bus at the bus stop.
Me espero en la parada hasta que	I wait at the bus stop until
llega el autobús.	the bus comes.

2 The pronominal forms of some verbs change the meaning of the verb:

dormir	to sleep	**dormirse**	to go to sleep
hacer	to do, make	**hacerse**	to become
ir	to go	**irse**	to go away
poner	to put	**ponerse**	to become, get, turn, put on
volver	to return	**volverse**	to become; to turn round

Se durmió en seguida.	He went to sleep at once.
Se hace tarde.	It's getting late.
Se fue ayer.	He went away/left yesterday.
Don Quijote se volvió loco de tanto leer de libros caballerías.	Don Quixote went mad from reading too many romances of chivalry.

3 The pronominal forms of **estar, caer, morir, olvidar** are worth noting.

a Estarse

The pronominal form is used for the imperative of **estar** and in the sense of **quedarse**, 'to stay':

Estáte quieto.	Be still.
Se estuvo trabajando toda la noche.	He continued (i.e. 'stayed') working all night long.

b Caerse

The pronominal form of **caer** (to fall), **caerse**, means 'to fall down', by accident:

Este año Viernes Santo cae en mi cumpleaños.	This year Good Friday falls on my birthday.
BUT	
Se cayó de la escalera.	He fell off the ladder.

c Morirse

The pronominal form is used to suggest a greater personal involvement:

Se le murió la madre.	His mother died.
Me moría de vergüenza.	I was dying of shame.

d Olvidarse

The pronominal form is nearly always used. The verb agrees in number with the thing forgotten:

Se me ha olvidado la dirección.	I've forgotten the address.
Se le olvidaron las llaves del coche.	He forgot his car keys.

4 Some verbs are used only in the pronominal form in Spanish but have no reflexive meaning in English, e.g. **atreverse** (to dare), **quejarse** (to complain), **jactarse** (to boast):

No me atrevo a decirle que su perro ha desaparecido.	I daren't tell her that her dog has disappeared.
No me quejo de la comida sino del servicio.	I'm not complaining about the food but the service.

31.4 Se used to express the passive voice

The reflexive pronoun **se** is frequently used to express the passive in Spanish:

La guerra se declaró en 1936.	War was declared in 1936.
Las aceitunas españolas se venden por todo el mundo.	Spanish olives are sold throughout the world.

(For a fuller description of the passive see Part II, 30.1).

Exercises

1 Rellena los espacios con uno de los verbos del recuadro en la forma correcta:

aprovecharse	ponerse	hacerse	volverse	atreverse
morirse	quitarse	sentirse	dormirse	jubilarse

a Mi abuelo _____ hace cinco años después de 40 años con la misma empresa.

b Estos días no _____ a salir sola por la noche.

c Mi querido perro _____ de repente mientras estábamos de vacaciones.

d ¡Todos los días _____ loco con el canto de este gallo tan de mañana!

e ¡ _____ el abrigo y pasa al salón!

f Son las once de la noche. Ya _____ tarde.

g Llegó tarde a la oficina, _____ de la ausencia del jefe.

h Ayer el niño _____ escuchando el cuento de hadas.

i Después de oír la noticia, _____ muy felices.

j Cada vez que me examino _____ muy nervioso.

2 Traduce al español:

a We'll meet tomorrow at 10 a.m.

b Get dressed, Miguel!

c My handwriting is like my mother's.

d They sat down on a bench and looked at the moon.

e I realise that nothing will be done quickly.

f He shrugged his shoulders.

g We didn't remember what day it was.

h I'm pleased to meet you.

i He ate it all up.

j You have to approach the headmaster for the answer.

32 The infinitive

Remember:

In Spanish the infinitive:

- consists of one word, which is invariable in form, e.g. **mirar**, **beber**, **escribir**.
- can also function as a noun.
- is often used after prepositions.

32.1 Verbs of perception

The infinitive may be used after verbs of perception such as **ver, oír** and **mirar**.

La vi entrar en el hotel.	I saw her go into the hotel.
Oímos llegar el coche.	We heard the car arrive.
Estaba mirando pasar a la gente.	He was watching the people go by.

32.2 The infinitive as an imperative

The infinitive is often used as a substitute for the imperative (see Part II,25.3):

No dar de comer a los animales.	Don't feed the animals.

32.3 The infinitive after prepositions

The infinitive is used after certain prepositions or prepositional phrases with a particular meaning:

1. **Por** is used with the infinitive in the sense of 'through + ing':

Por ser tan bueno le quiere todo el mundo.	Everybody loves him because he's so good.

2. **De** is used with the infinitive in the sense of 'if' (see Part II, 24.1):

Te pondrás anémica de comer tan poco.	You'll get anaemic if you eat so little.

3. **Sin** when followed by the infinitive, can have an adjectival function (see Part II, 4.3.2):

Lleva tres meses viajando sin parar.	She's been travelling non-stop for three months.
Una factura sin pagar.	An unpaid bill.

4. **Nada más** is followed by the infinitive in the sense of 'as soon as', 'just after':

Nada más llegar fueron a ver a sus primos.	As soon as they had arrived they went to see their cousins.
Nada más aceptar que era homosexual cambió su vida.	As soon as he accepted that he was gay his life changed.

32.4 A translation problem

 Learners are often unclear about the translation of the preposition 'to' in sentences of the type 'It is easy to believe ...'.

There are two types of sentence:

a where the infinitive is followed by an object or clause. In this case 'to' is not translated:

Es fácil aprender español.   It is easy to learn Spanish.

b where there is no object after the infinitive. In this case 'to' is translated by **de**:

El inglés es fácil de aprender.   English is easy to learn.
Ese problema es difícil de resolver   That problem is difficult to solve.

32.5 Verb + preposition

There follow lists of verbs which can be followed by the infinitive (a) directly, without the intervention of a preposition; (b) by **a**; (c) by **de**; (d) by **en**; (e) by **por**; (f) by **con** and (g) by **para**.

The lists given below cover the most common verbs. For an exhaustive list of verbs in each category please refer to a more detailed grammar.

a No preposition

conseguir	to succeed (in doing)	**parecer**	to seem (to do)
deber	to have to (do)	**pensar**	to intend (to do)
decidir	to decide (to do)	**permitir**	to allow to do
desear	to want/wish (to do)	**preferir**	to prefer (to do)
esperar	to hope/wait/expect (to do)	**prohibir**	to forbid (to do)
hacer	to make (someone do)	**prometer**	to promise (to do)
intentar	to try (to do)	**querer**	to want (to do)
lograr	to manage (to do)	**recordar**	to remember (to do)
mandar	to order (to do)	**saber**	to know (how to do)
necesitar	to need (to do)	**sentir**	to be sorry (to do)
olvidar	to forget (to do)	**temer**	to fear (to do)

b Verb + **a** plus infinitive

acercarse a	to get near to	**conducir a**	to lead to
acertar a	to happen to	**contribuir a**	to contribute to
acostumbrar(se) a	to accustom to	**decidirse a**	to decide to
acudir a	to go to	**dedicarse a**	to dedicate oneself to
animar a	to encourage to	**dirigirse a**	to head towards,
address			
aprender a	to learn to	**disponerse a**	to prepare to
apresurarse a	to hasten to	**echarse a**	to begin to
arriesgarse a	to risk (doing)	**empezar a**	to begin to
aspirar a	to aspire to	**enseñar a**	to teach to
atreverse a	to dare to	**enviar a**	to send to
ayudar a	to help to	**invitar a**	to invite to
bajar a	to go down to	**ir a**	to go to
comenzar a	to begin to	**mandar a**	to send to
negarse a	to refuse to	**subir a**	to go up to
obligar a	to oblige to	**venir a**	to come to
romper a	to burst out	**volver a**	to (do) again
salir a	to go out to		

c   Verb + **de** plus infinitive

acabar de	to stop (doing), to have just	**hartarse de**	to be fed up with (doing)
acordarse de	to remember	**jactarse de**	to boast of (doing)
alegrarse de	to be pleased about	**maravillarse de**	to marvel at (doing)
avergonzarse de	to be ashamed of (doing)	**olvidarse de**	to forget to
cuidar de	to take care to	**parar de**	to stop (doing)
dejar de	to stop (doing)	**terminar de**	to stop (doing)
encargarse de	to take care of, see to	**tratar de**	to try to
guardarse de	to be careful not to		

d   Verb + **en** plus infinitive

coincidir en	to coincide in (doing)	**interesarse en**	to be interested in (doing)
complacerse en	to take pleasure in (doing)	**ocuparse en**	to be busy (doing)
consentir en	to consent to	**pensar en**	to think about (doing)
dudar en	to hesitate to	**porfiar en**	to persist in (doing)
empeñarse en	to insist on (doing)	**quedar en**	to agree to
esforzarse en	to strive to	**tardar en**	to take time in (doing)
insistir en	to insist on (doing)	**vacilar en**	to hesitate in (doing)

e   Verb + **con** plus infinitive

amenazar con	to threaten to	**soñar con**	to dream of (doing)
contentarse con	to be happy to do		

f   Verb + **para** plus infinitive

prepararse para	to prepare oneself to

g   Verb + **por** plus infinitive

acabar por	to end up by (doing)	**luchar por**	to fight/struggle to
comenzar por	to begin by (doing)	**optar por**	to opt/choose to
empezar por	to begin by (doing)	**suspirar por**	to long to
esforzarse por	to strive to	**terminar por**	to end up (doing)

Exercises

1   Rellena los espacios, cuando sea necesario, con una de las preposiciones del recuadro. ¡Cuidado! en algunos casos no se necesita preposición:

por	para	con	de	a

a   Comencemos _____ lavar los platos.

b   Prepárate _____ salir dentro de cinco minutos.

c   Cuando era joven soñaba _____ ser un gran músico.

d   Intentamos _____ descubrir la causa de su ansiedad.

e   Hijo, trata _____ pensar en tu futuro.

f   Siento _____ tener que informarte que no conseguiste el empleo.

g   ¡Luchemos _____ nuestros derechos!

h   Juan se olvidó _____ decirte que no iban al bar.

i   No sabíamos adónde ir y terminamos _____ no hacer nada.

j   ¿No me dejas _____ acompañarte?

2 Traduce al español:

a Seeing is believing.

b On finding the bar they immediately rang their friends.

c Ecological change threatens to destroy the planet.

d If you try to change your diet you might damage your health.

e We've just won a holiday in Japan!

f I don't want to tell you what to do.

g We saw them going into the hotel.

h I heard my boss saying that he was going to give Manolo the sack.

i Italian is an easy language to understand.

j It isn't possible to give you an answer today.

33

The past participle

Remember:

- In Spanish the past participle is an essential part of compound perfect tenses (**haber** + past participle) and the passive voice (**ser** + past participle).
- The past participle also functions as an adjective.
- The past participle agrees in gender and number *except* when used with **haber** to form the perfect tense.

33.1 Verbs with two past participles

Some verbs have two past participles, one regular and the other irregular. The regular form is used as the past participle in various forms of the verb; the irregular form *acts only as an adjective*. Here are some common examples:

verb		*regular past participle*	*irregular past participle*	
absorber	to absorb	**absorbido**	**absorto**	absorbed
bendecir	to bless	**bendecido**	**bendito**	blessed
confundir	to confuse	**confundido**	**confuso**	confused
despertar	to wake up	**despertado**	**despierto**	awake, bright
maldecir	to curse	**maldecido**	**maldito**	cursed
soltar	to release	**soltado**	**suelto**	loose

El asesino anda suelto.	The murderer is roaming free.
Ese profesor es un bendito.	That teacher is a saint.
Encuentro un poco confusa tu teoría.	I find your theory rather confusing.

33.2 Active and passive meanings

 Note that some participles have two adjectival meanings, one 'active' the other 'passive'. The former are used with **estar** and the latter with **ser**:

	estar	ser
aburrido	bored	boring
cansado	tired	tiring
desconfiado	distrusted	distrusting
divertido	entertained	entertaining

33.3 The 'absolute' construction

The past participle is often found in the 'absolute' construction, i.e. one in which the past participle has a *different subject from the main verb:*

Dicho esto, los chicos se marcharon.
Nacido su hijo, siguió trabajando.
Terminada la faena, los amigos descansaron.

This being said, the boys left.
After her son was born she carried on working.
Having finished the chores, the friends took a break.

33.4 Tener with the past participle

Tener is occasionally used in place of **haber** as the auxiliary verb with the past participle, to form compound tenses in the past (see Part II, 17.4)

33.5 Lo with the past participle

The neuter article **lo** is used in combination with the past participle as an adjective, e.g. **lo ocurrido**, in which the meaning of **lo** is 'the thing which' or 'what' (see Part II, 2.3).

Lo prohibido (title of a novel by Galdós)
Lo dicho: volveremos dentro de dos días.
Tenemos que actuar en consonancia
con lo acordado.
Lo hecho, hecho está.

(lit. 'The forbidden thing')
As we said, we'll be back in two days' time.
We have to act according to what
was agreed.
It's no use crying over spilt milk (lit. 'What is
done, is done').

Exercises

1 Utiliza un participio pasado en diferentes funciones gramaticales: (a) como adjetivo: un nombre + participio pasado, (b) en una frase que contenga *ser* o *estar* + el participio pasado y (c) en una frase que contenga un tiempo compuesto del pasado. Utiliza los participios pasados siguientes: *empezado, terminado, abierto, hecho, puesto, prohibido, querido:*

Ejemplo: roto   (a) una ventana rota
                             (b) La ventana del dormitorio está rota.
                             (c) Los chicos han roto la ventana.

2 Traduce al español.

a I've put your jeans in the washing machine.

b The work having been done, they all went home.

c What a boring concert!

d Have you any loose change?

e I had distrusted him from the beginning.

f Exhausted, the two women decided to walk no further.

g The dinner had been prepared while they were at work.

h They still had not made any progress with the negotiations.

34

The gerund

Remember:

The Spanish gerund:

- is a kind of adverb, modifying the verb
- describes actions taking place at the same time as the action of the main verb
- emphasises the duration of the verb
- is called the present participle in English

34.1 Verbs followed by the gerund

In addition to the verbs **estar**, **seguir** and **continuar** (see Part I, 34.2), the following verbs are frequently used with the gerund:

ir + gerund

This construction is used to insist on the gradualness of the verbal action:

Iba engordando un poco más año tras año.	He got a bit fatter year after year.
Vete corriendo que vas a perder el autobús.	Run or you'll miss the bus.

llevar + gerund

The use of this construction stresses the continuity of the verbal action up to now:

Llevo ocho meses viviendo en Madrid.	I've lived/been living in Madrid for eight months.
Llevaban dos años exportando vino a Rusia.	They'd been exporting wine to Russia for two years.

andar + gerund

This construction emphasises an activity which lacks a sense of direction:

Felipe anda buscando un electricista de confianza.	Felipe is going round looking for a trustworthy electrician.
Mi marido anda reparando el coche.	My husband is tinkering with the car.

venir + gerund

This construction indicates a gradual action which started in the past and continues into the present:

Hace bastante tiempo que vengo diciéndote que debes consultar al médico.	I've been telling you for quite some time that you should go to the doctor.
Le venía diciendo a Ana lo buena que es la música de Sabina.	I've been telling Ana how good Sabina's music is.

34.2 Adjectival use of the gerund

1 The gerund is increasingly being used in an adjectival sense in modern Spanish, especially after the verb **haber**. This usage is considered grammatically incorrect:

Hay una chica esperando.	There is a girl waiting.
Había una pareja mirando hacia el cielo con un telescopio.	There was a couple looking at the sky with a telescope.

Note: in the first sentence above '**... una chica que espera**', and in the second '**... una pareja que miraba ...**' are usually considered more acceptable.

2 Two gerunds, **hirviendo** (boiling) and **ardiendo** (burning) can be used as adjectives and so are exceptions to the rule. They remain invariable:

agua hirviendo	boiling water
un bosque ardiendo	a burning wood

34.3 The gerund after verbs of perception

After verbs of 'perception', especially **ver**, **oír** and **mirar**, the gerund may qualify the object of the main verb.

Les vimos nadando en el mar.	We saw them swimming in the sea.
Había oído a los hombres hablando en el bar.	He'd heard the men talking in the bar.
Mira a los abuelos del pueblo jugando al dominó.	Look at the old people of the village playing dominoes.

34.4 The 'absolute' construction

In this construction the gerund stands separately within a kind of adverbial clause:

Siendo así, no te puedo ayudar.	This being the case, I can't help you.
Estando yo en Londres, me es difícil ponerme en contacto con ella.	Since I'm in London, it's difficult for me to get in touch with her.

34.5 The English present participle and the Spanish gerund

The English present participle (ending in *-ing*) frequently functions as a noun. As such it is often translated by a noun in Spanish, and not by a gerund.

Speed-dialling, remote controlling, thrill seeking, instant coffee drinking, rapid responding, we have begun to measure our daily lives in microseconds. Whoah! Is it any wonder we've lost the knack of doing nothing?

The Guardian, 16.09.00 (adapted)

La **marcación** rápida, el **control** remoto, la **búsqueda** de emociones fuertes, el café **instantáneo**, las **respuestas** rápidas, hemos empezado a medir nuestras vidas en microsegundos. ¡Basta! ¿No es de extrañar que le hayamos perdido el gusto al no **hacer** nada?

Exercises

1 Rellena el trozo siguiente con verbos de la lista en gerundio:

acercarse	apartar	decir	querer	aproximarse
esperar	observar	mirar	aguardar	sortear

Una mujer cubana

Me asomé al balcón, _____ (1) pasar a la gente habanera. Al cabo de unos minutos identifiqué a una mujer que permanecía quieta en el mismo lugar. Al poco rato se echó a andar hacia el hotel. Aquella mujer seguía _____ (2) y entonces gritó lo que ahora ya oía:

–¡Eh! ¿Pero qué haces tú aquí?

Me sobresalté al entender lo que estaba _____ (3), pero no tanto porque me lo dijera cuanto por el modo de hacerlo, lleno de confianza, furioso, como de quien se dispone a ajustar unas cuentas con la persona más próxima a quien está _____, (4) y que le enoja continuamente. Fue como si en mí hubiera reconocido de pronto a la persona que llevaba _____ (5) quién sabe cuánto tiempo. Había cruzado la calle, _____ (6) los pocos coches sin buscar un semáforo. Seguía _____ me (7) y _____ (8) un poco la vista, como si tuviera algún problema de estrabismo. Entonces gritó otra vez: –¿Pero qué haces tú aquí? ¿No sabes que te estaba _____ (9) desde hace una hora? Se siguió _____ (10) hacia mí, cada vez más indignada al no recibir respuesta.

Source: Javier Marías, Corazón tan blanco (adapted)

2 Traduce al español:

a We heard the children singing in the street.

b We've been travelling on this bus for hours.

c Swimming every day will make you fit.

d What are you thinking about at the moment?

e Things end up finding their true place sooner or later.

f He wrote to her asking her to come to Chile.

g From my window I could see the plane approaching slowly.

h They were putting the coins into a fruit-machine.

i 'Come in,' I said, trying to make my voice sound calm.

j She carried on laughing for a long time.

35

Negation

Remember:

- To express a simple negative in Spanish **no** is placed before the verb.
- Other negative words may be placed before or after the verb. If they come after the verb **no** must precede the verb.
- Spanish frequently forms 'double negatives': **no ... nada** (lit. 'not ... nothing') is translated by 'not ... anything' or 'nothing', depending on the context.

35.1 Words with a negative meaning

In addition to the negative words listed in Part I (Section 35.1) the following words/phrases also have a negative meaning:

alguno	no
apenas	hardly, scarcely
en ninguna parte/en ningún sitio	nowhere
en mi vida	never

Alguno/a

Alguno/a has the same meaning as **ninguno/a** when placed after a noun, but is more emphatic (see Part I, 35.1.4).

No dio contestación alguna.	He gave no answer (at all).

Apenas

Apenas means 'scarcely', 'as soon as/no sooner':

Apenas la veo/No la veo apenas.	I scarcely see her.
Apenas llegó/hubo llegado salió para buscar a sus amigos.	Scarcely/No sooner had he arrived than he went out to look for his friends.

En/Por ninguna parte

Aunque he mirado por toda la casa, no lo encuentro en ninguna parte.	Although I've looked all over the house, I can't find it anywhere.

En mi vida

En mi vida commonly acts as a negative phrase:

¡En mi vida he visto cosa semejante! ¡No he visto tal cosa en mi vida!	I've never seen such a thing in my life!

35.2 Negative words with sin

1. Negative words used after **sin** have the meaning of 'anything', 'ever', etc.:

Sin nadie que le ayude ...	Without anyone to help him ...

2. **No** is not necessary before the verb if **sin** precedes it:

No podemos darte una opinión sin saber nada del caso.	We can't give you a view without knowing anything about the case.
Sin vacilar ni un momento se marchó.	Without hesitating for even a moment, she left.

35.3 Negative words after comparatives

Negative words used after comparatives have the meaning of 'anything', 'any', etc.:

Marisa cocina mejor que nadie.	Marisa cooks better than anyone.
Me gusta el fútbol más que nada.	I love football more than anything.
Gregorio ha trabajado más que ninguno de nosotros.	Gregorio has worked harder than any of us.

35.4 Idioms

nada más	nothing else/more
de nada	not at all, don't mention it
pues nada	all right/OK
para/por siempre jamás	for ever and ever
ni idea	no idea
ni que decir tiene que	needless to say

Exercises

1   Llena los espacios con un negativo adecuado:

a _____ he visto nada parecido.

b _____ remedio parece adecuado para resolver ese problema.

c Ángel no quiso hacer el servicio militar. Yo _____.

d Hemos buscado el libro por todo el país pero no lo podemos encontrar en _____ parte.

e Pedro, ¿sabes dónde se ha ido Nicolás? ¡ _____ idea!

f De todas las chicas Arantxa juega al tenis mejor que _____.

g _____ Clara hubo llegado al nuevo colegio se puso a llorar.

h No tengo _____ miedo de viajar en avión.

i El día de la huelga esperábamos manifestaciones en la calle, pero no pasó _____.

j Los economistas creen que el euro va a salir de la crisis, pero _____ se sabe.

2   Traduce al español:

a She hasn't heard anything about her examinations.

b They haven't even started to build the house.

c What do you mean? Nothing special.

d Hardly anybody spoke about the war.

e Nobody here does anything to help the unemployed.

f That has nothing to do with what we were saying.

g I have never spent so much time working at the computer.

h I would not like to know anything about that.

i She applied for the job without knowing anything about what it involved.

j I need you more than ever.

Adverbs

Remember:

- Adverbs give more information about the action of verbs.
- Adverbs indicate manner, time, place or degree.
- Many adverbs are formed by adding **-mente** to the feminine singular adjective, e.g. **sincera** > **sinceramente**.

36.1 Uses of adverbs

1 When two or more adverbs are linked by the conjunctions **y**, **ni** or **pero**, only the last of the adverbs adds the suffix **-mente**:

Se pusieron de acuerdo honrada y libremente.	They came to an agreement freely and honourably.
Sin la ayuda de otros países Rusia no podía sobrevivir ni política ni económicamente.	Without the help of other countries Russia could not survive politically or economically.

2 Adverbs are often closely linked to adjectives and affect their meaning:

Javier es una persona muy ocupada.	Javier is a very busy person.
Está locamente enamorado.	He's madly in love.
Era un chico típicamente español.	He was a typically Spanish boy.
Haces tu trabajo mucho mejor que antes.	You do your work much better than before.

3 Adjectives can sometimes have the same function as adverbs. In this case they will usually agree in gender and number with the subject:

Mis tíos viven contentos en Londres desde 1980.	My uncle and aunt have lived happily in London since 1980.

4 Some adverbs have the same form as, and a similar meaning to, the adjective:

	adjective	adverb
alto	high	aloud, loudly
bajo	low	quietly
barato	cheap	cheaply
claro	clear	clearly
derecho	straight	straight
duro	hard	hard
fatal	fatal, awful	awfully

igual	equal	the same
limpio	clean	fair
rápido	quick	quickly

No hables tan alto.
Prefiero hablar bajo.
En Internet se compra barato los billetes
de avión.
Vaya derecho.
Lo ha hecho fatal.
¡Me da igual que vuelvas a casa o que te
quedes en la calle!
Si no juegas limpio …

Don't speak so loudly.
I prefer to speak quietly.
You can buy air tickets cheaply on the Internet.

Go straight on.
He's done it terribly badly.
It's the same to me whether you come back
home or stay out in the street!
If you don't play fair …

5 The adverb **recientemente** is shortened to **recién** before certain past participles, including **casado, hecho, llegado, muerto, nacido** and **salido**:

los recién casados
Maite, recién llegada del aeropuerto …
un coche recién estrenado

the newly-weds
Maite, recently arrived from the airport …
a new car

6 For adverbs of comparison see Part I, 5.1(2).

7 Position of adverbs and adverbial phrases (see also Word order, Part II, 40.2).

In general, adverbs and adverbial phrases are placed just before or just after the words they modify:

Fuimos ayer al castillo.
También he borrado los mensajes antiguos.
Quiero que la cena esté pronto esta noche.
Casualmente hoy iba a llamarte por teléfono.

We went to the castle yesterday.
I also have deleted my old messages.
I want dinner to be early tonight.
As it happens I was going to phone you today.

Exercises

1 Completa las siguientes frases con uno de los siguientes adverbios. Piensa en todas las posibilidades:

atrás	detrás	después	delante	arriba y abajo
cerca	lejos	antes	ahora	

a Elisa, no te coloques tan _____ que no te vemos.

b Mi novio vive _____ y yo _____ .

c No sabemos quiénes están _____ pero sí _____ .

d Lo siento, te oigo muy _____ .

e Podía oír los pasos pero cuando me volví no había nadie _____ .

f Esas cosas sólo pasaban _____; _____ ya no pasan.

g Las mujeres y los niños que salgan _____, los hombres_____ .

h Estuvimos todo el tiempo paseando _____.

i Ayer vi a tu hijo de _____ ¡Qué alto está!

j _____ de saludarnos salimos a tomar el aperitivo.

k Nos han sentado muy _____; yo no voy a ver nada.

2 Traduce al español:

a Speak quietly, please.

b She's a typically English girl.

c Some South American countries are socially and economically deprived.

d Your brother is behaving badly today.

e I can't take the examinations seriously.

f Go straight ahead, take the second left and then the first right.

g She carried out the tasks quickly and carefully.

h It's all the same to me.

i You can buy this television more cheaply here than anywhere else.

j He answered the questions intelligently.

37

Prepositions

Remember:

- A preposition is a word that links nouns, noun phrases or pronouns to the rest of the sentence. In the sentence '*After* the party, we all went down *to* the beach *without* any thought of sleeping', the words *after*, *to* and *without* are prepositions.

37.1 Uses of specific prepositions

Personal a

1 Personal **a** may be used if the direct object can be associated with people:

El Rey se ha dirigido a la nación.	The King addressed the people.
Los escándalos del GAL desprestigiaron a los socialistas.	The GAL scandal discredited the socialists.

2 Personal **a** may be used with abstract words in order to avoid ambiguity:

El amor debe vencer al odio.	Love should overcome hatred.

Other uses of a

1 **A** is used in certain time expressions, such as **a poco de** (shortly after), **a los (n) días** ('n' days later), **al día siguiente** ([on the] next day):

A poco de volver a casa comenzamos a preparar la cena.	Shortly after returning home we began to prepare the dinner.
A los quince días el tiempo había cambiado completamente.	Two weeks later the weather had changed completely.

2 With verbs of motion followed by an infinitive and destination, the second **a** is translated into English by 'in':

En 2010 fui a vivir a Caracas.	In 2010 I went to live in Caracas.

3 With certain verbs **a** can mean 'from' or 'of':

Le robaron el bolso a mi mujer en pleno centro la de ciudad.	They stole the bag from my wife in the very centre of the town.
Quería comprarle el reloj al anticuario.	He wanted to buy the watch from the antique shop.
Tengo miedo a las arañas.	I'm afraid of spiders.

4   **A la** and **a lo** + adjective

A la and **a lo** followed by the adjective mean 'in the style/ fashion':

Tráigame de primero gambas al ajillo y de segundo pollo a la chilindrón.

I'll have prawns in garlic for my starter and chicken *a la chilindrón* (with red peppers) for my main course.

La mujer llevaba el pelo cortado a lo chico.

The woman had her hair cut in a boy's style.

Con

Con has two special meanings: 'in spite of' and 'if':

1   In spite of:

Con todo el dinero que tienen, nunca van de vacaciones.

Despite all the money they've got they never take holidays.

2   'If', 'by' when followed by the infinitive:

Con darme regalos así, crees que te voy a perdonar.

If you give/By giving me presents like this you think I am going to forgive you.

Cree que con sólo estudiar en los libros va a aprender a pronunciar bien.

He thinks that by only studying the texts he will learn proper pronunciation.

De

De has a very wide variety of uses:

1   In measurements: the construction **tener ... (centímetros) de ancho/largo/alto**, etc., 'it is ... (centimetres) wide/long/high, etc.:

La pista tenía 10 metros de ancho y 15 de largo.

The floor measured 10 metres wide by 15 long.

2   When indicating authorship of a book:

'Corazón tan blanco' de Javier Marías.

A Heart so White by Javier Marías.

3   To show one's occupation or stage of life:

Trabaja de azafata/camarera.
Durante cinco años hizo compañía a un hombre de letras.
De niño me encantaba la regaliz.

She works as an air hostess/a waitress.
For five years I was companion to a man of letters.
As a child I loved liquorice.

4   'With', 'in', in adjectival phrases:

una chica de ojos verdes
el hombre de los zapatos blancos

a girl with green eyes
the man in white shoes

5   'If' before an infinitive:

De can be used for a conditional construction (see Part II, 24.1):

De haber sabido que era boxeador, no habría empezado la pelea.
De haber llegado un poquito antes, hubieras visto a los primos de Alcorcón.

If I'd known he was a boxer, I wouldn't have started the fight.
If you had arrived a little earlier, you'd have seen our cousins from Alcorcón.

Des-de

Desde hace means 'for' with a period of time:

Vivimos en la misma casa desde hace 35 años.

We've been living in the same house for 35 years.

En

1 **El primero/el último** followed by **en** means 'the first/last, etc., to':

La última en saltar a la piscina fue Pepa.
The last one to jump into the swimming pool was Pepa.

Jorge y Amparo fueron los primeros en llegar.
Jorge and Amparo were the first to arrive.

2 With percentages **en** means 'by':

Los precios han subido en un 3,2%.
Prices have gone up by 3.2%.

Para

1 To indicate point of view:

Para mí no todos los hombres son iguales.
In my view (For me) not all men are the same.

Para él, las conclusiones del informe eran erróneas.
In his opinion the conclusions of the report were wrong.

2 **Para con**

Para con meaning 'for', 'towards', has a special use with feelings:

Siente mucha solidaridad para con los gitanos.
He feels a lot of solidarity with the gypsies.

Tiene mucha gracia para con las plantas.
He's got a flair for plants.

Tiene muchos detalles para con ella.
He gives her a lot of attention.

3 **Bastar para/faltar para** means 'to be enough (to do)'

Tres huevos bastan para hacer un bizcocho.
Three eggs are enough to make a sponge cake.

4 **Para que**

Para que means 'in order that', 'so that' and is always followed by the subjunctive (see Part I, 23.3):

Compran muchos juguetes para que sus hijos no se aburran.
They buy lots of toys so that their children don't get bored.

Por

1 **Por** is used for exchange:

Vendió su coche por trescientos euros.
He sold his car for three hundred euros.

Te cambiaré mi balón por el tuyo.
I'll swap you my ball for yours.

2 **Por** is used to express an approximate place or time: 'in', 'around', 'along':

– ¿Por dónde se va a la Plaza Mayor?
How do you get to the Main Square?

– Por allí.
That way.

Me movía con soltura por aquella casa que conocía desde la niñez.
I moved easily around that house I had known since childhood.

El perro extraviado erraba por las calles de la ciudad.
The stray dog wandered about the streets of the town.

Por Navidad.
At Christmas time.

3 **Por** can be placed before certain prepositional phrases to give a sense of movement to them:

por delante de	in front of
por encima de	above
por debajo de	below
por detrás de	behind

Volamos por encima de Chile.
We're flying above Chile.

Tengo que terminar este trabajo por encima de todo.
Above all I have to finish this work.

Pasaron por delante de la iglesia.
They went (round) in front of the church.

Por detrás del chalet hay un huertecillo y una balsa con peces.
Behind the chalet there is a little garden and a pond with fish in it.

4   **Por** followed by an adjective or adverb, with the verb in the subjunctive, means 'however (much/easy, etc.)':

No le veía por mucho que agitara la mano.   I did not see him, however much he waved.
Por difícil que sea …   However difficult it may be …
No lo quiere hacer por mucho que se lo pida.   He won't do it, however much you ask him.

5   **Ir (a) por**

Ir por means 'to go and get', 'to fetch'. **Ir a por** has the same meaning but is more colloquial:

Vamos a por la leche.   We're going to get the milk.
¿Me acompañas? Voy a por un paquete de   Will you come with me? I'm going to get a
correos y luego a por los niños al colegio.   parcel from the post office and then pick up
the children from school.

Exercises

1   Una de las tres preposiciones entre paréntesis es incorrecta. Subráyala:

a El perro saltó (por, a través de, sin) la ventana.
b María, mete la carne (para, dentro de, en) la nevera.
c A los niños les encanta jugar (con, debajo de, en) la arena.
d Creo que nos han llamado (para, hasta, a) cenar.
e No puedo estudiar (por, bajo, a causa de) la música.
f A los jóvenes les gusta estar (según, con, entre) los amigos.
g Tenemos que parar (a, para, tras) comprar leche.
h ¿Cómo viene tu novia? (por, en, con) avión.
i Deja que hable yo (con, por, en) tu padre.
j Me fui una semana (ante, a, para) descansar.
k Se fue deprisa (sin, en lugar de, cabe) decir adiós.
l He venido en el autobús (junto a, con, para) tu primo Sergio.
m Si queréis llegar pronto será mejor que vayáis (cerca de, por, a través de) Tomelloso.

2   Traduce al inglés las siguientes frases:

a La fiesta es a las nueve de la noche en casa de Cuqui.
b Hugo tiene miedo a las alturas.
c Lo siento, no puedo ir con vosotros porque estoy a punto de salir para Nueva York.
d Su novio trabaja de bombero y ella está estudiando para farmacéutica.
e Ya te dije que vendría por esa calle.
f Siempre lleva muchas cosas en el bolso.
g Me gustaría comprar una casa vieja de ladrillo y renovarla con materiales nuevos.
h Dentro de unos días llegarán de Alemania unos amigos de mis padres que son unos pesados.
i Tras comprobar que teníamos todo lo que necesitábamos montamos en el coche y salimos de viaje por España.
j En ese restaurante hacen el filete de ternera con patatas fritas mejor que nadie.

3   Lee otra vez los usos de **por** y **para** y rellena los espacios con la preposición adecuada:

a Ha venido al hospital _____ que le operen del corazón.
b Ha tenido un ataque al corazón _____ comer demasiado y no hacer ejercicio.

c _____ ti, cariño, haría cualquier cosa.

d Cariño, he traído estas fresas _____ ti.

e Dinos _____ dónde has venido.

f Dinos _____ qué has venido.

g Le han dado un premio _____ ser tan trabajador.

h El jefe ha dado una fiesta _____ los empleados.

i He comprado unos dulces _____ el hijo de Roberto.

j Pregunté _____ el hijo de Roberto.

k Velázquez pintó 'Las Meninas' _____ encargo del rey.

l Velázquez pintó 'Las Meninas' _____ complacer al rey.

m El niño solo lo hace _____ llamar la atención.

n Loli no lleva minifalda _____ llamar la atención.

o Ese paquete es _____ Lucinda.

p Manda ese paquete _____ avión.

q Voy a _____ los niños.

r Me llevo el paraguas _____ no mojarnos.

s Estoy _____ ver el partido hoy.

t He vuelto pronto _____ ver el partido.

u Entra _____ dentro enseguida.

v Entra _____ la puerta.

4 Lee el texto a continuación y rellena los espacios con las preposiciones del recuadro. Verás que hay más espacios que preposiciones. Esto se debe a que algunas de las preposiciones del recuadro se repiten en el texto una o varias veces. En algunos casos si la preposición elegida es **a,** si ésta va seguida de **el,** no olvides hacer la contracción.

con	de	por	a	en	para	tras	entre	ante	al

Diario de un arqueólogo español en Oriente

(1)_____ el mediodía la primera jornada (2)_____ trabajo (3) _____ Tall Abu Fahd había finalizado. Regresamos (4)_____el hotel (5)_____ tomar nuestra merecida ducha y reponer fuerzas. Como cada tarde, (6)_____ esa pausa nos desplazamos (7)_____ el museo arqueológico (8)_____realizar el trabajo (9)_____ gabinete, que básicamente consistía (10)_____ la limpieza, estudio, clasificación, datación, y dibujo (11) _____ los fragmentos (12) _____ cerámica encontrados. Allí nos aguardaba una primera y grata sorpresa: el material arqueológico recogido esa mañana era muy homogéneo, es decir pertenecía (13) _____ un mismo período histórico. Poco después nos encontramos (14) _____ la segunda sorpresa: ese período no era otro que el Bronce Medio. No teníamos la menor duda. Y (15)_____ los restos, además, no hallamos materiales más antiguos. Como si (16) _____ un puzle se tratara, las piezas empezaban (17) _____ encajar (18) _____ la perfección. La emoción, aún contenida, embargaba al equipo. (19) _____ todos nos rondaba la misma idea (20) _____ la cabeza… Estábamos (21) _____ una cuidad fortificada, fundada (22)_____ el Bronce Medio y (23)_____ un lugar antes deshabitado… Pero nos faltaba una pieza más (24) _____ descifrar el misterio: el canal (25) _____ navegación que tenía Dur-Yahdun-Lim. Analizamos (26) _____ detalle los mapas topográficos (27) _____ la zona… Y entonces lo vimos. La tercera sorpresa. Tall Abu Fahd se encontraba (28) _____ las cercanías (29) _____ un antiguo canal, hoy parcialmente desaparecido (30) _____ las tareas agrícolas. ¡Eureka! Lo teníamos: una inmejorable candidata (31) _____ ser la antigua ciudad (32) _____ Dur-Yahdun-Lim.

Source: Clio Año 5 Número 50 (adapted)

38 Conjunctions

Remember:

Conjunctions are of two types:

- *co-ordinating*, that is they link two phrases of equal weight: **y, pero,** etc.
- *subordinating*, that is they introduce a clause that is dependent on a main clause: **porque, cuando,** etc.

38.1 Uses of specific conjunctions

Ni

1   **Ni**, as well as meaning 'nor', can be used emphatically, meaning 'not even':

Ni lo había pensado.	I hadn't even thought of it.
¡De eso, ni hablar!	That's out of the question!

2   **Ni siquiera** also means 'not even':

¡Ni siquiera nos dejaba salir por la noche!	He did not even let us go out at night!
Teníamos tanta prisa que ni siquiera desayunamos.	We were in such a hurry that we didn't even have breakfast.

Sino que

When **sino** links two clauses it must be followed by **que**. As with **sino**, the two ideas exclude each other, but are not necessarily in opposition to each other:

No sólo era inteligente y simpático sino que además era riquísimo.	He wasn't only intelligent and nice, but very rich too.
No sólo no oía sus palabras sino que tampoco podía verle.	Not only did he not hear her words but he couldn't see her either.

Que

1   In speech **que** frequently appears at the beginning of a sentence:

–¿Vamos o no? –Que sí.	'Are we going or not?' 'Yes, of course we are.'
Que te calles, hombre, que ya has hablado bastante.	Be quiet, won't you! You've talked enough already.

2   **Que** is sometimes added to a phrase for emphasis:

Eso sí que lo sé.	I certainly do know that.

(3) **Que** is inserted between a repeated verb for emphasis:

Siempre vas corre que te corre. You are always tearing around.

(4) **Que** is usually omitted in business letters after the verb **rogar** (to request):

Les rogamos nos envíen las piezas lo más pronto posible. Please send the parts as soon as possible.

(5) **Que** is frequently followed by the subjunctive in an imperative construction (see Part II, 25.2):

Que apagues la luz, que ya es tarde. Turn off the light, it's late.

Entonces, luego

Entonces is often used in speech to mean 'so', in the sense of 'in that case'. **Luego** also means 'so', in the more consequential sense of 'therefore':

No llevas maleta, no vienes con nosotros entonces. You haven't got your case so you are not coming with us.

Venezuela está muy cerca del ecuador, luego lo normal es que haga mucho calor allí. Venezuela is very near the equator, so it is normally very hot there.

Exercises

1 Elige entre: *donde, cuando, cuanto, como, según*, de acuerdo con el sentido de las frases siguientes. Asegúrate de que añades acento a estas palabras cuando sea necesario:

a _____ más me lo explica, menos lo entiendo.

b Soriano, en _____ termine lo que está haciendo, vaya a buscar el correo.

c Te lo cuento _____ me lo contaron a mí, palabra por palabra.

d Quiero un piso _____ pueda tocar el piano a mis anchas.

e Iban sentándose _____ iban llegando.

f No me explico _____ se ha hecho médico.

g Para _____ vaya a tener nietos estaré hecha una viejecita.

h Me llevó a la casa _____ pasó su niñez.

i Esas ruinas son de _____ los moros.

j ¡_____ tiempo sin verle, D. Gonzalo!

k Quisiera montar un restaurante pero no tengo idea de _____ y _____ .

l Escribe _____ quieras, no hay límite de extensión.

2 Rellena los espacios eligiendo entre *pero, sino y si no*:

a Carlos es inteligente _____ tiene que trabajar más.

b Le cortaremos el teléfono _____ paga la factura.

c No es de Consuelo de la que estoy enamorado _____ de Beatriz.

d Levántate _____ quieres llegar tarde.

e _____ sacas el billete con antelación no es seguro que puedas viajar.

f No le he dicho que sea grave _____ que debe cuidarse.

g Quería haber hablado contigo _____ no te encontré.

h Las mujeres no son débiles _____ fuertes y sensibles.

i _____ fuera porque es hermano tuyo le hubiera mandado a freír espárragos.

j Es incapaz de dormir _____ toma una pastilla.

k ¡ _____ bueno! ¿a qué se debe esta sorpresa?

l No me quejo del trabajo _____ del trato que dan a los empleados.

3 Rellena los espacios vacíos con las palabras del recuadro:

cuando	dónde	y	aunque	porque	mientras	como	sino	cuando	si no

_____ (1) nos enteramos de _____ (2) había estado nos enfadamos mucho. Ella, que no es tonta, sabía el porqué de nuestro enfado y _____ (3) no sentía remordimiento se portó _____ (4) si lo sintiera. _____ (5) tanto llegó la noticia.

Según el periódico la policía había entrado en el club y había detenido a todo el que se encontraba allí. Los amigos _____ (6) conocidos de Teresa estaban aún en la comisaría, no solo detenidos _____ (7) además con una ficha que iba a convertirlos en sospechosos. Ella nos miró con humildad _____ (8) _____ (9) hubiera salido _____ (10) lo hizo, antes que los demás, hubiera terminado igual que ellos.

39

Diminutives and augmentatives

Remember:

- Diminutives are used to express small size.
- Augmentatives are used to express large size.

A feature of diminutives and augmentatives in Spanish is that they frequently do not refer to size at all, but to an emotional attitude on the part of the speaker. For example, they can communicate affection, friendliness, irony, distaste, loathing. Diminutives and augmentatives therefore make a huge expressive range possible.

39.1 Uses of diminutives and augmentatives

1   Diminutives frequently express friendliness and affection and are used in informal and relaxed situations:

Un momentito, por favor, el doctor está atendiendo a los pequeñines.	Wait a moment please, the doctor is seeing to the little ones.
¿Qué tal si nos tomamos una cervecita con unas tapitas?	How about having a pint and a few tapas?
Mañana es domingo y te quedarás en la camita un ratito más.	Tomorrow is Sunday so you can stay in bed for a little bit longer.
Mi pobre gatito está muy enfermo.	My poor cat is very ill.
Le he traído un regalito, doctor, por lo bien que se porta conmigo.	I've brought a little present for you, doctor, for treating me so well.

2   Augmentatives often have connotations of unpleasantness, heaviness or ugliness:

palabra	word	**palabrota**	swear word
casa	house	**casota, casucha, caserón**	a house in bad state of repair
zapatos	shoes	**zapatones**	heavy shoes
pelos	hairs	**pelotes**	untidy hair
vaso	glass	**vasote**	big, ugly glass

3   The **-azo** suffix often refers to:

a   A blow of some kind:

puño	fist	**puñetazo**	punch
balón	ball	**balonazo**	a hit with a ball
bomba	bomb	**bombazo**	a bomb blast

b   A political coup:

el tejerazo	the attempted coup in Spain in 1981,
un golpazo	led by Colonel Tejero a coup d'état

4   In addition to those diminutive suffixes listed in Part I, 39.1, the following are also found:

-ete	viejo	old man	**vejete**	little old man
-ín	pelo	hair	**pelín**	a little, a bit
-iño	querido	dear	**cariño**	darling

Some of these diminutives have geographical preferences:

In Andalucía the preferred diminutive is **-illo/a.**
In Aragón **-ico/a** are used more often.
In Galicia the preferred diminutive is **-iño/a.**

5   Some suffixes do not convey any particular idea of size or emotion, but denote another word:

ventana	window	**ventanilla**	car/train/plane window
bolso	bag	**bolsillo**	pocket
cintura	waist	**cinturón**	belt
rata	rat	**ratón**	mouse

In the last example the augmentative ending actually denotes a smaller animal.

6   Usually the diminutive and the augmentative are of the same gender as the word from which they are derived, but occasionally there is a change of gender:

el camión	lorry	**la camioneta**	van
la espina	thorn, spine	**el espinazo**	backbone
el pescado	fish	**la pescadilla**	whiting

7   Adverbs may also take a suffix, which intensifies the meaning, especially in Latin-American usage:

ahora	**ahorita**	now
cerca	**cerquita**	near
al lado	**al ladito**	beside
encima	**encimita**	above
pronto	**prontito**	early

Exercises

1   Elige del recuadro de abajo un diminutivo o aumentativo y rellena los espacios en las frases siguientes:

campanazos	campanilla	cochinillo	dedicos	gigantesco	jamoncico
pastillita	pastillotas	patatiñas	patatitas	pequeñita	
pulpiño	relojito	relojazo	Rosita	violón	

a Nos han recomendado este bar gallego porque hacen un _____ y unas _____ bravas muy ricas.

b Él piensa que lleva un _____ estupendo pero a mí me parece un _____ de lo más normal.

c Cuando vayas a Segovia debes tomar un _____ con _____ en el restaurante de Cándido.

d Me tengo que tomar una _____ para poder dormir. Menos mal que es _____ porque no podría tomarme esas _____ que hacen ahora.

e El _____ de Teruel está para chuparse los _____ .

f Cuando sonaban los _____ en la iglesia, el marqués llamaba al criado con la _____ .

g La hermana pequeña, _____ tocaba el violín, Ana, la mediana, tocaba la viola y el _____, Alfredo, el _____ .

2 En este texto muchos nombres y adjetivos aceptan diminutivos. Cambia el texto añadiendo diminutivos donde puedas:

Paco y Carmen consiguieron ahorrar un *dinero* y se han comprado una *casa* en el campo. La *casa* es *pequeña* pero muy linda. Tiene un *comedor* con bastante espacio para una *mesa*, cuatro *sillas* y dos *sillones*. La *cocina* aunque sea pequeña es muy alegre y tiene mucha luz, y el *cuarto* de baño contiene todo lo necesario. A los niños les han puesto dos *camas iguales* que son una monada. En el *salón* hay una chimenea para poder encender un *fuego* en el invierno. *Paco*, que siempre ha sido muy *apañado*, ha puesto unas *cortinas* monísimas en todas las ventanas. A mí, lo que más me gusta es el *jardín*. *Carmen* tiene *manos* de jardinera y lo tiene lleno de *flores* silvestres de todos los colores. La verdad es que es una *casa* la mar de cuca.

3 Añade diminutivos y aumentativos donde convengan:

a Jorge está malo, voy a tomarle la temperatura.

b Tu padre está hecho un viejo muy simpático.

c Préstame algún dinero para un café.

d Llevaba un vestido con flores lila y un cuello de encaje.

e Han tenido un bebé precioso con los mismos ojos que su madre y las mismas ganas de comer que su padre. Será un hombre como él.

f Hubo un lleno impresionante en el teatro porque Javier Bardém es un actor genial.

40 Word order

Remember:

- Word order in Spanish is more flexible than in English.
- Verbs tend to be placed near the beginning of a sentence.
- Never end a Spanish sentence with a preposition.

40.1 The position of direct and indirect object pronouns

When a special emphasis is placed on a direct or indirect object it is repeated as a pronoun before the verb (see Part I, 7.3).

40.2 The position of adverbs

1   Adverbs are usually placed either directly before or directly after the verb:

Hablas bien el español.	You speak Spanish well.
Retira un poco los papeles, porque	Move the papers back a bit
vas a ensuciarlos.	or they'll get dirty.
Normalmente, los españoles cenan	Spaniards generally have supper
mucho más tarde que los demás europeos.	much later than other Europeans.

2   Adverbs should not be placed between an auxiliary verb and a participle:

Siempre he creído que ella volvería.	I have always believed that she would come back.
[He creído siempre … is also correct.]	
Juan Miguel se ha levantado rápidamente	Juan Miguel quickly got up from the chair.
de la silla.	
Nunca me ha pagado una copa.	He's never bought me a drink.

In English and French it is usual for adverbs to split a compound tense. 'I have always believed …' '*J'ai toujours cru …*' In Spanish this is not the case: **Siempre he creído …**

3   It is usual to place a word or phrase which one wishes to highlight at the beginning of a sentence:

Ayer la vi en el Corte Inglés.	I saw her yesterday in the Corte Inglés.
Desde niña me dan miedo los relámpagos.	I'd been frightened by lightning since I was a child.
Después de acabar la dictadura, España	Spain began to change dramatically when
empezó a cambiar de manera vertiginosa.	the dictatorship was over.

A partir del día que le conocí, mi vida cambió por completo.	My life changed completely from the day I met him.

In questions, a word or phrase that the speaker wishes to emphasise is often placed before the question and followed by a comma:

Y tu padre, ¿cómo está?	How is your father?
La moneda única, ¿es o no es una buena idea?	Is the single currency a good idea or not?
El diccionario, ¿lo tienes tú?	Have you got the dictionary?

Exercises

1 Cambia las frases siguientes enfatizando la parte más importante, colocándola al principio según el modelo:

Ejemplo: ¿Te han gustado las flores?

           Las flores, ¿te han gustado?

a ¿Ha llegado ya el cartero?

b No me ha gustado nada esa película.

c Me sienta muy bien ese color de pelo.

d ¿Has cerrado ya el ordenador?

e Los niños aprenden bastante en las escuelas privadas.

f El vino de Jerez les gusta mucho a los ingleses.

g Se cansa mucho de trabajar por la noche.

h ¿Han abierto ya la exposición?

i He perdido la cámara de fotos.

j Llevo trabajando en la misma empresa quince años.

2 Traduce las siguientes frases al español. Ten en cuenta que hay más de una posible traducción en cuanto al orden de las palabras:

a The amazing thing is that without any formal education he became an Internet millionaire.

b She has always gone swimming after work.

c My mother has never voted Conservative.

d I very rarely eat red meat and only occasionally fish.

e Blas has supported Real Betis since he was a child.

f The fire brigade turned up to put the fire out.

g Could you please bring us two more coffees?

h I don't suppose you have seen the book that Carla bought me.

Verb tables

Names of tenses

English	Spanish
present indicative	presente (de indicativo/de subjuntivo)
imperfect	pretérito imperfecto (de indicativo/de subjuntivo)
preterite	pretérito indefinido
future	futuro
imperative	imperativo
conditional	condicional
infinitive	infinitivo
gerund	gerundio
participle: present	participio: presente
past	pasado
compound tenses:	tiempos perfectos:
perfect	pretérito perfecto (de indicativo/de subjuntivo)
pluperfect	pretérito pluscuamperfecto (de indicativo/de subjuntivo)
past anterior	pretérito anterior
future perfect	tiempos futuro perfecto
conditional perfect	condicional perfecto

Regular verbs

hablar

imperative familiar	present indicative	imperfect indicative	preterite	future
habla	hablo	hablaba	hablé	hablaré
hablad	hablas	hablabas	hablaste	hablarás
	habla	hablaba	habló	hablará
	hablamos	hablábamos	hablamos	hablaremos
	habláis	hablabais	hablasteis	hablaréis
	hablan	hablaban	hablaron	hablarán

conditional	present subjunctive	imperfect subjunctive	gerund
hablaría	hable	hablara/ase	hablando
hablarías	hables	hablaras/ases	
hablaría	hable	hablara/ase	**past participle**
hablaríamos	hablemos	habláramos/ásemos	hablado
hablaríais	habléis	hablarais/aseis	
hablarían	hablen	hablaran/asen	

comer

imperative familiar	present indicative	imperfect indicative	preterite	future
come	como	comía	comí	comeré
comed	comes	comías	comiste	comerás
	come	comía	comió	comerá
	comemos	comíamos	comimos	comeremos
	coméis	comíais	comisteis	comeréis
	comen	comían	comieron	comerán

conditional	present subjunctive	imperfect subjunctive	gerund
comería	coma	comiera/ese	comiendo
comerías	comas	comieras/eses	
comería	coma	comiera/ese	**past participle**
comeríamos	comamos	comiéramos/ésemos	comido
comeríais	comáis	comierais/eseis	
comerían	coman	comieran/esen	

vivir

imperative familiar	present indicative	imperfect indicative	preterite	future
vive	vivo	vivía	viví	viviré
vivid	vives	vivías	viviste	vivirás
	vive	vivía	vivió	vivirá
	vivimos	vivíamos	vivimos	viviremos
	vivís	vivíais	vivisteis	viviréis
	viven	vivían	vivieron	vivirán

conditional	present subjunctive	imperfect subjunctive	gerund
viviría	viva	viviera/ese	viviendo
vivirías	vivas	vivieras/eses	
viviría	viva	viviera/ese	**past participle**
viviríamos	vivamos	viviéramos/ésemos	vivido
viviríais	viváis	vivierais/eseis	
vivirían	vivan	vivieran/esen	

Irregular verbs

andar

imperative familiar	present indicative	imperfect indicative	preterite	future
anda	ando	andaba	anduve	andaré
andad	andas	andabas	anduviste	andarás
	anda	andabas	anduvo	andará
	andamos	andábamos	anduvimos	andaremos
	andáis	andabais	anduvisteis	andaréis
	andan	andaban	anduvieron	andarán

conditional	present subjunctive	imperfect subjunctive	gerund
andaría	ande	anduviera/ese	andando
andarías	andes	anduvieras/eses	
andaría	ande	anduviera/ese	**past participle**
andaríamos	andemos	anduviéramos/ésemos	andado
andaríais	andéis	anduvierais/eseis	
andarían	anden	anduvieran/esen	

caber

imperative familiar	present indicative	imperfect indicative	preterite	future
cabe	quepo	cabía	cupe	cabré
cabed	cabes	cabías	cupiste	cabrás
	cabe	cabía	cupo	cabrá
	cabemos	cabíamos	cupimos	cabremos
	cabéis	cabíais	cupisteis	cabréis
	caben	cabían	cupieron	cabrán

conditional	present subjunctive	imperfect subjunctive	gerund
cabría	quepa	cupiera/ese	cabiendo
cabrías	quepas	cupieras/eses	
cabría	quepa	cupiera/ese	**past participle**
cabríamos	quepamos	cupiéramos/ésemos	cabido
cabríais	quepáis	cupierais/eseis	
cabrían	quepan	cupieran/esen	

caer

imperative familiar	present indicative	imperfect indicative	preterite	future
cae	caigo	caía	caí	caeré
caed	caes	caías	caíste	caerás
	cae	caía	cayó	caerá
	caemos	caíamos	caímos	caeremos
	caéis	caíais	caísteis	caeréis
	caen	caían	cayeron	caerán

conditional	present subjunctive	imperfect subjunctive	gerund
caería	caiga	cayera/ese	cayendo
caerías	caigas	cayeras/eses	
caería	caiga	cayera/ese	**past participle**
caeríamos	caigamos	cayéramos/ésemos	caído
caeríais	caigáis	cayerais/eseis	
caerían	caigan	cayeran/esen	

conocer

imperative familiar	present indicative	imperfect indicative	preterite	future
conoce	conozco	conocía	conocí	conoceré
conoced	conoces	conocías	conociste	conocerás
	conoce	conocía	conoció	conocerá
	conocemos	conocíamos	conocimos	conoceremos
	conocéis	conocíais	conocisteis	conoceréis
	conocen	conocían	conocieron	conocerán

conditional	present subjunctive	imperfect subjunctive	gerund
conocería	conozca	conociera/ese	conociendo
conocerías	conozcas	conocieras/eses	
conocería	conozca	conociera/ese	**past participle**
conoceríamos	conozcamos	conociéramos/ésemos	conocido
conoceríais	conozcáis	conocierais/eseis	
conocerían	conozcan	conocieran/esen	

dar

imperative familiar	present indicative	imperfect indicative	preterite	future
da	doy	daba	di	daré
dad	das	dabas	diste	darás
	da	daba	dio	dará
	damos	dábamos	dimos	daremos
	dais	dabais	disteis	daréis
	dan	daban	dieron	darán

conditional	present subjunctive	imperfect subjunctive	gerund
daría	dé	diera/ese	dando
darías	des	dieras/eses	
daría	dé	diera/ese	**past participle**
daríamos	demos	diéramos/ésemos	dado
daríais	déis	dierais/eseis	
darían	den	dieran/esen	

decir

imperative familiar	present indicative	imperfect indicative	preterite	future
di	digo	decía	dije	diré
decid	dices	decías	dijiste	dirás
	dice	decía	dijo	dirá
	decimos	decíamos	dijimos	diremos
	decís	decíais	dijisteis	diréis
	dicen	decían	dijeron	dirán

conditional	present subjunctive	imperfect subjunctive	gerund
diría	diga	dijera/ese	diciendo
dirías	digas	dijeras/eses	
diría	diga	dijera/ese	**past participle**
diríamos	digamos	dijéramos/ésemos	dicho
diríais	digáis	dijerais/eseis	
dirían	digan	dijeran/esen	

dormir

imperative familiar	present indicative	imperfect indicative	preterite	future
duerme	duermo	dormía	dormí	dormiré
dormid	duermes	dormías	dormiste	dormirás
	duerme	dormía	durmió	dormirá
	dormimos	dormíamos	dormimos	dormiremos
	dormís	dormíais	dormisteis	dormiréis
	duermen	dormían	durmieron	dormirán

conditional	present subjunctive	imperfect subjunctive	gerund
dormiría	duerma	durmiera/ese	durmiendo
dormirías	duermas	durmieras/eses	
dormiría	duerma	durmiera/ese	**past participle**
dormiríamos	durmamos	durmiéramos/ésemos	dormido
dormiríais	durmáis	durmierais/eseis	
dormirían	duerman	durmieran/esen	

estar

imperative familiar	present indicative	imperfect indicative	preterite	future
está	estoy	estaba	estuve	estaré
estad	estás	estabas	estuviste	estarás
	está	estaba	estuvo	estará
	estamos	estábamos	estuvimos	estaremos
	estáis	estabais	estuvisteis	estaréis
	están	estaban	estuvieron	estarán

conditional	present subjunctive	imperfect subjunctive	gerund
estaría	esté	estuviera/ese	estando
estarías	estés	estuvieras/eses	
estaría	esté	estuviera/ese	**past participle**
estaríamos	estemos	estuviéramos/ésemos	estado
estaríais	estéis	estuvierais/eseis	
estarían	estén	estuvieran/esen	

haber (auxiliary verb)

imperative familiar	present indicative	imperfect indicative	preterite	future
–	he	había	hube	habré
–	has	habías	hubiste	habrás
	ha	había	hubo	habrá
	hemos	habíamos	hubimos	habremos
	habéis	habíais	hubisteis	habréis
	han	habían	hubieron	habrán

conditional	present subjunctive	imperfect subjunctive	gerund
habría	haya	hubiera/ese	habiendo
habrías	hayas	hubieras/eses	
habría	haya	hubiera/ese	**past participle**
habríamos	hayamos	hubiéramos/ésemos	habido
habríais	hayáis	hubierais/eseis	
habrían	hayan	hubieran/esen	

hacer

imperative familiar	present indicative	imperfect indicative	preterite	future
haz	hago	hacía	hice	haré
haced	haces	hacías	hiciste	harás
	hace	hacía	hizo	hará
	hacemos	hacíamos	hicimos	haremos
	hacéis	hacíais	hicisteis	haréis
	hacen	hacían	hicieron	harán

conditional	present subjunctive	imperfect subjunctive	gerund
haría	haga	hiciera/ese	haciendo
harías	hagas	hicieras/eses	
haría	haga	hiciera/ese	**past participle**
haríamos	hagamos	hiciéramos/ésemos	hecho
haríais	hagáis	hicierais/eseis	
harían	hagan	hicieran/esen	

ir

imperative familiar	present indicative	imperfect indicative	preterite	future
ve	voy	iba	fui	iré
id	vas	ibas	fuiste	irás
	va	iba	fue	irá
	vamos	íbamos	fuimos	iremos
	vais	ibais	fuisteis	iréis
	van	iban	fueron	irán

conditional	present subjunctive	imperfect subjunctive	gerund
iría	vaya	fuera/se	yendo
irías	vayas	fueras/eses	
iría	vaya	fuera/ese	**past participle**
iríamos	vayamos	fuéramos/ésemos	ido
iríais	vayáis	fuerais/eseis	
irían	vayan	fueran/esen	

leer

imperative familiar	present indicative	imperfect indicative	preterite	future
lee	leo	leía	leí	leeré
leed	lees	leías	leíste	leerás
	lee	leía	leyó	leerá
	leemos	leíamos	leímos	leeremos
	leéis	leíais	leísteis	leeréis
	leen	leían	leyeron	leerán

conditional	present subjunctive	imperfect subjunctive	gerund
leería	lea	leyera/ese	leyendo
leerías	leas	leyeras/eses	
leería	lea	leyera/ese	**past participle**
leeríamos	leamos	leyéramos/ésemos	leído
leeríais	leáis	leyerais/eseis	
leerían	lean	leyeran/esen	

oír

imperative familiar	present indicative	imperfect indicative	preterite	future
oye	oigo	oía	oí	oiré
oíd	oyes	oías	oíste	oirás
	oye	oía	oyó	oirá
	oímos	oíamos	oímos	oiremos
	oís	oíais	oísteis	oiréis
	oyen	oían	oyeron	oirán

conditional	present subjunctive	imperfect subjunctive	gerund
oiría	oiga	oyera/ese	oyendo
oirías	oigas	oyeras/eses	
oiría	oiga	oyera/ese	**past participle**
oiríamos	oigamos	oyéramos/ésemos	oído
oiríais	oigáis	oyerais/eseis	
oirían	oigan	oyeran/esen	

pedir

imperative familiar	present indicative	imperfect indicative	preterite	future
pide	pido	pedía	pedí	pediré
pedid	pides	pedías	pediste	pedirás
	pide	pedía	pidió	pedirá
	pedimos	pedíamos	pedimos	pediremos
	pedís	pedíais	pedisteis	pediréis
	piden	pedían	pidieron	pedirán

conditional	present subjunctive	imperfect subjunctive	gerund
pediría	pida	pidiera/ese	pidiendo
pedirías	pidas	pidieras/eses	
pediría	pida	pidiera/ese	**past participle**
pediríamos	pidamos	pidiéramos/ésemos	pedido
pediríais	pidáis	pidierais/eseis	
pedirían	pidan	pidieran/esen	

pensar

imperative familiar	present indicative	imperfect indicative	preterite	future
piensa	pienso	pensaba	pensé	pensaré
pensad	piensas	pensabas	pensaste	pensarás
	piensa	pensaba	pensó	pensará
	pensamos	pensábamos	pensamos	pensaremos
	pensáis	pensabais	pensasteis	pensaréis
	piensan	pensaban	pensaron	pensarán

conditional	present subjunctive	imperfect subjunctive	gerund
pensaría	piense	pensara/ase	pensando
pensarías	pienses	pensaras/ases	
pensaría	piense	pensara/ase	**past participle**
pensaríamos	pensemos	pensáramos/ásemos	pensado
pensaríais	penséis	pensarais/aseis	
pensarían	piensen	pensaran/asen	

poder

imperative familiar	present indicative	imperfect indicative	preterite	future
–	puedo	podía	pude	podré
–	puedes	podías	pudiste	podrás
	puede	podía	pudo	podrá
	podemos	podíamos	pudimos	podremos
	podéis	podíais	pudisteis	podréis
	pueden	podían	pudieron	podrán

conditional	present subjunctive	imperfect subjunctive	gerund
podría	pueda	pudiera/ese	pudiendo
podrías	puedas	pudieras/eses	
podría	pueda	pudiera/ese	**past participle**
podríamos	podamos	pudiéramos/ésemos	podido
podríais	podáis	pudierais/eseis	
podrían	puedan	pudieran/esen	

poner

imperative familiar	present indicative	imperfect indicative	preterite	future
pon	pongo	ponía	puse	pondré
poned	pones	ponías	pusiste	pondrás
	pone	ponía	puso	pondrá
	ponemos	poníamos	pusimos	pondremos
	ponéis	poníais	pusisteis	pondréis
	ponen	ponían	pusieron	pondrán

conditional	present subjunctive	imperfect subjunctive	gerund
pondría	ponga	pusiera/ese	poniendo
pondrías	pongas	pusieras/eses	
pondría	ponga	pusiera/ese	**past participle**
pondríamos	pongamos	pusiéramos/ésemos	puesto
pondríais	pongáis	pusierais/eseis	
pondrían	pongan	pusieran/esen	

querer

imperative familiar	present indicative	imperfect indicative	preterite	future
quiere	quiero	quería	quise	querré
quered	quieres	querías	quisiste	querrás
	quiere	quería	quiso	querrá
	queremos	queríamos	quisimos	querremos
	queréis	queríais	quisisteis	querréis
	quieren	querían	quisieron	querrán

conditional	present subjunctive	imperfect subjunctive	gerund
querría	quiera	quisiera/ese	queriendo
querrías	quieras	quisieras/eses	
querría	quiera	quisiera/ese	**past participle**
querríamos	queramos	quisiéramos/ésemos	querido
querríais	queráis	quisierais/eseis	
querrían	quieran	quisieran/esen	

saber

imperative familiar	present indicative	imperfect indicative	preterite	future
sabe	sé	sabía	supe	sabré
sabed	sabes	sabías	supiste	sabrás
	sabe	sabía	supo	sabrá
	sabemos	sabíamos	supimos	sabremos
	sabéis	sabíais	supisteis	sabréis
	saben	sabían	supieron	sabrán

conditional	present subjunctive	imperfect subjunctive	gerund
sabría	sepa	supiera/ese	sabiendo
sabrías	sepas	supieras/eses	
sabría	sepa	supiera/ese	**past participle**
sabríamos	sepamos	supiéramos/ésemos	sabido
sabríais	sepáis	supierais/esen	
sabrían	sepan	supieran/esen	

salir

imperative familiar	present indicative	imperfect indicative	preterite	future
sal	salgo	salía	salí	saldré
salid	sales	salías	saliste	saldrás
	sale	salía	salió	saldrá
	salimos	salíamos	salimos	saldremos
	salís	salíais	salisteis	saldréis
	salen	salían	salieron	saldrán

conditional	present subjunctive	imperfect subjunctive	gerund
saldría	salga	saliera/ese	saliendo
saldrías	salgas	salieras/eses	
saldría	salga	saliera/ese	**past participle**
saldríamos	salgamos	saliéramos/ésemos	salido
saldríais	salgáis	salierais/eseis	
saldrían	salgan	salieran/esen	

seguir

imperative familiar	present indicative	imperfect indicative	preterite	future
sigue	sigo	seguía	seguí	seguiré
seguid	sigues	seguías	seguiste	seguirás
	sigue	seguía	siguió	seguirá
	seguimos	seguíamos	seguimos	seguiremos
	seguís	seguíais	seguisteis	seguiréis
	siguen	seguían	siguieron	seguirán

conditional	present subjunctive	imperfect subjunctive	gerund
seguiría	siga	siguiera/ese	siguiendo
seguirías	sigas	siguieras/eses	
seguiría	siga	siguiera/ese	**past participle**
seguiríamos	sigamos	siguiéramos/ésemos	seguido
seguiríais	sigáis	siguierais/eseis	
seguirían	sigan	siguieran/esen	

sentir

imperative familiar	present indicative	imperfect indicative	preterite	future
siente	siento	sentía	sentí	sentiré
sentid	sientes	sentías	sentiste	sentirás
	siente	sentía	sintió	sentirá
	sentimos	sentíamos	sentimos	sentiremos
	sentís	sentíais	sentisteis	sentiréis
	sienten	sentían	sintieron	sentirán

conditional	present subjunctive	imperfect subjunctive	gerund
sentiría	sienta	sintiera/ese	sintiendo
sentirías	sientas	sintieras/eses	
sentiría	sienta	sintiera/ese	**past participle**
sentiríamos	sintamos	sintiéramos/ésemos	sentido
sentiríais	sintáis	sintierais/eseis	
sentirían	sientan	sintieran/esen	

ser

imperative familiar	present indicative	imperfect indicative	preterite	future
sé	soy	era	fui	seré
sed	eres	eras	fuiste	serás
	es	era	fue	será
	somos	éramos	fuimos	seremos
	sois	erais	fuisteis	seréis
	son	eran	fueron	serán

ser (continued)

conditional	present subjunctive	imperfect subjunctive	gerund
sería	sea	fuera/ese	siendo
erías	seas	fueras/eses	
sería	sea	fuera/ese	**past participle**
seríamos	seamos	fuéramos/ésemos	sido
seríais	seáis	fuerais/eseis	
serían	sean	fueran/esen	

tener

imperative familiar	present indicative	imperfect indicative	preterite	future
ten	tengo	tenía	tuve	tendré
tened	tienes	tenías	tuviste	tendrás
	tiene	tenía	tuvo	tendrá
	tenemos	teníamos	tuvimos	tendremos
	tenéis	teníais	tuvisteis	tendréis
	tienen	tenían	tuvieron	tendrán

conditional	present subjunctive	imperfect subjunctive	gerund
tendría	tenga	tuviera/ese	teniendo
tendrías	tengas	tuvieras/eses	
tendría	tenga	tuviera/ese	**past participle**
tendríamos	tengamos	tuviéramos/ésemos	tenido
tendríais	tengáis	tuvierais/eseis	
tendrían	tengan	tuvieran/esen	

traer

imperative familiar	present indicative	imperfect indicative	preterite	future
trae	traigo	traía	traje	traeré
traed	traes	traías	trajiste	traerás
	trae	traía	trajo	traerá
	traemos	traíamos	trajimos	traeremos
	traéis	traíais	trajisteis	traeréis
	traen	traían	trajeron	traerán

conditional	present subjunctive	imperfect subjunctive	gerund
traería	traiga	trajera/ese	trayendo
traerías	traigas	trajeras/eses	
traería	traiga	trajera/ese	**past participle**
traeríamos	traigamos	trajéramos/ésemos	traído
traeríais	traigáis	trajerais/eseis	
traerían	traigan	trajeran/esen	

valer

imperative familiar	present indicative	imperfect indicative	preterite	future
vale	valgo	valía	valí	valdré
valed	vales	valías	valiste	valdrás
	vale	valía	valió	valdrá
	valemos	valíamos	valimos	valdremos
	valéis	valíais	valisteis	valdréis
	valen	valían	valieron	valdrán

conditional	present subjunctive	imperfect subjunctive	gerund
valdría	valga	valiera/ese	valiendo
valdrías	valgas	valieras/eses	
valdría	valga	valiera/ese	**past participle**
valdríamos	valgamos	valiéramos/ésemos	valido
valdríais	valgáis	valierais/eseis	
valdrían	valgan	valieran/esen	

venir

imperative familiar	present indicative	imperfect indicative	preterite	future
ven	vengo	venía	vine	vendré
venid	vienes	venías	viniste	vendrás
	viene	venía	vino	vendrá
	venimos	veníamos	vinimos	vendremos
	venís	veníais	vinisteis	vendréis
	vienen	venían	vinieron	vendrán

conditional	present subjunctive	imperfect subjunctive	gerund
vendría	venga	viniera/ese	viniendo
vendrías	vengas	vinieras/eses	
vendría	venga	viniera/ese	**past participle**
vendríamos	vengamos	viniéramos/ésemos	venido
vendríais	vengáis	vinierais/eseis	
vendrían	vengan	vinieran/esen	

ver

imperative familiar	present indicative	imperfect indicative	preterite	future
ve	veo	veía	vi	veré
ved	ves	veías	viste	verás
	ve	veía	vio	verá
	vemos	veíamos	vimos	veremos
	veis	veíais	visteis	veréis
	ven	veían	vieron	verán

conditional	present subjunctive	imperfect subjunctive	gerund
vería	vea	viera/ese	viendo
verías	veas	vieras/eses	
vería	vea	viera/ese	**past participle**
veríamos	veamos	viéramos/ésemos	visto
veíais	veáis	vierais/eseis	
verían	vean	vieran/esen	

volver

imperative familiar	present indicative	imperfect indicative	preterite	future
vuelve	vuelvo	volvía	volví	volveré
volved	vuelves	volvías	volviste	volverás
	vuelve	volvía	volvió	volverá
	volvemos	volvíamos	volvimos	volveremos
	volvéis	volvíais	volvisteis	volveréis
	vuelven	volvían	volvieron	volverán

volver (*continued*)

conditional	present subjunctive	imperfect subjunctive	gerund
volvería	vuelva	volviera/ese	volviendo
volverías	vuelvas	volvieras/eses	
volvería	vuelva	volviera/ese	**past participle**
volveríamos	volvamos	volviéramos/ésemos	vuelto
volveríais	volváis	volvierais/eseis	
volverían	vuelvan	volvieran/esen	

Compound verbs

The following common verbs conform to the same rules for spelling as the irregular verbs from which they are derived:

atraer	to attract	distraer	to distract
contradecir	to contradict	mantener	to maintain
convenir	to agree to	proponer	to propose
deshacer	to undo	reponer	to put back
detener	to stop	retener	to retain
devenir	to become	satisfacer	to satisfy
disponer	to arrange	suponer	to suppose

Key to Exercises

Part 1

Note: Answers are not given for those exercises which require an unpredictable response

1   Pronunciation, accents, spelling and punctuation

3 **(i)** **hard c**   *calor*   *campo*   *caramba*   *cubo*

  (ii) **soft c**   *cena*   *ciudad*   *palacio*   *policía*   *cerilla*   *ciencia*   *celos*   *dice*   *obsceno*

  (iii) **hard and soft c**   *destrucción*   *cinco*   *acceso*   *bicicleta*   *cicatriz*   *conciencia* *circunstancia*

4 **(i)** **hard g**   *gol*   *gordo*   *elegante*   *liga*   *orgullo*   *guerra*   *lugar*   *Miguel*   *pegué*

  (ii) **g like Spanish *jota***   *girasol*   *gerente*   *gitano*   *genial*   *gimnasta*

  (iii) **g like 'gw'**   *agua*   *guapa*   *averiguar*   *vergüenza*   *guardián*   *halagüeño*

5   *Diphthong*

  Yes: *ruina*   *variable*   *miedo*   *pues*   *destruido*   *hacia*   *pienso*   *luego*
          Ceuta   *ciudad*   *neurosis*
  No: *feo*   *correo*   *caer*   *peatón*   *poner*   *cara*   *chimenea*   *leer*   *jaleo*

6   *Accent*   *No accent*

Accent		No accent	
águila	riquísimo	fue	visiones
también	sofá	dijo	examen
ambición	imágenes	encantador	bailar
héroe	teléfono	saludable	ausencia
ambigüedad	subterráneo	destruido	local
jardín	caído	maestra	espejo
autobús		arroz	
comían		general	
interés		capaz	

7

last syllable	penultimate syllable	antepenultimate syllable
renegón	gato	crítica
rapaz	caramba	apéndice
autobús	alférez	retruécano
acordeón	golondrina	cántaro
Luis	Sevilla	antílope
coliflor	repique	Córcega
atención	mantequilla	dátiles
repostería	paella	altímetro
	pozo	
	dormitorio	
	alberca	
	lucero	

8 Isabel II es la número 60 de los reyes de Inglaterra, y la sexta reina. Su tío fue Eduardo VIII, quien abdicó en 1936 para casarse con una divorciada. Su padre, Jorge VI, dejó de ser duque de York para convertirse en rey después de aquella abdicación. Durante la dramática segunda guerra mundial la famila real se quedó en Londres, a pesar de la posible invasión alemana de la capital. Un año antes de los Juegos Olímpicos de Londres en 1948 Isabel había contraído matrimonio con el griego Felipe, quien renunció a sus derechos al trono griego. Existe parentesco entre el Príncipe Felipe y la reina Sofía de España.

9

English	Spanish
Monday	lunes
March	marzo
French	francesa
Spanish-American	hispanoamericana
A Hundred Years of Solitude	Cien años de soledad
Colombian	colombiana
Réquiem for a Spanish Peasant	Réquiem por un campesino español
Aragonese	aragonés

10 -¿Dígame?
-Buenos dias. ¿Es ahí la Embajada americana?
-No, señor. Esto es el restaurante Banderas.
-¿Está Vd. seguro? Me han dado este número para la Embajada americana y se trata de un asunto muy urgente.
-Mire, señor, le digo que esto no es la Embajada. Esto es el 91 4 61 79 01, un restaurante mejicano, y si no tiene intención de reservar una mesa, lo mejor será que cuelgue Vd.
-Perdone. Buenas tardes.
-Buenas tardes.

2 Articles

1
el	los/las	el
la	los	los/las
la	las	la
la	las	la
el	el	los
las	los	la
los	los	la

2
las	la	el	la	el	la	la	el
la	los	el	la	la	la	la	
el	el	la	las	las	la	la	
la	el	el	el	los	los	los	

3
la	el	la	la	la
la	la	la	los	la
el	la	la	la	los
los	la	la	la	la

4 **a** (-)/la **b** (-)/el; (-)/la **c** una **d** el **e** un/el **f** (-)/la **g** las **h** los **i** unos/los **j** (-) *or* un

3 Nouns

1
masculine	*feminine*
coraje	*mano*
tren	*gripe*
estrés	*moda*

policía *(policeman)*	cerveza
mapa	maldad
ojo	corbata
mercado	salud
dolor	sensibilidad
	foto
	biblioteca
	discusión
	policía *(policewoman/police)*
	costumbre
	tendencia
	televisión
	cena

2   la profesora – el amigo – la jefa – la escocesa – el perro – la socia – una nadadora – el andaluz – un cubano – una programadora

3

los franceses	las verdades
los tsunamis	las pieles
las madres	las posibilidades
los atletas	los reveses
unos lápices	unas veces
los reyes	los violines
las situaciones	las naciones

4

Common nouns	*Proper nouns*
suerte	Ángel
(el) pequeño	Ricardo
hermanos	Antonio
madre	Machado
casa	Zaragoza
gente	Microsoft
problemas	
escuela	
maestro	
beca	
Instituto	
(el) inglés	
matemáticas	
Universidad	
informática	
trabajo	
esperanza	
cargo	
director	
companía	

5   **a** el día   **b** una patente   **c** la mano   **d** la television   **e** el mapa   **f** un traje   **g** unas tapices   **h** el cliente

4   Adjectives

1   **a** moreno;   **b** difíciles;   **c** rápido;   **d** idénticos;   **e** dulce;   **f** electrónico;   **g** rayadas;   **h** abierta;   **i** sanos;   **j** fácil.

2   **a** unos ratones electrónicos;   **b** unas ciudades españolas;   **c** unas tareas difíciles;   **d** unos trenes franceses;   **e** unos pinchadiscos buenos;   **f** unos museos encantadores;   **g** unas mañanas grises;   **h** unos gobiernos corruptos;   **i** unas mañanas primaverales;   **j** unos grandes artistas.

3　**a** mi perrito es muy simpático;　**b** su padre era feliz;　**c** el chico es trabajador;　**d** tu amigo es carpintero;　**e** el gato no estaba enfermo;　**f** un hombre extraordinario;　**g** el niño bilingüe;　**h** un señor gallego.

4　**a** inglesa;　**b** alemanes;　**c** ruso;　**d** catalana;　**e** portuguesa;　**f** española;　**g** italiana;　**h** francés.

6　guapos y felices; generosos; excelentes; aplicados; muy protegida; muy bien pagado; carísima; importantes; Muchas; elegantes; ocupados; fantástico; buena.

5　Comparison

1　Suggested answers

a Un elefante es más grande que un ratón.

b Mónaco es más pequeño que Estados Unidos.

c El azúcar es más dulce que la sal.

d Los ingleses son más rubios que los españoles.

e Un lobo es más feroz que una oveja.

f Un coche es más rápido que una bicicleta.

g La luna es más fría que el sol.

h Una naranja es más redonda que un plátano.

i Las colinas son menos altas que las montañas.

j Un policía es mejor que un criminal.

2　Suggested answers

Carlos tiene menos hermanos que Charo.
Carlos vive en una vivienda más pequeña que Charo.
A Carlos le gusta más su trabajo que a Charo.
Charo es más trabajadora que Carlos.
A Charo le gusta más la televisión que el cine.
Carlos es más atrevido que Charo.
Charo se acuesta más temprano que Carlos.
Charo tiene más amigos británicos que Carlos.

3　**a** tantas … como　**b** tan … como　**c** tantos … como　**d** tan … como　**e** tanta … como　**f** tan … como　**g** tan … como　**h** tan … como　**i** tanta … como

4　Suggested answers

a No, América del Sur es menos rica que Europa.

b No, Estados Unidos es el país más rico del mundo.

c No, Holanda es menos montañosa que España.

d No, Finlandia es un país más moderno que Grecia.

e No, la monarquía española tiene tanto poder como la británica.

f No, Alemania es el país más grande de Europa.

g No, una copa de vino no cuesta tanto como un coñac.

h No, la moda italiana es más elegante que la sueca.

i No, los coches franceses son tan potentes como los alemanes.

j No, Bilbao es la ciudad más contaminada de España.

5 Suggested answers

a ¿Cuál es la montaña más alta del mundo?

b ¿Quién es el escritor inglés más famoso de todos?

c ¿Cuál es el mayor productor del aceite de oliva del mundo?

d ¿Cuál es el país más poderoso económicamente del mundo?

e ¿Cuál es el más popular de los nuevos productos tecnológicos?

f ¿Cuál es la estrella más cercana de nuestra galaxia?

g ¿Cuál es la temporada más fría del año?

h ¿Cuál es la temporada más cálida del año?

i ¿Cuál es el grupo pop más famoso del siglo veinte?

j ¿Cuál es el continente más pobre de nuestra época?

6 Suggested answers

Elena es mayor que Clara.
Elena habla más lenguas que Clara.
Elena es más alta que Clara.
Clara tiene menos experiencia que Elena.
Elena tiene menos títulos que Clara.
Elena tiene más responsabilidades familiares que Clara.
Clara tiene más libertad que Elena.
Clara tiene menos confianza que Elena.
Clara es más tímida que Elena.
Elena sonríe menos que Clara.

6   Numerals

1

24	109	16
54	1909	14
775	38	23
1.001.106	49	507

2 siete; quince; veintiuno; veintinueve; treinta y siete; cincuenta y tres; sesenta y nueve; setenta y nueve; ciento tres; doscientos/as ochenta y seis; mil treinta y nueve; ochenta y cinco; cuarenta y ocho; trescientos/as treinta y dos; catorce; ocho; noventa y nueve; ciento trece; quinientos/as; novecientos/as seis; cien; un millón.

3 primero; tercero; décimo; cuarto; segundo; séptimo.

4 dieciséis; cien; quinientos; treinta y una; doscientos cincuenta; setenta y cinco; un millón; novecientas.

5 **a** a las veintidós horas y siete minutos/ a las diez y siete minutos de la tarde

b a las doce/ al mediodía

c a las cero horas y quince minutos/ las doce y cuarto de la noche

d a las once horas y quince minutos/ las once y cuarto de la mañana

e a las veinte horas y treinta y cinco minutos/ las ocho y treinta y cinco de la tarde

6 **a** primer, cincuenta y ocho   **b** diecinueve, sesenta   **c** tercer, seis   **d** nueve, cuarenta y cuatro
e nueve, setenta y cinco   **f** séptimo/último, cuarenta y tres

7　Personal pronouns

1　**a** Lo echamos.　**b** ¿Las has plantado?　**c** Los compramos.　**d** Lo borramos.　**e** Los ha traído.
f La metí en la puesta.　**g** La ha buscado.　**h** No la conozco.　**i** No lo he leído.　**j** Lo han
sacado.　**k** ¿Las has visto?

2　**a** Le devolveré el libro.　**b** Las saludaremos.　**c** ¿Les instalamos los televisores?　**d** Le pagué el
alquiler　**e** Elisa le hizo un pastel....

3　**a** Se las dio.　**b** Carlos se la devolvió.　**c** Se la daré.　**d** Se las entregaremos.　**e** Se los he comprado.

4　**a** ... delante de ella.　**b** Según él ...　**c** ... sin ellas.　**d** ... para nosotros　**e** Detrás de ellas ...

5　**a** Sí, lo tengo.　**b** Sí, lo he cambiado.　**c** Sí, se lo he dado.　**d** Sí, se lo he contado.　**e** Sí, voy
a decírselo.

6　**a** Sí, dámelo.　　　　　　　　　　　　No, no me lo des.

　　b Sí, pónmela.　　　　　　　　　　　No, no me la pongas.

　　c Sí, démelo/dáselo.　　　　　　　　No, no me lo dé/ se lo des.

　　d Sí, devuélvanosla/devuélvesela.　　No, no nos le devuelva/se la devuelvas.

　　e Sí, llévemelo.　　　　　　　　　　No, no me lo lleves.

8　Demonstrative adjectives and pronouns

1　estas; esas; aquellas (botellas)
este; ese; aquel (tema)
este/esta; ese/esa; aquel/aquella (artista)
este; ese; aquel (cuello)
estas; esas; aquellas (manos)
este; ese; aquel (día)
estos; esos; aquellos (pulmones)
este; ese; aquel (hotel)
estas; esas; aquellas (niñas)
esta; esa; aquella (moto)
estos; esos; aquellos (peces)
esta; esa; aquella (cárcel)
este; ese; aquel (té)
esta; esa; aquella (foto)
este; ese; aquel (rincón)

2　**a** aquel　**b** ese/este　**c** ese　**d** ese/aquel　**e** estos　**f** esta

9　Possessive adjectives and pronouns

1　**a** sus　**b** su　**c** nuestra　**d** vuestro　**e** su　**f** tu　**g** su　**h** nuestros　**i** sus　**j** sus

2　**a** su　**b** sus　**c** nuestro　**d** su　**e** su　**f** vuestra　**g** tu　**h** nuestros　**i** su　**j** sus

3　**a** suyas　**b** nuestro　**c** suyo　**d** mía　**e** vuestros　**f** tuyas　**g** suya　**h** suyo　**i** suyo　**j** suyo

10　Relative clauses 3

1　A4 B5 C2 D1 E3

2　**a** la que　**b** el que　**c** las que　**d** la que　**e** los que

3　**a** que　**b** que　**c** las que　**d** quien　**e** el que　**f** lo que　**g** la que/quien　**h** que/quien　**i** que　**j** lo que

4　**a** Vimos llegar al cartero, quien/que traía muchas cartas.

　　b He visto un nuevo software que te ayuda a bajar material de Internet.

c Hemos alquilado un piso antiguo que nos encanta.

d La puerta, que no tenía buena cerradura, fue forzada.

e Carmen, quien/que canta flamenco los jueves por la noche, es una chica simpatica.

f Nacho, quien/que no sabía quién había ganado la copa, acaba de llamar.

11   Interrogatives and exclamations

1   A4 – B7 – C1 – D5 – E3 – F8 – G6 – H2

2   **a** Qué   **b** Cuál   **c** Quién   **d** Qué   **e** Cuál   **f** Qué   **g** Cuál   **h** qué   **i** Cuántas   **j** Dónde/ Cómo   **k** Adónde   **l** Por qué   **m** Cuánto   **n** quién   **o** qué

3   Possible answers

a ¿ Cuánto cuesta(n)?   **b** ¿Con quién estaban hablando?   **c** ¿Qué hora es?   **d** ¿Dónde vivís/viven?   **e** ¿Cómo estás?   **f** ¿Por qué no va(s)/viene(s) a la Costa Brava?   **g** ¿Cómo se (te) llama(s)?/ ¿Quién es/eres?   **h** ¿Qué has dicho?   **i** ¿Adónde vais/vamos?   **j** ¿Cuántos años tienes?

12   Indefinites

1   **a** alguien   **b** algunas   **c** algo   **d** alguna   **e** algo   **f** algún   **g** alguien   **h** Algunas   **i** alguna   **j** algún

2   **a** demasiado   **b** bastante   **c** Todo   **d** demasiada   **e** todos   **f** bastante   **g** demasiado   **h** Todas   **i** toda   **j** bastante

3   **a** otra   **b** mucho   **c** poca   **d** poco   **e** Mucha/Poca   **f** muchas   **g** otro   **h** pocas   **i** poco   **j** otra

14   Present tense

1   Possible answers

a Los niños duermen mucho.   **b** Escribes novelas.   **c** Terminais a las seis.   **d** D. Ramón fuma en pipa.   **e** Trabajo en Iberia.   **f** La plaza está en el centro.   **g** Desayunan a las ocho.   **h** Corremos mucho.   **i** Maruja ve la televisión.   **j** Jaime y yo vamos a la piscina.

2   llamo – Soy – Vivo – Tengo – llaman – vamos – vive – cogemos – lleva – prepara – comemos – quedamos – volvemos

3   A4 – B7 – C1 – D2 – E3 – F8 – G5 – H6

4   **a** Soy   **b** Tengo   **c** vivimos … tiene   **d** Vamos … está   **e** salimos … volvemos   **f** va   **g** estoy … nado   **h** hablo

5   **a** calentar/calienta   **b** jugar/jugamos   **c** costar/cuestan   **d** encontrarse/se encuentran   **e** acostarse/ Me acuesto   **f** empezar/ empieza   **g** preferir/Prefieres   **h** pensar/piensas   **i** cerrar/cierran   **j** calentarse/se calienta   **k** volver/vuelvo   **l** soler/suelen   **m** tener/tenéis   **n** tener/tienen   **o** pensar/ pensamos

6   Possible answers

a A mí me gusta montar a caballo.
A Marta le gusta montar a caballo.
b De vez en cuando cocino en casa pero prefiero comer en restaurantes.
De vez en cuando cocina en casa pero prefiere comer en restaurantes.
c Me acuesto temprano los días laborables pero los fines de semana me divierto mucho por la noche.
Se acuesta temprano los días laborables pero los fines de semana se divierte mucho por la noche.
d No me gusta nada ir al campo; prefiero pasar mi tiempo libre en casa escuchando música pop.
No le gusta nada ir al campo; prefiere pasar el tiempo libre en casa escuchando música pop.
e Nunca juego al tenis, pero sí practico la natación.
Nunca juega al tenis, pero sí practica la natación.

15 Future tense

1

infinitive	yo	tú	él/ella/Vd.	nosotros	vosotros	ellos/as/Vds.
mirar	miraré	mirarás	mirará	miraremos	miraréis	mirarán
escribir	escribiré	escribirás	escribirá	escribiremos	escribiréis	escribirán
perder	perderé	perderás	perderá	perderemos	perderéis	perderán
tener	tendré	tendrás	tendrá	tendremos	tendréis	tendrán
salir	saldré	saldrás	saldrá	saldremos	saldréis	saldrán
querer	querré	querrás	querrá	querremos	querréis	querrán
hacer	haré	harás	hará	haremos	haréis	harán

2   **a** irás   **b** Escribiré   **c** comeremos   **d** Volveréis   **e** haré   **f** habrá   **g** se levantará   **h** hará   **i** daré   **j** podrás

3   **a** hablaré   **b** vendrán   **c** iré   **d** examinaremos   **e** echaré   **f** diré   **g** llamará

16 Conditional tense

1

infinitive	yo	tú	él/ella /Vd.	nosotros/as	vosotros/as	ellos/ellas/Vds.
cerrar	cerraría	cerrarías	cerraría	cerraríamos	cerraríais	cerrarían
pedir	pediría	pedirías	pediría	pediríamos	pediríais	pedirían
volver	volvería	volverías	volvería	volveríamos	volveríais	volverían
tener	tendría	tendrías	tendría	tendríamos	tendríais	tendrían
poder	podría	podrías	podría	podríamos	podríais	podrían
hacer	haría	harías	haría	haríamos	haríais	harían
saber	sabría	sabrías	sabría	sabríamos	sabríais	sabrían

2   **a** tomaría   **b** encantaría   **c** molestaría   **d** darían   **e** contestaría   **f** podríais   **g** aconsejaríamos   **h** haría   **i** diría   **j** viajaría

3   Suggested answers

  a Yo, en tu lugar, me pondría el (vestido) rojo.

  b Yo, en tu lugar, me quedaría en Apple.

  c Yo, en tu lugar, le compraría unos guantes.

  d Yo, en tu lugar, escogería la Complutense.

  e Yo, en tu lugar, se lo diría.

4   haría – tendríamos – vendería – compraría – iría – podrían – buscaría – Estaría – acabaría

5   'Si no estuviera enfermo, este año terminaría y obtendría unas notas magníficas. Luego iría a las islas Galápagos y vería todos los animales interesantes que hay allí. Nadaría con los delfines y contemplaría el perfecto cielo azul desde las rocas. De las islas me trasladaría a Costa Rica y pasearía por el parque natural más hermoso de Centro América. A mi vuelta a Tarragona tendría tiempo de disfrutar de mis amigos y también me prepararía para el próximo curso. El año que viene sería el último de mi carrera y entonces sería biólogo.'

17 Perfect tense

1   **a** he encontrado   **b** has querido   **c** habéis limpiado   **d** han ido   **e** ha puesto   **f** hemos roto   **g** has abierto   **h** ha vuelto   **i** he absuelto   **j** hemos dicho   **k** ha traido   **l** se han levantado

2   **a** han empezado   **b** se ha despertado   **c** ha preparado   **d** ha comenzado   **e** se ha acostado   **f** ha ganado   **g** he visto   **h** han tenido   **i** hemos escrito   **j** ha investigado

3   **a** ¿Has comenzado...   **b** ¿Han vuelto...   **c** ¿Ha puesto...   **d** ¿Habéis cenado?   **e** ¿Ha hecho... **f** ¿Has hablado...   **g** ¿Habéis visto...   **h** ¿Habéis oído...   **i** ¿Ha recibido...   **j** ¿Han resuelto Vds....

4   han construido; ha atraído; ha llegado; se ha terminado; Ha comenzado; han sido.

18 Preterite tense

1

infinitive	yo	tú	él/ella/Vd.	nosotros/as	vosotros/as	ellos/ellas/ Vds.
llevar	llevé	llevaste	llevó	llevamos	llevasteis	llevaron
volver	volví	volviste	volvió	volvimos	volvisteis	volvieron
ocurrir	[ocurrí]*	[ocurriste]*	ocurrió	[ocurrimos]*	[ocurristeis]*	ocurrieron
mirar	miré	miraste	miró	miramos	mirasteis	miraron
coger	cogí	cogiste	cogió	cogimos	cogisteis	cogieron
hacer	hice	hiciste	hizo	hicimos	hicisteis	hicieron
salir	salí	saliste	salió	salimos	salisteis	salieron
querer	quise	quisiste	quiso	quisimos	quisisteis	quisieron
poner	puse	pusiste	puso	pusimos	pusisteis	pusieron
venir	vine	viniste	vino	vinimos	vinisteis	vinieron
ver	vi	viste	vio	vimos	visteis	vieron
ir	fui	fuiste	fue	fuimos	fuisteis	fueron
ser	fui	fuiste	fue	fuimos	fuisteis	fueron
saber	supe	supiste	supo	supimos	supisteis	supieron
comprar	compré	compraste	compró	compramos	comprasteis	compraron
llamar	llamé	llamaste	llamó	llamamos	llamasteis	llamaron
traer	traje	trajiste	trajo	trajimos	trajisteis	trajeron
tener	tuve	tuviste	tuvo	tuvimos	tuvisteis	tuvieron
romper	rompí	rompiste	rompió	rompimos	rompisteis	rompieron
irse	me fui	te fuiste	se fue	nos fuimos	os fuisteis	se fueron

* The asterisked forms of **ocurrir** do not exist, since it is only used impersonally, like **llover** (to rain).

2   **a** compré   **b** fue   **c** llamamos   **d** corrió   **e** hicieron   **f** obtuvisteis   **g** pasaste   **h** escondimos **i** deshice   **j** pareció

3   **a** chateamos   **b** conseguí   **c** bebieron   **d** Hablamos   **e** salí   **f** Trabajaste   **g** Recibisteis **h** contactaron   **i** hubo   **j** dijo

4   **a** empezó   **b** aburrió   **c** pusieron   **d** contestó   **e** aprobó ... dieron   **f** perdimos   **g** estuviste **h** reconocieron   **i** trajo

5   descubrió – fue – consiguieron – pudo – tomó – llamó – ordenó – entró – celebraron

19 Imperfect tense

1

infinitive	yo	tú	él/ella/Vd.	nosotros/as	vosotros/as	ellos/ellas/Vds.
encontrar	encontraba	encontrabas	encontraba	encontrábamos	encontrabais	encontraban
saber	sabía	sabías	sabía	sabíamos	sabíais	sabían
escribir	escribía	escribías	escribía	escribíamos	escribíais	escribían
decir	decía	decías	decía	decíamos	decíais	decían
ver	veía	veías	veía	veíamos	veíais	veían
ser	era	eras	era	éramos	erais	eran
pasar	pasaba	pasabas	pasaba	pasábamos	pasabais	pasaban
querer	quería	querías	quería	queríamos	queríais	querían
dar	daba	dabas	daba	dábamos	dabais	daban
salir	salía	salías	salía	salíamos	salíais	salían

2 **a** vivíamos **b** había **c** era **d** paseábamos **e** era … mudaban **f** nos alojábamos … se veían **g** viajaba … leía … se dormía

3 **a** llevaban **b** era **c** tenía **d** salíamos … permanecía **e** visitaba … charlaba **f** estaba **g** trabajaba … ganaba **h** se acercaban … estudiaban

4 **a** podía … se estropeaba **b** había **c** era **d** teníamos **e** trabajaba … tenía **f** estaba … entendía **g** vivíamos … íbamos **h** se reía … tenía **i** parecía **j** navegaba … cogía … iba

20 Preterite and imperfect contrasted

2 **a** se acercaba … esperaban **b** Hubo … siguió **c** Se bebió … se marchó **d** me levantaba … me marchaba **e** vimos … estábamos **f** Me puse … no aguantaba **g** salimos … estaban **h** Conocí … asistíamos **i** llamó … estaba **j** se cayó … se rompió

3 **a** viajaban … descubrieron **b** dormía … robaron **c** construyó **d** hiciste/hacías … dijo … iba **e** se comió … había **f** se sintió … tuvo **g** Hacía … esperábamos **h** venía … jugaba **i** invitaba **j** estuvimos

4 El ladrón entró por la puerta, **(c) que estaba abierta,** subió al piso de arriba y cogió todas las joyas **(f) que había en una caja en el armario (d) y que tenían un valor sentimental incalculable**. El ladrón lo dejó todo en orden **(a) ya que se trataba de un ladrón muy considerado**, y salió **(e) mientras D. Benito y Doña Luisa charlaban tranquilamente en el salón**. Los dueños tardaron mucho tiempo en darse cuenta del robo **(b) porque a Doña Luisa no le gustaba ponerse joyas.**

21 Compound tenses

1

infinitive	yo	tú	él/ella /Vd.	nosotros/as	vosotros/as	ellos/as/ Vds.
hablar	he hablado	**has hablado**	**ha hablado**	hemos hablado	**habéis hablado**	**han hablado**
conocer	**he conocido**	has conocido	**ha conocido**	**hemos conocido**	habéis conocido	**han conocido**

infinitive	yo	tú	él/ella /Vd.	nosotros/as	vosotros/as	ellos/as/ Vds.
ir	**he ido**	**has ido**	ha ido	**hemos ido**	**habéis ido**	han ido
poner	he puesto	**has puesto**	**ha puesto**	hemos puesto	**habéis puesto**	**han puesto**
vivir	**he vivido**	has vivido	**ha vivido**	**hemos vivido**	habéis vivido	**han vivido**

2

infinitive	yo	tú	él/ella/Vd.	nosotros/as	vosotros/as	ellos/as/ Vds.
mirar	**había mirado**	habías mirado	**había mirado**	**habíamos mirado**	habíais mirado	**habían mirado**
poder	había podido	**habías podido**	**había podido**	habíamos podido	**habíais podido**	**habían podido**
volver	**había vuelto**	**habías vuelto**	había vuelto	**habíamos vuelto**	**habíais vuelto**	habían vuelto
escribir	había escrito	**habías escrito**	**había escrito**	**habíamos escrito**	habíais escrito	**habían escrito**
romper	**había roto**	habías roto	**había roto**	habíamos roto	**habíais roto**	**habían roto**

3

infinitive	yo	tú	él/ella/Vd.	nosotros/as	vosotros/as	ellos/as/ Vds.
cerrar	habré cerrado	**habrás cerrado**	**habrá cerrado**	**habremos cerrado**	**habréis cerrado**	habrán cerrado
venir	**habré venido**	habrás venido	**habrá venido**	**habremos venido**	habréis venido	**habrán venido**
beber	**habré bebido**	**habrás bebido**	habrá bebido	habremos bebido	**habréis bebido**	**habrán bebido**
abrir	habré abierto	**habrás abierto**	**habrá abierto**	**habremos abierto**	habréis abierto	**habrán abierto**
decir	**habré dicho**	habrás dicho	**habrás dicho**	**habremos dicho**	**habréis dicho**	**habrán dicho**

4

infinitive	yo	tú	él/ella/Vd.	nosotros/as	vosotros/as	ellos/as/ Vds.
comer	habría comido	**habrías comido**	**habría comido**	habríamos comido	**habríais comido**	**habrían comido**
sacar	**habría sacado**	habrías sacado	**habría sacado**	**habríamos sacado**	habríais sacado	**habrían sacado**
hacer	**habría hecho**	**habrías hecho**	habría hecho	**habríamos hecho**	**habríais hecho**	habrían hecho

infinitive	yo	tú	él/ella/Vd.	nosotros/as	vosotros/as	ellos/as/Vds.
ver	habría visto	**habrías visto**	**habría visto**	habríamos visto	**habríais visto**	**habrían visto**
cubrir	**habría cubierto**	habrías cubierto	**habría cubierto**	**habríamos cubierto**	habríais cubierto	**habrían cubierto**

5 **a** había hecho; **b** he despertado; **c** había aterrizado; **d** había esperado; **e** había tomado; **f** había dejado; **g** habrás puesto.

6 habían ido; había perdido; había puesto; había olvidado; había tenido; había averiado; habían vuelto; habían cogido.

7 **a** habrá llegado; **b** habrás salido; **c** se habrá creado; **d** habremos pagado; **e** habrán abierto

22 The subjunctive

1

infinitive	yo	tú	él/ella/Vd.	nosotros/as	vosotros/as	ellos/ellas/Vds.
mirar	mire	mires	mire	miremos	miréis	miren
creer	crea	creas	crea	creamos	creáis	crean
escribir	escriba	escribas	escriba	escribamos	escribáis	escriban
saber	sepa	sepas	sepa	sepamos	sepáis	sepan
ir	vaya	vayas	vaya	vayamos	vayáis	vayan
poner	ponga	pongas	ponga	pongamos	pongáis	pongan
querer	quiera	quieras	quiera	queramos	queráis	quieran
encontrar	encuentre	encuentres	encuentre	encontremos	encontréis	encuentren
pedir	pida	pidas	pida	pidamos	pidáis	pidan
ser	sea	seas	sea	seamos	seáis	sean
poder	pueda	puedas	pueda	podamos	podáis	puedan
abrir	abra	abras	abra	abramos	abráis	abran
dar	dé	des	dé	demos	déis	den
preferir	prefiera	prefieras	prefiera	prefiramos	prefiráis	prefieran
venir	venga	vengas	venga	vengamos	vengáis	vengan

2

infinitive	yo	tú	él/ella/Vd.	nosotros/as	vosotros/as	ellos/ellas/Vds.
dar	diera	dieras	diera	diéramos	dierais	dieran
desear	deseara	desearas	deseara	deseáramos	desearais	desearan
tener	tuviera	tuvieras	tuviera	tuviéramos	tuvierais	tuvieran
necesitar	necesitara	necesitaras	necesitara	necesitáramos	necesitarais	necesitaran
decir	dijera	dijeras	dijera	dijéramos	dijerais	dijeran

infinitive	yo	tú	él/ella/Vd.	nosotros/as	vosotros/as	ellos/ellas/ Vds.
beber	bebiera	bebieras	bebiera	bebiéramos	bebierais	bebieran
poner	pusiera	pusieras	pusiera	pusiéramos	pusierais	pusieran
poder	pudiera	pudieras	pudiera	pudiéramos	pudierais	pudieran
haber	hubiera	hubieras	hubiera	hubiéramos	hubierais	hubieran
estar	estuviera	estuvieras	estuviera	estuviéramos	estuvierais	estuvieran
hacer	hiciera	hicieras	hiciera	hiciéramos	hicierais	hicieran
llamar	llamara	llamaras	llamara	llamáramos	llamarais	llamaran
conocer	conociera	conocieras	conociera	conociéramos	conocierais	conocieran
traer	trajera	trajeras	trajera	trajéramos	trajerais	trajeran
parecer	pareciera	parecieras	pareciera	pareciéramos	parecierais	parecieran

3 **a** cantes **b** digan **c** estés **d** vayamos **e** venga **f** entre **g** vaya **h** dejen **i** sepa **j** comamos

4 a/l – b/g – c/k – d/h – e/i – f/j

5 **a** fueran/fuesen **b** abriera/abriese **c** hiciera/hiciese **d** trabajara/trabajase … terminara/terminase **e** pudiera/pudiese

6 (examples of possible endings)

a … no llegues tarde a la cita. **b** … cesen todas las guerras del mundo. **c** … tus amigos vengan mañana. **d** … cojamos el autobús. **e** … los pilotos vayan a la huelga. **f** … yo les devuelva el dinero. **g** … tus amigos vayan/vengan de vacaciones con nosotros. **h** … abra la puerta si llega (él) primero. **i** … la seleccion española gane la copa mundial otra vez. **j** … lo haga Elena.

23 Continuous forms of the verb

1 está andando; están comiendo; estás escribiendo
estoy haciendo; estamos bebiendo; estás leyendo
se está levantando; estáis mirando; estaba hablando;
estábamos estudiando; está cayendo; estabas jugando;
está pidiendo; están destruyendo; estamos abriendo

2 **a** está pintando; **b** duerme; **c** estoy hablando; **d** está trabajando; **e** hacéis; **f** estaba grabando; **g** estaba duchando; **h** viene; **i** Estábamos desayunando; **j** llaman

3 (En este momento), los músicos se **están preparando** para el concierto. El pianista **está practicando** unas escalas y los miembros de la orquesta le **están escuchando**. Como siempre, todos **están esperando** la llegada del director, un señor muy distraído. Mientras tanto éste **está buscando** en vano dónde aparcar el coche. Los espectadores **están entrando** poco a poco a la sala. Todos **están vistiendo** sus mejores ropas y **están pensando** que el concierto será excelente. Todos **están charlando** animadamente y **están encargando** bebidas para el intermedio. Los acomodadores **están llevando** a los espectadores a sus respectivos asientos. Todos, músicos y público, **están deseando** que empiece el concierto.

24 If-clauses

1 **a** escribo **b** gusta **c** invitan **d** es **e** pasáis **f** gustan **g** llego **h** hace **i** está **j** son

2 **a** serán **b** estará **c** se mojará **d** tendrás **e** correrás **f** sabrás **g** habrá **h** cogeremos **i** podrás **j** podrás

3 **a** hubieran dado/habrían sido **b** hubiera ganado/habría estado **c** hubiera salido/se habría mojado   **d** te hubieras gastado/habrías tenido   **e** te hubieras entrenado/habrías corrido   **f** hubieras estado/habrías sabido   **g** hubieras hablado/habría contado   **h** hubiera salido/habríamos cogido   **i** hubieran instalado/habrías podido   **j** hubieras visto/habrías podido

4 **a** tuviéramos   **b** daría   **c** regalara   **d** cambiaría   **e** vendrías   **f** vivieran   **g** estaría   **h** pidieran   **i** harías   **j** hubiera

25 The imperative

1 **a** mira … mire;   **b** habla … hable;   **c** sube … suba;   **d** pon … ponga;   **e** bebe … beba;   **f** acuéstate … acuéstese;   **g** duerme … duerma;   **h** sal … salga;   **i** levántate … levántese;   **j** cállate … cállese;   **k** pon … ponga;   **l** vístete … vístase;   **m** ven …venga

2 **a** llamad … llamen;   **b** mandad … manden;   **c** ingresad … ingresen;   **d** pagad … paguen;   **e** poned … pongan;   **f** cerrad … cierren;   **g** comprad … compren;   **h** cambiaos … cámbiense;   **i** venid … vengan;   **j** divertíos …   **k** diviértanse

3 **a** No mires la pintura;   **b** No escribas la tarjeta;   **c** No leas el periódico;   **d** No digáis lo que pensáis;   **e** No escuchéis la música   **f** No te conectes a Internet;   **g** No salgas a la calle;   **h** No cierres la ventana;   **i** No cojas la pelota;   **j** No saques la foto;   **k** No vayáis al colegio;   **l** No pongas la tele;   **m** No elijas un contrato de prepago;   **n** No me cuentes cómo pasó;   **o** No hagas la cama;   **p** No huyas;   **q** No eches la piedra;   **r** No recargues el móvil;   **s** No busquéis la llave;   **t** No limpiéis el suelo

4 **a** No me digas tu número;   **b** No cojas el teléfono;   **c** No lo pagues en metálico;   **d** No os levantéis;   **e** No te despidas;   **f** No me lo dé mañana;   **g** No se acomode;   **h** No te olvides del pasado;   **I** No os divertáis;   **j** No te vayas

5 Siga andando por esta calle, tome la segunda a la derecha, tuerza a la izquierda después de la gasolinera, baje por la colina, suba las escaleras y luego tuerza a la derecha. Verá el hotel delante de usted.

26 Spelling changes in verbs

1

	infinitive	1st person singular	1st person plural	3rd person plural
a	empezar	empiezo	empezamos	empiezan
b	poder	puedo	podemos	pueden
c	despertar	despierto	despertamos	despiertan
d	soñar	sueño	soñamos	sueñan
e	querer	quiero	queremos	quieren
f	dormir	duermo	dormimos	duermen
g	verter	vierto	vertemos	vierten
h	torcer	tuerzo	torcemos	tuercen
i	sentir	siento	sentimos	sienten
j	conseguir	consigo	conseguimos	consiguen
k	reír	río	reímos	ríen
l	conocer	conozco	conocemos	conocen
m	coger	cojo	cogemos	cogen
n	leer	leo	leemos	leen
o	satisfacer	satisfago	satisfacemos	satisfacen
p	destruir	destruyo	destruimos	destruyen
q	poner	pongo	ponemos	ponen
r	caer	caigo	caemos	caen
s	conducir	conduzco	conducimos	conducen
t	actuar	actúo	actuamos	actúan

	infinitive	1st person singular	1st person plural	3rd person plural
a	sentir	sentí	sentimos	sintieron
b	caer	caí	caímos	cayeron
c	reír	reí	reímos	rieron
d	seguir	seguí	seguimos	siguieron
e	buscar	busqué	buscamos	buscaron
f	pagar	pagué	pagamos	pagaron
g	comenzar	comencé	comenzamos	comenzaron
h	preferir	preferí	preferimos	prefirieron
i	traducir	traduje	traducimos	tradujeron
j	reñir	reñí	reñimos	riñeron
k	hacer	hice	hicimos	hicieron
l	decir	dije	dijimos	dijeron
m	ver	vi	vimos	vieron
n	saber	supe	supimos	supieron
p	poner	puse	pusimos	pusieron

3 a tiene b cierras c pierde d se acuerda e se duerme f vienen g encuentro h vuelves i siento j juega

4 a pedí b cayó c durmió d se divirtieron e midió f corrigió g llegué h busqué i nació j trajeron

27 Modal verbs

1 a tienes que b tenemos que c tiene que d tengo que e tenéis que f tiene que

2 a puede b debes c puede d puedes/puedo/podemos e puedes f Debe g puedo h deben i puedo j puede

28 *Gustar*-type and impersonal verbs

1 a gusta b encantan c duele d Falta e hacen f molesta g interesa h gusta i cuesta j duelen

2 a ellos/Vds. b mí c ti d le e les f os g nosotros h le i mí j le

3 a Sí, le gusta/No, no le gusta. b Sí, me gusta/No, no me gusta. c Sí, les molesta/No, no les molesta. d Sí, nos interesa/No, no nos interesa. e Sí, me gusta/No, no me gusta. f Sí, le gusta/No, no le gusta.

29 *Ser* and *estar*

1 a está b estás c somos d estás e es f es g están h son i soy j están k es; está l Está m está n son o estáis p es q Es r están s está t son

2
- los perros **son** feroces/felices; los perros **están** hambrientos
- caminar **es** agradable
- las películas **son** aburridas/optimistas
- el Rey **es** de familia muy antigua/malísimo/agradable; el Rey **está** de mal humor
- nosotros **somos** de familia muy antigua/optimistas/felices; nosotros **estamos** hambrientos/ de mal humor

- la silla **es** de madera
- este tren **es** malísimo; este tren **está** atrasado
- Clara **es** de familia muy antigua/soltera/agradable; Clara **está** cansadísima/de mal humor
- Los jóvenes **son** de familia muy antigua/optimistas/felices; los jóvenes **están** hambrientos/de mal humor
- El tiempo **es** malísimo/agradable; el tiempo **está** malísimo/agradable
- Tú **eres** de familia muy antigua/ atrasado/ malísimo/ agradable; tú **estás** atrasado/cansadísima/de mal humor
- Su hija **es** de familia muy antigua/soltera/agradable; su hija **está** cansadísima/de mal humor
- Las noticias **son** aburridas/optimistas
- El País está a **la venta**

3   **a** (estar);   **b** (ser);   **c** (ser/estar);   **d** (ser/estar);   **e** (ser);   **f** (estar);   **g** (estar);   **h** (ser/estar);   **i** (ser/estar);   **j** (ser)

4   A es; está; es; es; está; es; es; es; es
    B es; está; es; es; es; está; es; es; está

5   Horizontales   Verticales
    (2) eras   (1) eres
    (4) está   (2) era/son
    (5) soy   (4) sea

30   Active and passive

1   **a** destruida   **b** trasladado   **c** construido   **d** derramada   **e** arreglado   **f** dejadas   **g** devorado   **h** devuelto   **i** impreso

2   **a** La cámara captó las imágenes.   **b** Los terroristas secuestraron al embajador.   **c** Construyeron las casas con ladrillos fabricados cerca de Madrid.   **d** Un grupo de arqueólogos halló los restos de una iglesia visigótica.   **e** Destinaron la colecta a las víctimas del terrorismo.   **f** El mecánico revisó el autobús.   **g** Pagaron un millón de euros para liberar al embajador.   **h** Ayer los diplomáticos resolvieron la crisis.   **i** Una empresa británica destruyó las armas.   **j** Almacenaron los residuos en depósitos de seguridad.

3   **a** El delincuente fue detenido por la policía.   **b** El señor Ramos ha sido nombrado presidente del club.   **c** La cena fue pagada por la compañía.   **d** La compañía de gas fue multada por el gobierno.   **e** La oficina fue cerrada por el jefe a las seis.   **f** Los pisos fueron vendidos en febrero.   **g** El chico fue mordido por el perro.   **h** El mundo ha sido cambiado por la tecnología.   **i** El puente fue construido en 1995.   **j** La llegada del Rey fue esperada por todos.   **k** La abuela fue devorada por el lobo.

4 Romero was a private detective who had been thrown out of the police. His former colleagues gave him a lot of respect because his wife had been murdered by a psychopath and, as a result, he had made himself a promise that he would devote himself to defending innocent people who were threatened by unscrupulous individuals. That morning, while he was deep in thought, a client knocked on the door. He said 'Come in' and a tall, beautifully dressed woman, with long, silky blonde hair, entered. She asked: 'Are you Mr Romero, the detective? Romero felt as if his life would be changed from that moment on.

31 Pronominal verbs

infinitivo	yo	tú	él/ella/Vd	nosotros/as	vosotros/as	ellos/ellas Vds
levantarse	me levanto	te levantas	se levanta	nos levantamos	os levantáis	se levantan
acostarse	me acuesto	te acuestas	se acuesta	nos acostamos	os acostáis	se acuestan
entenderse	me entiendo	te entiendes	se entiende	nos entendemos	os entendéis	se entienden
vestirse	me visto	te vistes	se viste	nos vestimos	os vestís	se visten
hacerse	me hago	te haces	se hace	nos hacemos	os hacéis	se hacen
ponerse	me pongo	te pones	se pone	nos ponemos	os ponéis	se ponen
encontrarse	me encuentro	te encuentras	se encuentra	nos encontramos	os encontráis	se encuentran
sentirse	me siento	te sientes	se siente	nos sentimos	os sentís	se sienten
sentarse	me siento	te sientas	se sienta	nos sentamos	os sentáis	se sientan
divertirse	me divierto	te diviertes	se divierte	nos divertimos	os divertís	se divierten

a me acuesto; **b** te bañas; **c** nos vemos; **d** os levantáis; **e** se siente; **f** me despierta; **g** se reúnen; **h** me ruborizo; **i** te acuerdas; **j** se enfada.

32 The infinitive

1 **a** poner **b** volver **c** ir **d** llegar **e** ver **f** resolver **g** comprar **h** divertirse **i** amanecer **j** leer

2 Suggested answers

a A mí me gusta *viajar*.

b Mañana a las dos de la tarde vamos a *ir de compras*.

c El tren tardó una hora en *llegar*.

d Iremos a la piscina después de *comer*.

e Beber demasiado puede *dañar la salud*.

f Espero *terminar la tarea la semana que viene*.

g Aunque no quieras, tienes que *acompañarme al aeropuerto*.

h Cuando le vimos, acababa de *levantarse*.

4 estudiar – ser – llegar – financiar – visitar – pedir – ser – recuperar – aumentar – interesar – convencer – vender – invertir – traer – equipar – llegar

33 The past participle

1 **a** parado; **b** querido; **c** conseguido; **d** ido; **e** escrito; **f** roto; **g** abierto; **h** construido; **i** oído; **j** leído; **k** caído; **l** dicho; **m** permitido; **n** descubierto; **o** visto; **p** hecho; **q** detenido; **r** llamado; **s** compuesto; **t** resuelto

2 **a** hecha; **b** cerradas; **c** casada; **d** apagadas; **e** encontrado; **f** hablado; **g** divorciado; **h** roto; **i** interpretada; **j** traído

34 The gerund

1 **a** esperando **b** conociendo **c** cumpliendo **d** viniendo **e** amaneciendo **f** poniendo **g** pudiendo **h** creyendo **i** eligiendo **j** hiriendo **k** pidiendo **l** corriendo **m** yendo **n** destruyendo **o** vistiendo

2 **a** leyendo **b** divulgando **c** avanzando **d** trabajando **e** mejorando **f** bajando **g** hundiendo **h** haciendo

3 **a** On arriving we greeted her.

b S(he) had an accident when (she(he) was) crossing the street.

c This is the best shopping centre in the district.

d S(he)/I was reading calmly when Ana arrived weeping.

e He failed the examination because he was seen copying.

f What are you saying?

g Smoking, drinking and eating too much is bad (for you).

h Carol likes singing in the morning.

i The telephone's ringing!

35 Negation

1 **a** No nos llama nunca, ni nos manda mensajes nunca **b** No saben nada de la cultura del sur de España **c** No ha querido nadie ir al festival de Benicassim conmigo **d** No creo que este año vayamos a ganar la copa tampoco **e** Hoy no van al mercado ni Fernando ni Sofía.

2 **a** Eso nadie lo sabe. **b** Nunca me molesta que fumes. **c** Tampoco lo creo. **d** Apenas le conocemos. **e** Nada de lo que han comprado tiene valor.

3 Suggested answers:

a Federico nunca habla del pasado. **b** Los domingos nunca los paso trabajando en el ordenador. **c** Ninguno de mis amigos va conmigo a Segovia mañana. **d** En la esquina nunca hay nadie sospechoso. **e** Yo tampoco me marcho.

4 **a** I never say anything. **b** When we return home there will not be anything to do. **c** Nobody had ever given him/her such a beautiful present. **d** I saw the film yesterday and I didn't like it either. **e** I don't believe in any politician.

36 Adverbs

1 **a** evidentemente **b** regularmente **c** secamente **d** ricamente **e** dulcemente **f** difícilmente **g** abiertamente **h** lealmente **i** electrónicamente **j** últimamente

2 **a** a veces/hoy **b** frecuentemente/a veces **c** enseguida **d** Siempre … antes **e** siempre **f** Ayer **g** nunca **h** después **i** tarde **j** Después/Hoy

3 Possible adverbs

a adelante ... atrás **b** adentro/afuera/aquí **c** a lo lejos **d** cerca **e** arriba **f** aquí/acá **g** en /por todas partes **h** afuera/dentro/aquí/allí **i** aquí

37 Prepositions

1 **a** al ... a **b** de **c** por **d** en ... con **e** desde **f** de **g** a **h** de **i** por ... por **j** para **k** de **i** con **m** hasta ... de **n** a **o** con ... por **p** en ... a

2 **Horizontales:** 1 hacia 2 a 3 desde 5 para 8 en
Verticales: 1 de 2 por 3 hasta 5 ante 8 sin/con

38 Conjunctions

1 **a** u **b** y **c** y **d** u **e** o **f** y **g** o ... o **h** y ... e **i** e **j** o **k** u **l** e **m** y **n** u

2 **a** cuando/mientras **b** cuando **c** cuándo **d** cuándo **e** cuando/mientras **f** mientras **g** Mientras **h** Mientras **i** cuándo **j** cuando **k** mientras **l** Cuando **m** mientras

3 **a** porque **b** por qué **c** Por qué **d** por qué **e** porque **f** por qué **g** Por qué **h** porque **i** porque **j** por qué **k** porque **l** Por qué **m** porque

39 Diminutives and augmentatives

1 **a** niñita; **b** palomita; **c** perrita; **d** copita; **e** pajarito; **f** lucecita; **g** piecito; **h** cordoncito; **i** faldita; **j** poemita; **k** descansito; **l** trenecito; **m** bomboncito; **n** cancioncita; **o** piscinita

2 **a** cobarde **b** pobre **c** señor **d** soltera **e** abeja **f** broma **g** guapo **h** azul **i** pesado **j** paella **k** vino **l** barca **m** avión **n** fortuna **o** mujer

40 Word order

1 Suggested answers:

a Bebe San Miguel, ¿no?

b ¿A qué hora quedamos?/¿Dónde quedamos?

c ¿Has preparado la lección/la comida ... de hoy?

d Perdón, ¿dónde se puede coger un taxi?

e ¿Te has puesto en contacto con Almudena?

f En Madrid no hay ninguna librería barata, ¿verdad?/Los libros en FNAC son muy caros, ¿no?

g ¿Sabes si ya se puede comprar el DVD de la última película de los hermanos Cohen?

h ¿Les apetece tomar una copa?

i ¿Dónde está el pescado?

2 **a** I've never heard anything so stupid.

b Twenty more unexpected guests turned up as if by magic.

c How much did you say you paid for this house?

d I've told you already that Consuelo doesn't like going out at night.

e It's too hot here.

f Sara has met the friends you spoke to me about.

g My family always supports me in my decisions.

h (*Alternative for*) When will we see you again?

i She/He bought her/himself a new pair of shoes.

Key to Exercises

Part 2

Note: Answers are not given for those exercises which require an unpredictable response.

2 Articles

1 **a** En la estación de Atocha se puede coger el tren rápido a Sevilla. **b** Gonzalo ha conseguido el puesto de director gerente. **c** Para tomar la mejor paella lo mejor es ir al restaurante La Pepica. **d** No puedo salir contigo porque tengo el examen de gramática mañana. **e** Ayer conocí a la chica de mis sueños en la fiesta de Lola. **f** Le han puesto la multa por atacar al sargento Roldán. **g** Este fin de semana me he gastado las tres mil pesetas que me quedaban en el club Dorma.

2 cars/los coches; televisions/los televisores; telephones/los teléfonos; performance/el rendimiento; electronic components/los componentes electrónicos; all parts/todas las piezas; time/el tiempo; people/la gente; everyday activities/las actividades diarias; driving/el conducir; technology/la tecnología

3 1 El; 2 la; 3 unos; 4 (el) del; 5 la; 6 un; 7 el; 8 Las; 9 los; 10 los; 11 (el) al; 12 una; 13 unas; 14 el

4 **a** uno de los móviles **b** (un miembro d)el ejército **c** (una parte de) la casa **d** (un miembro de) mi familia **e** el cuarto de baño **f** uno de los libros de estudio **g** una (de las) fruta(s) **h** (un miembro de) la justicia **i** un deporte **j** un alimento **k** un lugar de diversión **l** un entretenimiento **m** un lugar para comprar **n** un(o de los) combustible(s) **o** una parte de la crisis económica **p** una parte de Windows

5 **a** … lo mucho que me costó meterle esa idea en la cabeza. **b** … lo super arreglado que va siempre. **c** … lo poco que le gusta dar buenas notas al profesor de historia. **d** … lo bonita que resultó la boda. **e** … lo cochambroso que era el hotel en el que nos quedamos. **f** … lo muy enferma que ha estado Eugenia. **g** … lo mucho que beben los jóvenes hoy en día.

6 **a** El café no es bueno para la salud **b** Estudio (estoy estudiando) Informática **c** Los españoles son patrióticos **d** El italiano es una lengua hermosa **e** El restaurante estaba lleno de gente joven **f** El suelo estaba cubierto de nieve **g** Mi hermano es jardinero **h** No tengo dinero **i** Hablo ruso todos los días **j** No habla inglés muy bien **k** El Dr González (está) al teléfono **l** Se está cortando el pelo **m** ¡Tráeme otra copa! **n** La cocina/comida tailandesa.

3 Nouns

1 1 el 2 la 3 la 4 el/la 5 el 6 el 7 el/la 8 el 9 el 10 el/la 11 el/la 12 el/la 13 el/la 14 la 15 el 16 la 17 el/la 18 el 19 el 20 el 21 el 22 la 23 el 24 el 25 la 26 las 27 el 28 los 29 la 30 la 31 el 32 la 33 la 34 el 35 la

lista (a)	lista (b)	lista (c)	lista (d)
un cangrejo	un/una cantante	un rey	un dependiente
una rana	un/una franquista	un toro	un pintor
una persona	un/una testigo	un héroe	un escocés
un personaje	un/una piloto	un príncipe	un gato
un bebé	un/una delincuente	un varón	un ministro
un delfín	un/una guía	un duque	un mendigo
una pantera	un/una modelo	un yerno	un cirujano
	un/una deportista	una madrina	
	un/una corresponsal		

2

3

vendedor	venta	médico	medicina
artista	arte	músico	música
filósofo	filosofía	concertista	concierto
industrial	industria	florista	flor
actor	actuación	cocinero	cocina
diseñador	diseño	burócrata	burocracia
agente	agencia	académico	academia
twitero	twiter	político	política
corresponsal	correspondencia	director	dirección
delincuente	delincuencia	saxofonista	saxofón

4 Adjectives

1 oscura (noche); afilado (lápiz); fuerte (cerveza); guapa/alegre (chica); roja (flor); feroz (león); alto (edificio); alegre (fiesta); extranjero (idioma); cálido (verano)

2 **a** costera **b** hotelera **c** incomprensibles **d** irremediable **e** estudiantil **f** sin vender **g** poco inteligente **h** sin afeitar

3 1 ateo 2 masón 3 **políticas** 4 concurrida 5 profunda 6 del cielo 7 femenino 8 numerosos 9 apocalípticas 10 encinta

4 1 tranquila 2 agotado/cansado 3 maldito 4 deprimentes 5 templado 6 helada 7 pequeño 8 inesperado 9 trasera 10 necio 11 cotilla 12 encendidas 13 culpable 14 agotada 15 viejo 16 destartalado 17 ligerita 18 rápida 19 siguiente 20 desvelado 21 fríos 22 inquietantes 23 estropeados 24 cansado/agotado

6 **a** un madrileño **b** mi viejo amigo **c** una historia divertida **d** ¡el pobre Jorge! **e** los rojos **f** la Reina misma **g** ¡Felices Navidades! **h** los franceses **i** caras sonrientes **j** los últimos días

5 Comparison

2 **a** ilusiones **b** bien **c** amigos **d** rápidamente **e** placer **f** derechos **g** suerte

3 **a** de lo que **b** del que **c** de las que **d** de lo que **e** de la que **f** de los que

5 **a** Sus hijos son educadísimos. **b** Le compró una pulsera carísima. **c** Su casa estaba limpísima. **d** Tuvo un accidente gravísimo. **e** La comida italiana es riquísima. **f** El bebé lloraba porque estaba cansadísimo. **g** Mis padres estaban enfadadísimos porque volví tardísimo.

6 Numerals

2 **a** diez **b** cien **c** veinte **d** ciento ocho **e** veintidós **f** veintiuno **g** mil ocho **h** seiscientos

3 **a** quinto **b** séptimo **c** primero/segundo **d** cuarta **e** décimos

5 **a** El rey Felipe segundo **b** El siglo xix/diecinueve **c** el tercer milenio **d** El papa Juan veintitrés **e** El 25 aniversario de la asociación **f** el 400 aniversario del nacimiento de Velázquez **g** el octavo piso **h** en el séptimo cielo **i** el Tercer hombre **j** la reina Isabel primera **k** las primeras flores de la primavera **l** Enrique octavo **m** el 4 de julio **n** mi 18 cumpleaños

8 Demonstrative adjectives and pronouns

1 **a** aquel/ese **b** aquello **c** este … aquel **d** esa/esta/aquella **e** este **f** este **g** esta **h** esta … aquella

2 1 ese 2 Ese 3 este 4 este 5 aquella 6 los que 7 estos 8 este 9 los que 10 estos

3 **a** Este ordenador funciona mejor que ese. **b** Quisiera resolver eso de la ventana rota de una vez por todas. **c** De los dos argumentos, prefiero este. **d** Todos los que quieran ayudar con la fiesta, venid conmigo. **e** No me gusta aquel edificio. **f** Esa gente nunca deja de quejarse. **g** He pensado mucho en ese asunto. **h** Los que apoyábamos el gobierno estuvimos decepcionados. **i** Esas fotos son buenas, pero estas son mejores. **j** ¡No digas eso! No es verdad.

9 Possessive adjectives and pronouns

1 1 su 2 mi 3 sus 4 mis 5 mi 6 tu

2 **a** el mío **b** tuyo **c** mi **d** la nuestra **e** nuestra **f** los tuyos **g** las mías **h** tuyo **i** vuestro **j** su

10 Relative clauses

1 **a** el que **b** cuya **c** cuyo **d** la que/donde **e** la que **f** lo que **g** cuyos **h** cuya **i** lo que **j** cuando **k** la cual

2 **a** Todo lo que/cuanto sabemos es que van a llegar mañana. **b** Hay los que gastan y los que ahorran. **c** Allí es donde vivíamos antes. **d** Ramón, cuya madre era enfermera, ya es catedrático de medicina. **e** Esta es la razón por la cual hice la pregunta. **f** Carmiña es la que puede darte la información correcta. **g** Sofía, cuyos niños van a un colegio privado, es más pobre de lo que piensas. **h** Todo lo que te puedo decir es que intentaré ayudarte. **i** Raimundo, quien es cocinero en el Ritz, va a dar una fiesta. **j** Estaba yo en Méjico el año en el que ocurrió el terrremoto.

11 Interrogatives and exclamations

1 **a** cómo **b** cuántas **c** qué **d** quién/dónde **e** cómo/por qué **f** cuál **g** qué…cuánto **h** cuándo/cómo **i** qué/cuántos **j** qué

2 **a** ¿Sabes adónde vas? **b** ¿Qué cantantes te gustan más? **c** ¿Cuál prefieres? **d** Pregúntale al hombre cómo se va a la plaza mayor. **e** ¡Qué fiesta tan/más estupenda! **f** ¿Cuál es la revista que estás leyendo? **g** ¿De quién es la cartera en la mesa? **h** No sabemos qué/lo que están haciendo. **i** ¿Para qué sirve hablar contigo si no me escuchas? **j** ¿A quién le diste la cámara?

12 Indefinites

1 **a** todos **b** otra **c** todos … otro **d** otro **e** todo **f** algún **g** algo **h** algunos **i** cualquier **j** todo

2 **a** Podría llegar en cualquier momento/en todo momento. **b** Tiene otra hermana. **c** La decisión fue aprobada por todos los que asistieron a la reunión. **d** Algunas personas estaban allí antes de las ocho; otras tres llegaron más tarde. **e** No se podía encontrar las llaves en parte alguna. **f** Tiene familia en todas partes, pero principalmente en Argentina. **g** Todos los profesores necesitan vacaciones.

13 Verbs

14 Present tense

1 **a** digo **b** pone **c** tiene **d** conozco **e** duele **f** están **g** tienes **h** suben **i** cuenta **j** voy

2 La policía llega al bar a medianoche. Los agentes hablan con el dueño, quien les explica cómo mejor coger a los criminales. Entran por la puerta de atrás e interrumpen el reparto de armas y objetos robados. Los criminales intentan huir por todos lados, pero los detienen a todos sin que nadie pueda escapar. Luego van a la comisaría y con eso se termina la redada.

3 **a** Te espero aquí desde hace cinco horas. **b** Llevamos 20 años viviendo en Barcelona.
c Tienen su SEAT Marbella desde 1985. **d** ¿Desde cuando estás en Bilbao?
e Hace mucho tiempo que no nos vemos. **f** París me gustaba tanto que por poco compro una casa allí.

15 Future tense

1 **a** diré **b** llegará **c** tendrás **d** hará **e** estarán **f** traerán **g** irás **h** cerrarán **i** podré **j** saldrá

2 **a** tendrán **b** cerrará **c** aprobaré **d** podréis **e** abrirá **f** pondrán **g** subirán **h** se reunirá **i** iremos **j** te quedarás

3 **a** Serán **b** Estará **c** Costarán **d** estará **e** Llegará **f** ganarán

16 Conditional tense

1 **a** aseguró/entregaría **b** dijeron/podrían **c** estaba/aumentaría **d** anunció/habría **e** estaba/estarían

2 **a** 2 **b** 6 **c** 5 **d** 1 **e** 9 **f** 3 **g** 7 **h** 4 **i** 8

3 **a** ¿Podrías poner la mesa? ¿Querrías hacerme el favor de poner la mesa? **b** ¿Querrías hacerme el favor de no subir la escalera corriendo? **c** ¿Podríais esperarme un momento? ¿Querríais hacerme el favor de esperarme un momento? **d** Antes de salir ¿podrías quitar tus libros de la mesa? ¿Querrías hacerme el favor de quitar tus libros de la mesa? **e** ¿Podrías llevar el abrigo a la tintorería? ¿Querrías hacerme el favor de llevar el abrigo a la tintorería? **f** ¿Podría traer una zarzuela de pescado y un pollo al ajillo? ¿Querría hacerme el favor de traer una zarzuela de pescado y un pollo al ajillo? **g** ¿Querrías hacerme el favor de no poner los pies en el sillón? **h** ¿Podríais explicar al policía que fue un accidente? ¿Querríais hacerme el favor de explicar al policía que fue un accidente? **i** ¿Podríais coger el mapa por si os perdéis? **j** ¿Podrías decirle a tu madre que tienes novio?

17 Perfect tense

1

a	llegó	**b**	han anunciado	**c**	viajé
d	se ha marchado	**e**	he leído	**f**	se ha levantado
g	nos casamos	**h**	he podido	**i**	se anunció
j	hemos tenido	**k**	has visto /me encontré	**l**	se ha estrenado
m	perdió	**n**	se han abierto	**o**	ha hecho

2

a	has puesto	**b**	ha llovido	**c**	he visto
d	ha quedado	**e**	han abierto	**f**	he conocido
g	ha resuelto	**h**	has dicho	**i**	han trabajado
j	ha escrito				

3

1	se ha enfadado	2	he dicho	3	ha podido
4	ha devuelto	5	ha dicho	6	ha conocido

7	he enfadado	8	hemos sido	9	hemos pasado
10	ha podido	11	Ha tenido	12	he recordado
13	ha hecho				

4 **a** He ido al gimnasio regularmente. **b** Esperamos/Hemos esperado a tu padre desde las dos. **c** El cartero ha llamado dos veces. **d** Este año hemos ido a dos conciertos y a un festival de música. **e** El jefe trabaja en el proyecto desde ayer. **f** Acaban de comprar un coche nuevo. **g** Mis amigos no han visto la película todavía. **h** ¿Cuántos años hace que tocas la batería? **i** ¿Cuánto tiempo hace que no has comido? **j** ¿Cuántas veces te he dicho que no vuelvas a medianoche?

18 Preterite tense

1 **a** terminamos hace ... **b** Dijo que ... **c** Me costó ... **d** Le dije que ... **e** Se entrenaron ...

2 1 Se levantó 2 apareció 3 bajó 4 volvió 5 saludó 6 empezaron 7 se hizo 8 vio 9 Puso 10 Pe dieron cuenta 11 Pasaron 12 fueron 13 se quedaron.

3 a–m (... se retrasó el tren) b–t (... me puse enfermo) c–k (... me robaron todo lo que tenía en casa) d–r (... se inundó el cuarto de baño) e–s (... salió de fiesta con sus amigotes) f–n (... se estropeó hace más de un mes) g–p (... me dijiste que te gustan) h–o (... pedí gambas/... trajo un filete) i–q (... vi a tu novio con otra chica) j–l (... hubo un golpe de estado en Moldavia)

4 **a** La semana pasada fui con mis amigos a ver la película 'Todo sobre mi madre', de Almodóvar. **b** ¿Qué dijeron tus amigos de la película? ¿Les gustó? **c** Le conoció en Gerona. **d** Intentaron una y otra vez descubrir quién la había matado, pero no lo consiguieron. **e** Llegué a la oficina a las tres de la tarde y comencé a trabajar enseguida. **f** Cuando supe que había vuelto me puse en contacto con mi abogado enseguida. **g** Anoche Clara y Emilia trajeron algunas fotos de sus vacaciones en Marruecos. **h** La policía detuvo a dos terroristas en la frontera. **i** ¿Cómo reaccionaste cuando te robaron el coche? **j** La noticia de su accidente me asustó. No pude creerlo.

19 Imperfect tense

2 Era – era – podía – parecía – pudiera – era – producían – daban – encontraban – impresionaba – era – ponía – estaban – estaba – estaban – había – recogía – estaba – utilizaba – parecía – gustaba – era – disfrutaba – pensaban – eran.

4 **a** Cuando estaba en España me gustaba ir de tapas antes de cenar. **b** Hacía mucho tiempo que sabía lo que iba a pasar. **c** Jugábamos a las cartas mientras esperábamos el comienzo del partido. **d** Cuando llegaba el otoño paseábamos mucho por el bosque. **e** Mientras charlábamos en la sala de estar, mi madre trabajaba con el ordenador. **f** Estaba tan cansado que tuve que acostarme temprano. **g** No nos apetecía salir aunque hacía sol. **h** Nunca tocaba el piano cuando era joven. **i** Paco, ¿qué hacías/estabas haciendo cuando te vi ayer? **j** Angela solía nadar en el mar todos los días.

20 The preterite and imperfect tenses contrasted

1 **Texto A** 1 desencadenaron 2 se sublevó 3 se pronunció 4 fue 5 quedó 6 se enfrentó 7 Fue 8 murió 9 quedó 10 empezó 11 duró

Texto B 1 pasaba 2 tenía 3 tenían 4 preocupaba 5 vivía 6 fue 7 sonaban 8 iban 9 sufrieron

3 1 hubo 2 nació 3 dedicó 4 pasó 5 estaban 6 decidió 7 construyó 8 se inspiraban 9 pudo 10 dejó 11 tuvo 12 quiso 13 fue 14 nació 15 se inspiraban/inspiraron 16 describió 17 conocía 18 se declaró 19 quiso 20 aconsejaban 21 regresó 22 resultó 23 se condenó 24 cambió 25 nació 26 vivió 27 decidió 28 pensó 29 tenía 30 pensó 31 creyó 32 fueron 33 dieron

4 a Una amiga de mi hermana, a quien yo no conocía, entró y comenzó a hablar en voz alta.   **b** Me dijo que todos los veranos la gente celebraba una fiesta en su pueblo.   **c** Fue entonces cuando me di cuenta de que el coche iba demasiado de prisa.   **d** Cuando supimos que nuestra profesora estaba enferma le mandamos un ramo de rosas.   **e** Iban a dar las doce cuando se acordó de algo importante y se levantó.   **f** Cuando conoció a mi madre, trabajaba de camarero, un empleo que él se tomaba muy en serio.   **g** Hubo un tiempo en el que bailaban el tango todos los días.   **h** Cuando volví de Perú, descubrí que nadie sabía nada de la crisis.   **i** Era una noche de verano. En la plaza la banda se puso a tocar y comenzó la fiesta.   **j** Mi regreso del colegio era siempre igual: me olvidaba de los deberes, y mi ropa estaba sucia de pelearme con los otros niños. Mi madre se reía pero mi padre me reñía siempre.

5 **Logros – y consecuencias – con el GAL**

¿Qué esperaban conseguir aquellos políticos demócratas que, bien de forma pasiva o activa, aprobaron las operaciones del GAL? ¿Alcanzaron sus objetivos? Y si así fue, ¿a qué costo para la democracia española? Creo que podríamos decir que los objetivos de la guerra sucia eran tres: mantener al ejército y a la policía dentro de la democracia; dar un duro golpe a ETA, y sobre todo hacer presión para que Francia luchara contra el terrorismo en su *refugio francés.*

Hemos visto cómo el gobierno socialista se sentía bajo la enorme presión de las fuerzas de seguridad para que éste adoptara una línea más dura contra ETA. Andrés Cassinello, un general cuya cínica actitud hacia la democracia era bien conocida, dijo que el GAL era 'una campaña con imaginación, llevada a cabo con éxito'. Podemos imaginar que su punto de vista era ampliamente compartido por sus compañeros de armas, y que la creencia generalizada de que la guerra sucia contaba con el consentimiento del gobierno, proporcionaba una válvula de seguridad contra las enfurecidas frustraciones del ejército y de la policía. Por otra parte, ofrece una imagen triste de la dirección de un gran partido democrático como el PSOE, el cual prefirió calmar a los franquistas dentro de las fuerzas de seguridad, en lugar de eliminarlos.

21 Compound tenses

1 a Cuando llegamos a Honduras la huelga de pilotos había terminado.   **b** Cuando murió el general Franco había estado en el poder 36 años.   **c** Cuando empecé a fumar el gobierno aún no había prohibido la publicidad del tabaco.   **d** Cuando Lola empezó en este colegio aún no se había hecho ningún tatuaje.   **e** Cuando entré en casa mis hermanos ya habían puesto la mesa.

3 a Ya habrán contestado tu solicitud.   **b** Si hubieras ido al partido habrías visto a Laura.   **c** ¿Qué habría dicho tu jefe si lo hubiera sabido?   **d** Cuando se hubo lavado el pelo encendió la televisión.   **e** ¡No te procupes! Se habrá olvidado de la cita.   **f** En cuanto se hubieron sentado, el camarero trajo el menú.   **g** Había estado esperando a que instalaran banda ancha en su pueblo y eventualmente llegó.

22 The subjunctive

1
a mandaran	**b** ha aprobado	**c** se pongan
d hay	**e** podamos	**f** permitiera
g lleguen	**h** estuviera	**i** sabía
j quería		

2
| **a** terminéis | **b** llegue | **c** oigamos |
| **d** amanezca | **e** empiece | **f** esté |

3
a caiga	**b** ayudaran/asen	**c** pases
d llamaran/llamasen	**e** consiga/ofrezca(an)	**f** llegara(n)/ase(n)
g hubiera /ese	**h** mantuviera	**i** esté
j tenga		

5 a valoren/decidan; **b** pudiera; **c** despidan; **d** parezca; **e** consigan; **f** quiera; **g** tenga; **h** estropease; **i** publique; **j** ponga; **k** hubiera expulsado; **l** hiciera; **m** sea/sea/llame; **n** fuera/fuera/llamara; **o** describiese; **p** volviera; **q** duela; **r** llegara/estuviera terminado; **s** logren

1	viven	2	pueda	3	ven	4	tienen
5	pueden	6	controle	7	sean	8	supriman
9-	resulte	10	descansen	11	recuerda	12	clausure
13	imponga	14	admiten	15	será	16	quiera
17	empiece	18	escurra	19	gusten	20	soy
21	recomiendan	22	prefiero	23	niego	24	sean
25	proviene	26	presiden				

23 Continuous forms of the verb

1 **a** estaba estudiando **b** estaban fregando/estaban tomando **c** estábamos comiendo
d volvía **e** estuvimos **f** está haciendo
g ba … estaban bailando **h** teníamos **i** llevaba

3 **a** Llevamos dos horas andando. **b** Los chicos estaban jugando en el jardín cuando Martín volvió a casa. **c** Anoche estuvimos discutiendo la elección hasta las tres de la madrugada. **d** Ayer la seguí llamando en caso de que ella me necesitara. **e** Le estuve mirando durante unos segundos. **f** Cuando la vimos por última vez volvía de Valencia. **g** Seguía llorando y yo no sabía qué decir. **h** ¿Qué hacen este verano?

24 If-clauses

1 **a** comía **b** dejaras **c** hubieras … habrían **d** viniera **e** era **f** estaba **g** hubieran ganado **h** quería **i** supiera **j** hubieran podido
2 **a** haya **b** fuera **c** haga **d** dejes **e** admitan **f** pida **g** tuviera **h** sigas **i** dejes **j** fuera

25 The imperative

1 **a** Ponla/Póngala. **b** Cómelo/Cómalo. **c** Sácalas/Sáquelas. **d** Dímelas/Dígamelas. **e** No lo cojas/ No lo coja. **f** Hazlos/Hágalos. **g** Léela/Léala. **h** Dáselo/Déselo. **i** No se lo pagues/No se lo pague. **j** Apágala/Apáguela.

2 1 Coloca/Coloque 2 Añade/Añada 3 pon/ponga 4 fríelo/fríalo 5 vierte/vierta 6 permitas/permita 7 añade/añada 8 hiérvela/hiérvala 9 echa/eche 10 Haz/Haga 11 procura/procure 12 remueve/remueva 13 repártelo/repártalo 14 Haz/Haga 15 añade/añada 16 baja/baje 17 deja/deje 18 coloca/coloque 19 reduce/reduzca 20 déjala/déjela 21 coge/coja 22 oca/toque 23 disfrutadla/disfrútenla

3 1 Fíjese; 2 Lea/pregunte; 3 Compare/vea; 4 Recuerde; 5 regrese/Imagine; 6 compre; 7 Descubra; 8 Piense/Adminístrelo

4 **a** Salgamos ahora. **b** No me des tu contestación todavía, Carlos. **c** Recoged las botellas y ponedlas en la caja del reciclado, chicos. **d** No esperemos hasta mañana. **e** Dile lo que pasó. **f** Camarero, tráigame un poco más de agua, por favor. **g** Por favor, no den de comer a los patos./Hagan el favor de no dar de comer a los patos. **h** No me llames hasta las siete de la tarde, Rosa. **i** ¡Estáos quietos, niños! **j** Enciende\Encended la luz, está anocheciendo.

27 Modal verbs

1 **a** sé **b** habría podido **c** Quieres **d** podía **e** deberíamos/debiéramos/debemos **f** Debería/Debe **g** Podría **h** debería **i** puedo/podré **j** debemos

2 **a** Ángel debe de haberse marchado antes de que llegaran. **b** Quisiera aprender francés. **c** Solíamos ir a Francia todos los años pero ahora viajamos más lejos. **d** Sé jugar al golf pero no soy muy bueno. **e** Siempre deberíamos abrocharnos el cinturón. **f** Habría podido competir./Podria haber sido un contrincante. **g** A tu edad ya deberías saberlo. **h** En aquella época no podíamos ver que la democracia iba a triunfar.

28 *Gustar*-type and impersonal verbs

1   **a** gustaba   **b** duele   **c** molestó   **d** me ocurre   **e** toca   **f** encantó   **g** sobra   **h** cuesta   **i** me olvidó   **j** hacen falta

3   **a** Ayer mi hermana me enseñó su nueva pulsera pero no me gustó.   **b** Nos costó mucho trabajo organizar la exposición.   **c** El médico me puso una inyección pero no me dolió.   **d** Nos gustaría visitar Santiago el año que viene.   **e** Me molestaba que nunca cesara de quejarse.   **f** Se le cayó el libro.   **g** No nos convenía viajar a Cuba en el invierno.   **h** Esos vaqueros te sientan muy bien, Gonzalo.   **i** A mis amigos no les gusta pasar el tiempo en los bares.   **j** A mi hermana pequeña le duele mucho la cabeza.   **k** D. Alberto, me faltan mis notas.   **l** Lo que te hace falta son unas buenas vacaciones.   **m** No me importa mucho la televisión.   **n** A Chris le molesta si hablo español.   **o** A Carlos le gustan las ensaladas pero a mí no me gustan nada.   **p** ¿Le importa si cierro la ventana? No, no me importa en absoluto.   **q** Nos sobró mucha comida después de la fiesta.   **r** Les costó mucho trabajo encontrar el camino.   **s** Me extraña que no sepas que se casaron el año pasado.

29 Ser and estar

Crossword solution (Part I, 29).

1   1 es   2 está   3 es   4 es   5 ser   6 están   7 es   8 está   9 Es   10 es   11 es   12 estar

2   **a** Estará el   **b** estar   **c** estado en   **d** son son   **e** fue   **f** están, son;   **g** está   **h** estuvo   **i** está/está está;   **j** era

3   1 es   2 es/ha sido   3 Es   4 Está   5 es /fue   6 es/fue   7 eran   8 eran   9 es/fue   10 fue/ha sido   11 serían/fueron

4   **Title:** somos/son   1 están   2 están   3 es   4 es   5 era   6 Son   7 son   8 estaban   9 están   10 está   11 era   12 están   13 siendo   14 son   15 es

5   1 está   2 ser   3 es   4 está   5 son   6 ser   7 están   8 son   9 es   10 son

6   1 estoy   2 estás   3 soy   4 estar   5 estoy   6 esté   7 somos   8 éramos   9 es   10 sois   11 Somos   12 son   13 estar   14 ser   15 estar   16 estar   17 son   18 estás   19 es

30 Active and passive

1   1 se permite   2 se puede   3 Se espera   4 se dirijan   5 se comporten   6 se atenderá   7 será   8 se ofrecen   9 serán

2   **a** El teléfono lo inventó Alexander Graham Bell.   **b** La película *Tacones lejanos* la dirigió Pedro Almódovar.   **c** El Museo Guggenheim lo construyó un arquitecto estadounidense.   **d** Méjico lo conquistó Hernán Cortés en 1519.   **e** El banco Argentaria lo privatizaron en los años 90.

3   **a** se vendieron   **b**   se analizan   **c**   se ha establecido   **d**   se destruyó   **e**   se traducirán

4   **a** La decisión la tomó el Presidente/El Presidente tomó la decisión.   **b** Se le preguntó si tenía algo que decir.   **c** No se sabe nunca, ¿verdad?   **d** Se necesita(n) camareros.   **e** Aquí se compran coches de segunda mano.   **f** Se la llevó a/para ver a su abuela en el hospital.   **g** El aceite de oliva español se vende por toda Europa.   **h** Se decía que su padre era francés.   **i** Hacía tanto ruido que no se les podía oír   **j** Ayer bajaron las tasas de interés.

31 Pronominal verbs

1   **a** se jubiló   **b** me atrevo   **c** se murió   **d** me vuelvo   **e** quítate   **f** se hace   **g** aprovechándose   **h** se durmió   **i** nos sentimos   **j** me pongo

2   **a** Nos reunimos mañana a las diez.   **b** ¡Vístete, Miguel!   **c** Mi letra se parece a la de mi madre.   **d** Se sentaron en un banco y miraron la luna.   **e** Me doy cuenta de que nada va a hacerse rápidamente.   **f** Se encogió de hombros.   **g** No nos acordábamos de qué día era.   **h** Me alegro de conocerte.   **i** Se lo comió todo.   **j** Tienes que dirigirte al director para la respuesta.

32 The infinitive

1 **a** a/por **b** para **c** con **d** – **e** de **f** – **g** por **h** de **i** por **j** –

2 **a** Ver es creer.   **b** Al descubrir el bar enseguida llamaron por teléfono a sus amigos.   **c** Los cambios ecológicos amenazan con destruir el planeta.   **d** Si tratas de/intentas cambiar tu dieta podrías dañarte la salud.   **e** ¡Acabamos de ganar unas vacaciones en el Japón!   **f** No quiero decirte lo que tienes que hacer.   **g** Les vimos entrar en el hotel.   **h** Le oí decir al jefe que iba a despedir a Manolo.   **i** El italiano es una lengua fácil de entender.   **j** No es posible darle una respuesta hoy.

33 The past participle

2 **a** He puesto tus vaqueros en la lavadora.   **b** Hecho el trabajo, todos volvieron a casa.   **c** ¡Qué concierto tan aburrido!   **d** ¿Tienes suelto?   **e** Había desconfiado de él desde el principio.   **f** Agotadas, las dos mujeres decidieron no continuar andando.   **g** La cena había sido preparada mientras trabajaban.   **h** Todavía no habían progresado con las negociaciones.

34 The gerund

1 1 mirando   2 acercándose   3 diciendo   4 queriendo   5 aguardando   6 sorteando   7 observándo(me)   8 apartando   9 esperando   10 aproximando

2 **a** Oímos a los niños cantando en la calle.   **b** Llevamos horas viajando en este autobús.   **c** Nadar todos los días te pondrá en buena forma.   **d** ¿En qué estás pensando en este momento?   **e** Las cosas acaban encontrando su sitio verdadero más tarde o más temprano.   **f** Le escribió pidiéndole que viniera a Chile.   **g** Desde mi ventana veía el avión acercándose despacio.   **h** Iban metiendo las monedas en una máquina tragaperras.   **i** –Pasa – dije, tratando que mi voz sonara tranquila.   **j** Siguió riéndose por mucho tiempo.

35 Negation

1 **a**   nunca/en mi vida/jamás   **b**   ningún   **c**   tampoco
   d   ninguna   **e**   ni   **f**   nadie
   g   apenas   **h**   ningún   **i**   nada   **j**   nunca

2 **a** No ha oído nada sobre sus exámenes.   **b** Ni (siquiera) han comenzado a construir la casa.   **c** ¿Qué quieres decir? Nada de particular.   **d** Casi nadie hablaba/Apenas hablaba nadie de la guerra.   **e** Aquí nadie hace nada para ayudar a los parados.   **f** Eso no tiene (nada) que ver con lo que estábamos diciendo.   **g** Nunca he pasado tanto tiempo trabajando con el ordenador.   **h** No quisiera saber nada de esto.   **i** Solicitó el trabajo sin saber de qué se trataba.   **j** Te necesito más que nunca.

36 Adverbs

1 **a** lejos **b** cerca/lejos **c** delante/detrás **d** lejos **e** detrás **f** antes/ahora **g** antes/después **h** arriba y abajo **i** lejos **j** después **k** atrás

2 **a** Habla en voz baja, por favor.   **b** Es una chica típicamente inglesa.   **c** Algunos países sudamericanos están en desventaja social y económicamente.   **d** Tu hermano se está portando fatal hoy.   **e** No puedo tomar en serio los exámenes.   **f** Vaya todo derecho, tome la segunda calle a la izquierda y luego la primera a la derecha.   **g** Llevó a cabo las tareas rápida y cuidadosamente.

h Me da igual.   **i** Puedes comprar este televisor más barato aquí que en cualquier otro sitio.
j Contestó las preguntas inteligentemente/de modo inteligente.

37   Prepositions

1
a	sin	**b**	para	**c**	debajo de	**d**	hasta
e	bajo	**f**	según	**g**	tras	**h**	con
i	en	**j**	ante	**k**	cabe	**l**	para
m	cerca de						

2 **a** The party is at 9 p.m. at Cuqui's house.   **b** Hugo is afraid of heights.   **c** I am sorry, I can't go out with you because I'm about to leave for New York.   **d** Her boyfriend works as a fireman and she is studying to become a pharmacist.   **e** I told you I would come along that road.   **f** He always has plenty of things in his bag.   **g** I would like to buy an old brick house and renovate it using modern materials.   **h** In a few days some German friends of my parents who are really boring will arrive.
i After checking we had all we needed, we got into the car and left for a trip around Spain.   **j** At that restaurant they do steak and chips better than anybody.

3
a	para	**b**	por	**c**	Por	**d**	para
e	por	**f**	para	**g**	por	**h**	para
i	para	**j**	por	**k**	por	**l**	para
m	por/para	**n**	por/para	**o**	para	**p**	por
q	por	**r**	para	**s**	por	**t**	para
u	para	**v**	por				

4 1 Al 2 de 3 en 4 al 5 para 6 tras 7 al 8 para 9 de 10 en 11 de 12 de 13 a 14 con 15 entre 16 de 17 a 18 a 19 A 20 por 21 ante 22 en 23 en 24 para 25 de 26 con 27 de 28 en 29 de 30 por 31 para 32 de

38   Conjunctions

1 **a** Cuanto **b** cuanto **c** como **d** donde **e** según **f** cómo **g** cuando **h** donde **i** cuando **j** cuánto **k** any of these: cómo, cuándo, dónde **l** cuánto

2 **a** pero **b** si no **c** sino **d** si no **e** Si no **f** sino **g** pero **h** sino **i** Si no **j** si no **k** Pero **l** sino

3 1 cuando 2 dónde 3 aunque 4 como 5 Mientras 6 y 7 sino 8 porque 9 si no 10 cuando

39   Diminutives and augmentatives

1 **a** pulpiño … patatiñas **b** relojazo … relojito **c** cochinillo … patatitas **d** pastillita … pequeñita … pastillotas **e** jamoncico … dedicos **f** campanazos … campanilla. **g** Rosita … gigantesco … violón

2 Paquito Carmiña/Carmencita dinerito casita casita pequeñita comedorcito mesita sillitas silloncitos cocinita cuartito camitas igualitas saloncito fueguecito Paquito apañadito cortinitas jardincito Carmencita manecitas florecitas casita

3 **a** Jorgito está malito, voy a tomarle la temperatura.   **b** Tu papá está hecho un vejete muy simpaticón.
c Préstame algún dinerillo para un cafecito.   **d** Llevaba un vestidito con florecitas lila y un cuellecito de encaje.   **e** Han tenido un bebé precioso con los mismos ojazos que su mamá y las mismas ganazas de comer que su papá. Será un hombretón como él.   **f** Hubo un llenazo impresionante en el teatro y porque Javier Bardem es un actorazo genial.

40 Word order

1 **a** El cartero, ¿ha llegado ya?   **b** Esa película no me ha gustado nada.   **c** Ese color de pelo me sienta muy bien.   **d** El ordenador, ¿lo has cerrado ya?   **e** En las escuelas privadas los niños aprenden bastante.   **f** A los ingleses les gusta mucho el vino de Jerez.   **g** Trabajar por la noche le cansa mucho.   **h** La exposición, ¿la han abierto ya?   **i** La cámara de fotos la he perdido.   **j** Quince años llevo trabajando en la misma empresa.

2 **a** Lo raro es que sin tener ningún tipo de educación/título se haya convertido en millonario de Internet.   **b** Siempre ha ido a nadar después de trabajar.   **c** Mi madre nunca ha votado a los Conservadores.   **d** Casi nunca como carne roja y pescado; sólo de vez en cuando.   **e** Blas ha sido hincha del Real Betis desde pequeño.   **f** La brigada de bomberos llegó para apagar el fuego.   **g** Por favor, ¿podría traernos otros dos cafés?   **h** Supongo que no habrás visto el libro que me regaló Carla.

Index

English '–ing' 164, 302; gerund and **–nte** adjectives 163-164; **ir** + gerund 301; **llevar** + gerund 301; position of object pronouns 42, 43, 162; **seguir** and **continuar** + gerund 163, 301; spelling changes 116, 162; to form the continuous tenses 114, 163; translation of 'by + -ing' 163; use of **habiendo** 162; **venir** + gerund 301

Glossary of Computing & Mobile Phone Technology xiii-xiv

Glossary of grammatical terms ix-xii

gran(de) 24

gustar-type verbs 138-142, 282-283; Key ideas 140; **gustar** construction 139

haber de 136,

hacer que + subjunctive 110

hacia 182

hasta 182-183

hasta que 111

hay 140-141, 203

hay que 135, 136

hay quien 233

If-clauses 117-120, 272-274; Key idea 118; open conditions 118; unlikely or impossible conditions 118-119; missed opportunity 119; **si:** + present indicative 118, + perfect indicative 118, + preterite 118, + imperfect subjunctive 118-119,+ pluperfect subjunctive 119; equivalents of **si** 273; **hubiera** for **habría** 272; if = **como** + subjunctive 273; if = **de** + infinitive 273; **si** = 'whenever' 272; **si** meaning 'whether' 272; **si** used for emphasis 273

Imperative 121-126, 275-277; Key ideas 122; forms 122; familiar and formal imperative 122-125; formation of positive **tú** commands 122-123; irregular **tú** commands 123; formation of positive **vosotros** commands 123; negative familiar commands 124; positive **Vd.** commands 124; negative **Vd**. commands 124-125; position of object pronouns 125; **nosotros** imperatives 275; imperative **que** 275-276; infinitive as imperative 276; second-person familiar plural in Latin-American Spanish 276

Imperfect tense 95-98, 252-253; Key ideas 96; formation 96; irregular forms 98-97; subjunctive forms 109; in time expressions 252; replacing present 252; replacing preterite 252; replacing conditional 252; contrasted with preterite, 99-100, 254-257

Impersonal verbs 140-141, 282-283; Key ideas 140; verbs indicating the weather 140, 282; common impersonal verbs 141; **se** with impersonal construction 141

Indefinite article 14–15, 203-204; Key ideas 14; forms 14, 204; apposition 14; **un** before feminine noun 204; omission of 'some' 15; plural form **unos** 14; translation of **unos** 14; **unos** = approximately 14; with a qualified abstract noun 204; omission after: **con** and **sin** 204, **tener, llevar, ser** 204; omission before: **cantidad** and **parte** 204, occupations 14, **otro, tal, medio, qué** 15

Indefinites 66– 71, 237-238; Key ideas 66

Indirect object pronouns 43–44; Key idea 43; 'redundant' indirect object 44; position of indirect object 43; order of object pronouns 43; **se** replacing indirect object 43-44

Infinitive 154-157, 295-298; Key ideas 154; adjectives made from **sin** + infinitive 295; after: **acabar de** 156, **hay que** 156, prepositions 155-156, **tener que** 156, verbs of motion 155, verbs of perception 249; **volver a** 156, ; **al** + infinitive 155, ; alternative to subjunctive construction after certain verbs 266; as a noun 155; **de** + infinitive = 'if' 273, 295; following an active verb 155; infinitive as imperative 276, 295; perfect infinitive 155; perfect infinitive 155; **por** + infinitive = 'through –ing' 297; position of object pronouns 42,156; preceded by **nada más** 295; translation of 'to' of infinitive 296; verb: + **a** + infinitive 155, 296, + **con** + infinitive 297, + **de** + infinitive 155, 297, + **en** + infinitive 155, 297,, + **para** + infinitive 297,, + **por** + infinitive 297,, + infinitive without preposition 296

-ing verb ending in English 163-164

Interrogatives 61–3, 235-236; Key ideas 62; indirect questions 235

ir + a, future meaning,79, + gerund 301, **irse** 293

Irregular verb conjugations 323-333

-ísimo 29, 220

jamás 165, 167

leer 131

llevar 301, 246

lo neuter article 204; direct object pronoun 40, 42; followed by adjective 215; with possessive pronouns 231; with past participle 300

lo cual, lo que 58, 59

luego 316

mar 209

más que 27; **más de** 219; **más/menos del que** 220

mayor/más pequeño 219

medio 14, 223

menos que 27,

mientras 111, 264

mil 14, 35

millón (un) 35

Modal verbs 135-137, 279-281; Key ideas 135; translation of 'could'/'could have' 279-280; translation of 'should'/'should have' 280

morirse 293

mucho 66, 69

nada 165

nada más 305

Printed and bound by CPI Group (UK) Ltd, Croydon, CR0 4YY

23/10/2024

01777692-0005